T3-BUN-073

The Artless Word

The Artless Word

**Mies van der Rohe
on the Building Art**

*Fritz Neumeyer
translated by Mark Jarzombek*

*The MIT Press
Cambridge, Massachusetts
London, England*

This work originally appeared in German under the title *Mies van der Rohe. Das kunstlose Wort. Gedanken zur Baukunst*, © 1986 by Wolf Jobst Siedler Gmbh, Berlin.

This book was set in Helvetica and was printed and bound in the United States of America.

Library of Congress Cataloging-in-Publication Data
Neumeyer, Fritz.
   [Mies van der Rohe. English]
   The artless word : Mies van der Rohe on the building art / Fritz
Neumeyer : translated by Mark Jarzombek.
      p. cm.
   Originally published in German under title: Mies van der Rohe.
   Includes bibliographical references and index.
   ISBN 0-262-14047-0
   1. Architecture—Philosophy. 2. Architecture, Modern—20th
century. 3. Mies van der Rohe, Ludwig, 1886–1969—Criticism and
interpretation. I. Title.
NA2500.N3913 1991
720—dc20   90-47585
                                               CIP

Contents

Appendix:
Manifestos, Texts, and Lectures

Preface to the German Edition

This book, unlike other investigations into the work and person of Ludwig Mies van der Rohe, concerns itself more with his words than with his buildings. There is a simple explanation for this shift of interest. The writings of this great architect, which contain the key to his thought and to his architecture, have, compared to his buildings, remained largely unexplored.

Yet the Mies material in the Mies van der Rohe Archive at the Museum of Modern Art in New York, the Manuscript Division of the Library of Congress in Washington, and the archives in Chicago challenge us not only to follow Mies's thought to its sources but also to turn the word over to Mies himself by publishing all of his writings. This attempt to reconstruct Mies's conceptual edifice draws on another, so far unevaluated but authentic source, namely the markings left behind in his books in the form of underlinings. They afford insight into the spiritual dimension of his philosophy. Indeed, it would be almost impossible to demonstrate a close connection between philosophy and building were it not for Mies's private library of approximately 800 volumes preserved almost intact at the University of Illinois at Chicago in the Special Collections Department. The effort to establish a philosophical foundation for building in the age of technology makes Mies's statements important witnesses to a period of historical transition, whose importance has been unimpaired by the passage of half a century.

I am indebted to many persons who deserve more than the usual thanks. Gretchen Lagana of the University of Illinois Library, Special Collections Department, in Chicago and Pierre Adler of the Mies van der Rohe Archive of the Museum of Modern Art in New York have personally supported my work. I am also indebted to Dirk Lohan who continues Mies's architectural office in Chicago, not only for making private archival material very generously available, a circumstance that was of invaluable help to me, but also for his frankness. I also thank Franz Schulze of Lake Forest College, Chicago, author of an excellent recent Mies biography, for his cooperation and friendly encouragement, as well as Richard Pommer of Vassar College, Poughkeepsie, New York. I am further grateful to George Danforth and George Schipporeit, Mies's successors at IIT, and to Rolf Achilles of the Centennial Project of IIT, to all of whom I feel myself bound in friendship. I thank them for the confidence they have placed in my work and for the enthusiastic support I have received from them. To my American friends I dedicate this book.

Many others have participated in my work, directly or indirectly, especially Sergius Ruegenberg of Berlin, a longtime co-worker of Mies van der Rohe in the twenties, Tilmann Buddensieg of the University of Bonn, Werner Dahlheim and the late Hans Reuther of the Technical University of Berlin, Wolf Tegethoff of Kiel, and Theo Buck of Milan, as well as my Berlin Mies-friends Clod Zillich, Jasper Halfmann, Hans Kollhoff, Christoph Langhof, Ben Tonon, and Theo Brenner.

A generous grant from the Stiftung Volkswagenwerk enabled me to carry on my research, extending over almost two years, and undertake the required travels to New York, Chicago, and Washington. Ditta Ahmadi assisted in the preparation of the manuscript with critical patience. Publisher Wolf Jobst Siedler made it possible, for the first time, for a book on Mies to come out in Berlin, the city in which, between 1905 and 1938, he contributed so decisively to the architecture of our century.

Berlin
March 1986

Introduction:
Mies van der Rohe in the Historiography
of Modern Architecture

Each material is only worth what we make of it.
Mies van der Rohe, 1938

Mies van der Rohe participated in the dialogue on the "New Building" in its decisive historical phases not only as polemicist but also as critic. Sharing the basic convictions of modernism, he felt part of an avant-garde, an advance commando fighting for the development of a new art attuned to modern modes of living. By dismissing the ballast of inherited tradition and by accepting the demands of the epoch, he oriented his consciousness toward the threshold of a new age. This sensibility, in accordance with a modern spirit, opened itself to the future and embraced its new technology and construction methods.

In his very first statements from the early twenties, Mies had already accepted the inevitability of progress. But the fervor of his manifestos, which proclaimed his initial commitment to the new conditions, soon was accompanied by doubt that added a note of critical distance to his endorsement of modernism. It was not so much the acknowledging of the facts of the new epoch, with its own inventory of technology and economy, but the attitude man assumed toward these givens that became decisive in his view. Architecture therefore was no longer viewed merely as a matter of function and technology, as Mies had originally defined it in the twenties, but as a "life process," an "expression of man's ability to assert himself and master his surroundings."[1]

In the concluding words of his speech at the meeting of the Deutsche Werkbund in Vienna in 1930, Mies emphasized very emphatically that he rejected those mechanistic and functionalistic doctrines that were later to be equated with modern building:

The new time is a fact; it exists whether we say yes or no to it. . . . It is a pure given. . . . What is decisive is only how we assert ourselves toward these givens.

It is here that the spiritual problems begin.

What matters is not the what but only the how. That we produce goods and the means by which we produce them says nothing spiritually.

Whether we build high or flat, with steel or with glass, says nothing as to the value of this way of building.

Whether one aims for centralization or decentralization in urban planning is a practical question, not one of values.

But it is exactly this question of values that is decisive.

We must set new values and point out ultimate goals in order to gain new criteria.

For the meaning and justification of each epoch, even the new one, lies only in providing conditions under which the spirit can exist.[2]

Closeness and distance, call and warning, a yes and a no speak out of these sentences. Mies van der Rohe, who had by then, with the building of the Barcelona Pavilion and the Tugendhat House, risen to a prominent position within the ranks of modern architecture, accepted the function-orientedness of his age as a precondition that, while harboring its own potential, did not constitute in and of itself the proper theme for architecture. Fighting on two fronts, his skeptical rationalism opposed any type of unilateral reductiveness. One learns from the comments Mies made around 1930 that he refused to leave building in the grip of technology, but neither did he want to see it turned over to "clever speculation." Neither anonymous technical power nor acts of free interpretation by individualistic artists were accorded priority. "The building art"—so Mies printed in boldface—"is always the spatial expression of spiritual decisions."[3] And decisions, so one may add, demand criteria and principles: they demand intellectual rules based on a logic of order by means of which the relationship between fact and significance, between object and subject, can impart meaning to life.

According to Peter Blake, it is this emphatic sense of order, a characteristic typical of all Mies's buildings and projects, that enabled him to arrive at "architectural statements of such overwhelming precision, simplicity, and single-mindedness that their impact is that of a major revelation."[4] All Mies's statements, written, drawn, or built, are, each in its own way, declarations of principle or demonstrations of an idea. It is due to this consequentiality and perfectionism that Mies's work has found a firm place in the history of twentieth-century building. Mies's insistence on disciplined form and unhesitating liberality, on finality and objectivity, accounts for the captivating aura that surrounds his works and may also account for the emotional response Mies's work encountered, in the form either of acceptance or, occasionally, of virulent criticism. But beyond that, history has shown that only a few avant-garde projects and modern buildings have withstood the test of time as well as his—and that despite the ease with which the apparent Miesian simplicity blended with the anonymity of modern life.

In retrospect, Mies's projects appear almost inevitable in their compelling logic. That applies particularly to those utopian projects designed between 1919 and 1924 that practically catapulted Mies to the forefront of the avant-garde. His projects for Glass Skyscrapers, for an Office Building, for a Concrete Country House and Brick Country House introduced the so-called heroic phase of modernism, which reached its apex with the buildings erected between 1927 and 1929. The Weissenhofsiedlung, the Barcelona

Pavilion, and the Tugendhat House are outstanding achievements that established Mies van der Rohe's reputation as one of the great building masters of modern European architecture.

Extreme precision and consequentiality, extraordinary simplicity and generosity were the characteristic features of Mies's architecture. His buildings are platonic objects that seem to declare the universally valid principles of architecture. Conveying a pronounced sense of space, mass, and proportion, they not only invite contemplation but also call for a physical appropriation of space by movement. They reflect—as Mies expressed it in that fateful year 1933 in regard to the designs for houses with courtyards—"a measure of freedom" gained for the modern individual "that we will not relinquish any more."[5]

Mies conceived of building as arising out of a field of tension that consisted of intrinsic lawfulness on one hand and creative freedom on the other. It should afford the "required privacy combined with the freedom of open room forms"[6] and provide a "defining" but not a "confining space"[7] suitable for contemporary living. Behind this concept of space and architecture that defined "building" in a philosophical sense as a "giving form to reality"[8] stood for Mies the question of the "value and dignity of human existence," namely: "Is the world as it presents itself bearable for man? . . . Can it be shaped so as to be worthwhile to live in?"[9]

To elevate architecture into the expression of spiritual decision meant that it must first be conquered as idea. Only an "architecture of spiritual relations [Architektur der geistigen Beziehungen]" was autonomous enough to be secured against unilateral incursions of either a technical or a subjective kind. This concept of a self-reliant architecture arose out of an intellectual tradition founded in the eighteenth century in the architectural writings of Marc-Antoine Laugier and Carlo Lodoli and brought forward into the twentieth century by way of Gottfried Semper, Eugène-Emmanuel Viollet-le-Duc, Julien Guadet, Auguste Choisy, and Hendrikus Berlage. Mies's architecture with its enlightened postulate of an environment shaped by man himself arises out of this tradition.

Mies was to remain loyal to this rationalism, which had lost its basis in Germany after 1933, even after his emigration to the U.S. in 1938. Crown Hall (1950–56), Lake Shore Drive Apartments in Chicago (1945–50), and the Seagram Building in New York (1957) represent major milestones in the development of architecture right up to the present time.

Only in the final phase of his life and after his death on August 17, 1969, was Mies acclaimed one of the great building masters of the century. There was a drastic increase in the volume of commissions and the number of publications concerning his work in the last decade of his life. But back in 1947, when Philip Johnson published the first edition of his monograph on Mies van der Rohe, he was probably one of the least known pioneers of modernism. At that time, the sixty-one-year-old Mies had erected barely

twenty buildings and published a similarly modest number of terse statements and manifestos in dispersed and typically remote places. In contrast
to Le Corbusier, who had developed an extraordinarily rich publishing activity, Mies's aversion to self-promotion prevented him from making those propagandistic efforts by means of which Le Corbusier, Gropius, and other
leading representatives of the New Building attracted international attention
in their effort to disseminate their ideas and publicize their buildings.

The interest in Mies van der Rohe awakened by Johnson culminated in the
sixties in a series of monographs that largely followed in Johnson's foot-
steps. The latter had initiated a canonical interpretation of Mies that—cum
grano salis—was perpetuated in the works of Max Bill (1955), Arthur Drexler (1960), Peter Blake (1960), Werner Blaser (1965–72), James Speyer
(1968), Ludwig Glaeser (1969), Martin Pawley (1970), Peter Carter (1974),
Lorenzo Papi (1974), and David Spaeth (1985); it has not undergone
essential enrichment until the present time.[10] Only the monograph of Mies's
longtime friend and former Bauhaus colleague Ludwig Hilberseimer of 1956
constitutes a worthwhile exception.[11] Hilberseimer did not put the analysis
of buildings in the foreground but attempted to approach Mies's philosophy
from a theoretical point of view, setting it in the context of historical continuity ranging from Leon Battista Alberti's concept of concinnitas to Kasimir
Malevich's suprematist reduction.

In the last decade of his life, overwhelmed by commissions and honors,
Mies was turned into a mythic figure. A proud series of monographs and a
veritable flood of articles paid homage to him as master of modern building, around whom, not least on account of his retiring ways, a regular cult
developed. While friends and pupils wrapped Mies in a sort of aura, however, he experienced a downright cheapening at the hands of those epi-
gones who had risen from the ranks of everyday practice. The seductive
simplicity of the Miesian structure, which gave no clue to the arduous process of distillation out of which it arose, was narrowly codified and ultimately exhausted by commercial imitation.

The question of how far the publicistic propaganda contributed to this vulgarization of the architectural legacy is in itself worthy of investigation. In
each of the monographs one inevitably finds the identical basic inventory of
reproduced materials; dates are simply taken over. In those instances
where originals were no longer available, the authors simply made new
drawings. An example of this is the legendary blueprint reconstructions of
Werner Blaser for the Brick Country House, where the walls radiate far into
the landscape and the building substance dissolves into a complex of wall
screens. This painfully accurate blueprint, made by Blaser for his 1965
monograph during a period of contact with Mies himself, gives no clue as
to authorship; yet it largely determined the conception of this project, insofar as this reconstruction was readily accepted in other circles as a Mies
drawing.[12] That this reconstruction shows a number of differences and
deviations from the original, which exists only in badly reproduced copies,

and therefore perpetuates an incorrect rendering remained undiscovered until Wolf Tegethoff's publication in 1981, which has set new criteria for dealing with data and their analysis.[13]

The Mies school had succumbed to an uncritical fascination with its own hero. Respectful reproductions and misunderstood personal contact on one hand, and simplification and watering down of ideas and principles by commercial vulgarization on the other, resulted in an atmosphere of discomfort out of which arose in the sixties and seventies a critique not only directed toward Mies alone, but toward modernism in general. Pronouncements once cited as Miesian aphorisms now underwent provocative heretical transformations. The monkish homily "less is more," attributed by Johnson to Mies as personal motto,[14] had become a regular slogan supposedly summing up Mies. Robert Venturi expanded it in his *Complexity and Contradiction* of 1966 into a still respectful "more is not less."[15] For Sybil Moholy-Nagy, the question heading her essay "Has 'less is more' become 'less is nothing'?"[16] was simply a rhetorical one.

This change of attitude toward the dogmas of functionalism and purism delineated itself in the development of architecture since the late fifties in a demand for greater expressiveness and plasticity. Robert Venturi gave theoretical foundation to these trends in the sixties. Calling for a more context-enriched architecture in his "gentle manifesto," he pleads for a reclaiming of complexity. The vulgarized concept of "less is more"[17] has led, according to Venturi, to an architecture that has become anemic and boring and could be dispatched with "less is a bore." Venturi's theory of complexity and contradiction affirmed the delight in contradiction but decidedly denied—though this has hardly come to attention—incoherence and caprice, as well as picturesqueness and excess. Appreciation of complexity in architecture does not stand in conflict with demands for simplicity. Venturi recognized that the buildings of Mies van der Rohe opened valuable opportunities for the development of architecture but also that their selectivity and formal language represented a limitation.[18]

Critique concerned with more nuanced evaluation was drowned out by the more clamorous polemical arguments now attacking the icons of modernism. Bertrand Goldberg, one of the early dissidents of the Chicago School that had formed around Mies, confronted it with the defiant motto "rich is right." Stanley Tigerman, who also originated in these circles, illuminated this change of parameter with a photomontage to which he gave the title "Titanic." Meant ironically, but not without a symbolical play on reality, it showed Crown Hall, the incunabulum of modern steel and glass construction of the early fifties—a building that Mies himself had called one of his best[19]—sinking into Lake Michigan.[20]

The critical voices that accompanied Mies's work were seldom free of polemic. One can hear it reverberate in the question "Can one live in House Tugendhat?"—the title of Justus Bier's 1931 essay, in which he

The Titanic, 1978, photomontage by Stanley Tigerman.

spoke of display living and insufferable presentation style.[21] Of the critics of the succeeding period such as Joseph Rykwert, who denounced the campus of IIT in 1949 as a "slick, lucid, sickening scheme,"[22] one could form a separate chronicle. It would lead us from the journalistic battles that raged around the Farnsworth House,[23] to the aggressiveness against modernism typical of the McCarthy era, right up to Mies's last building, the New National Gallery in Berlin, which Julius Posener, carried away by a conflict between admiration and disdain, called a junk dealer's den (*Krambude*).[24] Fascination and polemic have their common roots in the problematic of the Miesian architecture that refuses to subordinate aesthetic considerations to social ones.

Both critics and admirers tended toward polarization. Reyner Banham saw the sterility of this tendency and summed up the situation with the question "Absolute good or absolute bad?" On one hand, a worldwide network of admirers elevated the buildings of Mies to the rank of absolutes of architectural perfection, seeing in them the emanation of an ideal Cartesian model; on the other hand, there were those who, like Lewis Mumford, perceived Mies as a Procrustes demanding that human nature adapt itself to his architectural idiosyncracies.[25]

These extreme judgments, rather than saying something about the architecture itself, indicated a confusion in the camp of the critics and could only lead to symptoms of exhaustion. While Mies entered upon a final phase of mastery—the purification of a mature concept of structure—his pupils, with Philip Johnson in the lead, began to deny him their allegiance. Johnson signaled this process of detachment in his 1955 publication of the lecture

"The Seven Crutches of Modern Architecture."[26] "What has happened to the Mies van der Rohe Fan Club?" was the consternated question with which Banham opened his essay "Almost Nothing Is Too Much" in 1962,[27] in which he once more reiterated the virtues of Mies's architecture.

The crisis around Mies cannot be explained merely by the general discomfort with modern architecture in the sixties. It was, one must conclude, to a certain degree created from within. The monographs on Mies were partially to blame for the manner in which Mies was presented and finally consumed. Mies's image had become static.[28]

Philip Johnson, who had been enthused over Mies in the twenties on account of his cool objectivity and his aloofness from the avant-garde movements of that period and who preferred him over Le Corbusier and Oud because he saw him as "less factorylike, more classical,"[29] established an image of Mies that was merely consolidated in the hands of his successors. Contradictions within the work, to the degree they were then noticeable, were played down; the early work had been subjected, presumably on Mies's own initiative, to a strict process of selection, and the twenties and thirties were presented as a preparatory phase for the mature achievement of the American years. The message superimposed over the oeuvre was one of timeless perfection, obsessive attention to detail, and a delight in expensive and luxurious material. In subsequent writing, according to the merciless summary of Richard Padovan, "ideas and whole phrases" were merely "lifted from one work of homage to the next," reducing to meaninglessness the one-sided and granite image of the great architect—now a monolithic symbol for universality and perfection—through constant repetition.[30]

Indeed, as Padovan points out, there exists only a single truly deviationist interpretation of Mies, namely that of Bruno Zevi, submitted in the pioneering work *Poetica dell'architettura neoplastica* (Milan, 1953). This turns out, however, to be no less unilateral than the canonizing approach via Johnson. Zevi does not follow the well-trodden path and the teleological model of a career moving in orderly progression toward a single aim—a theory that reads almost like Mies's own concept of the gradually unfolding form—but rather attempts to interpret Mies's career in terms of contradictory concepts: classicism and neoplasticism. Both concepts for Zevi are ideologically loaded; classicism is equated with despotism and rigidity; neoplasticism, as emancipation from the symmetrical axis and the traditional form-and-order concepts, is equated with freedom and democracy. Provided one accepts these definitions, one could view the development of Mies in terms of a parabola. At its apex stand the buildings of around 1930—the Barcelona Pavilion, the Tugendhat House, and the Model House for the Berlin Building Exhibition of 1931—which could be viewed as the realization of neoplastic aims formulated by the De Stijl movement. The ascending branch of this parabola would correspond, according to Zevi, to a phase of liberation from neoclassicism, the descending branch to a gradual sinking back into neoclassicism with the buildings after Barcelona. Mies, whose merit it was to have transposed the volumetric language of neoplasticism into spatial terms, relocked himself, according to Zevi, into the shackles of formalism. Rationalism regressed again to neoclassicism.[31]

The battle between classicism and neoplasticism in the work of Mies van der Rohe is much more complex than Zevi perceives it. It is not a single parabola but an ongoing oscillation, with many hesitations and changes of position,[32] as an exact analysis of buildings and ideas will show. The dialectical exchange between proclassical and anticlassical concepts and ideas is constantly present in Mies's work. Mies did not simply exchange old values for new ones, but continued the dialogue on successively new levels, as is evident from the simultaneity of neoclassical country houses and bold experiments. Even in the apex of the parabola the traditional values have by no means become obsolete. If one draws on sources such as the notebook of 1928, exploited here for the first time, that yields information as to Mies's readings, it becomes quite clear that Mies relied even at the high point of his career on established values. Not so much an exchange of old values for new ones but their synthesis is the presiding idea at the apex of the parabola. In accordance with the motto "Everything decisive happens despite" (Friedrich Nietzsche) that had been the maxim of Adolf Loos, one could reverse Zevi's argument and hold that it was the desire for a more profound traditionalism that led Mies to those works that formulated classical modernism around 1930.

The history of modernism in its entirety, from the enlightenment of around 1800 until the twentieth century, can be viewed as a comparable conflict, a perpetual dialogue of pro- and anticlassical concepts. However, one should not view this dialogue merely as a simple dualism between a liberating organicism and a repressive classicism, as Zevi postulates. In general, the proclassical tendency leans toward the essentially typical. It is countered by an anticlassical attitude that attempts to deny, as far as possible, that art is subject to the strictures of type. This configuration does not appear for the first time with the modernism of our century, which started in opposition to academism and classicism around 1900 but which simultaneously, under the sign of the Doric column, prepared the way for modern architecture. The contradiction between proclassical and anticlassical attitudes is intrinsically as old as architecture itself and is not unilaterally solvable. Just as the type as ideal can never be fully realized, so it can never be totally abolished without exposing architecture to anarchy, for it is already implicit in the basic principles of construction.

This conflict is evident throughout the history of the European building arts: in the eighteenth-century battle between the baroque tradition and the romanticism of English landscape gardening; or in the contradiction between cubic hermeticism and purposeful asymmetry in Karl Friedrich

Schinkel, who moved freely from absolute symmetry to Greek freedom in his urban architecture and his country houses influenced by the Italian villa type. These works with their pavilion system prefigure the panoramic conception of modern space that was taken up again as a theme by Mies, who realized it with the means of his own period.

The modernism of the twentieth century attempted to solve this conflict on a new level by liberating the classical building type from the polarity of inside and outside, from the enclosed interior space and the hierarchy of individual elements. The revolt against the classical principles aimed at replacing them with new, antithetical ones. The Vitruvian concepts of a clear separation of inside and outside and of concentricity were replaced by centrifugality and a free interplay of contrasting elements, an equilibrium of tensions rather than harmony.

If the work of Mies van der Rohe contains contradictory elements, it is due to the circumstance that the modernism of the twenties was itself burdened by a historical legacy. While Bruno Zevi's work breaks with canonical historicizing and opens up a broader perspective, it also reobstructs the view. The oversimplified identification of classicism (type, block, geometry) with authoritarianism, and the optimistic equation of the "free plan" with democracy, obstructs a more profound understanding of modernism—and not only of Mies van der Rohe. It is one of the productive ironies of this century's architectural history that only by rehabilitating classicism could a new modernism of considerable complexity and contradiction emerge.

Postmodernism, with its somewhat diffuse sympathy for history, has contributed to a renewed appreciation of classicism, as indicated by such mind-stretching terms as "postmodern classicism" or the daredevil proclamation of a "free-style classicism."[33] The architectural theories underlying postmodernism, demanding a semantic revamping of the term "classicism," indirectly answer the one-sided interpretation and ideological fixation of Zevian provenance. As "classicism without tears" (Charles Jencks), liberated from the oppressive overtones of its forerunners, it is supposedly differentiated from them by its free and nonpredetermined employment of forms.[34] This revolutionizing of the term "classicism" in the sense of a postmodern eclecticism, however, also throws new light on Mies's architecture. Not only because history is always present in it—a circumstance that should endear it to the postmodern point of view—but also because, after one has tired of those at best ironic quotation games, the desire for poetical serenity and structural honesty will awaken all the more. Thus the sayings of Mies retain an unexpected currency, for the problems he and his contemporaries faced touch us today more than ever.

The idea that history constitutes a potential and necessary enrichment of meaning—a thesis fundamentally called into question by the historiographers of modernism—is presently undergoing a rehabilitation. The traditional view of modernism is itself in need of revision, however. The across-the-board accusation that modern architecture was hostile to tradition and disdainful of context, that it resulted in uniformity and that it lacked sensitivity of scale, is partially the result of a dogmatically limited historiography. One-sided interpretation with a particular historical slant on modern architecture has exerted influence both on the level of perception and reception. For this reason, the critique of modern architecture must also include a critique of the historiography of modern architecture as disseminated by such influential teaching texts as Sigfried Giedion's *Space, Time and Architecture* (1941), in which the history of modernism is presented as unambiguous. That the type of history writing that sees history in terms of linear processes does not stand up to careful analysis has been proven by the brilliant essays of Wittkower's pupil Colin Rowe in the fifties; they prepared the way for a more critical interpretive attitude toward modernism in which the problems of historical continuity in particular come under scrutiny.[35]

In regard to the work of Mies van der Rohe, this implies that one must look not only for unity and universality, but also for discontinuities and reciprocal interactions. A critical view of the history of modern architecture indicates the need for a nuanced reappraisal. The research of our time has to occupy itself not only with modernism's break with tradition, but also with the complex and contradictory underground network of historical roots that nourished it.

"In their best work history is always present," said Aldo Rossi of those whom he viewed as his precursors, namely Adolf Loos and Mies van der Rohe, who for him represent modern architecture.[36] After one has experienced buildings ruled exclusively by the laws of functionalism, the reproaches raised against the architecture of Mies van der Rohe appear in a different light. In Rossi's eyes the rejection of primitive functionalism in favor of pure symbolism and pure poetry actually becomes a positive element, a specific quality of Miesian architecture. Particularly his insistence on creating art—already expressed in the term "building art" that he employed instead of "architecture"—made Mies one of the few able to create objects of timeless beauty despite the vagaries of the marketplace and the pressures of industry.[37]

"Throw light on the inner contradictions," demanded Richard Padovan in his spirited plea for a reinterpretation of Mies van der Rohe. Padovan's aim was not to devalue him but rather "to show him as a more interesting, more vulnerable, and today a more relevant figure than he has often been made out to be: an architect who not only reflected and shared in the struggles and conflicts of his time, but moreover embodied in the several phases of his career, every stage in the history of modern architecture."[38]

The abundance of publications on the work of Mies, made accessible by the *Annotated Bibliography and Chronology* of 1979 with its 732 entries,[39] only partially meets today's demands. The Mies van der Rohe Archive in the Museum of Modern Art in New York was only established in 1968. Publications that appeared before that date could not have benefited from these primary sources. The type of insight that can be gained by a thorough study of the bequest has been demonstrated by Wolf Tegethoff's work on Mies's villas and country house projects after 1922,[40] which has raised doubts about the reliability of present datings and attributions.

Mies's theoretical legacy has so far not been the subject of an independent study. Philip Johnson had attached a selection of Mies's most important writings to his monograph, thereby calling attention to this important aspect of Mies's activity. Today the programmatic announcements of the early manifestos belong to the fixed inventory of the architectural—and art historical—theory of our century. Practically no publication on the architecture of modernism can avoid making reference to them.[41]

It is therefore amazing that a comprehensive edition of the writings of Mies does not yet exist[42] and that those of his writings that are on hand in the archives of New York, Chicago, and Washington have not been published even by recent researchers. The modest volume of known writings has apparently not enticed anyone to subject them to special scrutiny. Compared to the volume of theoretical works delivered by his great contemporaries Le Corbusier or Frank Lloyd Wright, the writings of Mies are sparse.

As Lorenzo Papi has it, Mies did not want to add to "his constructive work a personal 'literature' that could have explained his thoughts and reasonings."[43] He was taciturn from an inner conviction; it was part of his *Weltanschauung* expressed in the phrase "The most important things can anyway not be discussed,"[44] an assertion that seems to echo the well-known concluding sentence of Ludwig Wittgenstein's *Tractatus logico-philosophicus*: "What we cannot speak about we must pass over in silence."[45]

Peter Blake has characterized Mies aptly as a "man of few words."[46] That such an expressive silence is an elemental part of Mies's reality structure is attested by both his written and his built declarations. Mies's frugal prose has its own horizon of values, the width of which has tempted others to burden his work retroactively with philosophical speculations. The short as well as confusing essay by Peter Serenyi, "Spinoza, Hegel and Mies,"[47] illustrates this type of misunderstanding, to which Mies himself had opened the doors by the persistent use of philosophical quotations from Thomas Aquinas and Augustine.

For Mies "the question as to the nature of the building art" was of decisive significance.[48] It led him to search for the truth "in the quarries of ancient and medieval philosophy."[49] From this question came the search for a spiritual orientation of architectural truth, without which there could be no clarity in the relationship between essence and appearance, necessity and possibility, construction and form. The problems of the building art cannot be viewed apart from the problems of being. Architecture must serve life not only practically but also spiritually and constitute a support for ideas that touch on the entire existence of man. In the realm of values lie the actual, decisive problems of architecture, and it is of this that architecture must speak in the language of the building art if it wants to participate in the larger discourse concerned with a new "genuine order."

This readiness to view things in a fundamental way, this concern with "genuine questions—questions about value and purpose,"[50] makes Mies van der Rohe's writings unique testimonies of the architectural theory of our century, for they point to problems that touch on the spiritual core of our period. For Mies, the actual task of the building art of our time consisted in the need to strive for a balance between man and civilization, technology and architecture, history and epoch; it must be motivated by the hope that "it should be possible to bring the old and the new forces of our civilization into harmony with each other."[51] The ongoing discussion in regard to contemporary problems demonstrates that this aim, then as now—and not only for architecture—has remained relevant.

"Today we are again occupied with stylistic forms; I want to warn that we have to be mindful of ourselves," wrote Sergius Ruegenberg, a longtime associate of Mies in the twenties, in his congratulatory address on the occasion of Mies's fiftieth birthday on March 27, 1936, which was published as an editorial letter in *Die Bauwelt*. Ruegenberg concluded with a sentence to which, a half century later, nothing needs to be added: "and if someone does not find himself, let me remind him of Mies van der Rohe."[52]

I The Double Work Field:
Architect as Author

The architect must be skilled in writing so that by written explanations [to his work] he can create a permanent memorial.

Marcus Vitruvius Pollio, Ten Books on Architecture, *c. 30 BC*

The phrase "create, artist, do not talk" remains always true.

H. P. Berlage, Gedanken über den Stil in der Baukunst, *1905*

"My main work has been the planning of buildings. I have never written nor spoken much."[1] Writing about architecture was apparently for Mies an enterprise full of inherent contradictions. This is already indicated by the brevity of his contributions, which leads one to conclude that he did not have a real love for writing; presumably thoughts were committed to paper under considerable resistance and only formulated in the first place due to some external pressure. The internal or external forces that led Mies to express himself publicly remain unknown, due to the fragmentary nature of the sources.[2] Only a reconstruction of circumstances allows us an insight into his motives.

Mies stepped in front of the public for the first time in the summer of 1922 with an article in a journal. Up to that time, the professional press had paid little attention to his architectural work. Only the Riehl House in Potsdam-Neubabelsberg, built in 1907, the first independent project of the twenty-one-year-old, and his competition entry for the design of a Bismarck Memorial had been noted.[3] Mies introduced himself as architect and author in the journal *Frühlicht*, edited by Bruno Taut, with an untitled article consisting of two designs for skyscrapers with dematerializing glass exteriors, accompanied by a short commentary.

The circumstance that led Mies to step in front of the public had probably been the Friedrichstrasse competition, which had been announced in December 1921 with the decision handed down early in 1922. Mies had participated with a radical entry that proposed a 20-floor glass skyscraper, which by the summer of 1922 he presented in two different versions. The design had met with complete noncomprehension on the part of the jury and had been laid aside as a utopian joke.[4]

This Glass Skyscraper project, which arose seemingly unexpected out of the work Mies had thus far produced, was also without precedent in the architectural background.[5] It represented the beginning of a series of designs that was to include the Office Building, Concrete Country House, and Brick Country House, in which the essential possibilities latent in the new construction methods and materials were explored in an aesthetic entirely related to their potential, bringing it to salient expression and denying any commitment to historical forms.

Traditional massivity had been totally overcome and the standard façade had been dematerialized into a unique play of light reflections on the glassy exterior that wrapped the structural skeleton in a transparent veil. This bold project revealed the creative possibilities of a longed-for futuristic architecture in programmatic form. Carl Gottfried, who introduced the glass towers of Mies van der Rohe in the journal *Qualität* in August 1922, celebrated their artistic form as "going beyond the times" and "contrary to all ornamental individualism," as "impersonal, timeless," and for that reason as "building art in the highest sense. In their heightened monumentality, scorn-

Ludwig Mies van der Rohe: Hochhaus

122

Three pages of Mies's article on glass skyscrapers, in *Frühlicht*, no. 4 (1922).

ing all traditional standards of measurements, they speak the language of a new time: The language of our time."[6]

That Mies introduced his glass visions in the journal *Frühlicht*, the forum of the expressionist movement, is not without particular significance. The crystalline stereometry of the skyscraper certainly seems to relate to the glass-and-crystal euphoria of expressionism. The glass polygons strive upward, in the eyes of the critic, with "towerlike, Gothic force" and show in their refractive, crystalline sharpness characteristics related to expressionism.[7] Perhaps one could view the watercolor fantasies of Hans Scharoun of 1920 as forerunners of Mies's skyscraper designs once the polygonal, crystalline structure behind the crackling, bursting, and overpowering surface had been laid bare. "High the transparent, the clear! High purity! High the crystal! and high and ever higher the flowing, the graceful, the sharp-edged, the sparkling, the flashing, the lightweight—high eternal building!" This emphatic heralding of a coming architecture, with which Bruno Taut

3

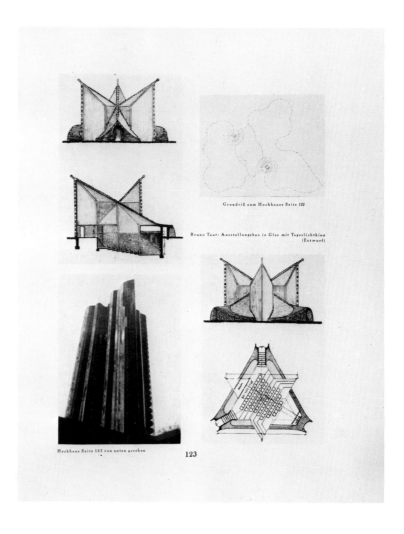

opened the first issue of *Frühlicht* in 1920,[8] furnishes attributes that—
stripped of expressionistic hyperbole and the mystical connotations of a
crystalline world architecture—might just as well have served to describe
the near expressionism of Mies's skyscrapers.

The apparent proximity to expressionism that might have suggested them
as a suitable topic for *Frühlicht* is, however, only superficial. Mies was one
of the few who, unlike Peter Behrens, Walter Gropius, and others, did not
retreat penitently from the tradition of a rarified prewar classicism into the
Bauhütten world of the medieval craftsman.[9] The glassy visions of the Miesian cathedral of the future did not harken back to medieval mysticism but
advanced the myth of a new time characterized by a preference for reason
and abstraction.

The villa projects of 1921, designed simultaneously with the skyscrapers,
prove that the principles of Schinkel's classicism, even after 1918, still
retained for Mies valid working ideas commensurate with honest building. It
was this imperturbable insistence on outdated principles that insulated Mies

Nur im Bau befindliche Wolkenkratzer zeigen die kühnen konstruktiven Gedanken, und überwältigend ist dann der Eindruck der hochragenden Stahlskelette. Mit der Ausmauerung der Fronten wird dieser Eindruck vollständig zerstört, der konstruktive Gedanke, die notwendige Grundlage für die künstlerische Gestaltung vernichtet und meist von einem sinnlosen und trivialen Formenwust überwuchert. Im besten Fall imponiert jetzt nur die tatsächliche Größe, und doch hätten diese Bauten mehr sein können als eine Manifestation unseres technischen Könnens. Allerdings müßte man auf den Versuch verzichten, mit den überlieferten Formen eine neue Aufgabe zu lösen, vielmehr ist aus dem Wesen der neuen Aufgabe heraus die Gestaltung ihrer Form zu versuchen.

Das neuartige, konstruktive Prinzip dieser Bauten tritt dann klar hervor, wenn man für die nun nicht mehr tragenden Außenwände Glas verwendet. Die Verwendung von Glas zwingt allerdings zu neuen Wegen.

Bei meinem Entwurf für das Hochhaus am Friedrichbahnhof in Berlin, für das ein dreieckiger Bauplatz zur Verfügung stand, schien mir für diesen Bau eine dem Dreieck angepaßte prismatische Form die richtige Lösung zu sein, und ich winkelte die einzelnen Frontflächen leicht gegeneinander, um der Gefahr der toten Wirkung auszuweichen, die sich oft bei der Verwendung von Glas in großen Flächen ergibt. Meine Versuche an einem Glasmodell wiesen mir den Weg, und ich erkannte bald, daß es bei der Verwendung von Glas nicht auf eine Wirkung von Licht und Schatten, sondern auf ein reiches Spiel von Lichtreflexen ankam. Das habe ich bei dem anderen hier veröffentlichten Entwurf angestrebt. (S. 122–23.)

Bei oberflächlicher Betrachtung erscheint die Umrißlinie des Grundrisses willkürlich, und doch ist sie das Ergebnis vieler Versuche an dem Glasmodell. Für die Kurven waren bestimmend die Belichtung des Gebäudeinneren, die Wirkung der Baumasse im Straßenbild und zuletzt das Spiel der erstrebten Lichtreflexe. Umrißlinien des Grundrisses, bei dem die Kurven auf Licht und Schatten berechnet waren, erwiesen sich am Modell bei der Verwendung von Glas als gänzlich ungeeignet. Die einzigen im Grundriß feststehenden Punkte sind die Treppen- und Aufzugstürme.

Alle anderen Unterteilungen des Grundrisses sollen den jeweiligen Bedürfnissen angepaßt und in Glas ausgeführt werden.

Mies van der Rohe

Mies van der Rohe:
Hochhausprojekt für Bahnhof Friedrichstraße in Berlin

Reklamebau des schwedischen Balletts
Berlin, am Potsdamer Platz

Laden Krielke in Schöneberg
von Arthur Götz

124

and secured him a high degree of independence against short-lived contemporary trends.

Mies retained a critical distance because he was unwilling to jettison old values as long as commensurate new ones had not yet been found. "The sudden liberation from ancient restrictions and aims," through which "even more lasting values have lost . . . clear definition," did not yet represent in itself a value system.[10] "In regard to the new, also, the attitude is not the same. Here also, it is the inner attitude of man that counts." This thought for a lecture, entrusted by Mies to his notebook, typifies his skeptical rationalism.[11]

The classicistic villa projects stand only in seeming contradiction to the bold glass fantasies of 1921. In reality they secured a continuity of development that, after 1924—after Mies had mastered in a series of prototypical, analytical designs the architectural possibilities of the new construction methods and materials—continued on without any immediately noticeable reference to those experiments in abstract form. The Mosler House in

The Double Work Field:
Architect as Author

5

Potsdam-Neubabelsberg, the construction of which began in September 1924, is the last example in which the classicizing tradition of Behrens is still visibly present. True, Mies reduced that reference to such extreme simplicity that the city surveyor's office felt it must interfere. One was afraid that the house "without embellishment . . . would appear like an army barracks" and would, on account of its blandness, disturb the urban image.[12]

"It is a futile endeavor to use contents and forms of earlier building periods today. Even the strongest artistic talent will then fail. We find again and again that excellent building masters fail because their work does not serve the will of the epoch. . . . In the final analysis, they remain dilettantes despite their great talent, for the élan with which one undertakes the wrong thing is irrelevant. It is the essential that matters. One cannot walk forward

Hans Scharoun, watercolor, 1920.

Mies's design for the Friedrichstrasse skyscraper, 1921.

The Double Work Field:
Architect as Author

7

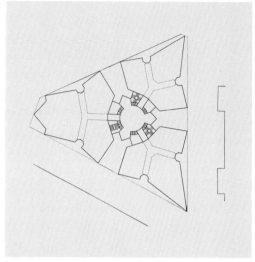

Sketch and ground plan for the Friedrichstrasse skyscraper, 1921.

while looking backward, and one cannot be the instrument of the will of the epoch if one lives in the past. . . . The entire striving of our epoch is directed toward the secular. The efforts of the mystics will remain episodes. Although our understanding of life has become more profound, we will not build cathedrals. . . . We do not value the great gesture but rationality and reality."[13] With these sentences published in 1924 in the article "Baukunst und Zeitwille!" (Building Art and the Will of the Epoch), Mies not only rejected misunderstood traditionialism but also refused to endorse a wrongly understood modernism of "aesthetic speculation," as expounded by an expressionism that, by 1922, had already passed its apex. The sky-scrapers in *Frühlicht* assumed, almost accidentally, a symbolic significance, for they signaled, with their sober sense of reality, the approaching end of the expressionist movement. The summer 1922 issue of *Frühlicht,* number 4 in the new series and the one in which Mies had spoken up for the first time, was the last publication of the journal.[14]

Escape into utopias, almost necessary after the traumatic war experience, now yielded to a mood that rejected fantasy for a new "enthusiasm for the immediately real."[15] The longing for harmony, projected by expressionism into the transcendental, now shifted to an equally invisible abstract realm that was, however, not metaphysically but rationalistically secured. The vanishing point of utopianism now shifted from the imaginary "cathedral of the future" to the reified, concrete world of the machine age, the *Zeitgeist* of which demanded visible realization according to a new definition of order.

It is this matter-of-fact sobriety, so much at odds with the quasi-religious, dreamy pathos of *Frühlicht*, that pervaded Mies's text. Compared to the illustrations of the bold skyscraper designs, the artless words appear almost defensive. Mies accompanied the extraordinary glass towers with plain sentences, according to which the towers' appearance was quite simply the result of the givens of the site, the manner of construction, and the optical effect of the glass panels. The lack of understanding Mies had experienced from a competition jury still swearing allegiance to the expressionist fashion[16] seemed to necessitate a justification that made the "reasonable meaning of the new form-giving" explicit.[17]

Mies described his concept and work method, which appeared to follow the principles of a deliberate theory, with the dryness of a manual. The design was explained in terms of a creative process that called for the interlocking of theoretical demands with formal decisions. "The writing and talking of artists about their work" was, as Theo van Doesburg explained in the introduction to his book on the Bauhaus, "the natural result of the general misunderstanding of the new art orientation by the lay public." Thus, the artists of the new direction considered it a "duty to support their work with words. . . . Theory followed the creative activity as a necessary sequel. Artists do not write *about* art, but *from within the domain of* art."[18]

This double requirement as outlined by Doesburg, namely "to give a logical explanation as well as defend the new art direction," was realized in the parallel rendering of text and project with which Mies introduced his work.[19]

Mosler House, Potsdam-Neubabelsberg, 1924–1926.

Halt

a an Größe und Intensität abnehmend, seitlich verschwindend

a in Lage und Intensität wechselnd, beginnt das neue Thema: Bewegung zweier Lichtqualitäten gegeneinander (Bewegung einer „Fläche" vor und hinter einer feststehenden Fläche

Anwachsen der vorderen Fläche

Schwinden der hinteren Fläche

Halt !!!

Zusammenfassen aller Vorgänge in einem

Schluß. Größte Licht-Menge und -Intensität

Hans Richter

gabemöglichkeit mit Hilfe eines kleinen Kondensatormikrophons. Der wissenschaftliche Nachweis, daß sogar weit kleinere Kapazitätsänderungen, als sie der Film erwarten läßt, für die deutliche Wiedergabe ausreichen, wurde 1920 durch einen kleinen Cylinderkondensatorfühler erbracht.

Aber vom sprechenden Film zur Optophonetik ist noch ein großer Schritt. Als erster hat der Erfinder des Antiphons, Plenner, in einer Schrift „Die Zukunft es elektrischen Fernsehers" diese Frage behandelt. Er sagt darin: „Kann der Lichtstrahl gezwungen werden, (mittels einer Selenzelle) Induktionsströme zu erzeugen oder zu verändern, so muß in die Leitung geschaltetes Hörtelefon solche inducierten Erscheinungen in Klänge verwandeln. Was also in der Empfangsstation als Bild eintritt, würde im Zwischenapparat als Ton erscheinen und wenn am Ursprung bewegte Bilder, sichtbare Vorgänge, aufgenommen werden, so müssen sich diese als eine Folge von Tönen kundgeben, und umgekehrt. Die Gestalt eines Vierecks muß bei akustischer Verwandlung ein anderes Tonbild hervorrufen, als das von einem Dreieck oder Kreis genommene, ein Würfel muß anders klingen als ein Kegel oder Prisma. Kristalle und Sterne werden zu reden beginnen, in welcher Sprache, in welchem Tongefäll? Das liegt noch gänzlich im Felde der Ahnung, aber aus dem Nichtwissen wird dereinst das Verstehen aufsteigen."

Nun liegt dieser Vorstellung, wie auch dem Tonbildfilm, ein Naturalismus zugrunde, um den es sich für uns heute keineswegs mehr handeln kann. Daß die Musik in ihrer letzten Form (auch die der Futuristen) unserer Weltbewußtheit nicht mehr entspricht, so wie ihr die akinetische Malerei nicht mehr entspricht, ist eine unleugbare Tatsache. Wir müssen also neue, für uns giltige Gesetze, eine neue Funktionalität für beide finden. Wir müssen die Zugehörigkeit der Formfunktionalität zu den Schwingungsintensitäten in einer grundlegenden Weise ermitteln, um über das Zufällige zu einer neuen Formverbindlichkeit zu gelangen.

Berlin   R. Hausmann

Dieser F m hat den Charakter einer gestaltenden Demonstration, in der bestimmte elem ntare Filmmöglichkeiten elementär entfaltet werden. Das Auftreten und die Dauer der einzelnen Figuren und Filmgruppen ist methodisch: Hellegkeitsgrade – Proportionen etc. etc.

Die Lichtverhältnisse haben qualitativen und quantitativen Charakter.

Dieser F m ... sind de facto Begrenzungen von Vorgängen in verschiedener Dimensionen (oder von Dimensionen in verschiedener Zeitfolge). In ihm gehen die "Formen" aus den Begrenzungen hervor – und ... zur Begrenzung bei Flächenvorgängen (als Material der Flächengen) vgl. die Fläche als Begrenzung bei Raumvorgängen. Die Lin e dient zur Begrenzung der Fläche ohne Begrenzung ist nicht darstellbar; daher verbrei de Linie (längliche Breite, Fläche und Quadrat (als einfachste und ökonomischste Fo m der Begrenzung).

Das eigentliche Konstruktionsmittel ist das Licht, dessen Intensität und Menge. Die Gestaltung der Lichtnatur im Sinne einer zusammenfassenden Ausschaulichkeit ist die Aufgabe für das Ganze.

Dieser F m ist also prinzipiell n i c h t ein solcher, der das □ und die □ als Kompositionsmittel gebraucht – etwa orchestriert und entwickelt –, sondern ein solcher, in dem □ und ... als Hilfsmittel auftreten. Der entscheidende Gehalt der Fläche etc., – die „Form" (ob abstrakt oder naturalistisch) ist zu vermeiden.

Die auf tretenden Formen sind weder Analogien noch Symbole, noch Schönheitsmi l.

Der F a vermittelt in seinem Ablauf (Vorführung) ganz eigentlich die Spannungen – d Kontrastverhältnisse des Lichts. Diese Verhältnisse bestehen zwischen h ll und dunkel, groß und klein, schnell und langsam, horizontal und vertikal etc. etc.

Es ist versucht, den Film So zu organisieren, daß die einzelnen Teile untereinander und zum Ganzen in aktiver Spannung stehen, sodaß das Ganze in sich ständig bewegllich bleibt.

Berlin

Jede ästhetische Spekulation,
jede Doktrin,
und jeden Formalismus

lehnen wir ab.

Baukunst ist raumgefaßter Zeitwille.
Lebendig. Wechselnd. Neu.

Nicht das Gestern, nicht das Morgen, nur das Heute ist formbar.
Nur dieses Bauen gestaltet.

Gestaltet die Form aus dem Wesen der Aufgabe mit den
Mitteln unserer Zeit.

Das ist unsere Arbeit.

B Ü R O H A U S

Das Bürohaus ist ein Haus   der Arbeit   der Organisation   der Klarheit   der Ökonomie.
Helle weite Arbeitsräume, übersichtlich, ungeteilt, nur gegliedert wie der Organismus des Betriebes. Größter Effekt mit geringstem Aufwand an Mitteln.

Die Materialien sind   Beton   Eisen   Glas.

Eisenbetonbauten sind ihrem Wesen nach Skelettbauten. Keine Teigwaren   noch Panzertürme. Bei tragender Binderkonstruktion eine nichttragende Wand. Also Haut- und Knochenbauten.

Die zweckmäßigste Einteilung der Arbeitsplätze war für die Raumtiefe maßgebend; diese beträgt 16 m. Ein zweistieliger Rahmen von 8 m Spannweite mit beiderseitiger Konsolauskragung von 4 m Länge wurde als das ökonomischste Konstruktionsprinzip ermittelt. Die Binderentfernung beträgt 5 m. Dieses Bindersystem trägt die Deckenplatte, die am Ende der Kragarme senkrecht hochgewinkelt Außenhaut wird und als Rückwand der Regale dient, die aus dem Rauminnern der Übersichtlichkeit wegen in die Außenwände verlegt wurden. Über den 2 m hohen Regalen liegt ein bis zur Decke reichendes durchlaufendes Fensterband.

Berlin, Mai 1923   Mies v. d. Rohe

G MATERIAL DER NÄCHSTEN NUMMERN:

Fiat ǀ Element und Erfindung ǀ Neue Optik ǀ Bauhandwerk u. Bauindustrie ǀ Topographie der Typographie ǀ Lunapark ǀ Photoplastik ǀ Kinderspielzeug ǀ Acrobatie des Schauspielers ǀ i ǀ Das neue Wohnhaus ǀ Die Internationale Verkehrszeichensprache.

Mies van der Rohe, "Office Building," published in G, no. 1 (July 1923).

His next publications followed the same pattern. In July and September 1923 Mies presented, in the first two issues of the periodical *G*—a letter that stood for the word *Gestaltung* (form-giving) and that received its programmatic meaning from the subtitle *Material zur elementaren Gestaltung* (Material for Elementary Form-Giving)—two additional breakthroughs: the design for his Concrete Office Building, which showed a continuous horizontal fenestration uninterrupted by supports, and the design for a Concrete Country House. Both projects demonstrated the constructive and aesthetic possibilities afforded by the cantilevering capabilities of concrete.

The double requirement was already evident in the visual presentation of the text's immediately intelligible arrangement. Before giving a "logical explanation" of the design by describing the construction and the resulting consequences, we find a proclamation assertively heralding the new art.

Any aesthetic speculation
any doctrine } *we reject.*
and any formalism

With this apodictic beginning dispatching with all prior art, Mies introduced his manifesto "Bürohaus" (Office Building). A bracket in the text encompasses the terms "speculation," "doctrine," and "formalism," which are canceled by an uncompromising "we reject" in widely spaced letters. The unequivocability of this gesture, dictated by an energetic will meant to suggest clarity, determination, and strength, is carried through in the subsequent lines that announce, in the full awareness of stating an eternal truth:

Building art is the spatially apprehended will of the epoch.
Alive. Changing. New.
Not the yesterday, not the tomorrow, only the today, is formable.
Only this building creates.
Create form out of the nature of the task with the means of our time.
That is our work.

Only now follows the heading "Bürohaus" and the actual text on the rendering of the design, couched in similarly general terms. The nature of the building task, the type, and the constructive thought determine the logical

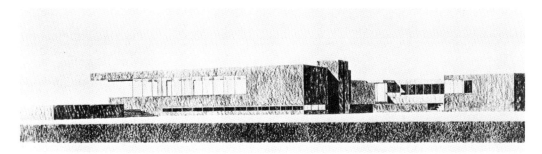

Concrete Country House, 1923.

G II

Sept. 23

MATERIAL ZUR ELEMENTAREN GESTALTUNG

HERAUSGEBER: HANS RICHTER. REDAKTION DIES. HEFTES: GRAFF, MIES v. d. ROHE, RICHTER. REDAKTION u. VERTRIEB: BERLIN-FRIEDENAU, Eschenstr. 7.

BAUEN

Wir kennen keine Form-, sondern nur Bauprobleme.
Die Form ist nicht das Ziel, sondern das Resultat unserer Arbeit.
Es gibt keine Form an sich.
Das wirklich Formvolle ist bedingt, mit der Aufgabe verwachsen, ja der elementarste Ausdruck ihrer Lösung.
Form als Ziel ist Formalismus; und den lehnen wir ab. Ebensowenig erstreben wir einen Stil.

Auch der Wille zum Stil ist formalistisch.
Wir haben andere Sorgen.
Es liegt uns gerade daran, die Bauerei von den ästhetischen Spekulantentum zu befreien und Bauen wieder zu dem zu machen, was es allein sein sollte, nämlich

BAUEN

M. v. d. R.

Der Versuch, den Eisenbeton als Baumaterial für den Wohnhausbau einzuführen, ist schon wiederholt gemacht worden. Meist aber in ungenügender Weise. Die Vorzüge dieses Materials hat man nicht ausgenutzt und seine Nachteile nicht vermieden. Man glaubte dem Material genügend Rechnung zu tragen, wenn man die Ecken des Hauses und die der einzelnen Räume abrundete. Die runden Ecken sind für den Beton gänzlich belanglos und nicht einmal ganz einfach herzustellen. Es genügt natürlich nicht, ein Backsteinhaus in Eisenbeton zu übertragen. — Den Hauptvorzug des Eisenbeton sehe ich in der Möglichkeit großer Materialersparnis. Um diese bei einem Wohnhaus zu ermöglichen, muß man die tragenden und stützenden Kräfte auf wenige Punkte des Gebäudes konzentrieren. Der Nachteil des Eisenbeton ist seine geringe Isolierfähigkeit und seine große Schall-Leitbarkeit. Es ist also notwendig, eine besondere Isolation als Schutz gegen Außentemperatur vorzusehen. Das einfachste Mittel, den Übelstand der Schallübertragung zu beseitigen, scheint mir darin zu liegen, alles das, was Schall erzeugt, auszuschließen; ich denke hier an Gummiböden, Schiebefenster und -türen und ähnliche Vorkehrungen; dann aber auch an eine Großräumigkeit in der Grundriß-

bildung. — Der Eisenbeton verlangt vor seiner Ausführung genaueste Festlegung der gesamten Installation; hier kann der Architekt vom Schiffsingenieur noch alles lernen. Beim Backsteinbau ist es möglich, wenn auch nicht gerade sinnvoll, sofort nach dem Richten des Daches die Heizungs- und Installations-Monteure auf das Haus loszulassen, die in kurzer Zeit das kaum errichtete Haus in eine Ruine verwandeln. Ein solches Verfahren ist allerdings beim Eisenbeton ausgeschlossen. Hier kann nur diszipliniertes Arbeiten zum Ziele führen.

Das oben abgebildete Modell zeigt einen Versuch, dem Problem des Eisenbeton-Wohnhauses näher zu kommen. Der Hauptwohnteil wird von einem vierstirnigen Bindersystem getragen. Dieses Konstruktionssystem wird umschlossen von einer dünnen Eisenbetonhaut. Diese Haut bildet sowohl Wand als Decke. Die Decke ist von den Außenwänden zur Mitte hin leicht geneigt. Die durch die Schrägstellung der beiden Dachhälften gebildete Rinne ermöglicht die denkbar einfachste Entwässerung des Daches. Alle Klempnerarbeiten kommen hierdurch, in Fortfall. Aus den Wänden habe ich an den Stellen Öffnungen herausgeschnitten, wo ich sie für die Aussicht und Raumbeleuchtung brauchte.

Mies v. d. Rohe

FIAT

Bau und Plan von den Herren Senator Giovanni Agnelli, Guido Fornaca und Ingenieur Matheo Trucco, Turin.

EINFAHRBAHN ÜBER DER FABRIK FIAT IN LINGOTTO.

Mit dem Ausbau und der Entwicklung der Automobil-Industrie entstand auch die Notwendigkeit, die Fahrzeuge vor der Ablieferung einer besonderen Probefahrt zu unterziehen, um die Sicherheit für ihre absolute Fahrbereitschaft zu gewinnen. Daher der Brauch, die Fahrzeuge auf der Straße auszuprobieren, bevor sie den Kunden ausgehändigt werden. Dieses bei einem beschränkten Fabrikationsumfang sehr einfache Verfahren schafft große Schwierigkeiten, wenn die Produktion über das Normale hinauswächst, denn es ist nicht leicht, einen zuverlässigen Stab von erfahrenen Einfahrern zu vereinigen, die, ohne einer ständigen und direkten Kontrolle unterworfen zu sein, für die volle Betriebssicherheit der Fahrzeuge, die man ihnen anvertraut hat, garantieren können. Außerdem verursacht die größere oder kleinere Entfernung zwischen der Fabrik und dem geeigneten Fahrgelände

Mies van der Rohe, "Building," published in *G*, no. 2 (September 1923), illustrated with a model of the Concrete Country House.

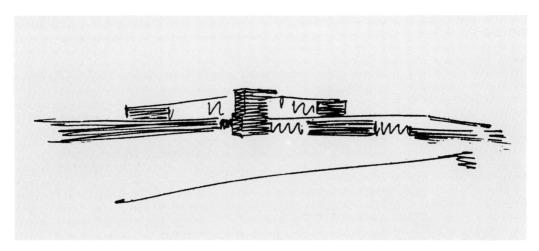

Sketch for the Brick Country House, published in the catalog of the Berlin Art Exhibition, 1924.

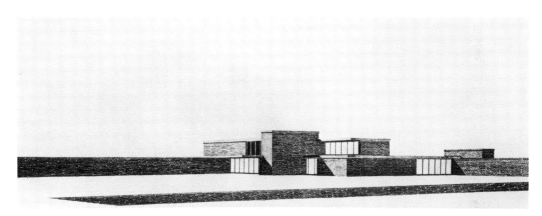

Brick Country House, 1924.

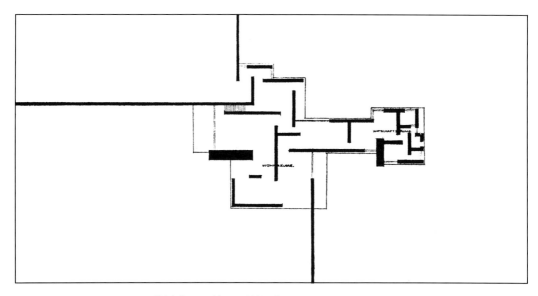

Brick Country House, 1924, plan.

explanation, which aims at describing the artistic process as a conceptually exact sequence. "Work," "organization," "clarity," and "economy" are its basic components. A framed citation by Karl Marx, "Art should change life, not interpret it," stands vertically on the inner margin, underlining the programmatic and activist tenor of the text.

The same arrangement is employed in the article accompanying the Concrete Country House on the title page of the second issue of G of September 1923, the editing of which, according to the masthead, Mies shared with publisher Hans Richter. Flanked by the monumental letters BAUEN, which frame the opening proclamation like a banner, Mies announces:

We know no forms, only building problems.
Form is not the goal but the result of our work.
There is no form in and for itself.
The truly formal is conditional, fused with the task, yes, the most elementary expression of its solution.
Form as goal is formalism; that we reject. Nor do we strive for a style.
Even the will to style is formalism.
We have other worries.
It is our specific concern to liberate building activity from aesthetic speculators and make building again what alone it should be, namely BUILDING [BAUEN].

The defensive, sober tone of the comments to the Glass Skyscraper Project has given way to an extraordinary self-assurance. The two texts in the avant-garde periodical G did not constitute a necessary justification to a third party, nor did they serve as an argumentative clarification in defense of creative possibilities.

In that agitated atmosphere that pervaded the period between 1922 and 1924, Mies, who had by now advanced to the forefront of the partisans of New Building with his bold and prophetic designs, developed what was for him a rare publicistic and propagandistic activity—and this not only as author of seven articles. Another activity that has so far received scant attention is Mies's collaboration on the periodical G, where he assumed extensive responsibilities, both as author and editor.[20] After 1924, its activities were conducted out of Mies's own office, as is indicated by the address "Berlin W 35, Am Karlsbad 24, Telephone Lützow 9667,"[21] and it has been proven that Mies made considerable efforts to secure its financial basis—by more or less successful attempts to obtain contributions from well-capitalized firms and contributors and, last but not least, by making contributions out of his own pocket.

An inquiry at the well-reputed *Frankfurter Zeitung* regarding an editorial participation on G remained without the desired effect. Mies had added to his petition a copy of G number 3 containing his essay "Industrielles Bauen" (Industrial Building), which was accompanied by an appeal for a fundamental change of dwelling forms. A photograph of Alfred Messel's Simon House (1900), located on the Matthäikirchstrasse in the Tiergarten, was chosen as example of the type of traditional house now being targeted. The rejection letter Mies received from the editor of the *Frankfurter Zeitung*, signed by Heinrich Simon, was not without a note of irony:

Dear Mr. Mies van der Rohe! I have glanced through your periodical, but believe that an editorial participation on our side cannot be contemplated. What is suitable for one does not suit all. I have absolute sympathy for such a radical publication, but it has no place in the framework of our publishing house. By a funny chance it was exactly the house of my mother that you chalked up in red, which has amused me greatly, but of course, it has in no way influenced my decision. With best regards, yours, Heinrich Simon.[22]

As the former *G* editor Hans Richter reported in his memoirs, Mies was "main co-worker" and as such the "only one who effectively influenced this 'hand-made' periodical, which I was able to keep afloat until 1926. This was due to his style, his personality, and his financial support."[23]

Richter was a painter, writer, and experimental film maker who had studied architecture from 1906 to 1909, had been in contact with the expressionist *Sturm* since 1912, had maintained close ties with dadaism, and had been a coworker on Theo van Doesburg's periodical *De Stijl* published since 1917; like Mies himself, he was a member of the Novembergruppe founded in December 1918. Mies had joined this artists' association in 1922. It had survived the disbanding of the *Arbeitsrat für Kunst* (Work Council for the Arts) in 1921 and Mies had been its president between 1923 and 1925.[24]

It was from this circle around the Novembergruppe, which distanced itself from the individualism of the expressionist ideology and engaged in a search for universally valid, suprapersonal, elementary concepts, that the periodical *G* arose.[25] One of its founders and coeditors was Werner Gräff, who maintained a close relationship with Theo van Doesburg. Van Doesburg visited Hans Richter in Berlin in the winter of 1920 and it is presumably from this period that we can date his first contacts with Mies.[26] In the beginning of 1921 van Doesburg settled for two years in Weimar, where he organized the opposition to the crafts-oriented teaching of Walter Gropius's Bauhaus. The third in this association of editors of the first number of *G* was the Russian architect El Lissitzky, who after completing his architectural studies in Darmstadt had returned to Moscow in 1914 and then attempted in 1920 to start a constructivist movement in Düsseldorf. It was on the initiative of Lissitzky that the van Diemen gallery showed the influential First Russian Art Exhibition in 1922, which introduced for the first time the work of the Russian constructivists in Germany.

Besides Mies, the main contributors of the periodical *G*, which published a mere six issues at irregular intervals between 1923 and 1926, consisted of

Title page of *G*, no. 3 (June 1924), with view of the Friedrichstrasse skyscraper.

Nr. 3

G

Juni 1924

Zeitschrift für elementare Gestaltung

Herausgeber Hans Richter

Redaktion: Gräff, Kiesler, Miës v. d. Rohe, Richter

G erscheint monatl., Preis für 1 Heft **1,50** Gm., Abonnement (6 Hefte) **8,00** Gm.

Redaktion: Berlin - Friedenau, Eschenstraße 7, Fernsprecher Rheingau 9978
Vertrieb: Berlin W 35, Am Karlsbad 24, Fernsprecher Lützow 9667

Masthead for *G*, no. 3.

El Lissitzky, Theo van Doesburg, Ludwig Hilberseimer, Raoul Hausmann, Hans Arp, and Kurt Schwitters. Additional contributions were furnished by Piet Mondrian, Kasimir Malevich, Viking Eggeling, Naum Gabo, Antoine Pevsner, Ernst Schöne, George Grosz, John Heartfield, Tristan Tzara, and Man Ray.[27] There was an especially close connection between *G* members and members of the Dutch De Stijl movement that had assembled around Mondrian, van Doesburg, J. J. P. Oud, and Gerrit Rietveld.

The fact that van Doesburg invited Mies in the summer of 1923 as the only non-Dutch architect to participate in the De Stijl exhibition in Paris in the fall of 1923[28] proves that people were conscious of a mutual commitment to a unifying artistic concept. The proximity between the *G* crowd and the De Stijl movement is already implied by the common references to the theoretical concept of elementary *Neue Gestaltung* (neoplasticism) as developed by Piet Mondrian. It was van Doesburg who wrote the leading editorial for the first issue of *G*, "Zur Elementaren Gestaltung" (On Elementary Form-Giving), and this relationship with *G* continued even after his departure from Weimar.[29] If van Doesburg concluded his letter to Mies with the phrase "I greet you and all friends of the square," it was not only a dadaesque flourish but also a symbolic play on the ideals of elementary purity and abstractness that, in ciphered form, characterized the Platonic-

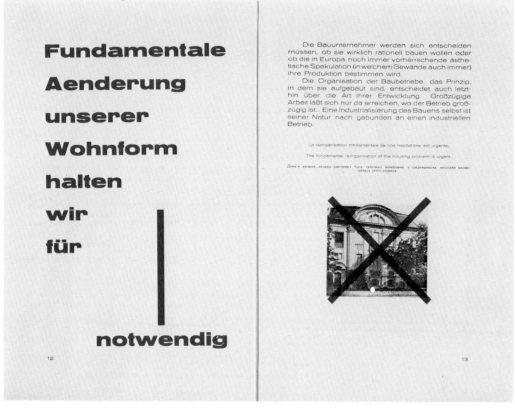

G, no. 3: an appeal for a fundamental change of dwelling forms, with the Simon House crossed out as an example of the old.

Poster for the Werkbund exhibition "The Dwelling," Stuttgart, 1927. Design by Willi Baumeister, Ludwig Mies van der Rohe, and Werner Gräff.

Mondrianesque world of universal harmony. The square, set in the heading of *G* next to the capital letter, referred to the brotherhood of the representatives of De Stijl and those of *G*. It served as motto for a specific artistic ideology much as the guitar was a favorite still-life motif serving as emblem for cubism.[30]

The two periodicals publicized each other: van Doesburg's monthly *De Stijl* presented *G* as "Het orgaan der Construcktivisten in Europa,"[31] and *G* recommended *De Stijl* to its readers as ranking "before all other art periodicals of the cultivated world . . . on account of its character and consequentiality. . . . If one generally looks to a publication for *information*, one looks to *De Stijl* for more; where others simply state, it sets aims and fights for them."[32] The latter also applied to the provocative orientation of *G* and the articles Mies contributed. Their avant-garde tenor did not aim at explanations but proclaimed the postulate of the new aims with revolutionary fervor.

By means of *G* and the Novembergruppe, Mies could take up contacts with the leading representatives of European modernism and publicize his own declarations of principle, both in drawings and in words. The Novembergruppe, which was represented by its own exhibit at the annual Grosse Berliner Kunstausstellung, also offered the opportunity to introduce radical experiments and compare them with the work of other modern architects, including those from abroad.[33]

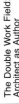

19

Advertisement for *G* in *De Stijl*, 6, nos. 6–7 (1924).

Advertisement for *De Stijl* in *G*, no. 1 (July 1923).

Mies could rightfully declare in 1924, on the basis of his axiomatic designs in which constructive thinking had been advanced as a basis for artistic formulation, that he knew of "no other work that is perceived so elementarily as construction and is so far removed from dusty magic without falling into the mistake of the artistic."[34] If this self-praise shows that Mies was, at that time, conscious of his historic achievement, it also shows that, though pleased with his role as leading advocate of the New Building, he became its spokesman only hesitatingly.

To entice him to make a publicistic statement, it was necessary, as Rudolf Schwarz said in 1929, to "get Mies started."[35] Several essays that had been promised were either never delivered[36] or else arrived too late,[37] and they were considerably shorter than had been agreed upon. The excuses reflected a program: "It is shorter than you expected, but I only wanted to stimulate building. All the rest comes of itself."[38] The key sentence, which could head all writings of Mies, was delivered in 1924 by Hermann von Wedderkop, editor of Der Querschnitt, when he affirmed the receipt of a manuscript by Mies with the phrase "excellent but much too short"—a judgment that practically anticipated the slogan "less is more," later used to describe Mies's buildings. "We had decided on 4 Querschnitt pages, but instead there are not quite 1½. I miss detailed explanations of your opinions, transpositions into the practical, particularly how the new house looks, especially the apartment house, all those problems of glass and reinforced concrete construction, of all of which nothing is mentioned. Can you not write it as a follow-up to the essay? But I would have to have it right away."[39]

Mies's answer to the editor was no less typical: "Since I am no writer, I find writing difficult; in the same time I could have completed a new design."[40]

Even the Bauhaus Book that was suggested to Mies by Walter Gropius in September 1925, since "it would be so important and nice if you would write this volume on your architectural ideas," did not come together in 1928 as announced by the publisher's prospectus.[41] Unrealized, too, remained the volume Mies was asked to contribute to the series conceived in 1925 by the Frankfurt neurologist Hans Prinzhorn: Das Weltbild. Bücherei Lebendigen Wissens (Image of the World: Library of Living Knowledge). This encyclopedic and ambitious undertaking was to consist of about a hundred volumes in "mass editions at reasonable prices" and was meant by Prinzhorn to give "a comprehensive rendering of the structure of the present world." Prinzhorn urged Mies in numerous letters and assured him that "then as now, it is very important to me that your Baukunst should be among the first three volumes, for one can very well demonstrate from it what the characteristics of the whole project are."[42]

Of all the opportunities that presented themselves, Mies apparently availed himself only of those that were unavoidable. He was caught in the wake of

Die Reihe wird in schneller Folge fortgesetzt.

IN VORBEREITUNG:

BAUHAUSBÜCHER

W. Kandinsky: Punkt, Linie, Fläche
Violett (Bühnenstück)
Kurt Schwitters: Merz-Buch
Heinrich Jacoby: Schöpferische Musikerziehung
J. J. P. Oud (Holland): Die holländische Architektur
George Antheil (Amerika): Musico-mechanico
Albert Gleizes (Frankreich) Kubismus
F. T. Marinetti und
Prampolini (Italien): Futurismus
Fritz Wichert: Expressionismus
Tristan Tzara: Dadaismus
L. Kassák und E. Kállai
(Ungarn): Die MA-Gruppe
T. v. Doesburg (Holland): Die Stijlgruppe
Carel Teige (Prag): Tschechische Kunst
Louis Lozowick (Amerika): Amerikanische Architektur
Walter Gropius: Neue Architekturdarstellung ● Das
flache Dach ● Montierbare Typen-
bauten ● Die Bauhausneubauten in
Dessau
Mies van der Rohe: Über Architektur
Le Corbusier-Saugnier
(Frankreich): Über Architektur
Knud Lönberg-Holm
(Dänemark): Über Architektur
Friedrich Kiesler
(Österreich): Neue Formen der Demonstration
Die Raumstadt
Jane Heap (Amerika): Die neue Welt
G. Muche und R. Paulick: Das Metalltypenhaus
Mart Stam Das „ABC" vom Bauen
Adolf Behne: Kunst, Handwerk und Industrie
Max Burchartz: Plastik der Gestaltungen
Martin Schäfer: Konstruktive Biologie
Reklame und Typographie
des Bauhauses
L. Moholy-Nagy: Aufbau der Gestaltungen
Paul Klee: Bildnerische Mechanik
Oskar Schlemmer: Bühnenelemente
Joost Schmidt: Bildermagazin der Zeit I
Die neuen künstlichen
Materialien

BAUHAUSBÜCHER

Die BAUHAUSBÜCHER sind zu bezie-
hen einzeln oder in Serien durch jede
Buchhandlung oder direkt vom

VERLAG

ALBERT LANGEN

MÜNCHEN Hubertusstr. 27

Bestellkarte liegt diesem Prospekt bei.

BAUHAUSDRUCK MOHOLY DIN C 5

Prospectus for Bauhaus Books by the publishing firm Albert Langen.

those principles he had evoked by his radically conceived designs, and people now expected him to take a public stand on these issues.

Invitations for speeches and requests for articles in the professional press increasingly testified to the interest that began to be taken in the architect Mies van der Rohe, who was expected to elaborate on the problems of the times. The spirit of the new building art wanted to be actively represented. And so it was that Mies gave a lecture on this topic on November 27, 1925, as part of a lecture series scheduled by the Kunstgewerbeschule of Bremen, in which the philosophers Nicolai Hartmann ("On the Revolution in the Ethical World Consciousness") and Romano Guardini ("The Crisis of the Will to Education and the Nature of Living Education") also spoke. However, Mies was soon to perceive all this flattering attention, on account of the concomitant attitude of expectation, as a burdensome obligation. In regard to his lecture in Bremen, he noted in a letter: "My lecture in Bremen was of course not brilliant. I have the impression that this circle expected extraordinary things of me and I had, of course, to be disappointing, since my perception of building is so very simple and, furthermore, I would necessarily refuse to hide myself behind fanciful theories only to satisfy an audience."[43]

Since the early twenties, Mies had worked with many renowned intellectuals and stood in a network of influences capable of exerting extraordinary stimulation, but which also called for an articulate expression of one's own views. Mies was committed to current debates by his active collaboration in the Novembergruppe since 1922, in the Deutsche Werkbund since 1924, and in the architects' association Der Ring since 1925. Furthermore, due to his collaboration at the periodical *G*, which perceived itself as the mouthpiece of the most important contemporary postexpressionist trends in Europe, he had direct contacts with the most prominent artists of the new art forms and with their thoughts.

Mies did not want to hide behind theories that explicated the work itself. A specific, rigid theory only shackled, in his opinion, the creative forces. From this point of view, one can understand the evasive commonplaces that are often found in his written testimonials and lectures, frequently triggering criticism. This occurred, for example, on the occasion of his lecture "The Preconditions of Architectural Work." The 1928 reviewer who "appreciatively admired the perceptual clarity and the convincing lines" but who lamented the dearth of "convincing amplitude of explicative detail" formulated the thrust of his critique by stating that "the creative artist van der Rohe has far more ideas than the lecturer Mies van der Rohe. This is beneficial for the building art of today, but less so for the audience of lectures."[44] However, this critique could not distract Mies from his convictions. "Is criticism then so easy? Is real criticism not just as rare as real art?"— with these questions Mies opened his lecture of 1930 "On the Meaning and Task of Criticism" in order to direct attention to "the preconditions of criticism" because "I believe that without adequate clarity on that issue real criticism cannot be practiced."[45]

Clarification had to be the first task of thinking; one must, first of all, "illuminate the spiritual and concrete situation in which we find ourselves, make it visible, order its currents."[46] Subsequently, ordering models have to be designed to serve as bridges into praxis, by means of which is it possible to create conditions within which the creative forces can unfold. This was the thrust of the conclusion of the lecture "The New Time" given at the Werkbund meeting of 1930, in which Mies saw meaning and justification of the new time exclusively in the way it offered "conditions under which the spirit can exist."[47] Only through the idea can the given world find meaning, and it is the noble task of architecture to demonstrate a correspondence to philosophical precepts by creating its own type of order. And this is how Mies expressed it on the occasion of his inaugural address as director of the architectural department of Armour Institute of Technology in Chicago in 1938, a speech that, better than any testimony, formulated his "philosophy of the building art": "We want to know what it can be, what it must be, and what it should not be. . . . But we want to give each thing what is suitable to its nature. We would do this so perfectly that the world of our creations will blossom from within. More we do not want; more we cannot do."[48] Theory as well as building praxis should not be an "object of clever speculation"[49] but should be fitted into the context of a larger world view and its concept of truth. The main proposition of the Miesian theory of art— insofar as that term is even permissible here—formulated in the beginning of the twenties, states: "absolute truthfulness and rejection of all formal cheating."[50] If there was a formula obligatory for postexpressionist modernism, then it was this sentence that pointed to the main concern of the artistic currents of that time, namely the unconditional demand to overcome the art of illusion as it had been practiced in the past by a re-creation of reality.

The negation of illusion and the call for truthfulness were, in spite of differences of interpretation, the common premise of a movement in which art was no longer assigned an imitative role in society but an essentially formative one. The new art was not satisfied with merely erecting an image of order to ward off chaos. It searched rather for universal principles by means of which the real objective world itself could be ordered. This was the constructive meaning of elementary form-giving, which did not want to represent or interpret but which, by the creation of "more exact relationships" (Mondrian), aimed at changing or re-creating reality itself. For this reason "knowledge of the time, its tasks and means, were necessary prerequisites for the work of the building artist," because the building art, so Mies emphasized over and over again, "is in reality only understandable as a life process."[51] It was this outlook that gave rise to the call to liberate "building activity from aesthetic speculators" and that concluded with that

Note on the back of Mies's manuscript "Building," 1923: "It is mainly our concern to liberate all building activity from aesthetic specialists. And make building again what it always has been. Building. Barbarians have approached the problem with the least imaginable measure of boldness. Cupboards that look like skyscraper models."

almost banal-appearing tautology of a nonpredicative sentence: "Make building again what alone it should be, namely BUILDING."[52]

This program of overcoming the world of appearances and of transposing art into a life praxis is based on an art theory by no means as radically new as one might suppose. It originated in the Platonic concept that truth renders testimony of itself. According to this concept, the beautiful is not the subjective creation of an individual but—as radiance of truth—ontological reality. "Beauty is the radiance of truth"—this postulate of the late-antique Neoplatonist Augustine, recorded for the first time in Mies's notebook in 1928, and later frequently quoted in debates and interviews, appealed in the twenties not only to Mies.

Truth, from the Platonic point of view, reveals itself, and therefore "Create, artist! Do not talk!" could be claimed by Mies as motto. To stand up for one's convictions is a necessity, but for the artist, as Mies emphasized at the end of a lecture, it is ultimately the "performance that matters."[53]

True art, Piet Mondrian explained in 1917 with arguments similar to those with which Plato condemned the Sophists, needs "in no way an explanation in words."[54] Mondrian, who had been heavily influenced by cosmogony and theosophy and who embedded the Platonic truth of the new art into a philosophical universalism, offered a corresponding explanation for that ambivalent relationship with the word that found its counterpart in the frugal prose of Mies van der Rohe.

Although the explicating word is superfluous, according to the Platonic theory of the self-revelatory nature of truth, making it unnecessary for the artist to add explanations to his own work, art should nowadays not remain silent, for "today's artist" so Mondrian has it, "ploughs a double work field."[55] He should testify to the truth not only through his work "but also through the word," more precisely though the "artless word." The only permissible form is a logical explanation by means of which "today's artist" can, in regard to his art, reach for the word. "Especially now, when the new in the form-giving praxis is so unknown, not yet common property, it appears necessary that the artist does that himself—later, let it be complemented or improved by the philosopher, the scientist, the theologian, or by whoever is able to improve or complement what has been said. For the time being, only those understand the new work methods who arrive at them by work. . . . Truth reveals itself, says Spinoza, but knowledge of truth can be achieved faster and more profoundly by means of words. . . . Thus the contemporary artist does not explain his work but he creates clarity in regard to the nature of his work."[56]

There were no work-related contacts between Mies and Mondrian as there were between Mies and van Doesburg.[57] Yet although Mies, when asked about the apparent relationship of his architectonic structures to the compositional principles of Mondrian, always energetically rejected a direct influence,[58] common properties cannot be denied. Both searched for a poetic formula for their Platonic concept of truth, both perceived clarity as a prerequisite. Their theoretical work reveals certain parallels insofar as the wordless art should be expressed by a metaphor-free, matter-of-fact, concrete language—by the employment of the artless word.

The written legacy of Mies van der Rohe, the published articles and the so far unpublished manuscripts, notes, and jottings, give an exact impression of the struggle for the formulation of these principles. Spiritual and formal perfection are here seen, much as in the building arts, as the ideal. The same can be said of the theoretical work of Mondrian. Hans M. Wingler gives a definition of this in the postscript to the reprint of the Mondrian Bauhaus Book of 1925 in a sentence that—also applicable to Mies—could not have been formulated more succinctly: he "was not particularly fond of writing, compared to the other protagonists of abstract art; he often repeated himself—and he compressed. This constant and imperturbable effort at condensation is what characterizes him as almost no one else."[59]

II Philosophy as Patron

1 The View into the Intrinsic

We must fathom the kernel of truth. Only questions into the essence of things are meaningful. The answers a generation finds to these questions are its contribution to architecture.

Ludwig Mies van der Rohe, 1961

For Mies, the world turned around this question of the intrinsic. The secret of life lay hidden in it. It alone supplied the key to an understanding of reality. Mies's "conscious professional career" began at that moment when the question as to the intrinsic nature of the building art appeared to him for the first time. This occurred around 1910, a period Mies retroactively described as "actually a confused time" for "nobody could or would answer the question as to the nature of the building art. Perhaps the time was not yet ripe for an answer. At any rate, I posed this question and was determined to find an answer to it."[1]

The answers Mies gave, both in his buildings and in his written statements, document the development of his thought and its striving toward universality. The "inquiry into the nature of the building art" was viewed as inseparable from the "inquiry into the intrinsic" and constituted the philosophical foundation of his architecture. In Mies's eyes, architecture could not be viewed as an isolated phenomenon, but only as expression and part of a *Weltanschauung*. The foundations of Mies's world view were, in the early twenties, already firmly established. On them Mies erected his philosophy of building that emerged not only in the buildings and projects of that decade, but also in the construction of his manifestos and statements.

Yet Mies stood in 1910 not nearly as alone with his "inquiry into the nature of the building art" as he would have us believe. Already around the turn of the century, long before the collapse of the old order in 1918, the question as to the nature of art had been posed by an avant-garde intent on jettisoning handed-down concepts and value systems. The rejection of the old, of course, brought with it the question as to the nature of the new. The need to understand one's own time became all the more urgent as the moral upheavals created by the world war had left a "sudden freedom" (Mies), a vacuum of values that called for new visions and utopias. If one was still content before the war with celebrating the dismantling of traditional art, the situation after 1918 called for definitions to help overcome the void. Reflections of an existential nature that had already moved into the field of vision at the end of the nineteenth century now demanded to be dealt with.

"A feeling for life must guide art, not the tradition of form"—this sentence of 1921 by the Dutch architect Jacobus Johannes Pieter Oud[2] reflects the consensus of a modern movement that had to articulate its own theories so that the driving forces of the present could be determined, organized, and shaped. Before phenomena could be dealt with one had to understand one's own time. According to Mies, "genuine questions" had to be asked,[3] questions that touch on the "innermost nature of the epoch,"[4] for only they were held suitable to the new time's "objective character" that revealed itself in its technical nature as "the great anonymous trait."[5]

The search for transcendent principles applicable to architecture was part of a broader search for the indispensable value system each generation must erect for itself. In the outstanding architectural and art theoretical writings of the early twentieth century, this search had already begun to delineate itself. A. Schmarsow's *Wesen der architektonischen Schöpfung* (Leipzig, 1894), Otto Wagner's *Moderne Architektur* (Vienna, 1896), H. P. Berlage's *Gedanken über den Stil in der Baukunst* (Leipzig, 1905) and *Grundlagen und Entwicklung der Architektur* (Berlin, 1908), and J. A. Lux's *Ingenieur-Ästhetik* (Munich, 1910) were all milestones pointing the way to a new attitude toward building. In these writings it was no longer the architect as inventor of forms who was seen as playing the decisive role; one searched instead for the patterns that were innate in the contemporary givens and for the constructive means that were available.

That the "confused time" around 1910 looked with particular interest toward the clarifying role of theory is attested by the publication of the first German edition of probably the most important work of "classical" architectural theory, namely Leon Battista Alberti's *Ten Books on Architecture*, in 1912.[6] Here one could find what amounts to an affirmation of the modern principles of functionality and simplicity. This text, which warns against literal copying of historical examples and suggests instead the assimilation of artistic intent, proposes an abstract and conceptual understanding of the building art. Then, there were the fundamental works of Heinrich Wölfflin, which addressed the problem of stylistic development in terms of a *Zeitgeist*, or spirit of the epoch.

Mies owned a 1917 edition of Wölfflin's *Kunstgeschichtliche Grundbegriffe* (1915); this book has remained in his collection, where one can also find the works of Alois Riegl and Wilhelm Worringer.[7] The sparse underlinings Mies left in these books—as compared with those in other philosophical works—support the assumption that he approached art and architectural theories without particular enthusiasm. Mies's devastating words on art historians in the early twenties further support that assumption.

The "inquiry into the nature of the building art" did not lead to art theoretical works but into the "quarries of antique and medieval philosophy," where he searched for the "nature of truth."[8] Mies set out in search of essences. It was the result of his inclinations and his background. His lack of academic learning set certain limits to his understanding of theoretical literature. The educational resources Mies could draw on were not so much scientific as philosophical-religious in nature. His education at the Catholic cathedral school of Aachen left him not only with a lifelong predilection for the buildings of the Middle Ages with their simplicity and severity, but with an equally strong attachment to a Neoplatonic world view. The cathedral school was followed by a two-year stint at a trade school, after which he began his apprenticeship in the paternal stonemason's shop.[9]

Here Mies came for the first time in contact with building and simultaneously with a "very small" but particularly significant, even decisive, "part" of architecture, as Adolf Loos affirms. Loos, who was also a stonemason's son, wrote in his famous essay "Architektur" (1909): "Only a very small part of architecture really belongs to art: the funeral stone and the memorial. Everything else, because it serves a purpose, should be excluded from the realm of art. Only when the great misunderstanding that art can be made serviceable has been overcome . . . only then will we arrive at the architecture of our time."[10]

Both Mies and Adolf Loos had been familiar from childhood on with that small segment of architecture that constitutes the main source of income for stonemasons. This contact acquainted them with the practical side of the building profession and made tangible the symbolic nature of all that is built: funeral stone and memorial in particular, dedicated to respectful commemoration, represent an absolute rhetorical architecture, elevated both in idea and form. The metaphysical is the core of their reality, the symbolical their intrinsic purpose, for they point beyond the visible and physical world to an invisible realm of numinosity.

It is this architecture of reverence that Mies transposed, in his own fashion, into the modern building art. The "respect for things and material"[11] that had been instilled in Mies in his apprenticeship years developed into a regular cult of quality in regard to everything material. It is indicative of a religious attitude toward the world that holds that things are precious and that perceives this preciousness as a trust. This philosophy of the material world expressed itself not only in a preference for costly stones, for travertine and marble and onyx—building materials Mies employed with a matter-of-fact ease matched by few modern architects—but in the handling of all building materials, which were accorded, down to the last detail, the full measure of handcrafted care.

In his apprenticeship years an encounter took place that affected Mies, according to his own testimony, in a very particular way. In the process of cleaning out his drawing table in the office of the Aachen architect Albert Schneider, where Mies worked for a short time, he came across a copy of Maximilian Harden's periodical *Die Zukunft* (The Future) and an essay on the theories of the French astronomer and mathematician Laplace, who in the eighteenth century had undertaken extensive research into the movements of the planets. Reading both texts with great interest, though their content far exceeded his understanding, as he admitted, Mies found his curiosity and intellectual interest awakened.[12] From this time on, beginning to pay attention to questions of a philosophical and cultural nature, he started to read intensely and began to think independently.[13]

The accidental encounter with the Berlin weekly *Die Zukunft*, which Mies read from then on regularly, brought him for the first time into contact with a previously unknown intellectual world. It was in *Die Zukunft*, the mouthpiece of anti-Wilhelminian rebellion, which had the reputation of being "the most read, most admired, and most hated of the political weeklies in Germany," that around the turn of the century one could find articles by the renowned art critics Karl Scheffler, Julius Meier-Graefe, and Alfred Lichtwark, the Danish literary critic Georg Brandes, and the Berlin historian Kurt Breysig.[14] The two latter were trend-setting Nietzscheans and trustees of the Nietzsche archives in Weimar, which under the aegis of Elisabeth Förster-Nietzsche used *Die Zukunft* as house organ. Furthermore one finds among the contributing authors such artists as Henry van der Velde and August Endell—both of whom can also be viewed as Nietzscheans[15]—as well as writers of the caliber of a Richard Dehmel, Stefan Zweig, Heinrich Mann, and August Strindberg. The economic historian Werner Sombart and the philosophers Georg Simmel and Alois Riehl round out the list of renowned contributors of those years.

Mies's first glance into *Die Zukunft* proved of symbolic significance. Volume 52 from September 27, 1902, reading almost like a prophecy of Mies's future, contained an essay by the Berlin philosopher Alois Riehl ("From Heraclitus to Spinoza") as well as a report by Meier-Graefe on the art exhibition in Turin[16] where Peter Behrens with his Egyptian-style and profoundly serious vestibule had caused a considerable stir.[17] Five years down the road Mies would come face to face with Alois Riehl and Peter Behrens, and these encounters were to have a decisive influence on his intellectual and artistic development.

What Mies read after this first brush with philosophy can only be reconstructed piecemeal. His statements on this matter are contradictory and cannot be ascertained with any degree of accuracy. Mies's claim of having owned 3,000 books at the time of his emigration in 1938 is disputed by Philip Johnson, who had close contacts with Mies in the twenties. Johnson claims that Mies did not read at all: "Anyway he had only three books."[18] The deciphering of a notebook from the year 1928, which is largely filled with excerpts, indicates that Mies not only read but actually studied certain texts closely. These writings on the philosophy of technology and religion resonate in his opinions of that period.

His formative background predisposed Mies toward the absolute and the metaphysical, and he consequently tended toward a corresponding world view. In the notebook of 1928 Mies remarked: "Only philosophical understanding reveals the true ordering principles of our service and thence the value and dignity of our existence."[19] Philosophical understanding had, in contrast to other modes of perception, the advantage of profundity and

Philosophy as Patron

33

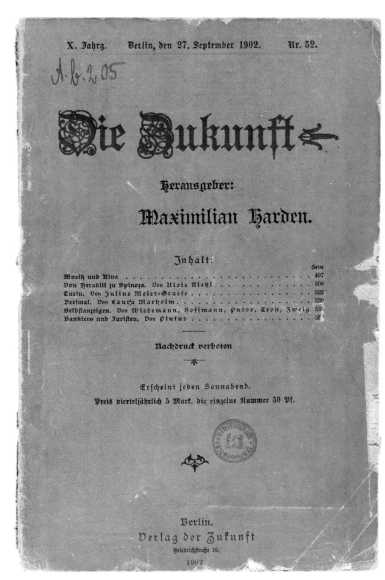

X. Jahrg.   Berlin, den 27. September 1902.   Nr. 52.

A.b.2.05

Die Zukunft

Herausgeber:

Maximilian Harden.

Inhalt:

Nachdruck verboten

Erscheint jeden Sonnabend.

Preis vierteljährlich 5 Mark. die einzelne Nummer 50 Pf.

Berlin.

Verlag der Zukunft

Friedrichstraße 10.

1902

Title page of *Die Zukunft*, no. 52 (September 27, 1902).

simplicity because it furnishes methods that permit the separation of the essential from the trivial. In this "restraint" lay the "only way" that would lead to insight and thus to "the creation of important architectural works."[20]

That philosophy has to be taken into account had already been emphasized by Vitruvius in the introduction of his *Ten Books on Architecture*. Only the study of philosophy produces the perfect architect of noble attitude, explained Vitruvius. Furthermore, philosophy "explains the nature of things."[21] Similarly, "the lonely seeker of truth," as Walter Gropius respectfully called Mies, appeared to lay claim to its values.[22] "If one wants to understand the epoch in which one lives," explains Mies, "one must come to understand its nature and not everything that one sees." "But," so he adds, "the essential is not easy to find, for the overall form unfolds itself very slowly.[23]

Ever since antiquity, architecture has been part and parcel of a philosophical thought edifice held to be in harmony with the general laws of being and with ultimate, objective principles, deriving therefrom its eternal laws. Only in the nineteenth century was this continuity broken, for in this epoch people were no longer able to fuse the new practical-technical givens with tradition-determined values and ideologies to arrive at a symbolic system with a justifiable world view. The inquiry into the "nature of the epoch," so passionately pursued by Mies and his generation, indicates that this context had been lost and that a self-understood relationship between the world of facts and the world of meanings no longer existed.

This loss of identity had manifested itself in the architecture of the late nineteenth century as a drastic contradiction between the forms of the academic, traditional styles on the one hand and the new typology of construction projects and building tasks on the other. The separation of "art form" from "core form" by means of which Carl Boetticher in the middle of the nineteenth century still sought to stem the gradual divergence between function and representation ended in an eclecticism that could not prevent, let alone abolish, the accelerating separation of construction from form and engineer from architect.[24] This fissure was only bridgeable by a fundamental reappraisal. Either function had to be legitimized and had to be viewed as an art form in its own right, as had been advocated by the Deutsche Werkbund before 1919, or one had to draw the uncomfortable conclusion, with Karl Kraus and Adolf Loos, that with respect to the serviceable things in life one simply had to suspend artistic demands.[25]

It became the task of twentieth-century architecture to redefine the interdependence of function and value, construction and form, and stake out a new base of support. Such an architecture, in the eyes of Mies, could only be realized if architects reformulated their discipline themselves. They had to display that heroic and "ascetic" frame of mind equated by Mies with the "thirst to partake of the fountainhead of being."[26]

2 From Accident to Order: The Way to Building

Art works, provided they withstand the forces of time, are in themselves, as it were, always there. No progress of a merely technological nature can kill them. They are alive, and, like all that is truly historical and valuable in an historical sense, they continually realize themselves; they continue their effectiveness and enter into a new interaction with each successive period. The thoughts of the great thinkers can be compared to such art works.

Alois Riehl, Philosophie der Gegenwart, *1908*

The Baumeister *forms a task by extracting from the modest requirements of the basic givens a spiritual content, thus releasing its form and movement into space, and then he projects the wall to the firmament and thereby renews creation. In many respects he is like the true scholar who absorbs the world into his contemplative soul and whose consciousness thus is larger than the cosmos, which only provides the space around which he wraps his soul.*

Rudolf Schwarz, "An Mies van der Rohe," *1961*

The chain of circumstances that had begun in Aachen with the discovery of philosophy in a drawing table drawer continued in Berlin in 1907: the very first commission Mies obtained as architect and executed under his own responsibility from design to execution was the house of a philosopher. The *Geheime Regierungsrat* Alois Riehl, professor of philosophy at the Friedrich Wilhelm University at Berlin, was Mies's first client. Born in 1844 in Bozen, Riehl had taught in Graz, Freiburg, Kiel, and Halle and was called to Berlin in 1905—the same year in which Mies departed for Berlin—where he was active until 1919.[1]

The particular set of circumstances and sympathies that may have led the renowned sixty-three-year-old professor of philosophy and his wife to commission the twenty-one-year-old "architect," who could point neither to a diploma nor to a practice, remains unknown. The professional or artistic qualifications of the young Mies do not seem to have played a decisive role. Apparently Mies had been able to convince his future patrons, who were "idealistically oriented"—meaning undogmatic—but who nevertheless did not want to play the role of guinea pigs,[2] by his personality and also through the proposed project itself. That the patron also liked to sponsor the career of his young architect is proven by the financing of an Italian trip of six weeks' duration Mies undertook in the company of Josef Popp, the assistant of Bruno Paul.[3] The friendly relations between the Riehl family and Mies that arose during the construction period presumably endured until Riehl died on November 21, 1924, in the house Mies had erected for him in Neubabelsberg near Potsdam.[4] Possibly it was his testamentary wish that Mies also build his funeral memorial.[5]

The rapport that existed between Mies and his first client is evident from a single, inconspicuous pencil entry made by Mies. On the occasion of Riehl's eightieth birthday on April 27, 1924, a printed invitation had been issued "to a limited circle of 100 friends and pupils" to "honor the revered man on April 27 by means of a speech and an honorary gift to convey their feelings of loyal devotion." That Mies belonged to this circle is proven by the circumstance that the invitation was among his papers. Donations— "even those that correspond to present German conditions"—should enable the celebrant to have, "besides a good book that might delight him, also a good old wine and some cigars on his birthday table" in those difficult times.

Why Mies was not mentioned on the printed congratulatory address listing friends and pupils is not known. Possibly it was an accidental oversight, or perhaps Mies had neglected to send in his donation in good time. What matters is that Mies counted himself in the circle of friends. In the margin of his copy of the congratulatory address, at the place where, in alphabetical order, his name should have been listed among the choir of congratulants and friends, he retroactively added a handwritten omission sign and his name "Ludwig Mies v. d. Rohe, Berlin."[6]

Through the Riehls, Mies gained access in 1907 to that new world of which he had first learned by reading *Die Zukunft*. The Riehls opened for him the doors to those circles out of which his later patrons were to come, intellectuals and artists, as well as men of industry and finance.[7] In Riehl's house Mies came in contact with the intellectual world of Berlin. Here he met among others Walther Rathenau; Werner Jaeger, the philologist of classical languages;[8] the art historian Heinrich Wölfflin—and also the latter's fiancée Ada Bruhn, whom Mies married in 1913;[9] the philosopher Eduard Spranger; and presumably also the philosopher of religion Romano Guardini, who noticeably influenced Mies's thoughts toward the end of the twenties.

Excerpt from the congratulatory address for the eightieth birthday of Alois Riehl: list of congratulants.

Alois Riehl, around 1914.

At first glance the Riehl House seems to resemble "the building style of 1800," the plain classicism of which Paul Mebes had so effectively called to the attention of his contemporaries in 1907 in his publications and which he recommended to the architects of Wilhelminian historicism on account of its Biedermeier clarity and simplicity.[10] The studied patrician reticence of the exterior, referred to by Mies, was well suited to a country house in the villa-suburb Neubabelsberg on the outskirts of middle-class residential Potsdam. In contrast to the neighboring villas built in the individualizing taste prevalent at the turn of the century, the Riehl House stood out by its pleasant inconspicuousness.

Mies's 1907 debut was discussed in the professional press in two illustrated essays. The journal *Moderne Bauformen* praised the generous impression made by the effective siting on the terrain and talked approvingly of its classical simplicity and clarity of design,[11] and Anton Jaumann, though still looking longingly back to the turn of the century, wrote with head-shaking approbation in *Innendekoration*: "It is the young generation, amazingly, that here preaches moderation; it corrects its teachers and surpasses them in exemplariness. . . . This work is simply so free of fault that one would never suppose that it is the first independent building of a young architect. . . . Certainly," prophesied Jaumann, impressed but imperturbable, "we will see in the next ten years a considerable number of excellent, well-executed, competent works from this 'coming generation,' but they will hardly be so amusing, so humanly gripping as the buildings of the last decade have been."[12]

Behind the solid authenticity of the Riehl House, which must have appeared to Jaumann like the work of a model pupil, hid a personal and novel concept, the intent of which could only be found if one looked beyond the surface. In the layering of volumes, the geometrizing of the forms, and the tightly stretched wall planes that were articulated by the precise incision of a pilaster beam structure, the intrinsic grammatical order of architectonic composition appears as if drawn on the surface in low relief. It is a skeleton structure that splits the function of the walls into either protective or supportive and that realizes itself structurally and spatially by means of a frame structure that dissolves the building volume on the narrow side into a full-width loggia.

The urge toward abstraction, implied by the precision of the geometrizing forms, is evident in the tension of a linear field of forces that stretches over the simple building volume and imparts to it, by means of this system of coordinates, its actual support. The bass chord is sounded by a continuous wall that defines, by means of an energetic line, the circumference of the garden terrain.

Spanning the terrain in almost monumental width, this extended wall diminishes, turns bracketlike at a right angle to the house, and encompasses the upper garden terrain which it shapes, in an embracing gesture, into a terrace.

Mies in front of the Riehl House, 1912.

"Riehl tombstone," entry in Mies's notebook.

From the other, lower side, this retention wall appears as a bare plane that secures the building visually on the sloping site. With openings provided only at the location of the house, the wall seems as if driven into the ground, guaranteeing the self-assuredness of the siting against the softly molded background of the natural surroundings. On this boundary line, nature is invited to intrude symbolically to soften the hard lines with its creeping vegetation. The pedestal with its stratifying effect beams out an imperturbable, almost majestic tranquility, as if it were created for eternity. On top of this podium rises, from an asymmetrical position, as apex of a hierarchical arrangement, a prominently positioned "classical" portico, composed of the posts of the loggia and the climbing, triangular gable.

Thus the side wall, ennobled by this architectonic symbol of dignity with its implication of centrality and hierarchical order, becomes the actual front of the house. Like a prostyle, its longitudinal axis rises from the blocklike massive podium, enriched by the tensions inherent in the spatial asymme-

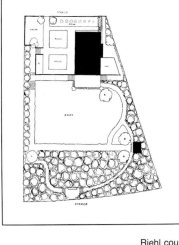
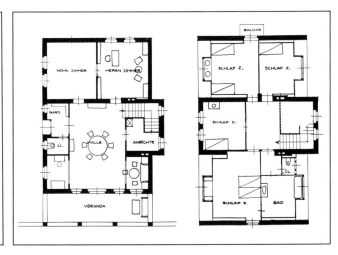

Riehl country house in Potsdam-Neubabelsberg, 1907, site plan and floor plans.

Alois Riehl's study.

Riehl House, parlor.

Riehl House, sitting alcove.

try and the disposition of massing and access arrangement. Instead of the academic principles of frontality and centrality, Mies stresses a primary order of a mutually intensifying interactivity between plastic appearance and spatial depth. From its exposed placement in the landscape, this country house as pavilion communicates with the depth of space. Rhetorically heightened, both as to form and content, its steps semiotically forward as an architectonic and plastic monument irrevocably fusing structure with space. Building and space complement and augment each other to form a whole.

Riehl House, view from the upper garden.

Riehl House in 1985.

The pavilion is the secret theme of the Riehl House. It is the leitmotif, as it were, pulled into the building from the side. The system of support pilasters, and in particular the lateral cornices that appear like inserted lintels, are indicative of this process of reinterpretation. Running across the length of the house, they impart a horizontal thrust that seems to extend beyond the end posts. After forming an angle around the gable, they are energetically cut through the profile, without any corner molding or other emphasis that would indicate their termination. The building volume, hovering as if on imaginary tracks, seems as if penetrated by these axes seemingly coming

43

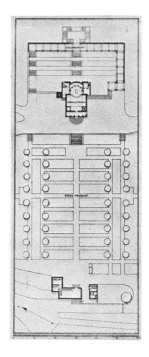

Peter Behrens, Hagen crematorium, 1907, ground plan and view.

Riehl House, view from the lower garden.

out of the infinite. The roof overhang, protruding proudly over the loggia, affirms the impression of a support-free, seemingly weightless cantilever effect, while the articulation of the pilasters, with their suggested support of the exterior walls, further encourages that impression.

One would exceed the permissible radius of interpretation if one were to perceive in these particulars the premonition of a coming architecture, the characteristic of which was to be a visual withdrawal of gravity and an opening up of volumes by means of continuous bands of fenestration resulting in a hovering balance.

What can be stated, however, is that already in Mies's first work two concepts are present, which one could describe as block type and open pavilion type. The concepts are in conflict with each other, interpenetrating but not yet brought to an independent and unified solution encompassing the entire building organism. The Riehl House is, in its overall appearance, dualistic. It presents two faces: in the frontal view it presents itself as a longitudinally oriented bourgeois residence that lies like a cube in front of the terrace garden; from the side, the volume dissolves into a pavilion positioned asymmetrically on a broad base, its volume opened up in a critical location by means of a pilaster system.

The pavilion theme was one of the first building tasks with which Mies struggled in Berlin. The clubhouse for the Berlin Lawn Tennis Club in Zehlendorf, entrusted to Bruno Paul, was erected concurrently with the Riehl House and is comparable to it. Both design and execution had been assigned to Paul's co-worker Mies.[13] Translated into another material and

Left, Bruno Paul, clubhouse of the Berlin Lawn Tennis Club, around 1908. *Right,* Peter Behrens, Elektra Boathouse of the Allgemeine Elektrizitäts-Gesellschaft (AEG) in Berlin-Oberschöneweide, 1911.

formal language and appearing under different conditions of purpose and space, we encounter here again the familiar image of the prostyle, this time, however, on account of a softly molded hip roof, deprived of the gable contour. Here, too, the building block is clearly articulated into a tripartite symmetry and the cubic volume is unilaterally hollowed out by a loggia that is rhythmically defined by its post and pilaster arrangement.

Even in the Werner House of 1913, Mies adheres to the pattern of a house type with a symmetrical front as advanced by the Riehl House. The formal language proves itself variable and easily adaptable to the wishes of the client, whose sympathies apparently tended in the direction of regional styling. The side loggia, which up to then had dissolved the building volume asymmetrically, now becomes a building part in its own right. It expands into a pergola that in turn extends into the garden, pulling the terrace garden toward the front of the house just as in Schinkel's Charlottenhof, which had been revised by Peter Behren's Wiegand House in 1912—a project in which Mies probably had participated.[14]

This dualism that manifested itself in the Riehl House in a double façade, in a conflict between block and pavilion, in a symmetrical concept and an asymmetrical positioning, also remains the dominant formal theme in the villas and country houses of the twenties. In the Barcelona Pavilion of 1929 Mies brought this dualism to a resolution on a higher plane of abstraction by means of a new equation.[15] There he achieved his aim of employing steel and glass, modern materials and building methods, to their full architectonic potential as "genuine building elements and as foundation for a new building art" (Mies). What had been foreshadowed and searched for in the Riehl House in 1907, but had there been barely suggested, was brought to fulfillment in a building in which classical and modern values fuse to a unique aesthetic experience.

Werner House, Berlin-Zehlendorf, 1913, exterior view and room with furniture by Mies.

Around 1930 Mies was able to realize his concepts. The new materials and methods, "genuine building elements," and their "space-toppling power" served the concept of an ideal art, for they offered that "measure of freedom in spatial composition that we will not relinquish any more. Only now can we articulate space, open it up and connect it to the landscape, thereby filling the spatial needs of modern man. Simplicity of construction, clarity of tectonic means, and purity of material shall be the bearers of a new beauty."[16]

The Riehl House demonstrates how conventional means can be transformed into elements of a clearly articulated spatial reference system. The house is posited in an original structured setting where it enters into a dialogue with a tension field of referential axes constituting the actual principles of architectonic order. The hermetic microcosm of the house with its precisely fitted interior spaces interacts with the equally well articulated immediate garden surroundings by means of the space-binding energy of these axes, which by final extension also draw in the dimensions of the open landscape. This concept of reference systems that imparts to the modest Riehl House of 1907 its particular generosity was to become the inimitable characteristic of Mies's architectural and formal language.

The Miesian principle of creation aimed at liberating things from their isolation and transposing them into an ordering system that imparts a higher meaning to its otherwise disparate elements. By means of this building order an architecture of spiritual references emerges. This philosophy of building transforms a simple mural extension into the spinal cord of an organism that unites house, garden, and surroundings. The wall extension defines site and place with a single, deliberate line. It furnishes the needed contrast to the plastic volumetricity, articulates the immediate surroundings, and responds to the wooded hillside on the opposite side of the lake. Mies designed a cadence that, with its far-reaching spatial rhythm, freed the

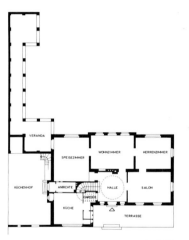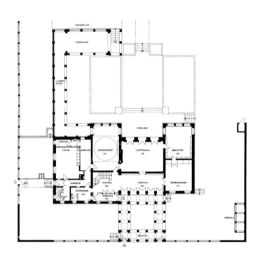

Left, Werner House, plan. *Right,* Peter Behrens, Wiegand House, Berlin-Dahlem, 1912, plan.

Left, sketch for the bedroom of the Werner House. *Right,* Peter Behrens, reception room in the German Embassy in St. Petersburg, 1912.

New National Gallery, Berlin, 1962–1967.

Farnsworth House, Plano, Illinois, 1945–1950.

architectural elements from their respective limitations only to release them into a larger context of transcendence.

The longing for unification and summarization, for harmony, stood in the center of this art, which called for participation in the cosmos and which conceived of itself as a metaphor for the great and the absolute. This was the lesson the stonemason's son from Aachen had brought with him to Berlin. In the Riehl House and in all later villas and country house projects, he aimed at unifying nature and human consciousness into a complementary whole in order to fill the need for another type of reality. The Riehl House marks the beginning of a development that was to end with the prostyle of the Farnsworth House of 1950–1955. The dialectic of structure and openness—the intellectual theme and the architectonic problem of the pavilion—crystallized into a sort of steel temple of the twentieth century that was no longer merely a place for living but a site dedicated to the contemplation of nature and a silent dialogue with the world. That part of the structure that embodies the meaning has stepped out of the confines of the wall of the Riehl House with its pilasters and found its way into a no longer reducible, totally glassed-in Platonic frame that, with its sand-blasted, seamless and faultless post system, comes only in symbolic contact with the ground, as if it were not of this world.

The designation of the Riehl House as "Klösterli" (little monastery), chosen by the patron—indicated by a stone plate inserted into the exterior plaster finish[17]—gave a perhaps not so accidental metaphor to a religious longing. The contemplative concentration that is conveyed by the placement of the house in the landscape and in the ambience of the interior spaces is indicative of a specific attitude that may very well have been shared by patron and architect in search of profound principles.

At the time Mies received the commission for the Riehl House, he was employed in the atelier of Bruno Paul, who had made a name for himself as caricaturist at the Munich *Simplicissimus* (a satirical periodical) and also as a leading German furniture designer. Paul's modern and solid, Prussian-styled Empire style made him a natural for the interior designs of modern ocean liners, the luxury of which was in keeping with his tastes.[18]

That Mies was misplaced in this environment was patently obvious. Paul Thiersch, his boss in Bruno Paul's studio, remarked appreciatively: "You should work for Behrens."[19] When the latter founded his Berlin atelier in 1907 and looked for colleagues, he could himself have taken note of Mies. Peter Behrens set up his atelier only a few blocks from the Riehl House in Neubabelsberg.

3 The "Great Form" and the "Will to Style"

With those who create, who harvest, and who rejoice I want to associate: the rainbow will I show them and all the stairs to the Superman.

Friedrich Nietzsche, Also sprach Zarathustra, *Prologue*

The coming style will be above all a style of redemption and of vital calm . . . a style of heroic monumentality. I want to call this style, in contrast to all the styles of the past, the style of perfected man.

Theo van Doesburg, Der Wille zum Stil, *1922*

Since the exhibition at the Mathildenhöhe in Darmstadt in 1901, Peter Behrens had become the leading spokesman for the new direction in art. In the eyes of his contemporaries he seemed exceptionally well suited to fulfill the longing of the epoch for its own style. Viewing art as "comprehensibly symbolic of a time's sensibilities toward life,"[1] he articulated the scientifically oriented turn away from historicism that had been ushered in by the art theoreticians August Schmarsow, Alois Riegl, and Heinrich Wölfflin, all of whom held that a new concept of style would have to be inclusive.[2]

Reversing the theory that wanted to distill objective statements of principle, idealizing abstractions, from cultural and intellectual processes, the artist Peter Behrens promoted self-objectivization, so that "all of life" would become "a great art equivalence" and "all can be ordered, chosen, and formed harmoniously, and be plugged into the larger circuits."[3] Peter Behrens formulated his artistic program analogous to Alois Riegl's *Kunstwollen* (will to art), known to him from his reading.[4] Both searched for that formula, that "agreement of all the elements of an art work with each other and with its innermost essence," that would reveal that "intrinsic lawfulness" that underlies life and art.[5]

In his lecture "Was ist monumentale Kunst?" (What Is Monumental Art?) of 1908 Behrens offered a more precise definition of an art that, subordinate to a greater law, is also the true expression of its time. The paired concepts "abstraction and empathy," employed by Wilhelm Worringer in the title of his influential dissertation,[6] reappeared in Behrens's argument of 1908: the largeness of the new style does not depend on preexisting or actual spatial expanse but on an "intensity" of shared "sensations." The monumental, so explained Behrens, depends "absolutely not on spatial size. The actual proportions are totally irrelevant. . . . a magnitude of this type cannot be expressed materially; it achieves its effect on a more profound level. . . . We can only sense it but we are nevertheless under its spell. We believe in it as if in a miracle."[7]

That Mies, during the time he worked for Bruno Paul, had come in contact with the work of Peter Behrens can be taken for granted. Behrens and Paul knew each other from their Munich years and had exhibited together in the Münchener Vereinigten Werkstätten für Kunst im Handwerk as representatives of the new applied arts movement.[8] After the turn of the century, both had turned from undulating art nouveau lines to a straight-lined style, and both had switched from the applied arts to architecture. The fact that Bruno Paul employed a co-worker of Behrens in 1907 as his office manager attests to that connection.

If one looks at the oeuvre of Peter Behrens executed before 1907 with the Riehl House in mind, the similarities with his crematorium in Hagen, erected in 1906–1907, become obvious. The crematorium was one of the first artistically executed buildings of this type ever to be built in Prussia. As Fritz Hoeber has demonstrated in his Behrens monograph, this building achieved "great fame . . . so that it belongs without doubt to the best-known works of its designer. Almost every time Behrens is mentioned, one refers to this modern San Miniato."[9] Even before the crematorium was erected, in 1906, a special folio with the design drawings, site plans, perspectives, and model photos had been published,[10] which might have been accessible to Mies as a source of inspiration at the time he designed the Riehl House. One can furthermore assume that Paul Thiersch, who was proud of having participated in the Hagen project as co-worker of Behrens,[11] called Mies's attention both to the building and to this publication.

The crematorium in Hagen and the Riehl House are similar in several respects. Both buildings, positioned halfway up a slope, interpret the site as a three-tiered terrace embankment; in both, a pedestal wall establishes the basis for the spatial configuration and heightens the plastic corporeality of the building. What Mies only implies analogically is declared by Behrens with overt, solemn self-confidence: the prostyle temple rises over the retention wall as a "massive gable structure" (Hoeber) that forms the apex of a strictly axial and symmetric composition.

What the critics found distinctive in this complex was equally applicable to Mies's Riehl House. Max Creutz spoke in 1908 of the "creation of an unrestricted feeling of spatiality" and ascribed the "allusion to the eternal," already noticeable during construction, to the circumstance that Behrens went beyond the spatial confines and fitted the structure into a larger, universal whole.[12]

The prostyle reference and the spatial interlocking thus seem, at first glance, to suggest a close connection between the crematorium and the Riehl House. On closer inspection, however, fundamental differences emerge. Although Mies and Behrens both searched for a clearly articulated, definite spatial linkage, they differed markedly in their respective perception of space and form.

The systematic geometrizing, to which Behrens subjected the building and its environment by means of a strict axiality of passage and a similarly severe treatment of the planes, was alien to Mies. This difference is by no means explainable by the dissimilarity of the building tasks and the assumption that the crematorium, as sacral structure, demanded such severe formal pathos. The exhibition architecture of Behrens, too, although designed for profane, short-lived events, is subjected to the same physical and spatial discipline. The exhibition hall he designed for the Northwest German Art Exhibition in Oldenburg in 1905 could, in its solemnity, easily be taken for a crematorium, and the crematorium, with its open and inviting loggia, is quite thinkable as an exhibition hall.

Peter Behrens transferred the experiences he had gained in the exhibition field into architecture. The crematorium presented itself as pavilion and made a dramatic statement of climax toward which all attention was directed. This building was intended not only to attract attention but to control it. It dominated the axially symmetric step formation, and the geometrical incrustations of the façade mirrored the absolute lawfulness of a tightly stretched spatiality with the crystal of the building volume itself as terminating apex.

This solemn staging of space and architecture, evoking the mood of a "pilgrim's procession,"[13] demonstrates the concept of the will to art that had been, at the turn of the century, passionately adopted by Behrens, under the influence of Nietzsche's "great style."[14] Commenting on his own residence on the Mathildenhöhe, Behrens noted in the exhibition catalog of 1901: "The rhythmical movement upward imparts an inner sense of elevation toward something"—a sentence one could also apply, as Hoeber did, to the crematorium.

The "Zarathustra style"[15] of Behrens set the scene, in Nietzsche's words, for "the stairs to the Superman" who built "life itself of posts and stairs": to "peer into far distances and blissful beauty—that requires height! and because it requires height, it requires steps and a struggle between steps and climber! Life wants to climb and, in climbing, to transcend itself."[16]

This is the meaning of Behrens's sentence, "We want to be elevated, not deceived."[17] The desire for a serious, high dignity raised the "solemn, final, unapproachable, eternal"[18] to the mythical source of the new art, thereby giving actuality to those classical qualities of the monument so familiar to Mies from his childhood. Heinrich Wölfflin, who, like all representatives of the cultural bourgeoisie, had been fascinated by the prophet and martyr figure Nietzsche,[19] had, by the turn of the century, already codified the "new conviction" and "new beauty" in his art theory. In his *Klassische Kunst* of 1899, he had equated it with a "feeling for the significant, the solemn, and the grand" on which the "noble," the "grand gesture," and the "classical calm" is based, the beauty of which is expressed through the "moderate," the "important," the "simple," the "comprehensive," the "clear," and the "regular."[20]

Monumental solemnity—so Behrens had it, totally in agreement with Nietzsche—aims at touching the emotions to move them to their profoundest. Behrens's architecture of worship pointed to that place "from which power issues forth or to which one tenders ardent veneration."[21] In this sphere of a first and a last, which lies like an undeviating matrix over and before all appearances,[22] the Dionysian is epitomized; it does not "ask for an art that one . . . can love and press to one's heart" but rather for one—as Behrens repeated after his prompter Nietzsche—"in front of which one sinks to one's knees, which makes us shudder, which overpowers our soul with magnitude."[23] This art of the heretical shudder does not seduce and does not smile, as a critic remarked in 1901: "It does not proffer itself, it does not come to meet us, we must go toward it and woo it; we must, even if we do so with some hesitation."[24]

Behrens's artistic and dramatic energy aimed for that will to style for which the art historian Alois Riegl had coined the term "will to art" (*Kunstwollen*). It seizes space, subjects the cube of air, only geometrically apprehensible, to an abstract mathematics of space,[25] and posits it symbolically at the feet of a temple that drapes itself by means of a geometrical, ornamental marble façade, as with an Apollonian veil. Like a crystal, this temple, dedicated to the power and veneration of the highest, rises on the stairs of Superman, who could here—as Nietzsche, the forerunner of a new interpretation of the antique, had desired it—stroll under colonnades, "looking up to a horizon defined by pure, noble lines, next to him the reflection of his transfigured self in shining marble, round about him solemnly perambulating or tenderly animated figures, talking in harmonious tones, accompanied by rhythmical gestures."[26]

Behrens's space is constructed mathematically, and his precise geometry suggests a "pathos of distance" (Nietzsche) that expresses the demand for a world that builds to suit its own spirit, that rises above nature and subor-

Peter Behrens, Exhibition Hall for the Northwest German Art Exhibition in Oldenburg, 1905.

Peter Behrens, book cover for Friedrich Nietzsche's *Also Sprach Zarathustra,* 1902.

dinates it to a higher aim. In Behrens's concept of the artistic possibilities inherent in the language of space and volume, we see a characteristic delineate itself that would ten years later become the dominating form-giving principle of modernism. As art liberates itself from the pictorial and the imitative to realize its unity with abstract universal laws, it must, quite consequentially, demand mathematically precise expression. Modern man confronts nature, by means of geometry, with his own rhythm. The elevation, transformation, and transcendence of organic functions in favor of abstract, spiritually more valid forms is his own cultural achievement. Nietzsche's aphorism "God is dead! We have killed him!" characterizes the mental state of modern man, who replaces the old religiosity with a belief in reason, science, and progress. "Spirit overcomes nature, mechanics supercede mere animalistic power, philosophy replaces religion": so sounds the unrelenting law stated without illusion by J. J. P. Oud in 1921, after the inevitable had taken place "with iron consequentiality."[27]

If one returns to the Riehl House from this excursus into the crystalline world of *Zarathustra,* it becomes clear that Mies's pavilion is still steeped in the spirit of a romantic world. Not only geographically, on account of its position above Lake Griebnitz, but also conceptually, the Riehl House is oriented toward Glienicke Park lying opposite it, which had been transformed by Karl Friedrich Schinkel and his congenial garden architect Peter Josef Lenné in the first third of the nineteenth century into a dreamscape in which architecture and nature are poetically wedded. As to the large concepts of plasticity and continuum in space, Mies and Behrens may have seen eye to eye, but in the manner in which these architectonic values are thematized, their differing ideological dispositions come clearly to the fore. In the Riehl House, both the natural and the built worlds retain their independent existences. Mies did not subscribe to the concept of a distancing super-order that asserts its will vis-à-vis nature in terms of Apollonian number harmony, from spatial rhythm to the ornamental plane geometry of the façade.

Behrens's concept of spatial rhythm is the result of abstract, cubistic thinking; Mies followed the laws of a natural plasticity, written by an invisible hand and made explicit by form, without, however, redeeming it. The unity of spirit and nature, striven for by Behrens by means of exact "logical construction" as "monumental synthesis through exclusively artistic means," much as Theo van Doesburg had formulated it in 1922 in *Der Wille zum Stil*,[28] was attempted by Mies by other means.

Mies did not subordinate architecture and nature to a universal measurement arrived at by analysis or act of will, but let spirit and nature coexist in their respective spheres of autonomy in which each is equivalent. He searched for a reconciliatory interpenetration of exterior and interior: a union of architecture and nature in which the built asserts itself as independent object by means of its plasticity and yet simultaneously unites with nature as part of a more comprehensive whole.

This unity of an absolute and a relative order, of which Schinkel had spoken,[29] is achieved by complex relationships of an organic rather than an abstract character. Geometrical-mathematical precision alone cannot bring about this result. Behrens equated order with the expression of a conscious act of will. Mies, by contrast, trusting in a unifying metaphysical truth, appeared to follow in his first work a lawfulness that is self-revelatory; the artist merely brings it to completion by assisting in the process of unfolding.

Truth can be formed but not autocratically commanded as an act of subjugation. To express this in the paired concepts Theo van Doesburg contrasted with each other in 1922 to describe the typicality of the old and the new will to style, one could say Behrens realized space as a modern "logical construction," while Mies worked with an untimely "lyrical constellation"; the "heroic monumentality" that, according to van Doesburg, would characterize the coming style should spell out "religious energy" but not "belief and religious authority."[30]

Unlike Behrens, Mies had, by 1907, not heeded Nietzsche's call for self-redemption exemplified by the motto: "Will liberates!"[31] Even later on, Mies retained his materialistic-metaphysical critical distance toward the concepts of an idealistic rationalism although these would, otherwise, exert considerable influence on him. "Will," as a category of the subjective, remained suspicious to Mies, who searched for the "intrinsic" and the objective. In his first manifesto Mies laconically countered van Doesburg, who was also influenced by Nietzsche's "will to style," with: "Even the will to style is formalism. We have other worries."[32]

Unknowingly, Mies had given, in the Riehl House, an analogy to that balance between necessity and freedom that the philosopher Eduard Spranger in his eulogy for Alois Riehl in 1924 had attributed to the latter's personality: "that touch of greatness, that breath of freedom that he needed for his inner world. Voluntary service was the content of his life. He was the critical Spinozist. . . . He knew nothing more sacred than the great thought of the universe into which God had poured all his strength. He too felt the gentle vault of necessity, a truly divine, rational necessity."[33] With this spiritual portrait of Alois Riehl one could also illuminate certain aspects of Mies's personality.

The idea that "voluntary service" is "a great privilege" that "unites one with the great dimension," and thus constitutes a guideline for life, may very well have been the common denominator that brought Mies and Alois Riehl together.[34] By means of this seemingly self-contradictory concept, free will—which Nietzsche did not want to see restrained by moral or ethical considerations—was to be harnessed to a commitment toward the natural order of the world. The "conflict between patron and artist, between materialist and idealist" or—to put it differently—between functional and sovereign reason, was summarized by Mies in notes for a lecture in 1928 by the resolve: "Not only self-revelation but also service."[35]

Mies searched for an equilibrium between a materialistic-metaphysical philosophy, a "hierarchy of objects," and an idealistic rationalism, a "hierarchy of awareness attitudes" that he liked to sum up with the words "service to value."[36] The main sources influencing Mies in that respect were the writings of Friedrich Dessauer, Max Scheler, Leopold Ziegler, and Romano Guardini, who all occupied themselves in the twenties with the "overthrow of values" (Scheler) as prophesied by Nietzsche, except that they simultaneously demanded a commitment to ethics, an attitude of "humility" and "serviceability toward the world."[37]

Behrens's type of idealism, with which Mies had come in contact in 1908, taught a greatness that was not a reward from higher forces but the result of willpower. The artist, as incarnation of ideal subjectivity, is called upon to impress the insignia of the idea upon the banal and common and thus elevate the world. Much as Nietzsche, Behrens did not believe in mystical powers but in fulfillment through the creative will, which, as "redeemer from the accidental" (Nietzsche), liberates man from the passive role of spectator and transforms him into an actor on the historical stage of mankind. This is how we are to understand the phrase "We want to be elevated, not deceived" by means of which Behrens, like Zarathustra, joined those "who create, who harvest, and who rejoice."[38]

Asked what he had learned in his years with Peter Behrens, Mies replied: "In one sentence, I could perhaps state that I have learned the great form."[39] This "great form," as leitmotif for all art at the turn of the century, stood for a concept of culture that wanted, by means of the will to art, to unify all cultural expressions of that period, something the art pluralism of the nineteenth century had been unable to achieve.

"Celebration of life and art" was Behrens's motto for that comprehensive culture (*Gesamtkultur*) that was to emerge as "symbol of a comprehensive sensibility" out of a stylized synthesis of nature and spirit, workday and feastday, and life and art.[40] This total art work of the "great form" reflects the influence of prophet Nietzsche's theory of aesthetic redemption of the spiritual life at the turn of the century. Many prominent representatives of the new architecture besides Behrens, such as Henry van de Velde, Bruno Taut, Erich Mendelsohn, August Endell, and Le Corbusier, or artists such as Filippo Tommaso Marinetti, Giorgio de Chirico, Henri Matisse, Max Beckmann, Wassily Kandinsky, Lyonel Feininger, Oskar Schlemmer, and many others, had also experienced Nietzsche's impact.[41]

The reception of Nietzsche as philosopher of culture was to no small degree precipitated by Alois Riehl, born like Nietzsche in 1844. Riehl was the first to come out with a book on the poetic, prophetic philosopher. His work, *Friedrich Nietzsche. Der Künstler und der Denker,* which appeared in 1897,[42] was the first monograph ever to appear on Nietzsche; Riehl's philosophical treatise was accepted for the series *Klassiker der Philosophie*

FRIEDRICH NIETZSCHE

DER KÜNSTLER UND DER DENKER.

EIN ESSAY

VON

ALOIS RIEHL.

STUTTGART
FR. FROMMANNS VERLAG (E. HAUFF)
1897.

The first published monograph on Nietzsche, written by Alois Riehl (Stuttgart, 1897).

Table of contents of Alois Riehl's *Einführung in die Philosophie der Gegenwart,* third edition (Leipzig, 1908).

and by 1909 had already reached its fifth edition and had been translated into various languages, contributing considerably to the image of Nietzsche at the turn of the century.

In his *Einführung in die Philosophie der Gegenwart* (1903), Alois Riehl paraphrased once more Nietzsche's philosphical-aesthetic thought, honoring him as the philosopher of life, whose aristocratic radicalism aimed to make "man great and independent" and "translate virtue into nobility." Riehl perceived in Nietzsche's world view, in which life is not merely affirmed but heightened, the "mirror of the modern soul" that "looks forward to future possibilities in life" by creating its own system of values and therefore its own culture: "Nietzsche 'sums up modernity': he has simultaneously fulfilled and surpassed it"[43]—an interpretation of Nietzsche affirmed by the importance he assumes in the discourse of today.[44]

That Mies was not only familiar with Riehl's writings but studied them carefully is proven by Mies's still-extant copy of *Zur Einführung in die Philosophie der Gegenwart,* which shows many underlinings in his hand.[45] His preoccupation with Nietzsche, which was encouraged by Riehl and by Behrens, shows the same basic tenor of rejection mixed with fascination that was also typical for Riehl. The relationship of Mies to his teacher Behrens was colored by a similar ambivalence.

Riehl's position toward Nietzsche was that of a neo-Kantian affirming the autonomy of the will—insofar as it embodies the principles of philosophical morality from Socrates to Kant—but rejecting the radical negation of morality that characterizes Nietzsche's stance. Nietzsche's consequent demand

Philosophy as Patron

59

for man's self-regulation and self-justification was greatly in conflict with Mies's rather religious mode of thinking, which saw the key for self-realization in service and obedience. On the other hand, the demand that "Life must be affirmed!"—which according to Riehl is the "first imperative of Nietzsche's morality,"[46] and which resurfaced in the manifestos of Mies and other artists of the period—contained itself the kernel of a religious attitude.

"Religion is simultaneously exaltation and surrender, dependence and overcoming," wrote Eduard Spranger in the festschrift for Alois Riehl in 1914, in reference to the irreligious Nietzsche who wanted to see "the longing for redemption" replaced by realistic activity, thus raising the question "whether Nietzsche's irreligiosity did not itself spring from religious roots." With Nietzsche, "all conditions for religiosity are present: an exalting of the world, above which rises a new awareness supported by inner feelings of strength—these are essentially the same characteristics that have brought forth the old religion. Whoever feels that great longing in the first place, this driving urgency hungering for satisfaction, whoever smarts under the transitoriness of life, in him religion is alive. Indeed, it is a sign of the very authenticity of his feelings that transmitted religion appears to him inadequate."[47]

If one views the last sentence of this citation with the fundamental beliefs of the building art in mind, one obtains a fairly accurate notion of Mies's position in the early twenties. It is notable for its refutation of any and all traditional theories or "moralities" of building, calling instead for a myth of "building" and "living" in which only a new attitude toward building was guaranteed. Even though no direct references to Nietzsche can be found in Mies's writing, his shadowy influence is nevertheless discernible in the background. In this respect Mies's acquaintance with the philosopher of religion Romano Guardini seems significant. Guardini, who had been teaching in Berlin since 1923, occupied himself intensely with the Antichrist aspects of Nietzsche, attempting to demonstrate that Nietzsche's postulate of life affirmation was equivalent to a new religious "attitude" toward the world—a thought that, after 1928, was also central in Mies's thinking. Mies, who demanded an "undistorted affirmation of life"[48] as the reflection of the consciousness of the epoch, in 1928 endorsed this religious longing that had been suggested by the thesis of the "human need for illusion" (Nietzsche) and the Dionysian myth of life in words that paraphrased all of Nietzsche: "It must be possible to heighten consciousness and yet separate it from the purely intellectual. It must be possible to let go of illusions, see our existence sharply defined, and yet gain a new infinity, an infinity that springs from the spirit. . . . But all that can only happen if we regain our belief in the creative powers, if we trust the power of life."[49]

Nietzsche's definition of culture as a "unanimity of styles comprising all expressions of a nation,"[50] repeated almost verbatim in the art theories and statements of Behrens, is based on the belief that art dominates life.

Nietzsche's famous sentence from his first work, *Die Geburt der Tragödie aus dem Geiste der Musik* (The Birth of Tragedy out of the Spirit of Music) of 1872, in which he stated that existence and the world seem eternally justifiable only as aesthetic phenomena,[51] already anticipated the turn-of-the-century aesthetic of the total art work.[52] Art is the only realm in which the lost unity can be regained. The attempt to achieve, by means of art, a new life praxis was based on the assumption of the primacy of the aesthetic.

The idea of the total art work derived from Nietzsche's thesis of an analogy between art and life. This thesis was to be emphatically affirmed by the aesthetic concepts underlying the art of the twentieth century. The avant-garde of modernism was ready, with Nietzsche, the destroyer of all values, to liberate art and theory from their ties with myth, from the bonds of morality, religion, and nature, and to release the promise residing in aesthetic form by way of art into a new life praxis that is "not the image of appearance but the unmediated image of will itself"[53] or, as Mies calls it in 1924, the "instrument of the will of the epoch."[54]

Behrens appeared predestined for the task of synthesizing art and life. His appointment to the artistic advisory board of the Allgemeine Elektrizitäts-Gesellschaft (AEG) in 1907 made him the first representative of modern "industrial" design. The modern total art work arose out of the collaboration between art and industry: from the letterhead of the firm to all its products, from the factory to the workers' settlements, it encompassed the world of machinery and daily industrial routines, all of which had to be raised to the "level of culture." Here, "celebration of life and art" was about to find its fulfillment.

III The Ambivalence of Concepts: Construction or Interpretation of Reality? Berlage or Behrens? Hegel or Nietzsche?

One rewards a teacher badly if one always remains a student. And why do you not want to pull on my garland? You were not yet in search of yourselves: then you found me. Now I ask you to lose me and find yourselves: and only when all of you have denied me, will I return to you.

Friedrich Nietzsche, Ecce Homo, How One Becomes What One Is

The atelier of Peter Behrens was, around 1910, among the best-known architectural offices of Europe. Here one could find the young generation of up-and-coming modernists. Walter Gropius, Adolf Meyer, Jean Krämer, Peter Grossman, and for a time also Le Corbusier were the most outstanding talents that worked next to Mies. Yet what kind of instruction Mies received from Behrens, and what significance that "marvelous feeling for form"[1] that Mies ascribed to his teacher had for his own development and for the clarification of his own design ideas, cannot be deduced from Mies's remarks.

In retrospect, it appears, Mies viewed these very decisive years of his coming into professional consciousness with strong reservations. In his homage to Frank Lloyd Wright of 1946, Mies recalled "Peter Behrens' significant creations for the electrical industry"; they were drawn on as proof that architecture is the realm of the objective: only "where objective limits made subjective license impossible" could the "valid solutions" of the time be found. This was the case, Mies stated, commenting on the renovation movement of 1910, in the field of industrial architecture, "but in all other problems of architectural creation, the architect ventured into the dangerous realm of the historical."[2]

Mies added a critical note to this appreciative acknowledgment of industrial classicism.

To some . . . the revival of classic forms seemed reasonable, and in the field of monumental architecture, even imperative. Of course this was not true of all early twentieth century architecture. Van de Velde and Berlage, especially, remained steadfastly loyal to their own ideals. . . . Nevertheless, we young architects found ourselves in painful inner conflict. We were ready to pledge ourselves to an idea. But the potential vitality of the architectural idea of this period had, by that time, been lost. This, then, was the situation in 1910,[3]

a period Mies later was to describe as confused.[4]

Apparently Behrens had not been able to come up with what Mies called a "real idea." "Real ideas," Mies explained on occasion of the dedication of Crown Hall on April 30, 1956, "are ideas based on reason, ideas relating to facts."[5] It could not be the task of the building arts, serving a real idea in the sense of this objective idealism, to "invent forms," as Mies called it, with a side-glance toward Behrens.

That will to style that should reform and ennoble life from the top down via the axis of aesthetics and synthesize into an "industrial culture," as proposed by Behrens and the Deutsche Werkbund, was apparently subsumed by Mies under the concept of formalism. The actual problematic of architecture lies in the realm of intrinsic, objective conditions and relations, which had to be defined and articulated but could not be commanded. "I

Peter Behrens in a charcoal drawing by Max Liebermann, 1911; Hendrik Petrus Berlage, 1910.

The atelier of Peter Behrens in Neubabelsberg, around 1910. Mies is third from right; left-most is Walter Gropius, next to him Adolf Meyer.

then understood that it is not the task of architecture to invent forms. I attempted to understand the nature of its real task. I asked Peter Behrens but he could give me no answer. He had never asked himself that question."[6]

This not very complimentary judgment of his erstwhile teacher points to a widely differing attitude toward building. In retrospect Mies credited not the "artist-architect" Peter Behrens, but the *Baumeister* Frank Lloyd Wright and Hendrik Berlage with the breakthrough experience. Berlage earned the highest esteem and admiration on account of his almost religious belief in ideals and on account of his upright character; Wright, whose work had been exhibited for the first time in Berlin in 1910 and had been republicized by Berlage in the twenties, was accorded by Mies the actual role of redeemer. "Here finally was a master-builder drawing upon the veritable fountainhead of architecture, who with true originality lifted his architectural creations into the light. Here, again, at last, genuine organic architecture flowered. . . . The dynamic impulse emanating from his work invigorated a whole generation. His influence was strongly felt even when it was not actually visible."[7]

The implications of the work of the Dutch master architect Berlage, with whom Mies had become acquainted over the house project for the art collector Helen Kröller in The Hague, lay for Mies in its "careful construction," which, "honest to the bone," revealed "a totally different attitude." Mies counted it an advantage that it had "nothing at all to do with classicism . . . nothing any more with the historical."[8] For this reason, Mies judged Berlage's 1898–1903 Amsterdam Exchange a "truly modern building," whereas Behrens had been of the opinion that "all that Berlage makes is passé."[9]

The aesthetics of analogy pursued by Behrens in the crossing of classical forms with the methods of technical-industrial production appeared to Mies as a signature style method of "form-giving" and therefore ill-suited as a basis for building. Berlage's criticism of the motto "appearance for essence"[10] supported the demand for a supposedly objective creative truth that must not be understood as form-inventing but as form-finding. Leaning on Gottfried Semper, whose materialistic theory was directed against the "arbitrary," since in nature "everything is necessitated by circumstances and conditions,"[11] Berlage proclaimed: "Now you artists, you not only have to be thrifty with your motifs, but you cannot even invent new ones. Just as nature reforms its archetypes, so you can only reformulate the original art forms; you cannot make new ones, and should you try, you will find that your work will have no lasting meaning, for you have become unnatural and untruthful."[12]

This confession of a belief in the "return of the eternally same" (Nietzsche) was also made by Behrens, albeit from his point of view with a reversed premise; the consequences he drew from this, though, differed noticeably from Berlage's.

H. P. Berlage in the hall of the Amsterdam Exchange (photo ca. 1925). *Top,* design for the cover of Berlage's *Grundlagen und Entwicklung der Architektur.*

For Berlage the question of honesty lay at the center and furnished the key words that were to reappear in Mies's statements in regard to building (*Bauen*) in the early twenties, unconditionally endorsing Berlage's prime rule. Mies probably did not get acquainted with Berlage's *Gedanken über den Stil in der Baukunst*—already published in 1905 and reissued in enlarged format in 1908 under the title *Grundlagen und Entwicklung der Architektur*—until his stay in Holland in 1912. The reading of this work left a long-lasting impression on him.

Berlage pointed to order as the "fundamental principle of style" and, referring to Viollet-le-Duc, promoted the anonymous medieval cathedral as forerunner for "rational construction." It was held out as example for the new art, for which the artist, as interpreter of the *Zeitgeist,* should lay the foundation.[13]

Mies sometimes followed Berlage's arguments verbatim.[14] Positions that the latter had advanced, against the background of the nineteenth century—the "century of ugliness"—echoed in Mies's pronouncements of 1922–23. Berlage's disgust with the "luxury buildings" and the "boulevards with the competition façades," the "villa quarters" and the "villa parks,"[15] found its parallel in the condemnation of buildings on the Kurfürstendamm and in Dahlem, that "total lunacy in stone" that Mies—no different from, say Bruno Taut or Le Corbusier in their estimation of the building art of the nineteenth century—called "dishonest, stupid, and insulting."[16]

When Mies, concluding this invective, raised "absolute truthfulness and rejection of all formal cheating" to the uppermost moral prerequisite,[17] he revealed himself as a loyal follower of the apostle of truth Berlage, who had preached: "The lie is the rule, truth has become the exception. So it is in spiritual life, so it is in art. . . . This pseudo-art, this lie, must be fought against so that we will again arrive at the essence of architecture rather than its appearance. We want this essence, this truth, and once more the truth, for in art, too, the lie has become the norm, truth the exception. We architects must therefore attempt to find our way back to the truth; that means we must understand again the very nature of architecture."[18]

Mies viewed Berlage's almost obsessive desire for intrinsic honesty with total sympathy. Berlage, who believed that religious energy forms the foundation of all creatures, wanted the void created by the "disappearance of upright piety"[19] to be taken over by "love for an ideal."[20] Whereas Behrens, the "architect of Zarathustra" (Buddensieg), saw the reevaluation of values as the specific task of modern man (according with Nietzsche's pronouncement "where one can no longer love, one should pass by!"[21], Berlage called for what Hegel—in reference to the relationship of art toward religion and philosophy—had described as an essentially rational theology: a philosophy that has to be understood as a "perpetual holy rite in the service of truth." For, according to Hegel, art, which occupies itself "with truth as the absolute object of consciousness . . . belongs to the absolute sphere of the spirit . . . and stands on one and the same ground with religion (in the stricter sense of the word) and philosophy."[22]

Influenced not only by Plato and Hegel but also by Schopenhauer,[23] Berlage categorically rejected all art that does not pursue an objective idea as "pseudo-art." The "factual, rational, and therefore clearly constructed" constitutes for architecture that particularly Hegelian "region of honesty" that should form the foundation for the new art. If the modern movement follows this interpretation of reason, then it functions "also with a religious tendency, with a religious longing, until finally longing becomes reality and a new world is born . . . not with a teleological idea, that is, not in the sense that it is religious, but with an ideal of this earth. But would the ultimate aim of all religions thereby not also move closer and would the Christian idea not also be served?"[24] The two "great aestheticians" Gottfried Semper and Viollet-le-Duc were called upon to legitimize objectivity. The principles of construction were canonized and became the embodiment of those great and simple laws of "true art" that control form and remain timelessly valid, a precondition of all formal beauty. If art and architecture, in particular, detach themselves from these fixed principles that are practically a law of nature, to enter upon a path to the arbitrary, then, according to Berlage's theory of salvation, "all is lost."[25]

And this is how Mies saw it almost fifty years later: "For over a century one has attempted, by thought and deed, to come to a closer understanding of the nature of the building art. In retrospect it becomes clear that all attempts to renew the building art from the formal direction have failed. Wherever important things occurred, they were of a constructive, not of a formal nature. This is doubtless the reason for the conviction that construction has to be the basis of the building art." Building, so it is noted in handwriting in the same document, is identical with the "simple deed," the "simple work process and clear building structure." "He who wants a building art must decide. He must subordinate himself to the great objective demands of the epoch. Give constructive form to them. Nothing more and nothing less. Building was always linked to a simple deed, but this deed has to hit the nail on the head. Only in this sense can one understand Berlage's saying BUILDING IS SERVING. . . . Let us not deceive ourselves. Many modern buildings will not stand the test of time. They may conform to all the general rules of the building art except the most fundamental one of 'building' [*Bauen*] and it is this last demand that will seal their fate."[26]

According to the Platonic-Hegelian concept of the objective idea one cannot obtain self-knowledge without a prior understanding of the order of things. The immanent guarantees the only valid model of eternal truth, the kernel from which the order of things reveals itself. The ultimate aim of architecture, as of all art, lies in an absolute value, detached from all that is subjective and temporal, embodying in its unsullied purity, as "objective demand" (Mies), the universal and eternal. This was the basis for that con-gruence of *adaequatio intellectus et rei* to which, as "identity of thought and thing," Mies, leaning on Thomas Aquinas, attributed a "truth relation-ship."[27] This identity of subject and object, idea and matter, that reconciles belief and reason leads to an idea of beauty that transcends eternal law and objectivity. The words of Augustine in regard to the revelation of beauty as the "radiance of truth," to which Mies referred again and again, point to this type of congruence that he called by the scholastic terms *ordo* and *adaequatio.*

Basing himself on these principles, Mies followed his mentor Berlage into the exemplary Middle Ages, held synonymous with all-powerful truth. Con-struction, interpreted as a metahistorical category of universal lawfulness, was declared to be the architectural principle of medieval building. With Viollet-le-Duc, such a factual, rational, and clear idea of construction had been established as the basis for a new art. Viollet-le-Duc's "Toute forme, qui n'est pas ordonnée par la structure, doit être repoussée" was copied by Mies in capital letters. Here was the basis for a "truthful attitude" on which one could found the building art.[28]

Much as Julien Guadet, who in his *Histoire de l'Architecture* of 1899 declared constructive premises to be the precondition for architecture, Berlage differentiated between "genuine" and "inauthentic" architecture. Against a norm that gives primacy to construction, the Renaissance had to appear as a "weak copy" of an original Roman art, in itself already "in a certain sense . . . suspect" because it "merely mirrored the formal values of the Greeks and not their spirit."[29]

How much more then were the neo-styles of the nineteenth century per-ceived as a dilution. This style architecture deserved, in the eyes of Ber-lage, at best to be suffered as a "love-lie." In the divergent interpretation of neo-Renaissance and neo-Gothic, the dogma became evident. While the former, as subjective style, could be compared to a grog, stretched in an act of desperation by the addition of water, the latter, an objective style, was judged by Berlage with lenient understanding. Of the two main stylistic trends of the nineteenth century, "only the neo-Gothic has been seminal since it redirected attention toward medieval art, which harbors the seeds of the future."[30] Mies, too, longed for a building style "that inherits the Gothic legacy. It is our greatest hope."[31]

Berlage was definitely partial toward the Gothic. He perceived in it "the triumph of an art fundamentally different from the classical" and the "roots of the art of a new time."[32] This dogmatic interpretation of history was meant to open the gate to the spirit of the Gothic, which would guide the architect on the right path toward a future, authentic building art.

At the same time, the way to the antique was blocked with words that warned against entering an alien world and ultimately questioned any refer-ence to the historic in general: "For we cannot possess the constructive spirit loved by the Greeks; and if we have love expressible by a corresponding concept of construction, then it must by necessity be totally different from theirs and consequently its expression must assume totally different forms."[33]

Hegel, too, pointing to both classicism and the Gothic, had warned in his *Ästhetik* against any well-meaning resumption of past artistic styles: "No matter how excellent we find the statues of the Greek gods, no matter how we see God the Father, Christ, and Mary so estimably and perfectly portrayed: it is no help; we bow the knee no longer."[34]

Berlage furnished Mies with the basis for a simple theory of the building art, from which persuasive arguments for a critique of Peter Behrens's architecture could be launched. How strongly Mies identified with these thought processes is here particularly explicit: the same reproaches Berlage leveled in his writings against Gottfried Semper now appear, this time in reference to Behrens, in Mies's words. It seemed easy to transfer the accusation of a "fatal sympathy for the High Renaissance,"[35] aimed at Semper, to the aristocratic Renaissancism of Behrens's architecture. Even the mixture of approbation and criticism Mies entertained in respect to his teacher Behrens was typical of Berlage's attitude toward Semper. On the one hand, he admired the lucidity of Semper's theory, which gave full scope to function and construction; on the other, he reproached him for not having "applied this consequentially to architecture."[36]

Mies entertained similar ideas with respect to Behrens. In the eyes of Mies, Behrens had achieved a considerable historical feat by having broken the spell nineteenth-century art had exercised over industry and construction and for having upgraded functional buildings into modern art objects; his limitations consisted in not having applied the new ideas rigorously enough. "But he did not seriously apply the method to other types of buildings" was Mies's comment on Behrens's Turbine Factory—"Funny. It takes quite a while before people realize what they are doing."[37]

From the perspective of Berlage's committedness, which Mies now literally made his own, Behrens was given credit for having employed the new steel and glass construction, without, however, exhausting all its possibilities, thus solving only half the problem. But more serious than a mere lack of consistency was the lack of authenticity of construction. The idealizing rhetoric suggested by the tympanum motif and corner pylons came, in their subjective will to style, dangerously close to what Berlage had called a "construction lie."[38] From the corner treatment of the Turbine Factory it is clear that Behrens put more value on formal expression than on constructive logic. Its tectonics called for a visually reassuring supporting mass, although the area is statically unburdened. "The nature of the technical is determined in its fulfillment. . . . He who builds a factory as if it were a temple lies and disfigures the landscape."[39] This remark, which almost sounded as if Berlage himself had leveled a devastating critique against

H. P. Berlage, office building, London, 1914.

Peter Behrens, Mannesmann Administration Building, Düsseldorf, 1911.

Peter Behrens, Administration Building of the Continental Works, Hanover, 1912.

Peter Behrens, German Embassy in St. Petersburg, 1912.

Mies, Office Building, 1923.

the Turbine Factory, was noted by Mies in his notebook in 1928, although he proudly announced that he had himself worked on the fenestration of the building's courtyard.[40]

If one reviews all Mies's references to Behrens, one senses an oppressive opinionatedness that denies any significant influence of the teacher on the student. And if one has to draw a conclusion from these utterances, it would not be farfetched to follow Berlage and extend his laconic verdict on Semper also to Behrens: "Pity the building arts."[41]

In practice, the opposite was the case; even if written and spoken statements largely deny any influence, Mies has proven to be a pupil of Behrens, not least by his urge to surpass him. That Mies had more than a mere personal appreciation for Behrens, and that this continued after the demise of the prewar ideals, is proven by several incidents. When Mies published in G no. 3 of June 1924 an article on "Industrial Building" that called for a radical reorganization of the building process "without concern for antiquated attitudes and convictions" and proclaimed that the industrialization of the building trades represents the "core problem" of "social, economic, technical, and even artistic questions," he illustrated his text with the picture of a "new type of hall structure" whose author was not the "design engineer" Berlage, but the "artist-architect" Peter Behrens. In the same publication, for the editing of which Mies was responsible, there was also an article by Ludwig Hilberseimer called "Konstruktion und Form" that also contained an example of a Behrens-style hall structure.

Apparently Behrens was one of the few still able to serve as example for the radical demands of modern construction as late as the mid-twenties. In

Peter Behrens, Turbine Factory of the AEG in Berlin, 1909.

Entry in Mies's notebook, 1928: "The nature of the technical is determined in its fulfillment./ The technical is alien to ornament. Technology as educator./He who builds a factory as if it were a temple lies and disfigures the landscape."

1924, Mies asked his former teacher to take part in an exhibition within the circle of the Novembergruppe.[42] In the same year, as a gesture of respect, Behrens was invited to take part in the building of the model housing settlement at Stuttgart-Weissenhof, which offered the European avant-garde, under the aegis of Mies, the opportunity to exhibit their work.

The overcoming of prewar classicism, practically synonymous with the name of Behrens, was not a mere personal matter, as Mies had it, but a historical process. Mies admitted that, after his encounter with Berlage, he had fought an inner battle to liberate himself from "Schinkel's classicism."[43] The "great detachment" (Nietzsche) from his teacher Behrens, who had initiated the veneration for Schinkel of 1910, now also extended to Schinkel himself, whose buildings Mies had described as exemplary and an "excellent example of classicism—the best I know."[44] While Mies declared Schinkel's museum publicly as a building from which one could learn everything about architecture,[45] he confided privately in his notebook: "Schinkel, the greatest building master of classicism, represents the end of an old and the beginning of a new time. With the Altes Museum he built a waning period. With his boring Gothic churches he was the forerunner of an unspeakably kitchy century, but with the Building Academy he introduced a new epoch."[46]

The detachment from neoclassicism and from the father figure Behrens was completed, at the latest, in 1929 with the Barcelona Pavilion. Yet at the very height of the liberation process, a new type of identification with the precursors emerged on a different level. The line of inheritance that an enthused art criticism had bestowed upon Behrens was now handed to Mies. Paul Westheim was the first to draw the new connection from Mies to Schinkel, to be later affirmed by Philip Johnson and others.[47] Westheim explained: "Mies initially understood Schinkel as speaking a specific formal language, as was generally held, but he soon discovered behind the classicist Schinkel that other Schinkel who had been, as to meaning, technology, and craftsmanship, the most eminent practical building master of his time, one who was never prevented by his ideals of the antique from planning his buildings as clearly and simply arising out of their proper frame of purpose. Mies, and in that he appears typical for the most promising of today's young architects, penetrates to the specifically architectonic in Schinkel; the classicizing formal language, the mere temporal aspect of Schinkel, becomes irrelevant. This means that Mies, who no longer shows any traces of the so-called Schinkel style, has to be looked upon as one of the most talented because most original of Schinkel's followers."[48]

And, indeed, it was Mies who had to redeem the hope the first decade of the century had placed in Behrens. Behrens's buildings followed clearly in the tradition of Prussian classicism and it was Schinkel[49] who was discovered, in 1910, to have been the forerunner of a modern mode of building. Schinkel prefigured what this time was looking for. Viewed from the per-

Karl Friedrich Schinkel, Charlottenhof Palace, Potsdam, 1826.

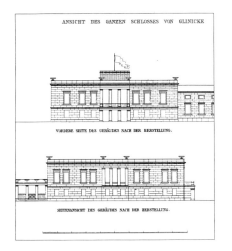

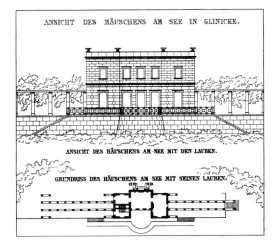

Karl Friedrich Schinkel, Glienicke Palace, Berlin, 1824, manor house and casino.

Design for the Kröller-Müller House, The Hague, 1912.

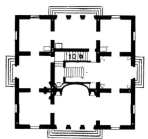

Karl Friedrich Schinkel, Pavilion, Charlottenburg Palace, Berlin, 1824.

Perls House, Berlin-Zehlendorf, 1910–1911.

spective of functional form, one could already make out in his works "definitely modern elements in the sense of today's purpose-oriented artist . . . ,
namely dispositions toward conscious, metropolitan functionalist
architecture."[50]

In assimilating industrial techniques, neoclassicism became the actual point
of departure for the new development. The fascination Behrens had exercised over the younger generation of architects can be ascribed to this
power of synthesis manifested by the fact that no other architect was occupied with such a large number of important commissions. His interpretation
of classicism was based on the thesis that an analogy can be drawn
between antiquity and modernism. The "elective affinity" between industrial
architecture and early antiquity[51] appeared to contemporaries like a promise that opened a "gate to heaven, . . . to a new, longed for heaven of our
own."[52]

Behrens had resorted to antiquity, much as Berlage had resorted to the
Gothic, not so much to revive its formal language as to revive the spirit of a
past epoch in order to bring up the spirit of one's own. Modern industrial
classicism, so it was hoped, would restore the lost continuity of meaning
disrupted by the nineteenth century and reestablish transcultural values
and "cultural associations" (Behrens). Plastic forcefulness was required to
bestow actuality and conviction to that transposition of values that aimed at
demonstrating the continuity and connectedness of the great design. Behrens linked the past and the present in a manner, so one critic has it in
regard to the industrial buildings and technical equipment, that evoked "the
curve backward to the classical codex" but just as deliberately pointed forward to the "steely presence"; his work thus "anticipates and searches for
the machines."[53]

By means of a deliberate reclamation of the formal values of antiquity, with
their rhetorical pathos and authoritative monumentality, one could rightfully
lay claim to objectivity. Much as Hegel was not so much interested in the
historical process itself as in the motivating laws that govern it, the modern
interpretation of antiquity with its urge toward abstraction revolutionized history, not because it distilled the Hegelian substrate of a universal construction of truth, but rather because it projected into history the contemporary
principle of an abstract will to form. Analogy constituted a bridge between
the reality of the past and the reality of the present, in order to link both
shores.

Already when the first indication of a Greek art influence became apparent
in the Düsseldorf work of Peter Behrens in 1905, Julius Meier-Graefe dis-
cerned the possibilities of a new aesthetic shining through the folly of that
analogy. Meier-Graefe posed the question of modernity as a question that
had suggested itself by Behrens's analogy but that was not to find its
answer until it was resolved by Mies two decades later: "Should it not be
possible to build in such a manner that not the form but only that cool,

Urbig House, Potsdam-Neubabelsberg, 1915–1917, garden and street façades.

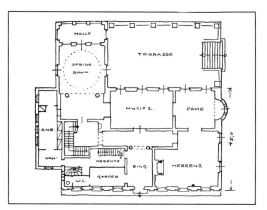 

Urbig House, plan, and condition in 1985.

Left, Urbig House, detail of street façade. *Right,* Peter Behrens, Wiegand House, Berlin-Dahlem, 1912, garden façade.

divine spirit of the Greeks would be resurrected?" This question had been evoked by the analogical possibilities existing between antiquity and modernism and had opened up a perspective that appeared to promise liberation from the restrictions of the historical. "The way to antiquity goes through our terrain. It must not end in Greece, but must bestow to our forms Hellenistic clarity, Hellenistic reason, or, let us simply say, the beautiful."[54]

The pupil who had repudiated his teacher brought the thesis of the master to completion. Mies articulated the potential latent in the analogy, giving an answer that had to resort neither to analogical imagery nor to the mediation of a specific extraneous formal vocabulary. He raised the classicizing curtain and revealed the secret archetype slumbering behind it, thus bringing to fruition the promise Behrens had awakened in regard to Schinkel.

With Mies, so wrote Sergius Ruegenberg, his co-worker from the twenties, in 1936, "the classical forms, profiles, and capitals . . . were abolished; what was important was the form and its expression, attained by intrinsic means"[55]—a statement that must be accorded considerable weight in view of the fact that Speer's classicism usurped the classical repertoire.

The "intrinsic form-giving" of Mies no longer resigned itself to a "borrowed existence" (Nietzsche) satisfied with bringing the epoch merely to the speaking point by means of a detour over historical terrain. The architecture of appearances was replaced by an architecture of being in which the new language was not merely brought to the point of speaking but spoke itself. Mies penetrated beyond the irrelevant temporal into the immanent—

into that sphere of the "specifically architectonic" (Westheim) that, both intrinsic and modern, created a new metaphor for epochal form-giving.

With his Turbine Factory whose "façade one never forgets" (Theodor Heuss, 1910), Behrens had awakened the awareness that visual and rhythmical values can be perceived separately from style.[56] With the Barcelona Pavilion, of which Behrens prophesied in 1929 that it would one day be counted the most beautiful building of the twentieth century,[57] Mies had expressed—with a space one never forgets—the modern sensibility. That this building has recently been reconstructed affirms its mythical status as a key structure of modernism. It expresses the sensibility of an epoch that, instead of the plane with its symbols, prefers genuine spatiality in which structure and composition, form and material, dynamic and static are fused.

The passage into antiquity, as sketched out by Meier-Graefe, diminished to a vanishing point in which past and future, primordial beginning and utopia, coalesced. It inspired the euphoric vision of a modernism that strove toward the beautiful in general, toward that essence of all styles that fused primordial beauty with new beauty by means of "simplicity of construction, clarity of tectonic means, and purity of material."[58] This transhistorical classicism promised an architecture that, in the words of J. J. P. Oud in 1921, "developed free of all impressionistic moods in the fullness of the light, to pure relationships, freshness of color, and organic clarity of form, and that on account of the absence of all irrelevancies surpasses even classical purity."[59]

Meier-Graefe's perceptiveness in regard to the developments of 1905, then barely discernible, did not stop at a sensibility to form. He was also in tune with the materialistic wing of the modern movement that, in its quest for rationality and influenced by the theories of Guadet, Berlage, and Wagner, insisted on rational construction. His opinion concerning the demands for honesty of function, purpose, and material should prove no less prophetic.

The criteria for a new architecture were not adequately served by a mere emphasis on rationality and rejection of ornament. However significant the liberation from ornament may have been—keeping in mind Meier-Graefe's argument as to the influence of antiquity—the way to construction, too, although lying in the realm of contemporary necessity, could not stop with the merely technological but had to lead beyond to a higher goal. Thus, he warned already in 1905 of an overemphasis on reason, an experience that the architecture of our century, dominated as it is by technology and functionalism, was not to be spared:

Now that we have finally arrived at reasonable attitudes, the danger is great that we obtain an art that is only rational, that fills all material and functional demands but that cannot prevent one thing: boring us thoroughly. Even the best of instructions still do not inform us how a house should be built so that it appears pictorial, plastic, engaging. And that

Feldmann House, Berlin-Grunewald, 1921–1922.

may very well be the reason why our so highly praised modern style appears so miserably deprived compared to all the others. Perhaps now that our style has become logical, it has become in its very logic as insubstantial as latticework through which the wind howls.[60]

In 1905 Behrens was counted as the great, perhaps only, exception. In the creative talent of this artistic outsider, who had been attacked as dilettante and rebel,[61] Meier-Graefe saw a latent regulative principle at work that guaranteed that things were not taken too literally. The decisive criterion, "the secret of all art" that cannot be attained "by purely logical means"[62] or—in the words of the Mies of the late twenties—"by calculation,"[63] depended on an equilibrium between the subjective and the objective, the old and the new, the individualistic and the rule.

This explains why Behrens, according to Mies, had viewed Berlage as outdated. Semper's critique of the constructive logic of the Gothic, withheld by Berlage from his readers despite his frequent Semper citations, already pointed to the problem that Behrens addressed but that was only to be solved by Mies on an advanced level. Semper had held that beyond the law of construction there is also the law of the perceiving eye that obeys its own rules of aesthetics and that searches for a sensible understanding of the static-constructive situations expressed by form. According to Semper, the Gothic had not solved the problem of bringing together both these demands harmoniously; only half the problem, the mechanical one, had been solved.[64]

"Just as there are physical laws, there are also artistic laws," explained Behrens in his lecture "Art and Technology" in 1910; it was frequently published and almost certainly was read by Mies. Behrens here countered indirectly the accusation of the "construction lie" by the concept of the

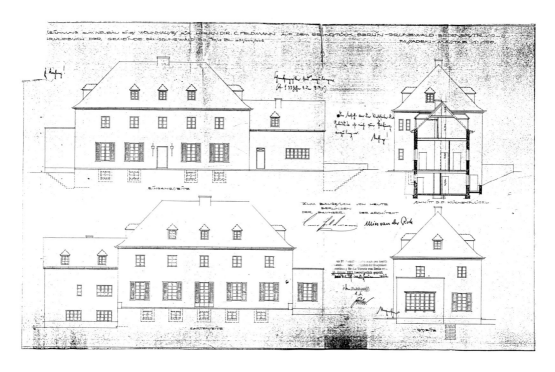

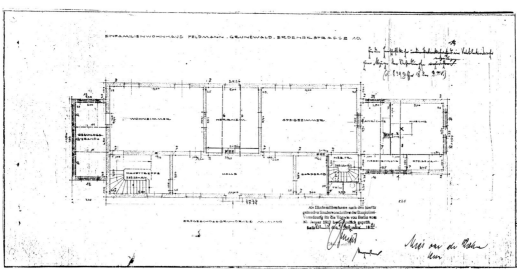

Feldmann House, view and plan from the records of the building commission.

84

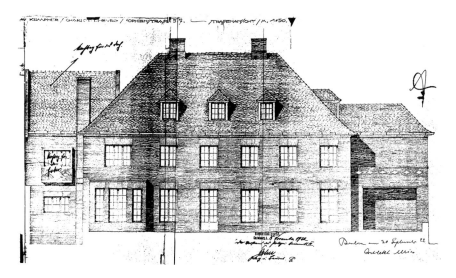

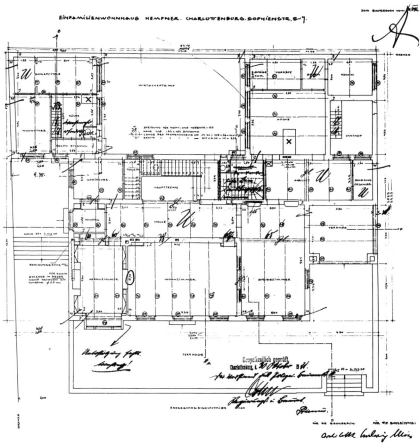

Kempner House in Berlin-Charlottenburg, view and plan from the records of the building commission, 1921–1922.

Eichstädt House, Berlin-Zehlendorf, 1920–1921.

"pseudoaesthetic" and accused a "certain school of modern aesthetics" of the mistake of wanting to derive "artistic form from function and technology. . . . No style can result from construction and material alone. There is no such thing as a materialistic style and there has never been one. The all-encompassing unity of an epoch arises out of a much larger complex of conditions than can be derived from these two factors alone. Technology cannot permanently be conceived of as an end in itself, but it assumes its significance and meaning when it is recognized as the most noble instrument of our culture. A mature culture, however, speaks only through the language of art."[65]

The antipodes Berlage and Behrens were unanimous in their demand that an elementary building art had to be reanimated, that contemporary contents had to fill it, and that its linguistic possibilities had to reflect the new conditions. If there was a common lesson they imparted to Mies, it was the call to solve this artistic task, to which Mies indeed devoted his entire effort. Thus, the general concepts of his teachers reached by way of divergent points of view a programmatical consensus. The restitution of geometry as a requisite for all architectural composition, the rigorous rejection of reproductive copying of characteristic style forms, and the expansion of architectonic form in "a factual direction"[66] were not only the prime rules for Berlage, but were also implicit in the industrial classicism of Behrens.[67] Berlage's plea for a rhythmical, geometrically composed architecture was of particular interest to Behrens, and in the *Grundlagen* of 1908 one could find indirect references to Behrens insofar as two student drawings from the architectural class of the Düsseldorf Kunstgewerbeschule, directed by Behrens, were reproduced as exemplary applications of the geometrical design method.[68]

The "geometrical basis" (Berlage) constituted a platform for divergent concepts. Berlage had been a devotee of the Egyptian number mysticism of triangulation and of the canonical lawfulness of cathedral structures, while Behrens paid homage to the "eternal laws of the square and the circle"[69] under the emblem of humanism. The one accepted the "living geometry" of the animal and plant kingdoms as his guiding light, seeing in them laws "that . . . make us shudder with reverence",[70] the other searched for the rhythmical laws of a spiritual force that enabled man to shape his life harmoniously, to make contact with the "larger currents" and thereby create a heroic art "before which we sink to our knees, that makes us shudder, that overpowers our soul by its magnitude."[71]

Behrens did not aim for an analogy with nature;[72] he made no effort "for the sake of nature to conceal an unmistakable rhythm." His form-giving did not follow a "truth of nature," as Berlage believed he detected in the objective law of the construction principle, but was oriented toward form-giving by means of rhetoric and style. This "truth of form" organized matter according to the artistic rules of measure and proportion. It did not eavesdrop on nature but set its own laws.

The antipodes Berlage and Behrens circumscribed two different worlds, and their divergence illustrates the crisis of consciousness that had already set in in the eighteenth century with the concept of individualism. Already Immanuel Kant had stated in 1780 that "reason does not draw its laws . . . from nature but dictates them to it."[73]

This "Copernican turn," as Kant proudly called it, also took place in the architectural theory of the eighteenth century with the spirit of enlightenment that opposed the inherited norms of nature and tradition. The dictum "Rules should not be based on what is but on what should be"[74] used by Abbé Laugier to introduce his *Essai sur l'architecture,* showed up the difference between the old and the new worlds and their respective architectures of reality. With the dawning of the industrial age, the conflict intensified between the traditional belief in a metaphysically guaranteed wholeness and the idea of an autonomous, rational individual that insists on imparting meaning to its own existence.

In the field of architecture, Berlage and Behrens embodied once more these opposites that had their roots in the discourse of the nineteenth century. Berlage, searching for ultimate truth and logical lawfulness, represented the point of view of metaphysical idealism (*Wesensphilosophie*); he stood in the shadow of Hegel and Schopenhauer, with whose writings he was familiar. Behrens, who did not ask for ultimate truth but for meanings, was influenced by modern existential philosophy, which was most emphatically propounded by Nietzsche in the latter third of the nineteenth century. In Nietzsche's eyes, the cultural achievement consists of a "plastic power" that brings about new values. Much as there is no truth in and for itself, art must not imitate natural law but function as a spiritual supplement that aims to overcome it.[75]

Berlage's method aimed at isolating the logical aspects of nature, of the entire, to discover fundamentals. What it found was the principle of the immanent, of a reality behind appearances existing a priori as "simple law-fulness" (Berlage). This "basic ideal idea" was laid bare by a process of abstraction that dismantled the layers of concrete reality hiding an a priori order with which the eternally true, pure building art coincided. Transposing this philosophical method to the field of architecture led necessarily to its dematerialization: the process of abstraction eliminated the object as form to distill the inherent from it. One must, so Mondrian described this Platonic procedure, "form with exactitude what shines through in nature only vaguely, and reductively destroy concrete appearances."[76] Geometry sym-bolized that ultimate sphere of an objective "basic ideal idea," to which "logical construction," identical with both natural truth and highest spiritual-ity, corresponded. In the absolute of truth was to be found the creative matrix of all being. Much as Hegel postulated an existing lawfulness, a *Weltgeist* that guaranteed the progressive development of history, Berlage endowed construction with a mythical power so that the law of historical progress might also guarantee a process of renovation in the building art.

Functionality and truth in construction spearheaded the attack against Vitruvian architecture. The transparent world of steel construction refused to subordinate itself to a canon of formal laws based on the concepts of monumentality and enclosed form depending on mass. Modern construc-tion called for a building art that must differentiate itself from the traditional in regard to appearances: it would—so Berlage sketched the physiognomy of the new form in an apt prophecy—remain flat on the exterior, its plastic articulation would derive from construction, and the architectonic space would be newly defined "as a more or less assembled complex of walls."[77]

Neoplatonism, which lived on via Berlage in the concepts of De Stijl and which spoke out of Mies's dematerialized "skin and bone buildings," pur-sued an image of immanence that cannot be interpreted by subjective, aesthetic means, but can only be constructed by universal, mathematically abstract means of expression. For this reason the word "aesthetic" might as well, as Berlage indicated, "quietly disappear from the architectural world."[78] This platform also found its apodictic champion in the Mies of the early twenties. He called for a "liberation of building activity from aesthetic speculators,"[79] something that sounded much like an iconoclastic battle cry aimed at mobilizing a crusade, as if the issue were the liberation of the building arts from thousands of years of oppression.

Behrens's creative principles, quite in contrast to Berlage's, were primarily based on aesthetics. In the dispute between object and perception, that is, in the wish of the object to be understood by means of its appearance, lies the access to reality and consequently the area of argument for this method of creating. Here art claims its rightful terrain in the form of poetic metaphor and by means of its linguistic instruments, rhythm, harmony, and proportion, or in Nietzsche's words it creates "reality *once more,* only selected, strengthened, and corrected."[80] Only the art work allows reality to be experienced by man as a self-created reality and, ultimately, as a "reflection of will."

This theory did not understand form as the manifestation of an order residing behind the world of appearances but as the result of a dialogue with appearances carried on in the imagination of man. Existential philosophy negates the existence of a reality beyond being that could be looked upon as a precondition for appearances and phenomena. Spirit is not based in a world behind things but in human perception, which encounters the world as an interpretative challenge. The enlightenment and the machine age demystified the old myths by the positivistic methods of modern science, rendering reality godless. Modern man, who has gained "an open look in the presence of reality,"[81] is forced by an act of "self-legislation" (Alois Riehl) to equip himself with his own, new ideals and "prepare a world suitable to his own existence."[82]

While Berlage, caught up in a Platonic-Hegelian predicament, could only wait "until a new world idea is born,"[83] Behrens as Nietzschean said "yes to reality," believing that one had to infuse new passions into values and "set to work *on that part of the world that is amenable to change.*"[84] This idealizing of what is given, by "directing the glance toward future possibilities of life,"[85] not only allowed the accommodation of contemporary trends in architecture but actually called for the inclusion of the machine world and a synthesis of art and industry. Without this epistemological premise, the aesthetic enthusiasm for utilitarian structures such as silos and cranes that had so invigorated the architecture around 1910 would remain just as inexplicable as the imagery of steamships, automobiles, and airplanes in the twenties.

To Mies, this reevaluative will that spoke in imagery and that employed aesthetic analogies was suspect. It stood in contradiction to that Platonism that sought the key to reality not so much in a manner of being as in a manner of perceiving. Heinrich Wölfflin had supplied a corresponding viewpoint in his *Grundbegriffe* of 1915. Wölfflin's thesis of a "history of seeing" opened up the traditional, historical imagery for formal reevaluation. His premise that "people probably have always seen as they wanted to see"[86] invited that relativism of viewpoints that ultimately permits one, as Zarathustra had it, "to ride on any simile to any truth."

Mies refused his allegiance to this approach, as it put the semblance of truth in place of the truth. If one built a factory like a temple, as Behrens did, or, even more extreme, juxtaposed a sports car to the Parthenon as equivalent, one must expect criticism. And even though Mies, faced with the choice, unhesitatingly preferred Le Corbusier over Schultze-Naumburg,

Peter Behrens, Wiegand House, Berlin-Dahlem, 1912, entry hall.

German Pavilion, Barcelona International Exposition, 1929.

Construction or Interpretation of Reality?
Berlage or Behrens? Hegel or Nietzsche?

it remained nevertheless "wrong of Le Corbusier to mingle his attitude with that of pure classicism."[87]

The dichotomy between construction and form embodied by Berlage and Behrens in their respective concepts of constructive form-finding and interpretative form-giving reemerged under new conditions in the New Building. Much like Berlage and Behrens, Le Corbusier and Mies agreed on what architecture should be but disagreed on what it is. Le Corbusier's definition of architecture as "the masterly, correct and magnificent play of masses brought together in light"[88] put its trust in the perceiving senses. Le Corbusier's buildings demonstrated a wealth of possibilities between mutually interactive volumes. Mies's dematerializing skin and bone structures strove to reduce reality to its very kernel, so that beyond all visual apprehension a preexisting inner order might crystallize.

The divergent orientation of these two architects is also evident in the function they assigned to geometry. In Mies's minimalism, the geometrical order of the supporting frame's posts and beams establishes a rhythm in empty space; Le Corbusier's purism by contrast saw geometry as the "language of architecture" and deployed the plastic volumes to appeal to the senses, so that the eye could partake, by way of cubistic purity, of the "joys of geometry."

Mies derived his credo from Berlage's theories that could be summed up by the simple formula "building is serving."[89] Le Corbusier, who liked to compare architects to poets, strictly rejected such functionalist concepts as unartistic. Their purpose lies in the realm of the practical rather than in that of art, which must not exhaust itself in the service of the material: "To those who . . . claim 'architecture means service,' we answer 'architecture means stirring the emotions.' And "—Le Corbusier added with a sidelong glance toward the critics who presumably had similar reservations toward his art as Mies had expressed in respect to Behrens's—"people have brushed us off as poets."[90]

Much like Behrens, Le Corbusier perceived buildings as metaphors for strength and moral support. According to his Dionysian definition of the art of building, inspired by Nietzsche's theory of tragedy, passion builds "drama out of inert stone."[91] It was this perpetual play of masses in the light that now had to be performed without the classical stage set. Just as Leon Battista Alberti had striven five hundred years earlier, the art of building had to realize its dramatic potential exclusively by means of form and arrangement. Le Corbusier saw the machine for living as a "palace" in which "each organ of the house, merely by means of its relationship to the whole, could stir us so movingly as to reveal the magnitude and nobility of an *intent*."[92]

This deliberate willing was not inward-directed—for example, toward a rendering of the structural building frame, to which Mies paid so much attention—but toward the imaginative possibilities of the architectonic. For Le Corbusier the metaphoric task of architecture, which must glorify the victory of spirit over matter, began with the "battle against gravity" that had to be translated into a "sensuous experience." In this drama lay, according to Nietzsche, the actual artistic meaning of the architectonic: buildings are supposed to render visible "pride, triumph over gravity and will to power. . . . Architecture is a kind of eloquence of power embodied in form."[93]

But it was Berlage whom Mies had styled the great educator in the field of architecture. To him he accorded the Nietzschean predicate of Superman, who, as "solitary giant,"[94] radiantly surpassed his contemporaries. But no matter how unequivocally Mies expressed himself for man and theory, it did not release him from the problematic of ambivalence. The unequivocal commitment to construction may have put the question of meaning into the background, but it did not answer it. Thus, the imaginary dialogue between two worlds, encountered by Mies at the beginning of his career, continued.

Even if Mies in the early twenties tried to extricate himself, by his uncompromising attitude that rejected all will to form as academic and speculative, his thoughts and statements remained ambivalent. In spite of the rhetorical impetus of denial, the executing impulses insisted on perfect form-giving and appearance—and thence on the rights of art.

These contradictions drove Mies's typical striving in all phases of his career. They challenged him to press for the simplest common denominator on one hand, while on the other to strive for richness. The absolutist desire for veracity and clarity originated in the conscious awareness of these profound contradictions and disruptions. Modern man, standing in front of a threatening "chaos" (Mies), must overcome "the loss of center" by creating a new structural framework of values. This contradiction between a belief in an a priori order and the modern demand for subjective self-regulation preoccupied Mies, who—like all modern men, according to Nietzsche—was torn by the resultant conflict of values; "sitting between the chairs" and confronted by both myth and enlightenment, he says both "yes and no in one breath." One could not find a more apt motto for Mies than Nietzsche's formula for happiness: "A Yes, a No, a straight line, a *goal*."[95]

IV Elementary Form-Giving:
Departure for the Limits of Architecture

1　"Beyond Architecture": On Eternal Building

It is mainly our concern to liberate all building activity from aesthetic specialists. And make building again what it always has been. Building.

Ludwig Mies van der Rohe, 1923

Our task steps up to us at each moment. Let us impress the image of eternity on our lives.

Friedrich Nietzsche, quoted by Alois Riehl, 1908

The most important assignment of life: to begin each day afresh, as if it were the first day—and yet to assemble and have at one's disposal the entire past with all its results and forgotten lessons.

Georg Simmel, Posthumous Fragments and Essays, *Munich, 1923 (in the library of Mies)*

By designing a series of projects that were for the most part self-gener-ated,[1] Mies left behind the familiar image of architecture. The designs made between 1921 and 1924, the Glass Skyscrapers, Office Building, Concrete Country House, and Brick Country House, were unique for that period in their logic, conception, and formal perfection. Exemplary, defini-tive, and yet fantastic in their precise poetry, they were both realistic and utopian at the same time; mature and totally thought through, they stood in the beginning of a development that had all the appearances of setting a norm for some time to come.

No less radical were the printed manifestos that accompanied these proj-ects; describing the New Building from a different angle, they reveal the spirit on which these prototypes of modern architecture were based. In their outspoken and strident tone, these first manifestos were as pioneering as the designs themselves. Both shared the fervor of an uncompromising diction that stressed an unrhetorical rolling-up-the-sleeves attitude. Clearly, work and idea, conviction and word are at the command of an identical will.

Like a Reformer, Mies nailed his thesis, so to speak, onto the door of the old church. He wanted nothing less than the renovation of the building art, from the root on up. The titles "Working Hypotheses" (1923), "Building" (1923), and "Building Art and the Will of the Epoch" (1924) suggest that a sober understanding of necessity is demanded from architects of the new age. The sought-after objectification of architectural form demanded strong beliefs. The architect's artistic freedom had to give way before the new desire for truth, which acquired the character of objectivity only according to the unambiguous rules of functionalism.

The renovation of the building art from its foundation up had to begin with the reestablishment of a fundamental morality of building. As its apostle, Mies entered the debate. Part of his program was, first of all, the rejection of a past, that had, after World War I, experienced a total collapse, a "heroic finale" (F. Dessauer). The purging of the building art from this history of decline began with a rejection of all aesthetic and symbolic references and contents. The clenched fist spoke, as it were, in the rhythmically insistent verdict of Mies: "Any aesthetic speculation, any doctrine, and any formalism we reject."[2]

This rejection not only repudiated traditional illusionistic art but also turned its back on any sort of theory or ideology, one could even say "religion," of the building art. Whether Taut's expressionism or Doesburg's neoplasticism, Mies in 1923 branded all concepts that strove for form, or, what was even more to be avoided, style, as "formalistic." From his perspective of the absolute, form could no longer claim any rights; it was laid aside with the laconic remark, "We have other worries," implying that the elimination of form had been long overdue. Form was no longer a factor in the catalog of architectural categories: "We know no forms, only building problems" was the appropriate phrase by which this symptom of decline was stricken from the new consciousness. "Form is not the goal but the result of our work. There is no form in and for itself. . . . Form as goal is formalism; and that we reject."[3]

This explains why it was practically self-understood that Mies wanted "nothing whatever to do with the aesthetic traditions of past centuries" and wanted to see "all theories" banned from the building arts.[4] What this inquisitorial method exempted from the purge remained ill-defined. A tautological explanation that came dangerously close to a banality, glorifying rather than defining, mystifying rather than enlightening, proclaimed: "It is our concern to liberate building activity from aesthetic speculators and make building again what alone it should be, namely BUILDING."[5]

A postscript in the manuscript shows an illuminating version of this sentence, putting Mies's understanding of history in the correct light: what mattered was "to make building again what it always has been. BUILDING." What should be and what is, the future and the eternal, so this already implies, fuse together. The new and the eternal beauty, as Mies explains elsewhere, are identical.[6]

The precondition for this redemption of the absolute and timeless was furnished by the philosophical method of abstraction. Concrete reality, a mere ephemeral layer of deception, had to be peeled from the essence of things so that the all-valid order of being could be laid bare. Reality should no longer merely be depicted, but should itself be shaped. This belief united the representatives of the early twentieth century over and above all differences they may have had otherwise. Much like Plato, who counted architecture among the original and creative rather than the imitative arts, the representatives of the new art called for an art in tune with universal laws. New Building, so Mies had it, progresses away from the aesthetic toward the organic, away from the formal toward the constructive.[7] The magical word "building" (*Bauen*) stands for such an image: conforming to a natural order and the lawful structuring of matter and its movement, it is followed by growth; it typifies the work of man that, resting on objective laws yet unfolding in freedom, realizes its own order. Thus, at least conceptually, the hoped-for fusion between an objective and a subjective order, held characteristic for elementary form-giving, had been redeemed.

Mies defined the word "building" only in the most general of terms and refrained from any specific explication, almost as if no further explanation were called for. "Building" signified for Mies a type of creating that arises "out of the nature of the task itself"[8] and that operates with the means typical of the epoch. It stood for a simple, obvious truth the validity of which did not need to be proven by theory or doctrine. Rather, a wisdom seemed to declare itself, based on an imaginary point, on which the "house of being" (Nietzsche) eternally built itself according to a hidden plan.

Mies shared the longing of his generation for a newly ordered world. The redemption myth connotation of the word "building" had first been employed by the expressionists. In April of 1919, Walter Gropius called upon the artists, in a pamphlet, to tear down the walls "that our false school knowledge erects between the 'arts' so that we may *all become builders again!*" The fall of our "function-cursed time" seemed predictable, since the time no longer understood the all-encompassing, animating meaning of building. As a result of this loss of meaning, men were condemned to live in "deserts of ugliness." "Let us understand this clearly: these gray, hollow, cheerless fakes in which we live and work will render an embarrassing testimony to posterity as to the hell-bent state of our generation, that forgot the great, the only, art: building."[9]

The reaction in 1919 against everything ideological and against earlier forms of knowledge and culture was the result of a vacuum of values. Only from the basis of a newly gained faith could the common, new "building thought" (Gropius) of the future be regained.

While the expressionists shifted toward the fantastic and turned their back on engineering, Mies, charting a course in the opposite direction, held fast to a bold realism that refused to heed a "call to building" appealing to subjective sensibilities and to emotional excess while turning a deaf ear on reality and the possibilities of contemporary renovation.

"Building," both as word and as concept, circumscribed for Mies a sphere of ideal purity that, untouched by "aesthetic speculation," guaranteed unblemished veracity.

The New Building must be anchored in unbreakable laws that due to their sovereignty command unswerving truthfulness and power of conviction. Here was that zero point that one could equate with "the intrinsic"; identical with the "archetypal source of being," it was able to nourish a "true building attitude." Thus Mies, in an archaizing act of abstraction, bent the bow backward toward fictive origins where the forms, as it were, took their beginning: "building" gropes to regain a lost condition of primordial innocence. This myth nourishes the belief in a building consonant with both an inner order and a presently effective force that, much like life, continually realizes itself. Thus, metaphysically charged with creative life force, "building" leads to a modern "building art" (*Baukunst*) in which echoes the great law of life to which the architect has to pay obeisance: "Their work shall serve life. Life alone shall be their teacher."[10]

Even the term "life," a rather romantic category of totalizing character, remained, initially in a similarly mysterious state of suspension, sharing with the word "building" a sort of exclusive preserve. The intent not to deceive oneself, which controlled the tenor of Mies's early manifestos, had its vanishing point in the origin and immanence myth, which remained itself, even if not an aesthetic, in any case a theoretical speculation. Mies's innermost nature seemed closer to the religious-mystical orientation of the expressionist ideology than to his own earlier stance that had aimed at a new reality and that had given his early projects that rationalistic and visionary quality.

A commitment to life and to a natural, eternal wisdom, or in other words "authenticity," was what Mies demanded above all else. The primacy of "building" declares the autonomy of architecture: an architecture that develops its own elementary grammar out of "inner necessity" (Mies) unaffected by the demands and theories made on it from the outside. With his belief in a building that does not need to redeem any theories but that fulfills the laws of life itself, and with his exquisite, formally accomplished projects, where form was explained in terms of a rejection of the laws of formality, Mies had departed for a realm of abstraction in which the immanent led its own authentic existence, untouched by human incursions. For Mies the only valid way, and the only exit out of that dilemma in which the prewar period with its conflicts was mired, was to penetrate into that realm in which the objective and the subjective were still in a state of harmonious coexistence. A new moral foundation for the building art had to be prepared.

The provocative tone with which Mies promoted his position indicated that he suggested—at least rhetorically—a *tabula rasa,* so that the lost myth of the primordial and truthful could be regained. It is out of this impulse that he dictated, on December 12, 1923, the following sentences for a lecture to be given at the meeting of the Bund Deutscher Architekten in Berlin:

In the country it is a self-understood usage to plow under a plot overgrown by weeds without considering the few grains that had managed to survive. We, too, have no other choice if we really strive for a new attitude toward building. . . . We demand . . . for the buildings for our time: absolute truthfulness and a rejection of all formal cheating.[11]

By calling for truthfulness and by alluding to a humble if rough, practically Darwinian law of life that still evoked natural, rustic forms, Mies was hunting for an order of being in which form and life are organically fused. The world is understood as a great divinely planned harmony. In placing his confidence in nature and faith, much as Berlage had done, who also wanted to show the way back to medieval architecture, Mies entered upon the way to building. At its end, however, was not a luminous "cathedral of the future" as the last and final aim of art[12] but a simple attitude toward building, which, with a glance toward the Middle Ages, held out factuality, service to the law of immanence, and personal dedication as preconditions for a timely building art.

That the medieval, with its dichotomy of world denial and hope, still maintained a certain relevance in the unstable years after 1918 was indicated by the easy reception of the Gothic elements in expressionism and the general revival of Neoplatonic notions in philosophy and science. In art history, too, this epoch found commensurate appreciation. Wilhelm Worringer had published his *Formproblem der Gotik* in 1912, a work acquired by Mies in a 1920 edition.[13] This was followed in 1917 by Karl Scheffler's *Vom Geist der Gotik,* and in 1922 Paul Ludwig Landsberg, a pupil of Max Scheler, submitted possibly the most important text on the subject, *Die Welt des Mittelalters und wir,* according to its subtitle, "A Historical and Philosophical Investigation into the Meaning of an Epoch." The 1923 publication of Hans Much's *Vom Sinn der Gotik* rounds out the series of influential publications that in the twenties found widespread distribution in several editions.[14]

Landsberg's study, written when he was only twenty years old, counts among the most important of the books that Mies intensively studied in the mid-twenties. This book, which gives an outline of Neoplatonic philosophy, may have been the volume that led Mies to "the quarries of antique and medieval philosophy" in order to find out "what truth really is."[15] That Landsberg's book was represented in two copies in Mies's library, both with numerous underlinings in pencil, reinforces this assumption.[16] What Landsberg searched for in the Middle Ages corresponded to Mies's quest. Much like Mies, who in 1924 rejected the expressionists' recourse to the Middle Ages with the remark, "the efforts of the mystics will remain episodes,"[17] Landsberg was far from "suggesting an impossible and unenjoyable 'return' to the Middle Ages" (underlined by Mies). A quote by Novalis preceding the text—"The meaning of the world has been lost, we have remained with the letter and have forgotten the appearing over the appearance"—circumscribes the goal Mies shared with Landsberg.

The "Middle Ages as a term of endearment" did not so much refer to a specific time period but to a "new love for the Middle Ages . . . that passes through our hearts like a wild tempest," that purifies us by offering "historical farsight" at the end of which the Middle Ages would appear as a "basic possibility for human existence," suggesting an analogy with "the spiritual conditions of the present time."[18]

Landsberg deliberately eschewed "modern" historical methods, relying instead on a supposedly medieval world view. According to this point of view, one did not embark upon an "inquiry into the coincidences of external events," one did not bother with the historical "how it really was" (Ranke), but one attempted to expose, "in the events of the past, how it eternally is." What made the Middle Ages so exemplary as a cultural epoch was unity and uniformity, that *ordo* that, according to Landsberg, "did not merely represent *a* coherent view of the world, but *the* coherent view of the world"[19](underlinings by Mies).

The "fervent attachment to the eternal that was peculiar to medieval man and that we are so bitterly in need of"[20] began to stand in for that passionate longing for the absolute that preoccupied Mies. Mies lined the margin of the following remarks with a double line: "But man is filled with the urge to perpetuate himself. . . . No 'return to the Middle Ages' can help us, no neomysticism, no neoscholasticism—only the rediscovery of the eternal in the world and in history and also in the Middle Ages. Only the eternal can be the ultimate example."[21]

Landsberg saw history as a "temporal realization of a trans-epochal, proto-ideal, and in the final analysis divine plan."[22] He found affirmation for his aprioristic concept of history[23] in Hegel's idea of a *Zeitgeist,* which, with its "pantheistic echoes," aims beyond individual epochs in search of an innate sense of the entire. Berlage, too, had called upon Hegel when he saw in art not the expression of an individual person but of the *Zeitgeist,* with the executing artist merely playing the role of interpreter.[24]

Mies, so it appeared, wanted to restrict the scope permitted the individual even more than Hegel had done. He spoke in 1924 not so much of *Zeitgeist* as of *Zeitwillen*—conjuring up an image of time's course as already mythologically predestined in the hidden suggestions of history. The sentence "The building art is always the spatially apprehended *Zeitwille,* nothing else"[25] seems to imply just such a mythic living force. This almost Schopenhaueresque "metaphysics of will" (Alois Riehl) removed will as a driving force from the conscious mind of the subject and attributed it to an innate essence, thus endowing it with those very characteristics withheld from the individual. Arthur Schopenhauer, to whom Berlage also was attracted, was no stranger to Mies. Already in his Aachen years his attention had been called to Schopenhauer by the architect Dülow, who apparently had been a Schopenhauer fan. It was Dülow who had invited the young Mies to dinner on Schopenhauer's birthday and had given him the advice to go to Berlin.[26]

Whether Mies had been able to follow the philosophical debate on the concept of will and take up a specific stance toward it is open to question.

Books by R. H. Francé.

Alois Riehl's essay "Schopenhauer und Nietzsche—Zur Frage des Pessimismus," which dealt with this question and which was available as a guideline, seemed to have met—according to the otherwise frequent underlinings—with no interest on the part of Mies. Mies's concept of will remained just as diffuse in its metaphysical coloring as his concept of building. Essentially, though, an attitude is implied that rejects the subjective in favor of a strict phenomenology. The individual is not seen as a source of truth but of error. He must give in to the objective, represented by the laws of nature and the commensurate *Zeitwillen,* which in turn leads to asceticism and a negation of will.

In this context can be explained the surprisingly strong interest Mies took in the writings of Raoul H. Francé, who had come to the attention of a large public through the series *Cosmos* published by the Society of the Friends of Nature in the early twenties. This author is represented in singular near-completeness[27] with over 40 titles in Mies's library. That Mies acquired the pamphlets and books of Francé practically systematically is shown by the order form to a book dealer toward the end of 1924, making inquiries as to the price and availability of the titles *Grundriss einer vergleichenden Biologie, Die technischen Leistungen der Pflanzen, Der Weg zur Kultur,* and *Grundriss einer objektiven Philosophie,* with a remark made by the book dealer on the bottom of the paper: "Mies v.d. Rohe, will telephone May 30."[28]

The writings of Francé were also read and debated among Mies's students at the Bauhaus, and it can be assumed that Mies absorbed many of the thoughts of this author he so highly valued and that they influenced his

Inquiries to a book dealer concerning titles by Francé. Note at bottom of first page: "Mies v.d. Rohe, will telephone May 30."

teaching. So writes the Bauhaus student Karl Kessler, one of Mies's last students, in a letter of June 16, 1933: "yesterday mies van der rohe dissolved the bauhaus due to financial difficulties . . . the bauhaus is dead, but the bauhaus spirit lives on . . . and that the direction of our solutions is good became clear to me on reading the book *bios* by raoul francé. What this biologist says in respect to engineering and that it must stand in harmony with world laws, just as with the smallest energy measure or with the law of harmony, that is bauhaus thought, that is bauhaus geist. for tuesday a steamer excursion is planned that shall give us once more the opportunity to discuss questions in regard to the future with mies v.d.r."[29]

The writings of Francé, several of which had already appeared before 1918, found their perfect sounding board in the intellectual climate of the early twenties. The moral indignation of the prewar years against individualism and greed for private profits and dominance, in which was seen the origin of the catastrophe, resulted in a general cultural pessimism that, in the final analysis, spoke against the modern view of a subject setting its own norms. The Middle Ages with their collective workshop communes were seen as models for the sublimation of the individual in favor of an anonymous generality; they symbolized an organic order that, much like nature itself, could be viewed as a region of innocence.

Francé's early work *Der Wert der Wissenschaft: Aphorismen zu einer Natur- und Lebensphilosophie* (The Value of Science: Aphorisms on the Philosophy of Nature and Life), which Mies owned in a third-edition volume of 1908, was ahead of its time insofar as it announced the demise of the strong, disciplined, ideal humanity that the Wilhelminian era had wanted to project for itself. *Der Wert der Wissenschaft,* in fact, critiqued Nietzsche on this very point. Francé held that Nietzsche was too beholden to the Wilhelminian cult of heroes and its myth of the Nibelungen. Though the Socratic nature of Nietzsche's thought could perhaps be accepted, his radical skepticism was declared by Francé to represent that paradigm of an unfortunate spiritual conduct of which "I want to warn." As a Socratic, Nietzsche had advanced to the utmost limit of self-destruction: "the collapsed Prometheus Nietzsche shows us the extreme of theoretical man." As "a great and noble sacrifice for mankind's coming centuries" Nietzsche could, according to Francé, be viewed as "a beneficiary for mankind, one could say a redeemer who, unaware of his act, sacrificed himself for their sake," provided one thing was learned from him, namely "how we must not live." It was the "luminous figure of Goethe" toward which Francé directed his gaze full of admiration and hope: Goethe, as Mies underlined, "as the author of *Zur Naturwissenschaft überhaupt* [Studies in the Natural Sciences], especially on morphology."[30]

If Georg Simmel and Alois Riehl, the turn-of-the-century discoverers of Nietzsche, saw in him above all, beyond the cult of genius, a proponent of ethics and of moral and cultural science, by 1918 the mood had undergone a pronounced change. Much as Mies condemned aesthetic speculation as a form of personal aggrandizement responsible for the decline of architecture, so Nietzsche was now seen as responsible for the decline of culture. Mies's attitude toward Nietzsche, as far as that can be established from the extant books, seems to have had that typical postwar emphasis propounded by Friedrich Muckle's book of 1921, *Friedrich Nietzsche und der Zusammenbruch der Kultur,* of which Mies owned a copy.[31]

Goethe's sentence "One must treat nature decently if one wants to benefit from it," quoted by Francé and underlined by Mies,[32] pointed to a principle that seems central to his world view. "Decent treatment" in respect to the givens at the place where two worlds intersect was for Mies an act of duty. The ascetic ideal of an education to humility[33] demands that one subordinate oneself to a larger, absolute lawfulness as opposed to a self-assured attitude toward a hypothetically changeable world. Only in the second half of the twenties was Mies willing to accord rights to both nature and idea in an attempt to complement his original position with the possibility of allowing people their own existential self-realization.

"The best one can do is to find a compromise between the I and this law [of ecology] and to adjust to it according to the invariables of the surroundings. That would result in a 'right'—meaning 'best possible'—way of life. More than the best possible is anyway not achievable." This sentence, underlined by Mies, appeared in a text by Francé called *Richtiges Leben: Ein Buch für Jedermann* (Correct Living, a Book for Everyone), published in 1924.[34] It promised its readers the key to the "right way of living," the rules of which were spelled out in the subtitle in the triad "lawfulness-equilibrium-adjustment." The right life demands "respect for the whole that, impenetrably complex, high and hostile, stands perpetually above us and in which we are posited [underlined by Mies]. . . . This respect for the whole must be embraced by us, so that we do not exceed the rights of man. It is, in the final analysis, the uppermost judge over the design plan of humanity. If it is missing, caprice will set in and poor, miserable man will swell up with hubris, become unaware of the order, break it, sin, become guilty"[35] (underlined by Mies).

In order to gain insight into the whole, one must search for the intrinsic; it is this search to which Francé accorded, with as much passion as if it were an issue between happiness and damnation, the ultimately monopolizing recognition: "It is characteristic of this insight that it concerns itself with only one issue, if it wants to decide a judgment. It is that disquieting, world-penetrating question: *What is*? that stops for nothing and must not stop, because the entire world will rise against that unfortunate one who deceives himself in respect to what 'really is' and who, seduced by alienating words or by his own imagination, acts falsely"[36] (underlinings by Mies).

And did Mies not, at the same time as these words were written, turn with the same uncompromising stance against "seduction" in the building art by any and all subjective theory and aesthetic speculation, against "alienating words" and "one's own imagination"?

"One must not be consumed by work. . . . Man is a harmonious creature—requiring change from work to rest—One must search out nature—You should love properly" (underlinings by Mies). These were the "five commandments of plasmatics" postulated by Francé as the biologically eternal laws of the correct way of life that determine the balance beyond which man is not permitted to transgress, either spiritually or materially. The harmony to be striven for brings with it *"thousands of resignations and self-denials"* (double lines by a vehement Mies in the margin), as it is the most stringent education to which man, then as now, has subjected himself, for it pursues a heroic goal: "the submission of the will to cognition."[37] It is not the will to power, referred to by Francé as the devil itself, but the "will to the disciplining of will," as it were, that was held out as the ascetic ideal of the new Superman acting in accord with objective laws.

Mies, in search of an absolute order that, according to E. Zederbauer's book *Die Harmonie im Weltall, in der Natur und in der Kunst,* builds itself up in step formation, found refuge in a biological parallel. The anatomical vocabulary of such terms as "skeleton" and "skin-and-bone structure" point in that direction. The biological analogy directs the aura of absolute values from the aesthetic toward the realm of being. Francé's writings such as *Das Sinnesleben der Pflanzen* (1905), *Die Pflanze als Erfinder* (1920), *Die Seele der Pflanze* (1924), *Die technischen Leistungen der Pflanze* (1919), and particularly *Das Gesetz des Lebens* (1921), may have encouraged Mies in that respect.

But his reading of the humanities also complemented this attitude. Natural science in the beginning of the twentieth century had brought to light many new facts, revealing the limited validity of our concept of space, time, and matter. This branch of knowledge confirmed the experience of the arts, that the classical terms to describe phenomena were no longer adequate. Thinkers such as Henri Bergson or Max Scheler, who had come to Mies's attention, took their starting points from the exact sciences when taking the "old but always new risk of metaphysics";[38] around 1920 they articulated the need of the epoch for a spiritual support system.[39]

To judge from the composition of his library, in which Johann Jakob von Uexküll, Werner Heisenberg, Karl Jaspers, and Erwin Schrödiger were represented with several works, Mies remained attached throughout his life to that coordination between nature, physics, and philosophy that had evolved in the twenties.[40]

Access to the intellectual discourse of the twenties had been facilitated by personal contact with Alois Riehl and his pupil and successor Eduard Spranger. In this intellectual arena Mies found his own metaphysical cast of mind affirmed, which, particularly in the harshness of its rejection of the speculative, proved to have its own religious energy. In the festschrift for Alois Riehl, Spranger called this an attitude of modern man, for whom the "strictness of . . . research [and] the realism of action" totally replace the "longing for redemption."[41]

The Miesian return to facts, to building, rested on a desire for belonging to a whole that could not be constituted simply as an intellectual phenomenon but had to be postulated as existing on a higher level. If one looks at the promises pronounced by the titles of books acquired by Mies, one discerns a mosaic of longings appearing behind the sober word "building" that imparts to it an entire horizon of significance. It is circumscribed by a "will to the whole" or a philosophy of the organic that has its center in the absolute, from where a bridge, built "from the eternal in man,"[42] reaches into the immediate present. It is in this remote place that we have to search for the roots of Mies's *Zeitwille*. Oswald Spengler, in his biologizing and Schopenhauerist pessimistic history of culture *Der Untergang des Abendlandes* (1920–1922), described history in terms of ascending and descending time periods. Into the mythical trajectory of an ascending period Mies wanted to plant building as expression of *Zeitwille*: "History is that which approaches man out of a dark past and wants by way of him to progress beyond into the future"[43]—a sentence that, underlined by Mies, appeared significant to him.

The path to the nature of things and to the laws of life aimed at an organic whole that preexisted as a dark, prehistoric matrix in matter itself. To illuminate it had been the ambition of modern science in the early twentieth century. Freudian psychology explored the individual conscience; Carl Gustav Jung's teaching on archetypes delivered a sequel with its theory of the collective subconscious; Johann Jakob Bachofen traced the content of archetypal symbols and religions. The myth of nature and history, the two reference points of the old world from which Vitruvian architecture took its point of departure and set its norms, experienced a brilliant theoretical renovation and was, through art and building, once more affirmed.

The principles of New Building were, as Hugo Häring, the theoretician of organic building who befriended Mies, wrote, not without tradition. "The tradition of the New Building, the tradition of building organically, is older even than architecture," for the "structural basics of organic building are elementary, are preexisting in nature, practically deeded to man."[44] This sounds similar to Spengler's mystic concept that has history come toward man out of a dark past. "Building" was hardly to be understood differently: it was an art fed by the archaic streams of the subconscious and the secret resources of being and, finally, not unsimilar to the world of antiquity, animated by nature deities, comprehensible only as part of cosmological speculation. For Häring, the history of cultures—and Mies certainly saw it no differently in those years[45]—had to be traced back to "a history of structures," and this development was held by him "to be irreversible. . . . For it is crucial that the idea of the organic structure is accepted in a cosmological sense. . . . For us, this is what building means, that there will be no more architecture. . . . On the terrain of organic structure one can only 'build.'"[46]

According to Häring's theory, which, with its concept of "achievement," subscribed to a similarly strict idea of "service," form was the result of the "intrinsic" dwelling within the object. Mies was in agreement with this point, which was referred to in Häring's terminology as "organic formalism" (*Organwerk*). A great part of Häring's theory may have been formulated under the influence of Mies, while, on the other hand, Mies may have obtained certain ideas from Häring. In 1923–1924 Mies allowed Häring to use a workroom in his atelier, and he carried on an active intellectual exchange with him. Despite their differing opinions on the relationship between form and function, both shared a belief in the intrinsic.

In a letter beginning "My dear Mies!" of January 22, 1925, Häring advised Mies not to accept the post of city building commissioner of Magdeburg as successor to Bruno Taut and encouraged Mies with the following sentences that emphasized their common goal: "I am of the opinion that we will soon obtain other offers. Unless you are motivated by economic considerations, it would, in my eyes, be a mistake to go to M. You know how important it is to be in Berlin in respect to what we want to accomplish. . . . I would miss you very much; our cooperation appears very valuable to me."[47] And in 1952 Häring recalled: "We marched from the very beginning in opposite directions, yet what we had in common played also a great role: this shared ground has not been lost, except that our ways retained their meaning; they lie in different endeavors."[48]

Both searched for the organic in building. Häring's *Organwollen* was remarkably receptive toward Mies's architecture. In the Barcelona Pavilion Häring saw cube and square reduced to their "true form grid," and this building appeared to him to possess an organic quality much "like the structure of plant growth."[49] Mies, however, who was in search of an "organic principle of order, that makes the parts meaningful and measurable while determining their relationship to the whole,"[50] confronted the organic form-giving of Häring with the same reserve he assumed toward all art trends of his time: an attitude that pronounced a yes and a no, nearness and distance, hope and doubt, occasionally simultaneously, suspecting everywhere a new formalism. In the following sentences, Mies accused both his colleagues Walter Gropius and Häring of formalism: "Gropius is, in his strict forms, almost as formal as Häring with his curves; with both, form is not always simply result. Gropius believes that he works constructively and Häring believes he is organic, but I believe both are to a large degree formalists; I see no difference between an animated and a severe form; Häring is, in respect to Gropius, a baroque nature, Gropius is, in respect to Häring, a classicist."[51] Yet this critique did not prevent Mies, in a 1924 lecture, from introducing Häring's design for the Garkau Estate next to Mies's own work as an illustration of "what we mean by elementary form-giving."[52]

Both Mies and Häring denied that form is the goal of form-giving. Form must, as it were, appear of itself, as the result of objective decisions, but it should not be brought about according to a specific theory of aesthetics.

With his three demands—"Form is not the goal but the result of our work. There is no form in and for itself; form as goal is formalism and that we reject. Form is conditioned by and intertwined with its task, yes, is its most elementary expression"—Mies saw himself, as he mentioned in a letter to Walter Jakstein of September 13, 1923, "in a position of outright contradiction to Weimar [meaning the Bauhaus] and all of what otherwise postures as modern."[53]

The problematic inherent in Mies's "categorical imperative" of form, which saw the How exclusively determined by the What, was pointed out by Jakstein in his reply to the manuscript sent to him by Mies: "Above all, the observation of these three demands seems a matter of conscience, for who could unequivocally determine whether he found the form as result of his work, or whether it was already aimed at? At least, it would require a very sharp eye. But which artist really knows how he set about his work and whether or not the Will to Form has not subconsciously influenced him?"[54]

2 Construction as Promise of Art: Building Art in the Raw

I want to learn more and more to see as beautiful what is necessary in things; then shall I be one of those who make things beautiful.

Friedrich Nietzsche, Die fröhliche Wissenschaft

We want to be free and not be exposed to the sad spectacle of those who throw themselves consistently into the spokes of the wheel of progress. But if we want to develop in the masses an awareness of the beauty of these new horizons, new lines, and new heights, it is necessary to awaken a delight in this natural beauty. . . . Whatever has to be done, let it be done joyfully; for freedom means to obey the necessary voluntarily and joyfully.

Josef August Lux, Ingenieur-Ästhetik, 1910

Naked construction is truth-compelling. Where it still stands without dress its skeleton shows, clearer and grander than the finished building, the bold construction in iron and reinforced concrete.

Erich Mendelsohn, Amerika. Bilderbuch eines Architekten, 1926

"Only skyscrapers under construction reveal the bold constructive thoughts, and then the impression of the high-reaching steel skeletons is overpowering."[1] So announced Mies when he first stepped in front of the public in the summer of 1922, in a sentence that already contained in a nutshell the typical aspects of his theory. This sentence indicates the starting point from which architectonic reality is to be perceived: it is not construction in its technical potential but the construction's appearance that is given an admiring glance. Mies's first and, one may conclude, primary interest is not so much ignited by the technical as by the aesthetic. It is his concern to redeem the aesthetic sensations triggered by construction's appearance and to translate them into architectonic reality.

In Mies's contemplation of the skyscraper, the aesthetic precedes the technical and not the other way around.[2] It is the aesthetic fascination with the "bold constructive thoughts" that anticipates the new possibilities dwelling in form and space. Mies does not approach construction from the point of its reality of purpose and function but from the intensity of experienced impression. This is why its condition "under construction" determined the final appearance of the building. The incomplete and not yet realized is seen aesthetically as the most satisfying state. The skeleton, with the severe grace of engineered construction clearly manifested, becomes the ideal. Lacking any rhetoric, it is bounded by the precision of an almost mathematical logic. Such virtues had already attracted defenders as early as 1900. In his well-known book *Moderne Baukunst* of 1908, for example, Karl Scheffler had succinctly described the ascendance of aesthetics over construction as propagated by the representatives of *Sachkunst* (object art), van de Velde, Obrist, and Muthesius.[3] That aestheticizing gaze at construction, favored by Mies in 1922, had already been explained by Scheffler: "Fantasy becomes productive; it influences the eye to ignore disturbing details, it completes the primitive, and it dreams the beauty still asleep in construction into art much as a flower before it breaks into bloom."[4]

Mies stood under the spell of a concept that the prewar architectural theorists called the miracle of new horizons, heights, and lines,[5] to which they, however, accorded only a secondary degree of beauty.[6] The tectonic experience conveyed by the "overpowering impression" of the "high-reaching" and the enthusiasm for the logic of the "bold constructive thought" endowed the naked construction frame with a quality that raised it to the level of an ideal architectural structure. In the raw structure of the steel skeleton, an intrinsic form seemed to manifest itself that implicitly forbade any masking or decoration.

With the raising of the walls, this impression is completely destroyed; the constructive thought, the necessary basis for artistic form-giving, is annihilated and frequently smothered by a meaningless and trivial jumble of forms. At very best one remains impressed by the sheer magnitude, and yet these buildings could have been more than just manifestations of our technical skill. This would mean, however, that one would have to give up the attempt to solve a new task with traditional forms; rather one should attempt to give form to the new task out of the nature of this task.[7]

Mies wanted to keep the skeleton free of all covering and confusing formal additions and treat it as a new type of experimental architecture with its own architectural form not harkening back to any other. Henry van de Velde had postulated such a functional form in 1901 and had demanded a total rejection of any and all ornament and pretense so typical of the epochs of the past. The purely functional form of technical equipment, of steamships and locomotives, was held up as prototype for modern form-giving. The character of their wayward beauty arose out of the congruence of form and function. The "honesty" of these objects was equivalent with their aesthetic quality. They could be perceived as beautiful due to their sobriety, for they were, in the eyes of van de Velde, exactly "what they should be."[8]

In the terms of this ethics of design, Mies's glass skyscrapers had freed themselves from the "straitjacket of historical style imitation," rejecting "any compromise with formal solutions borrowed from the building art." This demand had been raised by J. A. Lux in 1910 in his *Ingenieur-Ästhetik* in regard to the "hybrid" character of the American skyscrapers.[9] In his explanations Mies had raised naked construction to a norm that testified to the necessity of an "aesthetic of honesty" demanded by the frame construction. Rather than gloss over or hide the supposedly ugly appearance of construction, this aesthetic had to affirm construction and function.

860 and 880 Lake Shore Drive under construction, Chicago, 1948–1951.

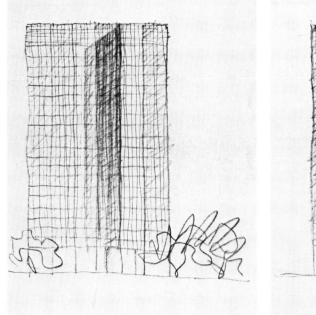

Pencil sketches for the Seagram Building project, Chicago, 1957.

Mies rejected as "nonsense" any attempt to salvage a higher aesthetic for the skeletal structures by means of artistic additions, much as Nietzsche had challenged historicists: "Off with your coats or be what you seem!"[10] Only an "increase of ideas rather than of material" would lead to the goal:

The purposes of our tasks are for the most part very simple and clear. One only has to recognize and formulate them, then they will lead of themselves to significant building solutions. Skyscrapers, office buildings, and commercial structures practically call forth clear, comprehensive solutions, and these can only be crippled because one repeatedly attempts to adapt these buildings to outdated attitudes and forms.[11]

The task that had to be solved was one of principle. The apodictic manner in which Mies staked out his position left little doubt as to that. The new construction image of a skeleton with its minimum of mass that touches the earth only by means of a few points of support called for a new definition of space and volume. The filigree pattern of free-span construction members that almost appear to surpass material limitations broke with the traditional view of inert, massive walls and rigid internal spaces that were the result of masonry construction. The building mass that had, under the old rules, been proportioned according to the rules of light and shade was now subject to different laws. The skeletal structure supported premises like those suggested by the contructivists Naum Gabo and Antoine Pevsner in their *Realist Manifesto* of 1920. This manifesto, which in certain passages dealing with the relationship of "time" and "life" reads almost like an anticipation of Mies's position, spoke the spatial language of the period. Volume has to be liberated from mass; the notion of mass as plastic and volume as painterly and plastic-spatial had to be overcome; only depth remained acceptable as spatial element.[12]

Even though Mies was collaborating with the circle of G people and substantially contributing to their magazine—which introduced itself in an ad in 1924 to the readers of the Dutch magazine *De Stijl* as "Het orgaan der Construcktivisten in Europa"[13]—he by no means wanted to be perceived as a constructivist. In Mies's notion of construction as an engineered, simple, right-angled support system indicative of anatomy, there was hardly room for the dynamic construction poems of the Russian constructivists. Indeed, Mies's categorical imperative of elementary form-giving that meant to "bring about a clear separation of attitudes" was particularly directed against the constructivists. That "ugly constructivist formalism" challenged Mies to clarify his position anew with all explicitness in the second number of *G*.[14]

Only a few weeks earlier Mies had expressed to Theo van Doesburg his concern that from the direction of the Weimar Bauhaus "a constructivist fashion might send a wavelike flood over Germany. I regret that very much because that would make the work of the real constructive artists much more difficult. One could see in Weimar how easy it is to juggle constructivist forms if one aims merely for the formal; there, form is goal, while in our work it is result. It appears important to me to demonstrate a clear separation between constructivist formalism and actual constructive work."[15] Doesburg, on a postcard from *De Stijl,* endorsed Mies's evaluation with a comment that brought Doesburg's tense relationship to the Bauhaus sharply into focus: "Dear Mies . . . I agree with you completely in regard to the Bauhaus. People turn *everything* into kitsch. Not one of the artists had the courage to attack. . . . These people have *done nothing* and will *always remain passive.* They only talk, but they do *nothing.* I am quite disheartened."[16]

The skeleton, standing for construction in general, filled the need of the new art of building and space. It brought the theoretical achievements of steel and concrete construction to their most common denominator and thus corresponded to the inner desires of the architects, who felt that the traditional architecture was finished. Le Corbusier had already invented such a system in 1914 with his Domino house, which consisted of two horizontal concrete slabs supported by set-back posts and connected by a staircase. This simplest of structures, meant for serial production, was the kernel around which one could evolve a new formal language. In the skeleton the dematerialization of a fixed body had progressed to its ultimate limits. This architectural extreme crystallized as a latticework of "mainly empty spaces" (Max Dessoir) that left only a pattern of pure lines and planes from which, along with mass, optical gravity seemed to be withdrawn.[17]

Thus the definition of space had to be thematized by means of the empty place, the opening rather than the wall. Instead of using brick fillers, Mies stretched gigantic, uninterrupted glass planes around his skyscrapers. He thereby abandoned the traditional principle of the wall enclosure into which openings were cut. The legibility of these planes remained confusingly ambiguous. They were simultaneously reflecting and transparent and changed, as Curt Gravenkamp still had it in 1930, "from a large window so to speak into a wall," or "into a wall that is only window. Actually, however, neither wall nor window, but something totally new that only now unlocks the ultimate potential of an age-old material."[18]

That the use of large glass planes permitting the construction skeleton to be externally visible brought with it its own problems became evident from Mies's subsequent experiments. The desired effect of transparency came about only under certain light conditions. The preserved model photos and representation drawings of his Glass House projects reveal the contradiction that resides behind the implied simplicity. ("The novel constructive principle of these buildings becomes clear if one employs glass in place of the now no longer supportive outer walls.") As Mies correctly noted, the use of glass called for "new approaches." Above all one had to decide between either achieving the desired light reflection or demonstrating the postulate of the construction principle, for the nature of the material did not allow both at the same time.[19]

Mies set the ideal image of the steel skeleton like a vision over a building art that was to be renovated from its foundation on up. In this very first and simplest of structures, all preconditions of his building philosophy were met. In his search for the intrinsic he had practically pulled from the building the skin that had traditionally constituted its garment. The experiments aimed at discovering expressive potentials in order to wed the new aesthetics with the construction. Viewing a skyscraper under construction as an aesthetic object came rather close to the philosophical confession of a dormant reality behind appearances. From this point of view the anatomy of the skeleton could be endowed with a "chaste beauty" (Scheffler) that it would be a sacrilege to cover by extraneous additions. Iron construction, written off by the nineteenth century as aesthetically hopeless even if absolutely necessary for practical reasons, was discovered by the twentieth century to possess a new "austere beauty" (J. A. Lux). While the generation of Semper perceived iron as inhospitable to the arts, critics like Scheffler around the turn of the century began to recognize the aesthetics of engineering implicit in iron construction. Scheffler went so far as to argue that iron contained the "traits of heroic monumentality."[20]

Forthrightly functional, the raw structure possessed a particular sort of beauty. Mies's skyscraper studies were based on this premise. Scheffler, already raising this issue in 1902 on occasion of the Berlin elevated street-car system then under construction, remarked this almost casually, basing himself on an observation that corresponded very nearly to that of Mies:

When the railroad was still under construction we experienced sensations here and there. . . . As long as the constructive intent was exclusively at work, the skeleton, still without its garment, showed the purpose and function of each part, and while the assembly began, as it were, at the intersection of problems of statics, the appearance, in its primitivity, had frequently the effect of an art promise. . . . In summary: one experiences these days the strongest architectonic impressions from half-finished projects. A raw structure without doors or windows, undressed, covered by the fine, dusty clay of the local bricks, with the unbroken tendency toward vertical thrust not yet hidden under plaster-of-paris ornaments, impresses one, in the monumental relationships between the large, undetailed massing, in all its somber primitivity, as beautiful—or at least as forceful.[21]

What Scheffler here pronounced paved the way for Mies's theory of the skin and bone structure, which derived a premonition of a coming architecture out of the matter-of-fact monumentality of the raw-structure method but which now demanded more than the mere rejection of historical dress and the prevention of irrelevancies. How this art promise of the raw structure could be redeemed was demonstrated by the bold skyscraper projects of Mies, the contours of which had already been schematically announced by Scheffler: did not Mies's projects show just that "unbroken tendency toward vertical thrust" of which Scheffler had spoken, and did they not gain, by the mere "energetic outline of their volume," a plastic explicitness of form, and finally were they not buildings "without windows" insofar as the windows had become walls? Under Mies's hands, the "austere primitivity" of construction-under-way was transposed into its positive counterimage: it gained crystalline elegance by constructive simplicity that made possible a "one hundred percent architecture of light,"[22] a vision that would, without an advanced technical culture, have been impossible.

The way to the new art was to be found in simplicity, in the primitive. The art promise of primitivity discussed by Scheffler was articulated by Adolf Behne in 1917 when he turned against any sort of pseudo-art and taste-mongering with the sentence "Understand the primitive in life, then art will arise on the horizon."[23] One could almost say the same of the belief in the intrinsic and in basic construction held by Mies. Raised to archetypal status and thus standing beyond any historical form, with its simple and typical traits arising only out of the meaningful and essential, tectonic composition found its contemporary expression in the steel skeleton.

Here the destruction of the object as appearance was completed right down to its ultimate intrinsicness, and an essentially simple structure remained as archetype, as fundamental as the molecular construction of the elements. As model of a primordial building plan, it could not derivatively be traced back to any historical form and the order of its compositional principles could, as a sort of genetic constant of all building, claim transhistorical validity. As Landsberg had it, its only prototype was in the eternal.

The simple lawfulness of elementary building, claimed by Mies in his theory of the skeleton and the skin and bones structure, was based on an archetypal principle of building that justified itself out of the conditions of purpose and material handling and was not dependent on any further theoretical explanation or legitimization. The anatomical anthropomorphism seemed seductively plausible: "A healthy building"—so Walter Gropius in a lecture in 1919—"requires a healthy bone structure, much as the human organism, and what the bone structure is for the human body, the technical-tectonic part of a building is in relationship to its appearance."[24] Against a background of biological analogies such as skin and bone structure, a literature that talked of the "technical achievements of the plants" could be conceived of as relevant.

"Primitive" building of ethnic cultures, arising out of climatic, biological, and geographical conditions, also offered possibilities for comparisons. For his already mentioned lecture at the Berlin Bund Deutscher Architekten of December 12, 1923, Mies had a slide collection composed exclusively of

Post and beam hut from Leo Frobenius, *Das unbekannte Afrika,* 1923.

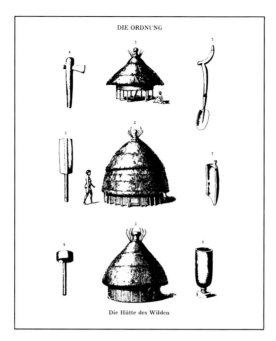

DIE ORDNUNG

Die Hütte des Wilden

"Tribal hut," reproduction from Le Corbusier, *Städtebau* (Stuttgart, 1926).

buildings from "outside the realm of the Greco-Roman culture," a selection he justified with: "I have done this on purpose, because to me an axe stroke in Hildesheim is *closer* than a chisel stroke in Athens." That this "closer" did not refer to a geographical but to an inner proximity was made clear in the subsequent slide lecture where the skin and bone structure was endowed with a family tree.

The examples drawn on by Mies were:
• an Indian tent: "This is the typical residence of a nomad. Light and transportable."
• a leaf hut: "Have you ever seen anything more perfect in terms of function and use of material? Is that not the best possible use of the jungle shadow?"
• an Eskimo house: "Now I take you into night and ice. Moss and seal skins have here become building materials. Walrus ribs form the roof structure."
• an Eskimo summer tent: "This fellow even has a summer villa. The building material is skin and bones."

A northern German farm house, a frame structure, was shown at the end of the sequence: "All the pictures I have shown correspond in every way to the needs of the inhabitants. This is all we ask for ourselves. Only the means that are of our time."

Only at the end of the lecture did Mies arch over to the present time, expressing his regret that there are no comparative buildings "equally responsive to the needs of modern man." In his final slide Mies showed a structure "of modern sensibility and [filling] those conditions that I also long for and strive for in our houses." The steamship *Imperator,* built in Kiel in 1912, was held up as an example: "A floating apartment building, created according to the needs and means of our time. . . . We would be enviable if we had buildings on dry land that would suit our needs equally well. Only when we experience the needs and means of our epoch so elementarily will we obtain a new building attitude."[25]

The primitive hut and the ocean liner were held out by Mies as models for purposeful form-giving. Both stood for that artless work built on an objective basis in which the plain primitivity of the past and the "sophisticatedly primitive grandeur of certain engineering projects" (Scheffler) of the machine age meet on an equal basis. Both searched for a fusion of purpose, construction, and form. In this endeavor, the uncivilized native and the modern engineer could shake hands across the centuries.

Adolf Loos, in his essay *Architektur* of 1908, had held a very similar concept of Western building art. Loos saw in the absence of decoration and in the freedom from ornament a symbol of unspoiled states of mind that he atttributed to peasants and engineers, for they built from within the security of their instinct in harmony with the universe without devoting thoughts to architecture. Somewhat later this picture of the engineer as a noble savage was undermined by the futurists. Yet the coming generation that had aspired to build like engineers, in a manner suitable to the machine age, still stood under the influence of this image.[26]

Le Corbusier's "machine for living" made this thesis into a spectacular concept. In his *Vers une architecture* of 1922, which met with great interest in the circle of the *G* people,[27] Le Corbusier attributed to the engineers that new contemporary "spirit of construction and synthesis." The engineers belonged in his eyes to the "most active creators of contemporary aesthetics" just because they believed themselves "far removed from any aesthetic activity"; furthermore, they were "in accord with the principles that Bramante and Raphael had applied a long time ago."[28] Even though the foreign language obstructed access to Le Corbusier's thought, the illustrations alone may have sufficed to convey to Mies Le Corbusier's hidden message. In this manifesto the entire arsenal of technical objects held by the machine enthusiasts of the prewar years as exemplary for the new object art was introduced: silos, factories, and cranes, motors and automobiles, airplanes and ocean liners—but also the "primitive temple" in form of a tent.[29] Le Corbusier held these strangely beautiful objects up for those "eyes that do not see" and put them more or less directly on equal footing with the significant structures of European history, the Parthenon and Pantheon, the Colosseum and the triumphal arch, the cathedral and the Campidoglio. The provocative comparison of the Parthenon with a sports car that viewed both as state-of-the-art precision products suggested a parallel between a modern engineering achievement and the building art of antiq-

M.S. *Imperator* under construction, installation of deck.

M.S. *Imperator*, 1912.

DES YEUX QUI NE VOIENT PAS...

I

LES PAQUEBOTS

PAESTUM, de 600 à 550 av. J.-C.

Le Parthénon est un produit de sélection appliquée à un standart établi. Depuis un siècle déjà, le temple grec était organisé dans tous ses éléments.

Lorsqu'un standart est établi, le jeu de la concurrence immédiate et violente s'exerce. C'est le match; pour gagner, il faut

Cliché Albert Morancé.   PARTHÉNON, de 447 à 434 av. J.-C.

faire mieux que l'adversaire *dans toutes les parties*, dans la ligne d'ensemble et dans tous les détails. C'est alors l'étude poussée des parties. Progrès.

Le standart est une nécessité d'ordre apporté dans le travail humain.

Le standart s'établit sur des bases certaines, non pas arbi-

Cliché de *La Vie Automobile.*   HUMBERT, 1907.

DELAGE, Grand-Sport 1921.

Pages from Le Corbusier's *Vers une architecture* (Paris, 1923).

"Antediluvian behemoth ready to jump": loading cranes from Werner Lindner, *Die Ingenieur-bauten* (Berlin, 1923).

uity. All veneration for the engineer aside, though, the artist's primacy remained uncontested. Poesy, and thus art, spoke the final word in the machine for living.[30]

Mies was yet far removed in 1923 from such a double position in which, beside the objective demands of the form-giving subject, the artist was seen as exercising a decisive function. The will to the absolute rebelled against having a subject as originator of a contemporary building art. Mies was on the march with those "simple, uncompromising ones," as Carl Einstein called them, "to a nearby, necessary task."[31] Mies dismissed the epoch of the bourgeois individual unsentimentally and pitilessly with the flourish: "The individual becomes less and less important; his fate no longer interests us." This sentence from "Baukunst und Zeitwille!"—written in 1924, but still echoing the activist tenor of 1919—affirmed one more time that the rules of the new architecture arose out of a collective spirit and were thus committed to a social goal. One had to overcome modern man's isolation and dislocation, as it stood at odds with the "objective character" of the times. It alone determined the "critical achievements in all areas," and the man of the new time had to adjust to it.[32]

For the architect this meant that he had to orient himself toward those building types in which that "great anonymous trait of our time" became manifest. The engineering buildings arose with "great natural ease without their builders becoming known"; they were "typical examples" of the "will of the epoch" and also pointed the way to the "technical means we will have to employ in the future." The optimism implied by this surrender to the will of the epoch that was expected to bring about the good by an autonomous process can be heard in Mies's conviction: the "demands of the time for realism and functionality" had only to be fulfilled consistently enough and without any regard for the traditional emotive contents, and then the utilitarian structures would develop of themselves, as "representatives of the will of the epoch" as it were, "into a type of building art" symbolic of its time. This autonomy of progress that demanded a conditionless surrender to the requirements of the present time corresponded to Mies's definition of the building art, which in the final analysis "is always the spatially apprehended will of the epoch, nothing else."

Everything depended on a clear understanding of this "simple truth." "One will have to understand that all building art arises out of its own epoch and can only manifest itself in addressing vital tasks with the means of its own time," stressed Mies with the self-assuredness of one who believes himself in intimate contact with the objective truth of the will of the epoch. Any deviation from this attitude that obscures this simple fact or loses sight of it is just as superfluous as the trivial decorations on the construction skeleton. The spirit of the epoch requires that glassy clarity and steely uncompromising attitude demonstrated by the skyscraper projects. The new matter-of-fact attitude appeals to "reason and reality" and opposes any romanticism that stands in the way of the unpathetic striving of the time "toward the secular."

Mies viewed the buildings of the past with the same sobriety. If one could relinquish that attitude of "romanticism" one could discover in the cathedral, in the "masonry structures of antiquity," and in the "brick and concrete constructions of the Romans" those "incredibly bold engineering feats" that stand witness to the will of the epoch. This will to construction perceived the Greek temple, as Ludwig Hilberseimer had it somewhat later in the third issue of *G* of July 1924, as "a perfect product of engineering in stone."[33] Le Corbusier by contrast had caused history to affirm his plastic will to form. Over and above construction, cathedrals and temples speak of a search for the Dionysian "drama, . . . a sensation of sentimental nature," as the decisive criterion of the building art. To assemble the stones for the Parthenon that had previously lain "inert in the quarries of Pentelicus, unshaped," one had to be, in Le Corbusier's eyes, "not an engineer, but a great sculptor."[34]

Construction—"that loyal safekeeper of an epoch's spirit," as Mies was later lovingly to describe it—represents that quality that reaches, as an eternal constant of building, beyond the epoch. As the "objective basis" for any development of building forms, it not only determines form but, as Mies had it, was "form itself."[35] The itinerary that was to lead to that "forming" principle had already been indicated by the representatives of the functional building method of 1910, when they demanded of building artists the courage to "become engineers again."[36] The engineer was honored as the actual architect of the modern period.[37] Thus building, and ultimately also the history of building, were seen through his X-ray eyes that penetrate to the elementary construction or the bones, as it were. For Mies, building as "work process" was basically a mythic act, "linked to a simple deed, but this deed has to hit the nail right on the head." Of course, this could only occur if the architect subordinated himself to the "great objective demands of the epoch," assisting them to assume spatial form.[38]

Mies's logic of the building art rested on this foundation. It inspired him to the bold abstractions that emerged in both his project drawings and his statements. Viewing building in this light, the connection between a primitive hut and an ocean liner could easily be drawn. Mies found a justification for his beliefs in the widely disseminated book *Die Ingenieurbauten in ihrer guten Gestaltung* (Buildings by Engineers in Their Good Form) published by Werner Lindner in the spring of 1923. The reasonings of this study are clearly noticeable in Mies's lecture of December 12, 1923. Shortly before, Werner Gräff had reviewed this book in *G* no. 2 of September 1923—in the same issue that carried the "Building" manifesto on its title page—complete with illustrations and quotes that were interchangeable with Mies's prose in the "Building" manifesto. The dictum "form is not the goal but the result of our work" that adorned the title page of this issue of *G* was echoed on the

Abb. 2. Feste Karsferia

Abb. 3. Wasserwerk Breslau

34

35

Pages from Werner Lindner, *Die Ingenieurbauten.*

last page where the message of Lindner's publication was summarized: "Form shall never be goal, but it is the *by-product,* so to speak, of a work executed according to function and above all the constructive potential of the available materials."[39] Gräff had already prophesied in the first number of *G* that "the new type of engineer will arrive"—the prototype of the modern, creative man with the unqualified characteristic "to think and form elementarily . . . , to make manifest, radically and uncontestably, the elements of each respective formal realm."[40]

Lindner's publication, brought out by the Deutscher Bund Heimatschutz (German Association for the Preservation of the Homeland) and the Deutsche Werkbund, was by no means motivated by an avant-garde intent; nevertheless, it inadvertently broke a lance for elementary form-giving. Arguments and proofs were furnished that lent support to the demands raised by Mies and Gräff in *G.* The terse, concentrated text, well supported by its morphologically progressive series of illustrations, explored the basics of "good form-giving." The quintessence of the study affirmed that not only engineering structures but ultimately "all building activity" is subject to immutable laws. "You can only build if you know how to construct" was, according to Lindner, the first law of building, and only on the basis of this premise could one even talk of a building art. Its task consisted in arriving at an aesthetic evaluation of the new construction and imbuing it "with a soul."[41]

The "ground rule for all good form-giving" that is "valid for all times and in all situations" calls for "a thorough assessment of the factual requirements . . . a clear differentiation between the essential and superfluous, and, built

Raw sulfur silo in Marseille from Werner Lindner, *Die Ingenieurbauten,* drawn upon by Mies for his "Baukunst und Zeitwille!"

on this, a skill, both practical and artistic."[42] Mies consistently represented this methodical progression of form-giving: first in his statements of principle, then in his concept of building, and later in the structuring of his teaching programs at the Bauhaus and the Armour Institute of Technology in Chicago.[43]

For Lindner, buildings by engineers made no "romantic concessions,"[44] a belief totally endorsed by Mies in his article "Baukunst und Zeitwille!" Lindner's publication devoted a special chapter to "Churches as Buildings by Engineers," perhaps encouraging Mies to categorize all buildings of the past under this heading.[45] The circumstance that Mies suggested for his "Baukunst und Zeitwille!," which was to appear in *Der Querschnitt* in the spring of 1924, "three meaningful illustrations" from Lindner's work—since "the spirit of our time" is revealed "almost exclusively by engineer-made buildings"[46]—proves once again how much stimulation Mies owed to this work. Moreover, Mies's raw-structure aesthetic also found affirmation here, for Lindner praised the raw-structure-like "skeletal condition of the completed iron assembly" as "exquisite" and only regretted that its convincing self-assurance crumbles into "the petty and unharmonic" after completion, as regards both detail and the total aspect: "the simpler and clearer the entire and all its details are formed, and the more obviously logic and function are expressed, the greater will be the effect." The ultimate proof for the "lasting effect of such plain forthright beauty" could be found in "well-formed old buildings."[47]

For Lindner, the key term to label the timelessly valid method of elementary form-giving was "organically developed construction." It corresponded to a "living building organism" that showed a "clear, organic, and harmonic organization with respect to both the inside spatial organization and the volume formation on the outside."[48] For Mies the "spirit of the new building art" existed in the "organic building method" that created "its formal values out of its function" and thereby—as there was no "new" or "old" functionality—obeyed the universal law of elementary form-giving.[49] The new art, trying to tie in with a primal order, wanted, according to its leading spokesman Piet Mondrian, to reconstruct all being "out of the universal, the profoundest essence of all being." The basic "principle of all form-giving of the future" could not nor needed to be invented; being universal it "is already present"; residing as a perpetual energy at "the core of all things," it need only be expressed by a contemporary consciousness.[50] This explains Mies's concept of a universal principle of building as something that "always has been" and "always should be," namely a process that corresponds directly to the task at hand and that is realized by the means of each respective period.

This secret of good form-giving, as Lindner attested, was employed by both the ancient and the modern engineer: without "chasing after effects" and without "contraband symbolism . . . unconcerned with guesswork and art mongering . . . factual and with natural responses." Works that arise out of such "organically developed construction" are understandable "at first glance as purposeful." They need neither "rhetorical enhancement nor explanatory comment," for in them the archetype becomes manifest and "wondrous, old prototypes of human resourcefulness and handiwork" are revived.[51] Such engineered, functional structures represent a phase one could describe in Nietzschean terms as an "innocence of becoming" or, as Erich Mendelsohn expressed it in poetic terms in his 1925 *Bilderbuch eines Architekten* (Picture Book of an Architect), as "childhood forms." Mendelsohn illustrated this metaphor with the picture of an American grain silo, representing so to speak its architectonic psychogram. These forms fascinated because they were "awkward, of primordial forcefulness, submissive to a dire need. Primitive in their purpose . . . startled by an overwhelming necessity, the preliminary phase as it were of a future world here still in its organizing state."[52]

These novel and startling engineering structures, not really comparable to any others, pointed to a lawfulness equivalent to the highest form of existence where "primitive force" and "protoforms of things to come" seemed to coincide. They could only be described in terms of a comparison to analogous archetypes: modern loading cranes appeared to Lindner as "gigantic monsters poised for attack" or "prehistoric behemoths." It is this affinity between mechanical and organic forms that helped to bring out the potential beauty of the purely mechanical. The obvious similarity of airplanes and submarines to dragonflies and fish was, according to Walter Riezler's 1926 essay "Die Baukunst am Scheidewege" (Building Art at the Crossroads), "instant proof" of the astounding and meaningful similarity between mechanical and organic forms, opening vistas to an encompassing, universal "uniformity of the world."[53]

It was on the image of such a primitive but authentic archetype that Mies based his 1923 lecture in which he drew an analogy between the primitive hut and modern engineering, between leaf hut and ocean liner. The primitive and the technological were summoned to the witness stand to testify for the new form-giving that did not want to imitate reality but recreate it according to a "primal order." In view of this shift from imitation to conception, the emphasis on the ethnological and technical was equivalent to an act of cognition. The primitive became the touchstone for modern art. Tribal art challenges forth the self-same question as engineering structures, namely to what extent they can even be regarded as art, insofar as classical art theory failed to account for either. In painting, Gauguin and Picasso had already found exemplary prototypes before 1914 that could be assimilated. Mies now attempted to introduce a similar process in architecture by falling back on the primitive "buildings" of Indians and jungle inhabitants. "Disgust with one's own art" led to this turn toward the primitive, according to Victor Wallerstein in *Das Kunstblatt* of 1917,[54] a judgment that also spoke out of Mies's words when he provocatively turned his back on that "total lunacy in stone" to divert attention from these "aesthetic junk heaps" toward elementary, primitive building.

What negro sculpture—newly called to attention by Carl Einstein, a one-time pupil of Alois Riehl and Heinrich Wölfflin, in his book *Afrikanische Plastik* of 1912[55]—was to art could be compared to what the simple native hut signified for Mies. For demonstration purposes, Mies supplied himself with the richly illustrated publication *Das unbekannte Afrika* (The Unknown Africa) by Leo Frobenius, which had appeared in 1923 and was laid out for a long time in Mies's office alongside Karl Friedrich Schinkel's volume of designs for Orianda.[56]

The immediacy of the primordial guarantees the authenticity of a vital building art. Mies's model of the skin and bone structure, a term in which one can hear Semper's garment theory reverberate—it also leaned on the art expressions of natives—only needed the approbation of suitable materials and purposes; "walrus ribs and skin" had to be exchanged for steel and glass. Mass, reduced to the minimal structure of post and beam (*Raumfachwerk*) constructed of steel "trunks" of industrial origin, embodied a technical variation of that magnified jungle shadow, wrested not from "natural" nature but from the "technical" nature of the industrial age. Technical ersatz nature replaced mimesis of nature.[57] With the help of girders, the "main nerve of iron architecture" (J. A. Lux), Mies copied the Laugerian native hut for the twentieth century; it lives on in the "fleshless ribs" (J. A. Lux) of the steel skeleton and its unadorned supports, which now come into the purview of art. The task facing the modern building artist was the conquest of the elementary iron language, the grammar of which, composed of angle irons, T-beams, or other girders, was determined by mathematical laws.

The poeticizing of the steel structure, rather than its constructive-technological potential, was largely to determine the building routines of the twentieth century. Even though Mies's initial statements had been in harsh contradiction to this approach, he worked it ceaselessly, from his first skyscraper project in the twenties up to his last commission, the New National Gallery in Berlin. His buildings are not really technical objects like those of the engineer, but ideals of the building art where—and that is by no means unproblematical—the demonstration of an idea came before the realization of the practical task. Mies delivered ideal "constructions" in the sense of aesthetic metaphors, in which the technical was sublimated to the artistic with eloquent precision.[58] William H. Jordy, in his essay "The Laconic Splendor of the Metal Frame," gave a penetrating summary of Mies's intention.[59] Much as Nietzsche's theory of aesthetics demanded, Mies treated "a familiar, perhaps commonplace theme"—the "everyday melody" of the steel skeleton—by circumscribing it inventively, elevating it and heightening it to a symbolic level in order to disclose in the original theme "a whole world of profundity, power and beauty."[60]

The Vitruvian primal hut according to Marc-Antoine Laugier, *Essai sur l'architecture* (2d ed., Paris, 1755).

Mies on the building site of the Farnsworth House. "Perhaps one accuses me of having reduced architecture to practically nothing. It is true that I have eliminated from architecture much that is superfluous, that I liberated it from a lot of trivia with which it was habitually decorated, that I have left only its function and simplicity. . . . A building with freestanding supports that carry the girders has no need of doors and windows—but on the other hand it is uninhabitable if it is open on all sides." Marc-Antoine Laugier, *Essai sur l'architecture.*

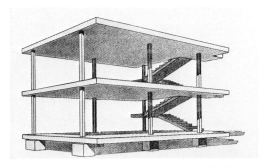

Le Corbusier, Domino construction system, 1914.

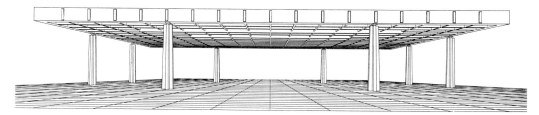

Mies, construction system for the Bacardi Office Building, Santiago, Cuba, project of 1957.

The preconditions for an artistic assimilation of a new type of construction by a new type of *Gestaltung* has been shown with great clarity by Herman Sörgel in his *Theorie der Baukunst* (Theory of the Building Art) of 1918. The iron structure demands a "new aesthetic attitude" and "its own corresponding aesthetic that must carefully take its characteristics into consideration and must not be prejudiced. . . . Those who deny the rationality factor in their critique of building aesthetics will never arrive at an appreciation of iron structure, for its beauty arises out of the internal static stresses of the post system. This post system [*Stabsystem*] must be aesthetically so composed that it appeals to reason, soul, and eye, thus making it gratifying: that is the artistic task."[61]

According to Sörgel, this could only be brought about if the architect was interested not only in construction, the "supports and internal bone structure of the material," but also "in the aesthetic fit" that lays bare the muscles and tendons of the building's organism. The aesthetic-anatomical outlook on construction, peculiar to Mies, demanded correspondingly changed sensibilities of perception and a reevaluation of sensibilities. Already in what Sörgel called the *Werkform* (the form of work in progress), the aesthetic qualities had to be discovered. This being "under construction," the fascination of which inspired the Miesian experiments of 1922, appeared to Sörgel as a process of appropriation that stimulated peculiar creative potential: "The construction appearance stimulates the fantasy toward new contents of mood and form. The struggle with the technical during the building process often yields unexpected aesthetic results."[62]

This sort of raw-structure aesthetic that—practically in reversal of the *Ruinenromantik*—aims at its own type of aesthetic experience, derived not from what had been but from what is in the process of becoming, from the unfinished and practically unreal, has to be accompanied by a reevaluation of aesthetic perception. "The new eye" (J. A. Lux) upsets the traditional; instead of noticing a devastation, it "perceives the rise of a new type of beauty" and registers "technical construction, art history to the contrary, as artistic, or at least aesthetic."[63]

Naked construction compels truth: "We can no longer view that as beautiful that is not also truthful!"[64] The abstract beauty of the construction appearance calls for someone who can stand up to this sort of beauty and who is not shocked but delighted by that shudder that overcomes him when looking at the bold measurements, the large-spanned voids of space, the terrifying thinness of the skeleton. This "new person" has to "carry within himself a sense for the proportion of the inner powers residing in an iron grid in order to absorb its full beauty."[65]

The modern industrial age calls for a man who, much like the steel frame itself, is "right-angled in body and soul"—an expression of Nietzsche's employed by Ludwig Hilberseimer when he characterized the Office Building of Mies.[66] This energetic, right-angled frame of mind has been written into the face of the heroic man of the Bauhaus age with Oskar Schlemmer's profile constructed out of angle pieces.[67] And, in a photographic portrait of the same time (p. 238), Mies presents himself in much the same way.

Oskar Schlemmer, emblem for the Bauhaus, 1923.

3 The Building Master of Today

We are! We will!

And we create!

Oskar Schlemmer, Manifesto to the first Bauhaus Exhibition, 1923

But we want to become those that we are, the new ones, the unique ones, the incomparable ones, those who create their own laws, those who create themselves!

Friedrich Nietzsche, Also sprach Zarathustra

Since 1914 many have acquired a brand-new intellectual outfit. Many begin, for the first time in their life, to think.

Henry Ford, My Life and Work, 1922

"Never have the building trades been more talked about than today, and never has one been further removed from understanding the nature of building. For this reason the question as to the nature of the building art is today of decisive importance. For only when it has been clearly understood can the struggle for the principles of a new building art be conducted purposefully and effectively. Until then it will remain a chaos of confusing forces."[1] This diagnosis of the architectural efforts of the time, made by Mies in the summer of 1924, gives a poor rating to the efforts of the modern movement. The restlessness of a period in search of itself with its diverse and often competing art movements and isms he summarily interpreted as a "chaos of confusing forces" that would remain sterile as long as there was no clear understanding of the "nature of building."[2]

The turbulent debates around the Bauhaus reflected the ferment in which the European avant-garde was caught up in the early twenties. The Dutchman van Doesburg chastised the expressionistically oriented arts and crafts trend of the early Bauhaus with furious polemics, culminating in a provocatively meant summons of a Congress of Constructivists and Dadaists to Weimar in September 1922. The final break between Itten and Gropius occurred in 1923. The appointment of the constructivist László Moholy-Nagy to the Bauhaus, which triggered Mies's already mentioned panicky fear of a wave of constructivist fashion, brought with it a reformulation of the Bauhaus idea under the motto "Art and Technique," which introduced a new—the actual—era of the Bauhaus. Three exhibitions in 1923, in which he participated with his Berlin works, drastically proved to Mies the extent of the pluralism of the new architectural movements: the Berlin Art Exhibition, in which El Lissitzky showed his Proun Room, the De Stijl Exhibition in Paris, and the International Architecture Exhibition in Weimar, in which Le Corbusier with his Cité Contemporaine was also represented.

From within this spectrum of concepts Mies conducted, with the imperturbable steadfastness of a religious founder, his battle for the foundation of the new building art, directed against all praxis-alienated building theory and against ivory-tower aesthetics in all its forms. The concept of functionalism, raised by Mies to a norm, was based on a philosophy that revolved around the idea of the intrinsic, or, as Mies circumscribed it, "the nature of the task," for without a grasp of these "first" relationships it was impossible to work in an authentic manner. This was the point where Mies's work thesis as touchstone of his ideology could be proven, for "probing for the immanent" (*Wesensforschung*), as Gropius called it, typified the new form-giving attitude (*Gestaltungsgeist*) that penetrated "to the bottom of things."[3] Intellectual matters too concerning the architecture of the epoch were primarily a sort of raw-structure rendering of the architect's frame of mind.

In this general trend, Mies's opinions differed much less from those of other artists of his time than he himself appeared to have thought. Neoplastic, constructivist, and functionalist concepts all based their discourse on a Platonic platform insofar as they believed in the idea of universal truth and strict objectivity. On the basis of such a history of ideas, something like a "Creative International," as suggested at the 1922 constructivist congress at Weimar, was quite conceivable.[4]

Mies entered into this general debate with propositions that revealed a pronounced preference for principles. The texts of the first manifestos and the accompanying drawings formed a propagandistic unit that could not fail to be effective. To the large-format original drawings—the perspectives for the Friedrichstrasse Skyscraper and for the Concrete Office Building measure over two meters!—corresponded a polemical expressiveness that, by means of a deliberate rejection of the traditional rhetoric, created the impression of aloofness. Text and drawings demonstrated forcefulness and brilliance; the omission of detail in word and image augmented their suggestiveness. The generalizing character of Mies's texts elevated the statements into an ideal sphere that sidestepped social problems and fused the realistic and the fantastic very effectively. With his "book drama"—for as such was his glass skyscraper still being viewed in 1928 by a critic[5]—Mies conveyed a precisely calculated image.[6]

With his programmatical propositions, Mies aimed no doubt at a direct effect. This is already attested to by the circumstance that he brought out his manifesto "Baukunst und Zeitwille!" in a periodical that counted among the most important organs of the new art—*Querschnitt,* published by Hermann von Wedderkop. The apparently purposefully inserted, reviewlike pointer to Mies's essay in the periodical *Der Neubau,* published by Walter Curt Behrendt, can also be considered part of this strategy.[7]

As is evident from the correspondence of those years, Mies privately criticized other modernists, but he restrained himself from taking public positions or leveling direct critiques. His manifestos, rendered in the tenor of a radical fundamentalism, only held forth on general principles and then proceeded, without any transition, to introduce his own projects. His lecture of December 1923 that reached from tribal art to the machine was based on this principle: in order to convey the existence of a vacuum of values after 1918 he totally blocked out the world that lay between the primitive hut and the ocean liner. Neither the achievements in the building art up to then nor anything of the past was worthy of consideration.

The intellectual problems occupying Mies turned around the question whether form is a direct outcome of purpose and construction, or—and he was to expand his position after 1927 by an existentially enlarged dimension—whether form is "derived from life or for its own sake."[8] Those memorable sentences in which Mies created epigrams for himself in the early twenties were not lacking in "Baukunst und Zeitwille!" In the manuscript of February 7, 1924, Mies noted down: "We do not solve formal problems but building problems, and form is not the goal but the result of our work. This is the essence of our striving."[9] This declaration separating entire worlds was the litmus test of his building ideology. It was held up to indicate the demarcation between real modern building and the old architecture.

Mies's notorious, almost pedantic insistence on this principle was justified from another side. In the first chapter of his text *Neues Wohnen—Neues Bauen* (1927), Adolf Behne, one of the most perceptive critics of modern architecture, put his finger on the sore point when he held, in agreement with Mies, that opinions divide into "two different directions or attitudes. . . . Form is not the first, but the last consideration in a healthy architectonic work process. . . . By thinking clearly, one has to *arrive* at good form, thus one cannot begin with form." While other publications of 1927 already announced the "triumph of the new building style," Behne's survey affirmed Mies's evaluation of 1924: "Let us be quite open: in surveying the achievements up to now, we cannot find a particularly bountiful harvest. But then, what is asked of the building masters is nothing less than a Copernican revolution."[10]

The architect, and next to him modern man who had chosen intellectual freedom, stood in front of this "Copernican revolution" that challenged forth independent thinking and an independent building art. The choice of a center of orientation from which form and idea emanate made the building art—as defined by Mies for the first time in 1926—a matter of "spiritual decisions."[11] The elementary concept of the immanence of form, so Mies continued his thought processes in the manuscript of "Baukunst und Zeitwille!," "still separates us from many. Even from most of the modern building masters. But it unites us with all the disciplines of modern life."

How the disciplines of modern life were recognizable has been made clear by Mies in the preceding essays: they were determined by the "objective character" of the "outstanding achievements" that gave structure to the epoch. The objective was indicated by the empirical reality and thus acceptable as preordained fact. "Not the yesterday, not the tomorrow, only the today is formable" was Mies's work thesis in 1923, which, with its unconditional realism, carried the metaphysical will of the epoch along as an invisible kernel. Nor did one's own existence need any justification from either the past or the future: "Today is the deed. We will acount for it tomorrow." And this was the maxim under which the constructivists wanted to conquer the present. "We leave the past behind like a corpse. We leave the future to the soothsayers. We grasp the today."[12]

"Real thinking" cannot be left to historians or prophets. Louis Henry Sullivan had already presented a similar argument in 1901: "You cannot think *in* the past, you can only think *of* the past. You cannot think *in* the future, you can only think *of* the future. But *reality* is of, in, by and for the present, and the present only. Bear this strictly in mind, it is highly important, it must lie at the root of your new education."[13]

The Miesian order of thinking followed this maxim, wanting to reconcile the essential and the existential, the eternal being and the present in a "truth relationship." This was the constant theme of Mies's modernism over the decades. With the question "Where do we go now?" that summarized the problematic of identity as it appeared to him, Mies confronted an epoch that was in danger of losing the immanent and thus itself.

The building of civilization is not simple, since the past, the present, and the future have a share in it. It is difficult to define and difficult to understand. What belongs to the past cannot be changed any more. The present must be affirmed and mastered. But the future stands open—open for the creative thought and the creative deed. It is against this background that architecture arises. Consequently, architecture should only stand in contact with the most significant elements of civilization. Only a relationship that touches on the innermost nature of the epoch is authentic. I call this relationship a truth relationship. Truth in the sense of Thomas Aquinas: as adaequatio intellectus et rei, as congruence of thought and thing.[14]

The authenticity of existence was the great problem toward the solution of which both art and philosophy worked. The synthesis of "Baukunst und Zeitwille!" required a conditionless acceptance of the present and a rebellious attitude toward the authority of history. That the structure of the present was "principally different from earlier epochs" was made evident by the new "work methods" that wrested the preconditions for making a living from the building trades. Mies believed that those who still recommend handicraft methods in the twentieth century in the assumption that they possess an innate ethical value have "no inkling of the interrelationships of the new time. Even handicrafts are only a work method and a form of economics, nothing more. . . . But it is never the work method but the work itself that has value."[15]

It would be difficult to conceive of someone more qualified than Mies to put a final end to the debate about the value of handicrafts that was still being conducted at the Bauhaus, for he was born into "an old family of stone-masons" and was familiar with the handicrafts "not only as an aesthetic onlooker," as he did not fail to emphasize.

My receptiveness to the beauty of handwork does not prevent me from recognizing that handicrafts as a form of economic production are lost. The few real craftsmen still alive in Germany are rarities whose work can be acquired only by very rich people. What really matters is something totally different. Our needs have assumed such proportions that they can no longer be met with the methods of craftsmanship. This spells the end of the crafts. . . . Whoever has the courage to maintain that we can still exist without industry must bring the proof for that. The need for even a single machine abolishes handicrafts as an economic form.

Theories that wanted to renovate art by means of handicrafts, as expounded by the expressionists and early Bauhaus members, were not proposed by practitioners but "by aesthetes under the beam of an electric lamp" and were presented on "paper that has been produced by machines, . . . bound by machines" for their "propaganda mission." According to Mies one should have "devoted only one percent greater care to improving the bad binding of the book and one would have done a greater service to humanity."

Historians—"people who lack a feeling for the essential and whose profession it is to concern themselves with antiquities"—always attempt to "set up the results of old epochs as examples for our time." Mies particularly hated the academic-historical faculty that sees the world through the "scholarly glasses of archaeology" (J. A. Lux); it provoked him to blunt polemics, that—like the following—were later eliminated from the manuscript. "And here again it is the historians that recommend an outdated form, always the same mistake. Here, too, they mistake form for essence." The representatives of an art theory alienated from living praxis, and the academic specialists in particular, were a thorn in Mies's side. The liberation of building from "aesthetic speculation and specialization" was part and parcel of his attack against the class of educated philistines who stood, like "the art lovers and the intellectuals . . . too remote from real life to draw meaningful conclusions."[16] Mies blamed the historians with obstructing insight into essential things because they confuse effect with cause. The art historian has given birth to the "academic belief" (Nietzsche) that "buildings exist for the sake of architecture," as Mies noted in his manuscript of 1924. Amazingly, there was a "total lack of historical understanding connected with this love for historical things," which has led to a complete misunderstanding of the "real interdependence of things, both what concerns the new and what concerns the old."[17]

"That eternal preoccupation with the past is our undoing." With this sentence Mies suggested in 1924 a rethinking of history, which, much as art, should be recommitted to the present: "Life confronts us daily with new challenges; they are more important than the entire historical rubbish." The present time needs—so Mies circumscribed the avant-garde with a sentence that could have fallen from the lips of Zarathustra—a "full-blooded generation," full of "power and grandeur":[18] "creative people who look forward, who are unafraid to solve each task without prejudice and from the bottom on up, and who do not dwell excessively on the results. The result is simply a by-product."[19]

This vitalistic self-assurance perceived history as nothing but the result of living, rather than the opposite. The consequence of such a reasoning would be: "In regard to art, a clear understanding of tradition means rebellion, not subordination."[20] In the last issue of *G* in 1926, the new understanding of history as a reaction to the failure of the historically cultivated intellectuals to cope with the world was poured into the formula: "*History is what happens today.* And only based on such a profound and affirmative understanding of today can the past again take on meaning."[21] Only what stands up to the probing gaze of today deserves to be called permanent. History has to go with the times. History writing either practices "living history"—"history of the motivating forces of an epoch"—or it remains, like the traditional history here under fire, an "epitaph on a funeral stone" and therefore "is to the artist 'of no concern' (or at best whether he is 'in it' or not). . . . Art history that is uncommitted warms us up only with central heating."

The hatred of academicism, inherited from Nietzsche, who derisively called it "the German education," was part and parcel of Mies's polemic against "our historical schooling." "We need no examples," wrote Mies in his manuscript of "Baukunst und Zeitwille!" only a few paragraphs after he had written about the exemplary engineer-made buildings. These buildings were held out as exemplary precisely because they were perceived as having no immediately preceding historical prototype.[22]

The engineer-made building embodies the new ideal without prototype and the eternally new under the banner of which the change of all values in favor of "life" must be undertaken. The "no" to tradition resulted from a "yes" to life, as that followed the eternal laws of the historical process and not the life-remote "school theory" (Mies). It is part of the nature of the historical process, in which both the eternal and the new coexist on equal footing, "that the certainty of the old must be sacrificed for the content of the new." "No ethical progress was thinkable" without this, as Mies underlined in a copy of Eduard Spranger's *Lebensformen*.[23]

"Each past deserves to be condemned." With this battle cry Nietzsche in 1874 had challenged the *Unzeitgemässen* (the untimely ones) to battle and thrown the gauntlet into the ring of historicism. Without courage for one's own existence, one cannot undertake the step into the present. The will to the present manifests itself in the confidence one places in one's own vitality and in the longing for a life free from the dictates of history. To be fit for living, man must have "from time to time the strength to break up and dissolve a part of the past."[24] Nietzsche's "first imperative" (A. Riehl)—the affirmation of life—points to the precondition one has to accept if one wishes to master one's own existence. According to Mies, it is "the duty of each generation to assume a positive attitude toward life, rather than remain caught up in dusty thinking."[25]

Mies's demand for an "undistorted affirmation of life"[26] corresponds to that linearity of consciousness held to be the property of modern man. The "big yes to everything" represents for Nietzsche *the* criterion for the "great style": a style—longed for by modern man—that is not "merely art, but reality, truth, *life*" itself.[27] The "practical sense" (*Tatsachensinn*), "the last and most valuable of all senses" (Nietzsche), ennobles the new man who sets his own laws for life and art and who does not go in search of them by theorizing or moralizing, or by engaging in the idealistic window dressing of classical education.

The will of the epoch, like Nietzsche's "will to life," circumscribes the creative principle, in which "the eternal joy of becoming itself"[28] is revealed. The rebirth of the creative principle was the ultimate aim of the new art; in essence it corresponded to a belief in "eternal recurrence" that Zarathustran teaching handed down from Heraclitus and the pre-Socratics. The belief in the eternally new perceived history as canceled (in the sense of a Hegelian antithesis) by a nonhistoricizing history.

Hans Richter, characterizing the new type of building artist, stated in a 1925 essay: "The old architect has nothing to give to his time any more. It is the new building artist who must realize it." The latter is more concerned with "creating actual relationships than mere symbols standing for them." The task of "the young generation all over the world" consists in affirming the "existence of the creative" and forcing its own time "into consciousness." The new "sense of the factual" that Richter spoke of, and the affirmation of the present and the belief in an eternally valid creative principle, were the trademarks of this "new building master." He was embodied in the person of Mies:

The new building master has to reckon with a new sensuousness [he must possess it]: with the sensuousness of a more consistent, more prejudice-free person, a gradually more practical and less sentimental society, a world of rapid mobility, a world of sharpest calculation; and he must do all that with the composure of a man who does not depend on occasional flashes of insight but who draws from a profound understanding. . . . He says yes to the time with all its preconditions and perspectives; the time as a sum of all possibilities alone appears to him just and reasonable, so that he accepts its tasks and limitations, he believes in the today by

*necessity and gives that body to it that it demands from him. . . . With him
a tradition begins to revive that once had been able to build pyramids,
and that will be able to recognize and master the tasks of an internationally organized society.*[29]

The possibilities for the building arts inherent in the times were demonstrated by Mies with a persistence that differentiated him from many of his
contemporaries. He drew his consequences without making concessions.
The spreading industrialization took over the building trades by necessity,
and this process of restructuring took place "without regard for old perceptions and values." Crafts-oriented building practices with their antiquated
finishing methods had to be fundamentally overhauled, much like the aesthetic perceptions themselves. This long-overdue procedure had to be
effected without undue sentimentality, and Mies was convinced that industrialization would destroy the building trades in their present form. But he
who regrets, so he adds, "that the house of the future will no longer be
erected by artisans must keep in mind that the automobile, too, is no
longer built by the wheelwright."[30] It is in the tenor of this statement that we
have to understand the final sentence of "Baukunst und Zeitwille!": "The
world did not become poorer when the stagecoach was replaced by the
automobile."[31]

Mies saw "the core problem of our time" quite correctly in the industrialization of the building trades.[32] In 1910 Walter Gropius had suggested to the
Allgemeine Elektrizitäts-Gesellschaft (AEG) a program for an industrial residential complex, and in 1918 Peter Behrens and Heinrich de Fries proposed a similar solution in *Vom sparsamen Bauen* (On Thrifty Building)
with a model for a garden city.[33] How far developments in this area had
progressed technically can be seen from the catalogs of American mail
order houses—also circulating in Europe—in which by 1910 one-family
houses were offered that could be assembled from ready-made parts at
favorable prices.[34] The need for mass housing had, under the increasing
pressures of a general housing shortage after the war, become an urgent
social task that was unsolvable without the novel methods of building economics and building techniques.

A first step toward a scientific-technical production method in the building
trades had been undertaken by Behrens in 1918–1919 with his concept of
a "group building method" that worked by means of a "simplification of work
procedures along the lines of the Taylor system."[35] But rationalizations of
this sort, which attempted to increase effectiveness by using larger sizes of
stone and more systematic planning, appeared in 1924 no longer far-
reaching enough. Industrialization of building had to begin on a new level.
The "first prerequisite" as Mies saw it was "finding a building material" that
could practically be distilled out of the conditions of industrial production
itself and that not only permitted but actually demanded a process of industrialization. Only thereby could one really rationalize the fabrication pro-

cess; and work on the building site—much like in an automobile assembly plant—would be "exclusively of an assembly type, bringing about an incredible reduction of building time. This will bring with it a significant reduction of building costs."[36]

The American automobile manufacturer Henry Ford had in 1920 brought the production-line method into the limelight, and by stimulating the stagnating machine industry had opened up new social perspectives. His belief that the automobile could be transformed from a luxury article to an article of mass production and the conviction that the production of this product could be totally revolutionized secured for Ford a place in history.[37] The extraordinary interest with which Henry Ford's book *My Life and My Work* was received in Germany—appearing in German in 1923 with the promising subtitle "The Big Today and the Bigger Tomorrow"—is proven by the thirteen editions it went through in the year of initial publication. Another twenty editions were to follow up to 1930.

The thought lay at hand that democratization, such as that of a vehicle the ownership of which had previously been viewed as a privilege, could also be applied successfully to building production. A hygienic, practical apartment was in the early twenties for many a luxury article that could be given, like the automobile, a new social dimension by revolutionizing the production processes.

There are indications that Mies owed to Henry Ford many of the thoughts he published in 1924 in his article "Industrial Building." Ford had stated in the introduction to his book that he intended to prove "that the ideas we have put into practice are capable of the largest application."[38] Ford and Mies, both self-made men, were principally in agreement. The method according to which Mies proceeded conformed to a process defined by Ford: "My effort is in the direction of simplicity. . . . Start with an article that suits and then study to find some way of eliminating the entirely useless parts. This applies to everything—a shoe, a dress, a house, a piece of machinery, a railroad, a steamship, an airplane. As we cut out useless parts and simplify necessary ones we also cut down the cost of making. This is the simple logic."[39]

Even Mies's call for a new building material—"It will have to be a lightweight material"—may have been inspired by Ford's thinking. In the systematic "reduction of weight" and in the development of new sorts of steel, like vanadium, exactly tailored for this purpose lay one of the secrets of the technical superiority of the legendary Model T that had come out in 1908. A distinct echo of this recipe for success from the automobile industry can also be heard in the theories of Le Corbusier, who prophesied that the house of the future would no longer be "this solidly-built thing" that has to survive for centuries but simply "a tool as the motor-car is becoming a tool."[40]

Presumably it was also thanks to Ford's book that Mies regarded the ideas of his teacher Behrens as inadequate in this respect. To Behrens's 1918 *Vom sparsamen Bauen* Mies, with Ford, could have replied: "The cure of poverty is not in personal economy but in better production. . . . Economy is the rule of half-alive minds."[41]

Ford's rule for the acceptance of the mechanical aspects of life was "an absence of fear of the future and of veneration for the past."[42] Similarly, Mies with his motto "Not the yesterday, not the tomorrow, only the today is formable" confessed optimistically to the creative force of technical inventiveness by means of which progress hews its own path. Should it be possible to complete this industrialization, Mies euphorically prophesied in 1924, then "the social, economic, technical, and even artistic questions will solve themselves."[43]

The belief in an independent creative process was not directed at the invisible world of meanings but at the world of practical purposes and needs. The building art arises out of this mechanical interpretation of being as a logical response to demands. Mies took literally Semper's sentence of 1843 that "art knows only *one* master, necessity."[44] A house, Mies summarily declared, should simply be developed out of its function, "namely organizing the activity of living," rather than "demonstrating to the world how far its owner has progressed in the realm of aesthetics."[45] Building site, sun exposure, room layout, and material constitute the givens out of which the "building organism" has to be formed. Admiration for the Cartesian thought processes of the engineer and for economic-logical solutions replaced the traditional principles of aesthetics and poetics in composition. The laconic sentence that accompanied the "Concrete Residential Building" is hard to excel in its renunciation of aesthetic design criteria: "I cut openings into the walls where I need them for view and illumination."[46] In contrast to this pragmatic realism, Le Corbusier's lyrical interpretation of openings—"The holes give much or little light, make gay or sad"[47]—seems hopelessly sentimental. Apparently here too Berlage's rigor had served as example: "The actual decoration of the walls is the windows," declared Berlage, adding at once, "one must of course only install them where needed."[48]

Mies recommended that the architect model himself on the engineer. This held true not only for special areas, such as the installation of reinforced concrete, where "the architect still had everything to learn from the shipbuilding engineer,"[49] but for structural building in general, which still awaited its own industrial revolution. It is in this light that we have to view Mies's attempt to obtain the participation of a ship's engineer for the competition for contemporary apartment buildings, arranged by the Bund Deutscher Architekten, so as "to make it evident that we are striving for an engineering instead of a handicrafts basis for modern apartment buildings."[50]

Mies had gladly given his "big yes" to the necessities of the present. The will of the epoch required matter-of-factness, objectivity, and a form-giving that corresponded to the constructive, technical, and practical requirements of the time. The determination with which Mies represented his ideas, the bellicose tone, and the implications of totality deliberately flaunted in all the declarations of these years, reflect a concerted effort to realize the desired unification of art and life, the comprehensive art work of one's existence. This had been the thesis of Nietzsche, who held that the necessity of one's existence should not merely be suffered, much less idealistically glorified, but should be reshaped with a new love. Henry van de Velde had delivered the same confession symbolically with his "Amo" for the generation of machine enthusiasts before Mies.[51] The new generation of the twenties reproached this stance for its aesthetic claims. The unification of art and life should not merely be reflected in promising pictures, but should become reality by means of a new art. This art wanted to be understood as "expression of creative energy that organizes the progress of mankind," and thus as "instrument of the general work process."[52] For this reason, the modern artists could compliment themselves: "Today, one can only speak of the builders of a new life."[53]

But next to this apotheosis of the means of one's own time that vibrates in Mies's early texts, there existed—still hidden—another theme. It was only to emerge as the unrestrained affirmation came up against its limitations and as doubts arose as to whether the application of the new means could actually bring about progress. This belief in progress that wanted to see the creative, urgent force rise autonomously out of the givens, as Mies saw with respect to the industrialization of the building trades, was questioned by him for the first time in that same year. The example of Ford became a lesson for Mies in two respects: it showed the logical principles according to which social production has to be organized, but it also showed that these objective principles had to be given limits by the subject. This is expressed in the concluding passage of the lecture manuscript of June 19, 1924:

Nothing illuminates more clearly the situation in which we find ourselves than the fact that Ford's book could trigger such a strong reaction here in Germany. What Ford wants is simple and illuminating. His factories show mechanization in dizzying perfection. We agree with the direction Ford has taken, but we reject the plane on which he moves. Mechanization can never be goal, it must remain means. Mean toward a spiritual purpose. While we want to stand with both feet firmly on the ground, we want to reach with our head to the clouds.[54]

V From Material through Purpose to Idea: The Long Path to the Building Art

1 Departure from the Will of the Epoch: Building Art as Spiritual Decision

Architecture means building art [Baukunst], uniting two concepts in its name: the expertise, the mastery of the practical, useful discipline, and the art of abstract beauty. It is liberalizing to see combined in one word the two concepts of practical usefulness and abstract beauty, which regrettably have often faced each other, especially in our time, with hostility. We have gone through times when they stood almost for opposite meanings. We have this time behind us and can state with satisfaction that the indications of a reconciliation become ever more evident.

Peter Behrens, Das Haus Peter Behrens, *1901*

In the early twenties the "significance of facts"[1] had for Mies a normative meaning: function and the treatment of materials were the uppermost laws of elementary form-giving. Objectivity was served and subjectivity overcome if one surrendered to the positivism of the givens and the conditions of the period. Mies demanded that the architect assume without reservations an attitude of "serviceability toward things," submitting unconditionally to the will of the epoch and offering himself as its instrument. The building master of today refused to compromise. Mies wanted nothing whatever to do with the "aesthetic traditions of past centuries."[2] Quite the contrary, a radical rupture with the past was the program.[3]

Ultimately, elementary form-giving aimed at a liberation from form and style as traditionally understood in favor of an "independent aesthetic-organic form-giving," as J. J. P. Oud called it, which could only be brought about by a "free art." This independent form-giving, severed from the oppression of prototypes and from the imitative principle, proceeds "less and less from the exterior to the interior, and more and more from the interior to the exterior," which means in the words of Mies that it forms itself "out of the nature of the task." These creations therefore are no mere "depictions" of transmitted ideal prototypes but step into life as "forms" in an autochthonous sense.[4]

In his theories of building Mies propagated such an artless "form," one that wanted to be understood not as the product of an intentional aesthetic but as the logical result of autonomous technological-mechanical conditions. Gottfried Semper's prophecy of 1852, "that the process of decomposition of existing art types" under the impact of industry and the social sciences must first be completed "before something good and new" can arise,[5] found its fulfillment in the disintegration of the traditional types and concepts in favor of the new "forms." These new forms took on varying shapes: with the futurists, the house became a machine; expressionists and functionalists approximated the forms of organic growth; constructivists replaced earthbound volumetricity with dynamic constructional poems that floated "aeronautically" in space, as Kasimir Malevich visualized it.[6] The neoplasticism of De Stijl dissolved space-containing volume into a system of freestanding wall segments; and the cubistic purism of Le Corbusier, who wanted to realize the Cartesian dream of a world full of precision and poesy, reduced the house to an abstract complex of pure stereometry.

The old forms and concepts, constituting a layer over reality, had to be broken so that reality could be reorganized according to new constructive principles. Mies, with his skin and bone structure, had progressed to the utmost border of architectonic disintegration. Construction is the elemental form of all building and demarcates—as the analogy to the skeleton implies—a threshold beyond which one could no longer talk of a "building." This no longer reducible structure obeys the new principle of a nonmimetic immanence. Out of it the technical forms of the machine age and the engineer-made buildings emerge as "the magnificent first-fruits of the new age."[7]

It is the task of the modern building artist to uncover the integral beauty of construction and material. The promise of a new art consists not in "aesthetic speculation" imaginatively added from the outside, but in a disciplined subordination to the conditions of material and functional method. The immanent beauty of the architectonic reveals itself through straightforward, logical construction and is most impressively evident in raw construction, for here the building material—not having been subjected to any will to form—appears in its "undraped" purity just as Semper had demanded it.[8] "The material is the key to the secrets of artistic beauty"[9] was the maxim of the materialistic aesthetic articulated for the twentieth century by J. A. Lux, updating Semper.

The artist of the new type of form-giving was bound to this premise and was expected, according to Theo van Doesburg, to adjust himself "to the world of machines." In short, one not only aimed at discovering, in a mechanical-technological way, the "style secrets of a knowledge of building material" (E. von Berlepsch, 1900), which after all had been respected in former times, but one aimed at "creating, when needed, new materials."[10] Mies, who in his plea for "industrial building" had presented the invention of new building materials as a central problem, concurred with Doesburg: "If the architect submits the design as a challenge (without aesthetic preconceptions) then it is up to the engineer to discover the material suitable for the implementation. The building art will never arrive at a full expression of creative time-consciousness if architects remain timidly and passively satisfied with existing materials."[11]

It was against this sort of passivity that did not even exhaust the possibilities of the already existing that Mies aimed the invective added with an irate flourish to the back of the manuscript of his manifesto "Bauen" of October 1, 1923: "Barbarians have approached the problem with the least imaginable measure of boldness." This reproach was directed against the architect and directly related to the discussion centering on the architec-

Left, the discovery of the exemplary functional structure: American grain silo in a widely disseminated and frequently reproduced photo of 1910. Reproduced, among other places, in the 1913 *Jahrbuch des Deutschen Werkbundes,* Le Corbusier's *Vers une architecture* (1923), Werner Lindner's *Ingenieurbau* (1923), and Adolf Behne's *Zweckbau* (1925). *Right,* the city as working apparatus: "The New City of the Future" of Mario Chiattone, 1914.

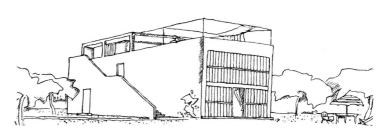

Le Corbusier, Maison "Citrohan," 1920.

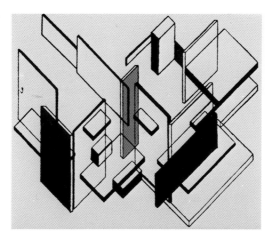

Cornelis van Eesteren and Theo van Doesburg, Maison Particulière, 1923.

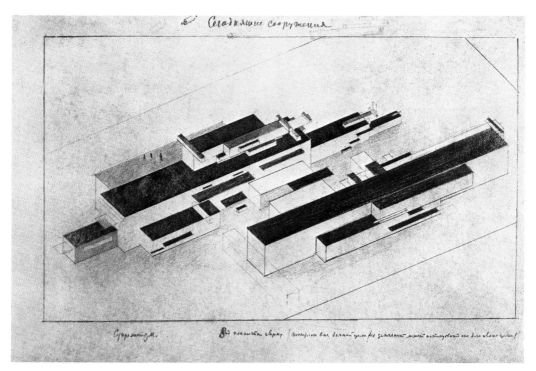

Kasimir Malevich, Architekton, 1923.

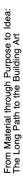
From Material through Purpose to Idea:
The Long Path to the Building Art

tural possibilities of the "Concrete Residential Building." The discipline this material exacts from the architect and the perspectives the deployment of ferroconcrete opens architecturally had previously been dealt with by Mies in his text. "Ferroconcrete requires the most precise planning before its execution." Only then can the "advantages of this material" be exploited and its "disadvantages" avoided.[12] Only by restrained, disciplined action, boldly oriented toward the future rather than toward the past, can the "favor of the material" (Wölfflin) be courted. This, however, was the work method of engineers, not of architects. They could be described, as Le Corbusier did, as "healthy and virile, active and useful, balanced and happy."[13] It was the engineer who conquered nature and who discovered, by mechanical-technological means, the materials "that made a new architecture feasible." The architect and the "so-called building art," however, had—according to Doesburg's polemic—"murdered" the material by "sentimentalizing reverie."[14]

The will of the epoch searches for *its* properties, and one of them must be the characteristic of making "the expression of subjective feelings practically impossible."[15] And though new material such as steel, glass, and especially concrete set practically no limits to the fantasy of the architect,[16] the worth of these materials was measured not in terms of the manifold possibilities of their picturesque plasticity, but rather in terms of their practicality and functionality. Thus elementarily employed, the new materials could be viewed as possessing a Miesian will to material, congenial with the will of the epoch with its stress on the objective and unambiguous. Mies's urban projects seemed to be exemplary in terms of this congruence. Curt Gravenkamp's reflections on Mies's department store designs resulted in a practically Wölfflinian maxim that affirmed the objective character of Mies's designs: "Each epoch reaches for that material that is typical for it. But the specific deployment of an architectonic material is also symptomatic for the spirit of a period."[17]

What Mies advocated was an anonymous type of building whose lapidary principle, expressed in the formula "The building art is the spatially apprehended will of the epoch, nothing else," proclaims a universal truth. The problem of meaning and the question as to what is meant by the means of the times remained in Mies's theory still largely bracketed out, for these problems touched on subjective value judgments. Function and material—raised by Mies to objective forces—were not mere conveyors of meaning, but already its very manifestation. In this epistemological monism, fact and meaning correspond to a theory of building that in its utilitarianism—"the purpose of a building is its actual meaning"—trusted that its hidden elementary law would lead to its meaning "in itself."[18]

Behind this "simple truth" of building, as uncompromisingly sober as it may have sounded in the early twenties, hid a mysterious logic of form. The myth of objectivity veiled its law; its realization remained wrapped in secrecy. For, according to Mies, the immanent form is not subjectively creatable but arises spontaneously from the conditions of life. The building master has to yield to these conditions and, for the sake of truth, renounce ascetically the aesthetic expression of self. "Significant and characteristic form" emerged, as Mies explained in the example of the urban expansion of Magdeburg by Bruno Taut, paradoxically "just because form was not striven for."[19] The new art's entering into existence was described by J. J. P. Oud in the following manner: "We perform our work conscientiously, take care of the smallest details, subordinate ourselves totally to the task, do not reflect on art, and see—one day the work is completed and emerges as—art."[20]

Mies had led the building art back to that absolute zero point from which it arises all of itself out of the conditions of simple building. A further reduction, exceeding these limits, was, as construction, not conceivable. This was the point of departure for a new process, later described by Mies as "the long path from material through purpose" into a new dimension: the world of spiritual values and meanings, the order of which was not materialistically determined and did not reveal itself in the existing world as "simple reality" but as an idea, first thought and then *created* by the acting subject.[21] "Genuine order," as Mies then called it, had its orientation center no longer unilaterally in *Sein* (being)—in materials and functions—but also, as it were, in *Sollen* (that which ought to be) and in *Schein* (appearances). Mies climbed the steps to *Baukunst* according to a virtually classical example, in a sequence already indicated by Vitruvius by the words *firmitas, utilitas,* and *venustas.*

Function, which in 1924 still exercised together with material a total lordship over building, appeared in 1927 in a different light. In "Baukunst und Zeitwille!" residential building was derived quite simply "to suit its purpose, namely organizing the activity of living." Three years later, Mies attached critical questions to his statement: "The apartment is a use item. May one ask for what? May one ask to what it relates? Obviously only to physical existence. So that all may proceed smoothly. And yet man also has the needs of his soul, which can never be satisfied with that . . ."[22] This demand added to the "hierarchy of objects" the "hierarchy of levels of perception" (*Erkenntnisebene*).[23] The value of function and organization was now determined from that direction, the dictate of which Mies sidestepped by means of a new definition: "Order is more than organization. Organization is the determination of function. Order, however, imparts meaning."[24]

This change in Mies's position, which represented a shift from the materialistic-postivistic What in favor of the idealistic and aesthetic How, began in 1925–1926. It had already been evident in the contradictions noticeable between proclaimed theory and actual design. The severe self-restriction in favor of the objective called for by Mies would have led one to anticipate drawings of a schematic nature, rather than those large-format perspectives that aimed at an aesthetic impact. No doubt, aside from all his enthusiasm for that much-proclaimed engineering style, there existed an extraordinary artistic effort.

And, if one looks very closely, one can even detect classicizing allusions, like symbolic relics. In his Concrete Office Building, Mies had articulated the externally "formless" building on the inside into a classical A-B-A rhythm. Not only in this subliminal emphasis of the building corners can one find traces of the academic tradition. The entrance solution, with its recessed portico with pillars and generous freestanding staircase, appears to follow classical examples and might remind the initiate of Schinkel's museum. Similarly difficult to discern at first glance are the step-by-step increasing protrusions of the floor levels that are barely noticeable on the reduced photographic reproductions but are noticeable on the 1.38m × 2.89m (!) original drawing—an irregularity that is betrayed by the increasing width of the corner windows in the ascending story levels. J. J. P. Oud had already pointed to the new plastic possibilities inherent in the concrete construction method that now permitted one to build not merely "from bottom to top inward only," but also "from bottom to top outward."[25]

That the virtues of classicism Mies had learned from Behrens had their practical applicability is again proven by this sophisticated detail. This hidden classicism permitted the artist Mies to do what his own dogmatic theory of building forbade. The plastic possibilities, so tempting to the artist, could be employed for aesthetic effect with good conscience without compromising the engineering character.

The impression of extreme subjectivity achievable by the cantilevering of planes had been demonstrated by Erich Mendelsohn's Einsteinturm. The plastic modeling and the fluid lines that recall the superstructure of a U-boat may have elicited the remark from Mies that ferroconcrete buildings are "neither pastry nor tank turrets," but, according to their nature, "skeleton structures."[26] But Mendelsohn continued to avail himself of the spectacular plastic possibilities afforded by the new construction techniques and

Left, main staircase of the Altes Museum, Berlin, by Karl Friedrich Schinkel. *Right,* door detail of Mies's Office Building.

Left, pattern deviation: detail of the façade of the Office Building. The increasing cantilever span can be read from the increasing width of the corner window. *Right,* swelling of the exterior wall of the Wiegand House by Peter Behrens, 1911.

the malleability of the materials in his department store projects, the Mosse House, and the Kemperplatz House. They offered welcome expressive means for rhetorical muscle flexing of astounding dynamic effect that appeared to claim for the building volume a gravity-free condition.

The slight protrusion Mies imparted, very carefully and, in comparison to Mendelsohn, actually timidly and with extreme discretion, to the floor levels of his Office Building was not in that sense an extraneously applied form of expression that exploited construction. Rather, it gave an indication of the constructive state of the building. Mies did not want to renounce form, but—like Berlage—did not want to concede special rights and privileges to it at the expense of construction. The actual lesson Mies learned from Behrens, nevertheless, was that a form had to be found that gave meaning and identity to construction, and Mies was not to forget it.

Mies arrived at a compromise according to which form was allowed its right only at second glance. The Office Building had an overhang but not one that was, like Mendelsohn's, expressly laden with plastic energy. The slight and gradual protrusions of the floor levels remain unobtrusive and almost unnoticeable. How much fantasy and sophistication a sublime form-giving of this sort requires has been convincingly demonstrated by Peter Behrens in his Wiegand House of 1912. Here, the outer walls of natural stone bow slightly forward in a soft curve and visually unburden in fluid elegance the massive volume of the building. One could interpret the wall treatment of Mies's Office Building as a similar, subversively classical gesture. The slight protrusion was discrete enough not to be viewed as fashionable formalism, but intensive enough to effect its own sort of aesthetic effect.

The exterior walls open toward the viewer with a slight, very restrained but elegant bow and thus appear to meet him spatially. The weighty building volume should not float—as Mendelsohn suggested—but remain attached to the earth yet open itself to space. The classical principle of a building volume firmly earth-related, yet comprising a room that opens up to space—that architectonic theme of pedestal and pavilion that Mies already had mastered before its time in the Riehl House—retained its validity. This principle stood for a dialectic in which the contradiction between heaviness and lightness, enclosedness and freedom are coaxed into a delicate balance. Such an equation could not simply be achieved with Berlage's constructional rigor as it echoed in Mies's theses. The classicizing references, which by implication can also be found in his skyscrapers,[27] indicate that Mies did not reject history nearly as radically in his buildings as he seemed to announce verbally with his emphasis on construction and materials.

The mechanical determinism speaking out of the rigid theories of building were not evident in Mies's designs, even if these were criticized for schematism. It was an impression that apparently was deliberately avoided. It would be difficult to explain why Mies, the apostle of construction, failed to provide a plan of the support system. In his skyscraper designs posts do not even appear in the ground plan, and the design for the Office Building was submitted without any plan whatever: it would have offered the eye no more than a framed raster of supports, and the rhythmic intervals would have called attention to the formally intended corner emphasis.[28]

The reduction of building to the basics of construction had consequences that by no means led automatically to aesthetically satisfactory solutions, as Mies had hoped. The "schematic" that was implicit in the task and therefore "finds its expression in form-giving"[29] had to be aesthetically sublimated. The method of classicizing assimilation, propagated by Behrens in response to the serial requirements of the times, proved its true usefulness and universality in Mies's raw-structure classicism of the early twenties. Mies might have found encouragement in that direction through his friend J. J. P. Oud, an admirer of Behrens, who suggested a similar, ahistorical classicism to spiritually immunize architecture in the twenties.

What the manifestos failed to announce, architecture revealed: Mies searched for a way that would reconcile the objective facts and givens with the world of the perceiving senses, which—as Leon Battista Alberti had pointed out centuries ago—are particularly sensitive to and indeed covetous of proportion and beauty and in that respect "insistent" and "fastidious."[30] That Mies allowed for the special rights of the eye was already obvious from the explanations that accompanied the glass skyscrapers. Their idiosyncratic form arose by no means out of constructive but out of aesthetic considerations. Visual impression and appearances were determinative, and the "danger of an effect of lifelessness" was hopefully forestalled by the play of light reflections.[31]

The architectonic design revealed characteristics that had so far gone untreated in Mies's theory. Only between 1924 and 1926 can one begin to notice a corresponding expansion in his positions and the attempt to find a rapproachement between two positions that seemed to strain in different

Erich Mendelsohn, design for Kemperplatz House, 1923.

directions. By 1927 the necessity to set limits had become the prevailing theme. The challenge confronting Mies and his times now was seen as a need "to raise tasks out of an atmosphere of the unilateral and the doctrinaire"[32] and to do justice to both the objective and the subjective.[33]

This is the tenor of Mies's foreword to the 1927 book on the Weissenhof housing project, which he started with the sentence: "It is not entirely senseless to specifically emphasize today that the problem of the new housing is a problem of the building art, in spite of its technical and economic aspects. It is a complex problem and therefore can only be solved by creative forces rather than by calculation or organization."[34] Mies, who had advocated in 1924 a fundamental reorientation of the building trades in favor of industrialization, expecting from it a solution to social, economic, and artistic problems,[35] now criticized in his attitude toward the Weissenhofsiedlung that "battle cry 'rationalization and typification'" that accompanied the "call for the economizing of the housing industry."[36] Rationalization and typification, the mainstays of industrialization, are "slogans" that, solving only marginal problems, fail to address the essential. Mies thereby not only abandoned the position he had established in his 1924 thesis advocating the industrialization of the building trades, but even undermined the initial program of the Weissenhofsiedlung itself, which aimed at demonstrating "to the public in exemplary manner"[37] the consequences of a "rationalization of all spheres of life" with all its technological, hygienic, and aesthetic advantages.

A naive hope in the liberating potentials of technology had given way to skepticism. The organizer of the Stuttgart experiment, in his official position, misses no opportunity to point out that the limits of the modern methods must be admitted.

The extent of the change from a materialistic toward an idealistic position that had taken place between 1924 and 1927 becomes evident if one com-

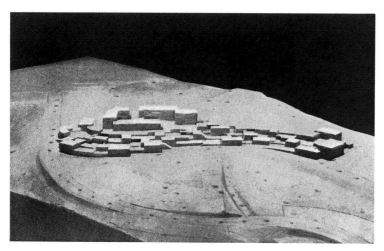

Initial study model for Stuttgart-Weissenhof, 1926.

pares two statements. Whereas in 1924 Mies still saw "the core problem of building in our time" reductively as a "question of materials," in 1927 he viewed the "problem of the new housing basically [as] a spiritual problem."[38] Criteria had to be regrouped according to a new scale of values: The "creative power," the spirit, is triumphant over calculation and organization. The problem of the new housing, Mies emphasized specifically, is "a problem of the building art . . . in spite of its technical and economic aspects."[39]

This declaration was preceded by the design for a site plan that, as urban precinct, attempted to "avoid everything schematic" and that in the execution of the buildings allowed to each contributor "as much freedom as possible to execute his ideas."[40] The loosely grouped building masses in their cubistic plasticity complemented the natural landscape; they were connected by terraces and structured to form a type of terrain sculpture. What resulted was an urban complex that, in its balanced distribution of volumes, appeared more like a Mediterranean agglomeration than a compound of typical, rationalized living units.

The conservative and populist critique after 1933 actually affirmed these spatial qualities by the very slander it directed against the Weissenhofsiedlung, reviling it as "suburb of Jerusalem" or "Arabville."[41] The southern ambience of graceful urban complexity, as compared with the coming period of row houses and monotonous zoning, appears like a reproachful memory. More than in the actual execution, this complexity came to the fore in Mies's first urban model. Here the Rosa Luxemburg and Karl Liebknecht memorial seems to fuse with the terrace house design of Peter Behrens, the row houses of Oud and Hilberseimer, and also with Bruno Taut's Stadtkrone. It was with good reason that Peter Behrens had been brought to memory in the Weissenhof book publication edited by Mies with an illustration of his terrace house design.[42]

The change that had taken place in Mies's position between 1924 and 1927 is evident in the manuscript for the lecture of March 17, 1926.[43] It is a document that signals a turning point in his life, testifying to his efforts to relinquish his so far one-sided point of view. Now as before, Mies promoted his position combatively. In the "chaos of confusing forces" the time was marked by "tragedy." The actual reason for this was that no "consequences" had been drawn from the "changes in living conditions." Again Mies explicated the basic tenets of his ideology. The materialistic, indeed Marxist interpretation of "culture" and building art as "result of very specific economic conditions without which it would either have failed to develop or would have developed differently" was nevertheless here being relativized, insofar as it would "of course" be wrong to assume that "economic change in a society" is automatically followed by a change in ideology.

In an analogous argument, part affirmation, part limitation, Mies now also corrected his attitude in regard to engineering buildings: "It is well known that certain technical requirements lead to new forms with powerful expressive qualities. Yet"—so he adds—"one must not confuse this with spiritual expression. It is beauty of a technical kind. Technical forms are the product of a technical, not a spiritual will. . . . In reality only creative forces can truly give form."

Under the banner of "spiritual will" a gradual but fundamental detachment was taking place. Mies began to argue in two different directions. He differentiated between "spiritual" and "material conditions," between "building for life in a general sense" and another type of building "intimately connected with specific spiritual atmospheres that we perceive as characteristic cultures," and finally between a "technical" and a "spiritual will." In this lecture manuscript Mies updated, with almost casual nonchalance and in long-familiar sentence structures, his definition of the building art. He saw it now no longer as "the spatially apprehended will of the epoch," but as that what supposedly it always was, namely "the spatial execution of spiritual decisions. . . . It has never been otherwise."

Architecture as will projected into space—this was the formulation of Mies's definition. And to this Nietzschean theory of art as reflection of the will, translated by Peter Behrens in 1910 into the pathos of the great unifying form, Mies was to remain loyal. Now only the subjective element had to be annulled by forcing the concept of will into the metaphysical, and the formula of 1923, "building is the spatially apprehended will of the epoch," was found. In 1926 Mies shifted emphasis and began to correct the process of

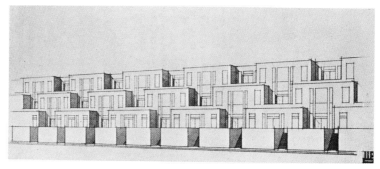

J. J. P. Oud, Row Houses on the Ocean, 1917.

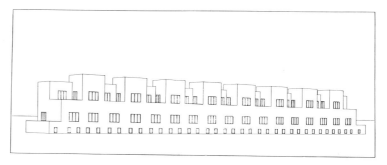

Ludwig Hilberseimer, Row Houses, 1924.

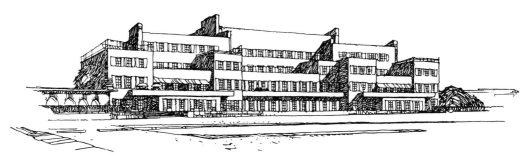

Peter Behrens, design for Terrace Housing, 1920.

will formation in gradual steps. The phrase "will of the epoch" was dropped from his vocabulary. The last time this anonymous guarantor of objectivity appeared was in this manuscript of March 17, 1926, in the opening passages of which Mies stated that "one cannot walk forward while looking backward" and that "one cannot be the instrument of the will of the epoch if one lives in the past." From that time on, the phrase never appeared any more in his statements.

The "spiritual will," the "spiritual decision" now take its position. This change was no semantic, superficial modernizing but the expression of a deep-reaching reevaluation. The building art is now seen as a relationship between object and subject, no longer as preordained by a higher will that makes itself manifest in facts. Rather there is a dialogue between givens and the building art that arises creatively out of the "entire fullness" of life "in its spiritual and concrete aspects."[44]

As the lecture of 1926 clearly demonstrates, Mies began to differentiate between spiritual and material conditions, between art and technology; indeed he did so by necessity. It is the logical outcome of Mies's new equation: "Building art as spiritual decision" presupposes an order, and indeed an order that does not anchor the spiritual in the immanence of things, in circumstances, but first of all in the consciousness of man, in will and in idea.

Mies informed himself of this basic difference in philosophical systems through a book that carried Mies's old and new position practically in its title: Dietrich Heinrich Kerler's *Weltwille und Wertwille. Linien des Systems der Philosophie* (World Will and Will to Value. Outline of a System of Philosophy). It appeared in 1925, just in time to enforce the turning away from the "will of the epoch," corresponding to Kerler's "world will," toward "spiritual will," corresponding to "will to value." Kerler pointed to the parting of the ways from which philosophical systems diverge in opposite directions. According to how the ontological problem, that is, the question of the nature of "the metaphysical quality of being," is solved, the ideologies separate into either a monistic world image of materialism that perceives the true nature of the "world of being" in matter, in the material, or a dualistic world image that sees in "the world of being" not the only world but one potentially open to a "much higher world independent of space and time," namely *the world of the spiritual values.*" This "source of value in the world, the culture, the spiritual" must not be seen as something that gushes forth from the "archetypal matrix, the absolute" but was explained by Kerler in the terms of a modern epistemology "pluralistically . . . as the combined effect of purpose-oriented individuals" (underlined by Mies).[45]

That Mies was interested in this theory stimulated by Schopenhauer and Nietzsche and directed against materialism is shown by the following sentences that he underlined:

The conduct of life is determined exclusively by those values found within us, and by nothing else. That is an eidetic truth. . . . The values, the realization of which determines the meaning of life, have been set by ourselves, and that is why they alone give us absolute certainty. Here we have solid ground under our feet, while all claims for nature or natural laws, quite contrary to the naive and materialistic assumptions, are and remain totally uncertain. . . . But materialism is not only disproved psychically—as opposed to physically—by an intuitive insight into the guaranteed fact of existence, but is actually a totally absurd ideology. Matter, the objects, are given to us only as images, as imaginings, as phenomenal material or content, but by no means, as the materialists claim, directly. . . . To state that matter exists, over and above the image, is metaphysics. . . . Matter is not the object but the condition of experience![46]

Mies saw himself confronted by a theory that was contrary to his ideology, but that was reminiscent of familiar, idealist positions of the prewar period. Kerler's philosophical discourse affirmed the *Kunstwollen* (will to art) of Riegl and Behrens and also Nietzsche's basic thesis that the world is only justifiable as an aesthetic phenomenon. For the world does not exist for man per se (*an sich*) but can only be experienced by the sense organs that, as Kerler explained, can only produce "their image" of the object world. Whom Mies had in mind when he wrote a capital B in the margin next to some underlined text passages will remain a secret. Certainly it cannot have been Berlage.[47]

"The naked fact is nothing more than the materialization of a possible idea. The naked fact is a medium for ideas only by reason of the 'order' that is applied to it"—so explained Le Corbusier.[48] Mies was to express himself similarly in 1930 on occasion of the Vienna meeting of the Werkbund when he spoke of the new time as a "fact" that proves its value only if it creates preconditions for the existence of the spirit.[49]

As to art and architecture, J. J. P. Oud's formula applied: "'Style' always presupposes a spiritual order, that is, a spiritual willing."[50] The understanding of these relationships forced Mies to reconsider his forthright theory of 1926 that saw building art as the result of treatment of material and response to function, and to examine the alleged equivalence of art and technology. That both phenomena are "intrinsically two different expressions" and that it would therefore be a "fallacy to assume that aesthetics could arise simply out of an ultimate, direct response to function"[51] had already been foretold by Peter Behrens in 1917, who had kept the synthesis of art and industry under scrutiny.

Mies concurred with his teacher in 1926. What he called the "will to the spiritual" (in contrast to "will to the technical"), without which beauty was inconceivable, was not dissimilar to the "will to form." Without it, the "coordination of great technical skill and profoundly felt art"—and so with the building art—could not be effected.[52]

2 1926: Stimuli, Critique, and Orientation

One thing is sure, the technological alone—and may the word be ever so univer-
sally perceived—will not of itself be enough to build a world.
Rudolf Schwarz, Wegweisung der Technik, 1929

To look upon architecture only from one angle, such as the rational-constructive
or the purely artistic, is a simplification and impoverishment.
Theo van Doesburg, "Die neue Architektur und ihre Folgen," 1925

He who expects the law of form only from construction and materials is like the
sorcerer's apprentice who was not master of the technical apparatus, the magic
broom, but its servant.
Edgar Wedepohl, 1927

Mies did not attain his reputation as a leading representative of the new
building art on account of his buildings, but through his bold architectural
visions and energetic manifestos. In the turbulent time between 1921 and
1925 he built only four modest villas in a classicizing style and renovated
one villa in Berlin-Westend.[1] These well-crafted structures, certainly deserv-
ing to be called honest works, do not incorporate anything novel yet are
not quite representative of the past either. Certainly they do not exemplify
Mies's announced building program and are to this day largely undocu-
mented. As far as the reputation of the new building master was concerned
they remained without impact.

The stabilization of the economy after the monetary reforms of 1924
brought many noticeable changes professionally. Mies's reputation had
firmed to the extent that he was considered in 1924–1925 as a candidate
for the post of director of the Kunstgewerbeschule of Magdeburg, the Kunstakademie in Breslau, and the Stadtbaurat of Frankfurt am Main.[2] In 1925
he also finally received commissions that enabled him to put his convictions to the test.

That the radical attitude of 1923 would lose some of its uncompromising
tenor in these reconstruction years was only to be expected. How tentative
the relationship between theory and practice really was became evident in
his first major commission, an apartment house (1925–1926) on the Afrikanische Strasse of Wedding in Berlin, traditionally an industrial and working class district. It was among the first such new settlements of the
Weimar Republic.

Anyone expecting the author of the plea for industrial buiding to seize the
opportunity to demonstrate new methods of mass fabrication, of rationalization or prefabrication, as Walter Gropius and Ernst May had done in the
same period, would be sorely disappointed.[3] The buildings, though executed quite conventionally with stuccoed walls, differed, however, from their
predecessors, particularly by their proudly recessed siting. Furthermore, the

façade, although resuming the traditional post and beam theme, gave on its wall a unique lesson in abstract principles of construction by means of rhythm, balance, proportion, and—not to be forgotten—perfection of detail.[4]

Mies was to occupy himself only once more with this theme, namely in his apartment block for the Weissenhofsiedlung. In general, Mies refrained from entering the main battlefield of the New Building, namely mass housing, which was held to be practically emblematic for the Weimar period and was viewed by all architects as the major social and artistic problem of the times. His doubts that the housing problem could be solved by emphasizing rationalization, standardization, and functionalism is best illuminated by his attitude toward the Weissenhofsiedlung, which speaks of disillusionment and resignation—the result of exaggerated hopes.

Mies stood by no means alone in this. Even before the excesses of a rationalized happiness had been condemned around 1930 by an enlightened critique and factuality and functionality had been recognized as "self-laid traps for the building art,"[5] there had been doubting and rejecting voices. Mies now joined them with his Stuttgart admonitions.

Between 1924 and 1927 Mies received important stimuli that were to guide his thinking into new tracks. In this respect Rudolf Schwarz must be mentioned. Mies met the Poelzig student, eleven years his junior, presumably in the early twenties in Berlin, where Schwarz was concluding his studies; they were to remain lifelong friends. Mies described Schwarz as a "great building master in the full sense of the word," whose "incomparably profound thinking" he greatly admired.[6] Schwarz, in turn, showed a commensurate respect for Mies, and no one else understood the philosophical implications of Mies's building in all its profundity better than Schwarz, who could illuminate it with a few pregnant phrases.[7]

Mies himself has indicated the extraordinary significance the encounter with Schwarz had for his development in the twenties. In the notes for his acceptance speech to the Royal Institute of British Architects in 1959, in which he looked back on his career, he particularly emphasized the year 1926. Three names are listed on a notecard that served him as memory guide for this speech: "In this peculiar year—1926: Schwarz—Max Scheeler—Whitehead."[8]

Rudolf Schwarz, the first-named, was active in the twenties in the Catholic youth movement Quickborn, which had its meeting place at Castle Rothenfels near Frankfurt. Among the leading personalities of the movement was the philosopher of religion Romano Guardini, who had been teaching at the University of Berlin since 1923. Mies was to take up contact with him also. Schwarz and Guardini shared, in the early twenties, the editorship of the periodical *Die Schildgenossen* (Comrades-in-Arms), in which Mies, urged on by Schwarz, was also to publish something eventually.[9] Mies became acquainted with the ideology of these thinkers through the essays of Rudolf Schwarz in *Die Schildgenossen*.[10] The position Schwarz assumed in respect to the "new things" of his times resolved those very contradictions that Mies had been unable to reconcile theoretically in his unilaterally expressed manifestos. Schwarz did not deny that the "new world" with its technical potential had its own sort of magnitude, but he professed "a great fear of things to come," particularly the tendency of the times to "become abstract"; this, in his eyes, made "grace, charm, playfulness, love, and humility" impossible. The word "rationalization" seemed to him "one of the most stupid slogans of our time" because it conveys only a mechanical, not a spiritual message.[11] Mies, who had expressed similar notions albeit in milder terms, could here only find encouragement.[12]

Attracted by the thoughts of Schwarz, who put spiritual concerns before materialistic ones, Mies gave new orientation to his own position. Schwarz saw the "true solution" to the existential anxiety of modern man exclusively in spiritual terms:

There is something called spirit. . . . There is not only brute force, and there is not only "soul"; there is also "spirit" . . . something quite ultimate . . . and it is this that is in tune with nature, and in it inanimate nature

Residential blocks, Afrikanische Strasse, Berlin-Wedding, 1926.

IN THIS PECULIAR YEAR - 1926
- Schwarz -
· MAX SCHEELER -
· WHITEHEAD -

Rudolf Schwarz, Church of Corpus Christi, Aachen, 1928. "The properly formed emptiness of space and plane is not merely a negation of pictorial representation but rather its antipode. It relates to it as silence relates to the word. Once man has opened himself up to it, he experiences a strange presence." Romano Guardini, 1929, on Rudolf Schwarz's Church of Corpus Christi.

discovers its worthy adversary. . . . This necessitates that we become free: that we stand at each moment both within time and above it. This demands an awareness that can say even today: I am the master. This demands that we commit ourselves to absolute freedom.[13]

Schwarz advocated an attitude that conceded neither to the coldly calculating and anonymous—equivalent with Mies's concept of will of the epoch—nor to its opposite, namely an "infusion of soul" into the new world by means of a façadelike "humane, bourgeois stratum"; he called rather for an attitude that truly confronts the "new things" and masters them.[14]

But a common ideology that tended toward a metaphysical and religious attitude toward the world was not the only thing uniting Mies and Schwarz.

What they shared was a search for the forming and the "building" of a reality that comes to terms with the salient phenomenon of the modern epoch, its technical aspect with all its consequences. The question of how the limits of progress should be defined—a question Mies had avoided up to then—took up a central position in Schwarz's thought. Like Mies, he was convinced that the technological contained the wonderful potential of an "archproduction."[15] In contrast to Mies, he emphasized very emphatically that this brought with it the obligation to set limits to technology. Technology has to be harnessed to become serviceable to man. For it is not the technological in itself that matters, but the orientation man gives to it.

What is at stake is the mastery of the objective forces by the human spirit. And it is the specific task of modern man to "control these forces." It was a task that seemed "more difficult than the work of the ancestors" who had "gained arable land from the wild forest, its animals and spirits."[16] Essays such as "Vom Sterben der Anmut" (Of the Demise of Grace), which Mies according to the markings seems to have read, vacillated between a Spenglerian pessimism anticipating the decline of the world and a Christian-optimist confession "do not fear!" Mies was receptive to this longing to lose oneself, to this hope of finding oneself. His thinking was not founded on theoretical knowledge but on genuine faith. Schwarz's thinking by contrast did not remain attached to transcendental flights but became practical and took up partisan positions in the immediate reality. The architecture of the period and its "immanent historicism" in its various manifestations he analyzed with amazing astuteness.[17] Like Mies, Schwarz was, in the early twenties, obsessed by a Messianic fervor "not only to beautify the world but to convert it"; he also seized upon the ocean liner as an example of "convincing authenticity and force" and criticized—not to Mies's displeasure—the father figure Peter Behrens.[18]

Schwarz's writings convey a thinking that alternates between two poles, refusing any type of unilateralness and absoluteness, any "doctrinaire shabbiness" (Schwarz). When Mies attempted in Stuttgart in 1927 to liberate building from "an atmosphere of the unilateral and doctrinaire," it was this attitude that he was paraphrasing.[19] Rudolf Schwarz was a pathfinder. His Wegweisung der Technik (Orientation by Technology) (Potsdam, 1929), the publication of which had been urged by Romano Guardini,[20] was referred to by Mies as a "way station in my development."[21] This text can rightfully be counted among the "significant, the meaningful programmatic writings of the second half of twenties";[22] Mies not only seized upon it right after its first availability in 1928–1929 but still consulted it in 1950, whether to help him in the ordering of his thoughts in regard to the building art or to silently take over some of its phrases in a speech manuscript.[23]

That the thoughts of Rudolf Schwarz—and here one has to add Romano Guardini, who is audible in the background—fell in the mid-twenties on fertile soil may partially have been due to the critique that was directed against Mies. Theo van Doesburg, for example, in his programmatic lecture "The New Architecture and Its Consequences" given in 1925 in Berlin, referred to Mies's imperative on "building" that by then, presumably on account of insistent repetition, was almost as well known as the skyscraper projects. Doesburg quoted the axiom "We know no forms, only building problems . . . etc., etc." and added briefly in a dry tone: "Only one must not confuse form and style."[24]

Already in 1922 Doesburg had expressed opinions in a lecture at Weimar that sounded like replies to Mies: "Building does not yet mean form-giving. Even a gradual rejection of everything superfluous . . . does not yet constitute a formful building; it is undecorated building. Formful building is something more." This applied also to the "anatomically oriented" building—as Doesburg quite typically called it—that restricts itself to "exposing . . . the skeleton of construction," for "constructive building alone does not yet constitute form-giving."[25]

"Form-giving," so Doesburg explained in his 1922 manifesto "Der Wille zum Stil"—to which Mies again appeared to reply in silent dialogue with his "even the will to style is formalism"[26]—means interpretation, simile, and symbol. Form-giving is not construction but "direct expression obtained by the characteristic means of art."[27] Doesburg accused Mies of confusing form and style and stressed that the new architecture does not reject form, but merely "the a priori accepted formal schema." The "purely constructive, anatomical architecture, which shows its skeleton on the inside and its skin on the outside," was basically nothing else but the consequence of that process of simplification that had started in the beginning of the century as a reaction against "decorativism" and that now, under the flag of a "return to rational construction!," led in turn to its own sort of unilateralness and impoverishment. Not only Mies but Le Corbusier, Mallet-Stevens, Tony Garnier, and others were seen as representing this development.[28]

"Architecture became naked, bones and skin . . . in Germany one actually talked of a bone and skin architecture, and one wanted no share in aesthetic speculation or formal problems. . . . Architecture was newly defined as functional organization of materials. Form was secondary, a by-product." Even in 1928, when Mies had already moved on to other convictions—and it was certainly he who was meant—Doesburg still continued to make war against the "function romantics," the glorifiers of purpose and construction. His last argument announced: "Man does not live in construction, but in an *atmosphere* that is evoked by the *surface!*"[29]

The most explicit critique of Mies's theme was formulated by Adolf Behne in his work *Der moderne Zweckbau* (The Modern Function Structure), which, though composed in 1923, did not find a publisher until 1926. It ranked among the most important publications up to then dealing with the

New Building and has retained its significance as key work on the discussion of the theory of architecture. Behne's merit was that he had undertaken a summary of all the various impulses that originated in the years from 1900 to 1923 and arranged them in their contextual sequence, whereby he stressed the various concepts of rationalism and functionalism, illuminating their respective dogmas and prejudices.

The summary of this discourse contained a critique of Mies, for Behne confessed candidly: "We find that the German building art is easily inclined to extremes that frequently change course and then give way to opposing extremes—consequences of inner insecurity."[30] Only a few paragraphs earlier the strict concept of factuality to which the "young generation of German architects" paid homage had been taken into focus. Behne cited as a prototypical axiom of this attitude the Miesian dictum: "Any aesthetic speculation, any doctrine, and any formalism we reject. . . . [Create] form out of the nature of the task and with the means of our time. That is our work." To which Behne responded: "To reject aesthetic speculation, formalism, and doctrine is necessary and even healthy—it only seems a fallacy (not infrequently encountered) to reject these things from the premise of an antiaesthetic position, even though we may rebel a hundred times a day against the aesthetics of the aesthetes. To reject aesthetic demands—which is not the same as aesthetic speculation—would mean to saw off the branch one is sitting on."[31]

The critique directed against Mies amounted to the allegation that he was obsessed by a "fear of form"[32] and that he was aiming for a materialistic, mechanistic aesthetic that equated building art with technology. J. J. P. Oud, with whom Mies had entertained contacts since 1924,[33] had admitted as much in his "Bekenntnisse eines Architekten" (Confessions of an Architect), which were headed by a "Yes and No" and consisted of self-critical aphorisms: "I announced that the artist had to put himself in the service of the machine but then I realized that it is the machine that has to be put in the service of art . . . I hate railroad bridges that resemble Gothic cathedrals, but the pure purpose-architecture of many a famous industrial building leaves me cold also . . . I understand why American silos are shown as examples of a timely building art, but I ask myself where in the structure art is concealed."[34]

Le Corbusier had written in 1920 in *L'Esprit Nouveau:* "It will be a delight to talk of architecture after so many silos, factories, machines"[35]—a sigh of relief that, after the translation of the widely known *Vers une architecture* (which also appeared in 1926 under the title *Kommende Baukunst*), may have come to the attention of Mies. Here the artist Le Corbusier addressed himself to a "commonplace among architects (the younger ones)" that alleges: "The construction must be shown," and another one, common in the same circles, that holds: "When a thing responds to a need, it is beautiful." To these he countered:

*But. . . . To show the construction is all very well for an Arts and Crafts
student who is anxious to prove his ability. The Almighty has clearly
shown our wrists and our ankles, but there remains all the rest!*

*When a thing responds to a need, it is not necessarily beautiful; it satisfies
only one part of our mind, the primary part, without which there is no
possibility of richer satisfactions; let us recover the right order of
events. . . .*

*Architecture is the art above all others which achieves a state of platonic
grandeur, mathematical order, speculation, the perception of the harmony
which lies in emotional relationships. This is the aim of architecture.*[36]

To judge by the publications, the year 1926 was an interim period given
over to programmatic critique. We find, added to the writings of Adolf
Behne and Le Corbusier in that same year, Oud's *Holländische Architektur*
(Dutch Architecture), which appeared as a Bauhaus Book and which completed the inventory. Oud took issue with the "uncritical admiration for
everything mechanical," viewing it as a dangerous regression, and
defended instead the concept of "form synthesis" that was viewed as sus-
tained by a "timely will to form." Obvious was a basic sympathy with the
thoughts of Behrens, even though Oud did not specifically single him out
by name: "Not *only* the technological and not *only* the aesthetic, not *only*
reason and not *only* sentiment, but the harmonic synthesis of both should
be the architectural aim . . . A miserable period that does not know how to
assimilate material progress spiritually!"[37]

Even Mies's hero Berlage, the great mentor of the modern Dutch building
art, was now drawn into the cross fire of criticism. After acknowledging all
his merits, Oud chalked it up against his teacher in 1929 that his forms, on
account of their restrictions, belonged intrinsically to the previous century
and were indebted to Viollet-le-Duc, since much "traditional ballast" was yet
attached to them. On one hand, the demands of construction were "still too
obtrusive," while on the other hand Berlage did not permit himself to be
guided "consequentially enough" by the requisites of construction that
might have permitted him "to arrive at corresponding new architectonic
forms."[38]

This choir of critical voices in 1926 was now joined by Heinrich de Fries, a
former co-worker of Peter Behrens, who articulated his dissatisfaction with
contemporary achievements of modern architecture by holding up once
more the shining example of Frank Lloyd Wright. The entire discussion on
form and construction, de Fries held, was an irrelevant nuisance. The
actual architectonic problem of spatiality, as could be learned from the work
of Wright, could only begin once this hurdle had been overcome.[39]

The year 1926 was, as Mies affirmed, not only a particularly significant
year but, as far as his own development was concerned, *the* decisive year:
"I would say 1926 was the most significant year. Looking back it seems

that it was not just a year in the sense of time. It was a year of great realization or awareness. It seems to me that at certain times in the history of man the understanding of certain situations ripens."[40]

In this year of coming to consciousness falls a decisive reversal.[41] Almost in affirmation of Behne's thesis that one tends in Germany to fall from one extreme to the other, Mies, presumably in this year, regrettably asked his co-worker Sergius Ruegenberg to clean up the Am Karlsbad office and throw away a heap of old drawings and tracings.[42]

3 Space for the Unfolding of the Spirit

Space is no empirical concept. For this reason the visualization of space cannot be derived from the conditions of external appearances by way of experience, for this external appearance is itself only possible by a thought process.

Immanuel Kant, Critique of Pure Reason, *1781*

The "problem of form" in architecture must be transposed into a "problem of space." Architecture is the form-giver of the entire spatial world, from the smallest spatial cell of furniture to the immense expanse of nature.

Herman Sörgel, Architektur-Ästhetik, *1921*

Among all the publications of the year 1926, one work in particular proved stimulating for Mies and must therefore be singled out, especially as this work attempted to interrelate architecture, philosophy, and the reformation of life. The work in question is the idiosyncratic tract of Bauhaus member Siegfried Ebeling that appeared in 1926 in Dessau under the peculiar title *Der Raum als Membran* (Space as Membrane). The work has been largely ignored by historians writing on the architecture of the twenties. Ebeling undertook the ambitious attempt to fundamentally rethink the conditions under which architecture can exist under the changed sensibilities toward life and nature. His premise opened up new horizons for Mies without forcing him to abandon his own convictions, for Ebeling based his theories of architecture on two spiritual fathers who had also influenced Mies himself: Friedrich Nietzsche and Raoul Francé.

The mention of these two names alone promised that this work would lead Mies to encounter his own thinking, so to speak, as a mirror image. The names stood for two decisive, successive phases of his development: Nietzsche, connected with the names of Alois Riehl and Peter Behrens, stood for the period up to 1918; Raoul H. Francé was the model for the time after 1918 during which Mies attempted to secure "building" on the foundation of natural lawfulness. Now he reencountered the protagonists of his building philosophy in the theory of Ebeling, proceeding arm in arm toward a new architecture.

As one might expect, the juxtaposition of these two names promised a theory of architecture that was as prophetic as it was idiosyncratic. Already the title *Der Raum als Membran* seemed to allude to the anthroposophical and cosmological ideology underlying the basic tenets of the early Bauhaus under Johannes Itten and Gertrud Grunow. Presumably Ebeling was a student at the Bauhaus at that time[1] and in 1926 stood still under its influence, recognizable by its unmistakable idiom.

Once one has penetrated the peculiarities of expression that hide the drift of the thought by a dense veil of mystery,[2] it suddenly becomes clear why Mies found the work of this original thinker so fascinating. Hurdles the contemporary reader has to overcome posed no serious obstacle for Mies. His close relationship with the *Organiker* Hugh Häring had made Mies familiar with the mental and linguistic practices of these circles, and extensive reading of the works of France—whose works abounded in Mies's library—facilitated the effort to follow the serpentine ways of a theory of "biological architecture."

Already in the beginning of this work, Mies found himself in familiar territory. The "definition of the house" in its "primal situation" was presented as the exemplary eternal, just as Mies had evoked it with his concept of building. To create a sense of measurement against which all existing and future architecture could be compared, it was useful to visualize "the primal activity of building a house as the fundamental form of architecture." This provides the basis for the "objective distance . . . to everything around us that architecturally meets with public interest."[3]

This is of course a traditional stance. Vitruvius's architectural theory also postulated the hut as the type model for the first house.[4] Mies with his skin and bone buildings stood directly in this continuity, in which the primitive hut and the vision of a simple and honest primal construction, in Berlage's sense, appears to realize itself as a natural truth of building.

However, Ebeling was not so much in search of an eternal tectonic truth and its formative law. His interest was not directed toward the architectonic object but toward the architectonic condition under the elementary circumstances of biophysical existence. Seen that way, the house in its "primal situation" looks something like this: It is a "relatively rigid multicelled volumetric body," that is more or less firmly attached on its underside to the earth and is adjoined on its other sides by a "thin medium" that is "permeated by a periodically varying light." The degree of "harmonious equilibrium between the three components" was the criterion that determined the architectural character and quality.[5]

In this elementary situation, the space of the house could be viewed as equivalent to a "skin" or a "membrane between men and exterior space." Retranslated into the biophysical ideology and its jargon, architecture was nothing but a methodical attempt to "equalize the three-dimensional, physically determined space of a three-dimensional, biologically determined membrane between our bodies, as plasmatic, labile substances, and the latently given yet biostructurally apprehensible emanation of the spheres."(!) Mies, evidently prepared for this sort of essentials, expressed his tribute to this definitional achievement by a mark in the margin.

Compared to Mies's skin and bone theory that stressed the primacy of structure, Ebeling's theory, viewing the building as a breathing organism, possessed a higher degree of abstraction. Not limited to any particular type of building or construction method, it was universal in that it was applicable to all or nothing. On this theory of building he erected, in graduated steps, his theory of architecture.

DER RAUM
ALS
MEMBRAN

Ebeling saw his membrane theory affirmed by the progress of technology in the building industry. The increasing importance of the technical aspects of building a house with all its installations proves that "architecture . . . has already been moving along these lines" and has become equivalent to an apparatus or technical organ. In particular the increasing mechanization of the household, "this type of *'neue Sachlichkeit,'*" worked counter to the traditional meaning of architecture with its appeal to the imagination by way of the symbol. It cannot be denied that, as a consequence of the comprehensive technical reorientation of society, architecture no longer served as a conveyor of meaning, but assumed the character of a piece of machinery, as Le Corbusier articulated it. Mies already had endorsed the loss of the symbolic function of architecture in the technological age by rejecting all "aesthetic speculation" and by advocating a surrender to objective forces that he called will of the epoch.

But while Mies believed that building, provided it serves function and material, would develop into a building art all by itself, as a reward so to speak, Ebeling, calling upon Nietzsche, demanded an act of architectonic self-redemption by active reevaluation.

The loss of symbolic function, according to Ebeling, occurred because architecture was no longer oriented toward humanity or toward "man as man." Rather it became a physiological instrument and related to a concrete "man of flesh and blood"—or, Ebeling added, a man "in full possession of an indefinitely increasable sensuousness."[6]

Correspondingly, a physical or biological sensibility would replace the traditional symbolic forms as an organizing and forming architectonic principle. "Rhythmical man breaks the shackles of the past" was the Nietzschean motto Ebeling had written over his text. All this was in tune with the demands of the youth of the twenties for a new naturalness. Gymnastics, dance, air, and light determined the new physicality of a "rhythmical culture," for which Nietzsche had supplied the motto: "We have rediscovered the body."[7] In a metaphorical sense this also applied to the architectural body. Liberated from the historical dress style, the buildings assembled themselves as naked volumes under the light, because, as Le Corbusier said, "we have acquired a taste for fresh air and clear daylight."[8]

Ebeling missed something in the architecture of his time, which "still stood where Nietzsche's prophetic protest had left it," something decisive—something that Mies also had wished to bring about with his manifestos— namely, as Mies marked in the margin, a "leap," an "inner jump into the primal region of forming." What had so far been achieved remained "at best a loving symbiosis with the great mother technology or proof of a certain 'Qui vive' in the dregs of society for which 'money and being human' are interchangeable values." But nowhere was there evidence of the "evolution of an arch-spirit who, with revolutionary dynamics, reaches deeply into the ultimate confrontation between man and world" (markings by Mies). To sum it up: "No incipient beginnings of an architecture that breaks down the fences into the future."[9]

By underlining the following sentences, Mies endorsed this judgment.

One emphasizes with heavy strokes the will to a new architecture without filling this will with a new content. One emphasizes form, not content. One steals glances at the engineer yet remains, even in the "most sober functionality," an aesthete. . . . No incipient beginning, as harsh as that may sound, is noticeable in the planning of our housing settlements. The procrustean bed of settlement planning became the winter and deathbed of architecture. More architects suffer from this tragic situation than the politically influenced public wants to have true. "To each man his own home" has become "to each man his own house at the lowest possible price." Politics therewith destroys the spiritual value of architecture.[10]

This last point in particular, doubting that a solution to the problem could be found in the methods of industrial building and planning, prefigured strongly the attitude of rejection Mies was to assume only shortly afterward in Stuttgart.

According to Ebeling, a fundamental "reevaluation of architecture" was direly needed to overcome "that unfortunate separation: here architecture, here technology, here art." The apparatuses "as technical wonders" were the manifest "exponents of the will of the epoch and its development tendency," and they stood in a "different type of world" that did not care whether a style was "historical" or "neutrally purified." The architectonic space as such remained untouched. This led quite logically to the idea of "reevaluating space in the spirit of the apparatus."[11]

Much as these technical installations were basically negative architectural elements, assembled, installed, or built unbeholden to the "idea" the architect wanted to express with his apartment blocks, so the entire space was to be visualized as being similarly independent. Analogous to the secondary technical elements, space was to be viewed "rather as a negative," a membrane "that only affords the physiological precondition,"[12] instead of "positively" as representative space.

This expressed in a nutshell the idea of a neutral space and architecture as a protective covering that Ebeling had observed in nature and plant life and dubbed the "bark principle" (*Prinzip Rinde*). This architecture makes do without the traditional semiotic signs and confines itself to the role of encasement or container, only proffering the "physiological precondition" with its "negative space"—*ein Raum ohne Eigenschaften* (a room without characteristics).

Ebeling's "space as membrane," inspired by that "exquisite book by Raoul Francé *Technische Leistungen der Pflanzen* . . . which will be better appreciated by the architectural sciences of the future" (markings by Mies),[13] anticipated the architecture of climate control and the energy-efficient ecology of "climatological differentiation." It prophesized "sun power installations" and utopian shields that "soften the ravages of earth's climate," anticipating Buckminster Fuller's geodesic dome of 1959. Beyond that, Ebeling's critique of the "instant-building method" for industrial structures, which appeared to him much too cumbersome in the "age of migration and mass movement," was eventually to be affirmed by the utopian high tech of "Plug-In-City" and, decades later, by mobile homes.

For Mies, the inspiration of this book lay not so much in the technical concept of its membrane theory that in essence dissolves the house into a "transition area for a continuous . . . force field,"[14] but in Ebeling's concept of space. Here their outlooks coincided, though arising out of different precepts. What Ebeling referred to as "negative space," namely the neutral, three-dimensional membrane that exists "free of all alien suggestions," corresponded to what Mies, rejecting "all aesthetic speculation," strove for when he accorded construction priority.

Mies's skin and bone buildings could be viewed as "negative architecture" insofar as they had cast off—a few subliminal references excepted—all traditional symbolism and characteristics of historical style; they might therefore be classified, in Ebeling's terminology, as "naturally purified." Yet precisely this was now made into a reproach by the critics of "anatomically oriented building," who asserted that "building does not yet mean form-giving."[15]

The criteria of form-giving as practiced by Mies remained undefined. The verbally flaunted antiaesthetic attitude rejected out of hand all deliberate form-giving and installed the "nature of the task" as pictorial norm, which, no further explicated, was assumed to speak for itself. Ebeling's concept of space opened up an avenue out of this dilemma of negative form-giving, as it claimed to be a building art without art. The creation of negative space that sets merely the physiological precondition, much as "building" under the dictates of construction only realizes the architectonic preconditions, should be viewed as a transitional phase, "a proto-stage of the activated space."

The logic of this ascending order was simple and compelling: the corrosion of symbols by the processes of technology hostile to tradition also cleanses space of "alien suggestions" and throws man back upon himself. Neutral space thereby offers the possibility for a new existence, a "being on one's own."[16] Space, emptied of meaning, could now be evaluated according to the Kantian category of the "condition of the possible," which means it could be newly organized and delimited according to one's own rules.

At this crucial point, Ebeling abandoned the terrain of the biological theory, dominated by Francé, to entrust himself to Nietzsche and his concept of self-redemption. This philosophy preached liberation from the spellbinding forces of alien powers in favor of autonomy, a "being for oneself," that guaranteed a new type of existence conforming to one's own inner needs.

Ebeling longed for an architectonic space that would do justice to one's relationship with one's body, one's being, and the eternity of the cosmos. This type of space had all the earmarks of having been personally designed by Zarathustra, as it was seen as responding to the need "for a space allowing free rhythmical dance movements and a Dionysian fervor of living, or, in reverse, permitting utmost concentration and mystical celebrations, offering undiminished views and admitting the light from the nocturnal sky for that serene, astrologically minded man"[17]—spatial desiderata endorsed by Mies's markings in the side margin.

In the same manner, Mies took note of the subsequent conclusion: "Should even a single occasionally occurring inner need be general in nature, this would impose on the architect the welcome compulsion to regroup the house organism dynamically around this need and examine its constructive consequences."[18]

However, this type of building, as the building of the present shows, is for the time being reserved for a future man; the architect presently is not ready to draw the required radical consequences. Locked in "between luxury, poverty, traditional bourgeois expectations, closet mentality, and machine splendor," he draws the "resultant" out of these "polarities," raises it to a doctrine, and advocates a middle ground of "unpretentiousness": "This marks him as representative of his time, but not as its goal setter."[19]

Such sentences mark the key issues of Mies's development as architect in the second part of the twenties: a turning away from mass housing, a rejection of the principles of economics, an insistence on highest quality, and finally the architecturally decisive realignment of interest away from construction to space.

Mies had already solved the second of Ebeling's two demands, namely "to regroup the house organism dynamically around . . . lifestyle and examine its constructive consequences." The reevaluation of construction that began in 1922 could only be completed by a further step. The promise of art latent in construction contained the possibilities not only of a new appearance of architecture but simultaneously of a new spatial grouping. Mies, so far, had only dealt occasionally with the interdependence of these factors.

The design for a Brick Country House of 1923–1924 was such an exception, as it revealed a totally new spatial concept. While the sober explanations Mies furnished of this project[20] indicate that the concept of the wall had to undergo a decisive reinterpretation, he failed to indicate by even a single word the consequences implied by this architectonic reevaluation. Only in 1929 did he turn again in this direction that had apparently been only of fleeting interest to him in 1924. The same could be said for the Glass Skyscrapers, the blueprints of which seem to take note only in passing of the newly gained spatial freedom. They remain "negative" spaces without specific qualities and of unlimited function, as not even constructive features were indicated in this vacuum.

Ebeling's theory of building was motivated by Zarathustra, whose clear gaze did not fasten on "free from what?" but on "free for what?," in order to impart a new rhythm to life. This type of freedom means more than merely being free from "certain spatial concepts," which Mies, without being more specific, had blamed in 1924 for those "impossible results."[21] If in 1924 architecture was unconditionally at the mercy of technology, the situation had reversed itself by 1928 when Mies announced: "We see in technology the possibility of liberating ourselves."[22] By the "space-toppling power" of steel and concrete construction, a "measure of freedom in spatial composition" had been obtained that made possible a "freedom for a new type of task": "Only now can we articulate space freely, open it up and connect it to the landscape. Now it becomes clear again what a wall is, what an opening, what is floor and what ceiling."[23]

By the reevaluation of space, by extirpating symbolism, by the appropriation of emptiness and by the metamorphosis of the negative space into a new "room full of rooms,"[24] Mies had created in the early twenties the pre-conditions for a new spatial perception. Now the spiritual factors, the content and the values had to be determined, according to which—in Ebeling's words—the house organism must be organized to reflect that new "lifestyle."

"The Preconditions of Architectural Work" was, significantly, the title of a lecture given by Mies in several locations in the spring of 1928, a lecture that was warmly welcomed by the public.[25] Already in the opening sentences that summarized his theses, the new direction became evident: "Ladies and Gentlemen! The building art is for me not a subject for ingenious speculation. I do not expect anything from theories and specific systems. But particularly nothing from an aesthetic attitude that merely touches the surface. The building art can only be unlocked from a spiritual center and can only be comprehended as a living process."

Mies had made this confession to a philosophy of life even more explicit a few months earlier in his letter on form to Walter Riezler, the publisher of the periodical *Die Form:* "We want to open ourselves to life and seize it. Life is what matters in all the fullness of its spiritual and concrete relations. We do not value the result but the starting point of the form-giving process. It in particular reveals whether form was arrived at from the direction of life or for its own sake."[26]

This "starting point of the form-giving process" that Mies considered so crucial gains its full meaning against the backdrop of Ebeling's work. The authenticity and intensity of life advocated by Nietzsche, and the forming powers of nature held out as examplary by Francé, had become criteria of a theory of form. Its main thesis, expounded here for Walter Riezler, was: "Only life intensity has form intensity." This definition represents, as it were, the combined result of both positions: of a naturalism that already recognizes the existing as form, and of an idealism of will that aims at a subjugation of the given. Mies delimits himself against both extremes: "The unformed is not worse than the overformed. One is nothing, the other illusion." His conclusion stated: "Real form presupposes real life. But not one that has been nor one that has been thought. Therein lies the criterion. This is why the question of classical or Gothic is as irrelevant as the question of constructivist or functionalist."[27]

The New Building represents, as Mies described it in his Stuttgart explanations, an "element of the larger struggle for new forms of living."[28] Adolf Behne saw it the same way: "Building is nothing else but the organization of space, so that life can unfold under the best possible circumstances. To think about good and right building means no more than to think about good and right living. For—to repeat it once more—the new architects do not want to impose some new forms of style, they want to contribute toward better organization of life."[29] The new arrangement of space around life—or to be more exact, around a specific idea of what life could be or should be, and therefore still an idea of life—moved after 1926 into the center of Mies's work. The social responsibility of architecture, as Mies perceived it, consisted in creating a suitable environment for new modes of living, rather than in the normative division of space according to the new methods of mass production.

It was the task of architecture to reflect the new attitude toward life by a "spatial execution of the changed situation."[30] The undertaking to reevaluate space upon which Mies had embarked had already begun in 1910 with Behrens's subtle dialogue around the concept of the Schinkel Villa. The process of opening up an enclosed plan was continued by Mies in the twenties with renewed vigor. In his essay "Mies van der Rohe. Entwicklung eines Architekten" of 1927, Paul Westheim afforded a glimpse of this phase of the development that was to come to completion in 1930, peaking with the Barcelona Pavilion, the Tugendhat House, and the model house for the Berlin Building Exposition.

According to Westheim, Mies's plan afforded "circulation that leads from room to room," resulting in an "overlapping of individual rooms." Mies articulated the available space "organically to the planned function," not unlike "modern office buildings where this has already become a standard practice" and where space was divided "according to the type of operation," with walls reduced to partitions. The plans of Mies's villas appeared to be basically "no more than a grid for overlapping spatial sequences" and the house itself, in the final analysis, "nothing but an enrobing of this spatial configuration."[31]

This attempt to "reshape the house into a dwelling organism"—which, to judge from Westheim's remarks, resulted in a mixture between apparatus and living organ—was continued by Mies after 1927, but with new principles and means. In his apartment block for the Weissenhofsiedlung, the walls assumed the character of room dividers. The "freedom of usage" afforded by the steel skeleton permitted Mies a commensurate freedom in regard to the interior spatial arrangement.[32] Movable wall segments, which could be unfolded according to specific spatial requirements, determined the blueprint. A model for this type of flexible dwelling had been given by Gerrit Rietveld in 1923 in the Schröder House in Utrecht, the upper story of which could be opened up into a single room or divided into five smaller ones.

With his Stuttgart experiment, Mies had begun that "space-dynamic re-arrangement" that had been called for by Ebeling. The flexible floor plan responded to a new mode of living described by Werner Gräff, Mies's comrade-in-arms, as consisting of a heightened demand for airiness, color, and mechanics, an inclination toward sports, and an increased social mobility.[33] The Stuttgart Werkbund Exhibition had been intended to demonstrate the possible dwelling forms and living styles of such a society, thus contributing to the "clarification of the will to dwell."[34]

The breakthrough to a totally new understanding of space first led to a further, systematic reduction and separation of elements: the Barcelona Pavilion of 1929 was the high point of this development. Space was no longer defined by limited segments but rather appeared itself to be set in motion. On the dotted grid of the steel skeleton, Mies composed a cadence of asymmetrical, freestanding wall segments, metamorphosing the structure into an interlocking configuration that breathed light and space and that did not correspond to any existing categories. This spatial experience was no longer explainable in terms of the old terminology, and even new terms such as flowing or open space circumscribed it only vaguely.[35]

In this building perfectly fusing the classical heritage and the promise of modern art, the reevaluation of construction that had begun in 1922 and the reevaluation of space that had already been incipiently under way before the war reached their final resolution. If Mies had declared in 1922 that the aesthetic function of architecture lay in construction appearance, by the time of the Barcelona Pavilion he emphasized spatial experience. In the blueprint one can now detect that membranelike transparent quality that had, up to then, been the trademark of the veiling glass skin. Its large planes and the unattached wall screens created an effect that was irritatingly open and restrictive at the same time.

With this poetical space that brings to mind the "space of *elsewhere*" of Gaston Bachelard's *Poetics of Space,*[36] the likes of which had not been known before, Mies entered his name in the genealogy book of the human habitat. Not the delimiting wall nor the tectonic system but space itself, or rather the spiritual principle of its delimitation, had become the actual work of art.

Mies "built" an aesthetics of space, the theoretical preparation for which reached back beyond the turn of the century. August Schmarsow had expressed the conviction in 1893 that the nature of architectural creation consists in the shaping of space. H. P. Berlage had pointed out in 1908 that the art of the building master consists in creating rooms by means of a "more or less assembled complex of walls." A building is not determined by the actual, immediately apprehensible formal presence, but by an "idea of architecture" that "manifests itself through and through in spatial terms,"[37] a saying by his mentor Berlage that encouraged Mies to remain loyal to the concept of the classical villa type even after 1919.

Herman Sörgel, basing himself on the writings of Camillo Sitte, August Schmarsow, Alois Riegl, A. E. Brinckmann, and Walter Curt Behrendt, attempted in 1918 with his *Architektur-Ästhetik* to pioneer a new architecture as spatial art. His maxim "The 'problem of form' in architecture must be transposed into a 'problem of space'"[38] summarized the concerns of the New Building. "Spatiality" is the true problematic of architecture, for in it lies "something . . . that universally for all times and styles" determines the essence of architecture.

The truly architectonic expresses itself "as a spatial relationship," the principle of which consists in carving a limited space out of an infinite one, thus forming a space within space.[39] Sörgel defined architecture as "the form-giver of the entire spatial world, from the smallest spatial cell of furniture to the immense expanse of nature." For this concept of a spatial continuum Mies's architecture seemed custom-ordered: "Only by perambulation can spatial forms be successively viewed and artistically apprehended."[40]

In Barcelona, space was not only equivalent with material, as had been aspired to in the plastic interlocking of body and space in the Schinkel Villa, but it was of even greater importance. A new "understanding for relational profundity" (Sörgel) triumphed over matter. The creative spirit had conquered matter and given it a new shape and therefore a new possibility for existence. The idea of a building had become the basis of its architectural reality. Mies had transposed the aesthetic function from body to space; a process that corresponded in this thinking with a shift from the "will" of the material to the idea. Rubio Tuduri made this point with his remark: "In the German Pavilion in Barcelona, architecture stops being matter. It becomes incantation and symbol."[41]

It seems futile to ask to what degree art theoretical works were important for the practical realization of Mies's aims.[42] His statements, containing only a few spare references to spatial problems, give us no answer.[43] The disinclination to engage in speculation remained typical for Mies's attitude.

If there was a single text from which Mies might have received stimulation as to the problematics of space, it could have been the small, handy volume of the well-known Jugendstil artist August Endell, which had appeared in 1908 under the title *Die Schönheit der grossen Stadt*. The self-taught Endell had made a name for himself in 1896 with his spectacular firstling, the Elvira photographic studio in Munich. Less known than his highly ornamental architectural work were the numerous art theoretical writings of this former student of philosophy and psychology.[44]

As a regular reader of the periodical *Die Zukunft* Mies might have taken note of Endell, who published for the first time in this periodical in 1905. In 1908 it also printed excerpts from his book *Die Schönheit der grossen Stadt*.[45] Endell, who had attended Theodor Lipp's lectures in Munich on the theory of empathy, was in pursuit of a phenomenon that he called the "life of space." It was difficult to render a clear conception of this "life of space" because it was not explicable from the point of view of traditional architecture.

In order to understand this phenomenon, a new mode of seeing was called for that was motivated by an "enjoyment of the visible" and a "love of the object." Endell turned this poeticizing way of seeing toward the metropolis, which appeared to him like a Nicolas Poussin moodscape. Endell viewed the city with the eyes of a painter who is less interested in its structures than in the visual phenomenon of "city" and who is fascinated by its atmosphere, its "light space," and its manifold appearances.

Seen from this point of view, the architectonic element shifts to space itself. Endell enlightened his readers as to the limitations of the standard way of seeing: "Thinking of architecture, one generally means the building elements, the façades, the columns, the ornaments, and yet all this is only secondary. What is important is not the form but its reversal, the space, the emptiness, that spreads out rhythmically between the walls that define it and the vitality that is more significant than the walls. If one can experience space, its directions, its measures, then the movement of emptiness is equivalent to music, and one can gain access to an almost unknown realm, the realm of the architect and the painter."[46]

Not only the approach to a basic aesthetic concept of space might have been facilitated for Mies by this work of 1908. If one compares Endell's book with the Miesian pronouncements of the early twenties, one is under the impression of having found the secret source that supplied Mies with his decisive ideas. Almost all the key terms of his manifestos had already been employed by Endell: The "love for the here and now";[47] the accusation against a period that had embarked upon an "escape into the past" and that had no true comprehension of either the old or the new;[48] the aversion toward philistines and "romantics of all types;"[49] and beyond that, the poeticizing of the raw structure consisting of "rhythmically arranged iron beams."[50]

But in yet another decisive point the trace leads us to Mies. Presumably Endell's writings were the pathbreaking stimulus to which Mies owed his design for the glass skyscraper project for the Friedrichstrasse. The effect of the play of light on large glass panes—which, according to Mies, guided his design to obtain "a rich play of light reflection"—had similarly fascinated Endell; the construction of a large curtain of glass skin, a "curtain wall" as façade, excited his curiosity. Endell visualized the effect such a glass structure would have on the urban landscape as it rose over the surrounding houses and appeared "above them . . . luminous . . . like a high, red-shining mountain" that is "enflamed to glaring fire by the evening sun."

This imagery was elicited by the Friedrichstrasse railroad station built in 1884 that was situated right opposite the site planned for the glass skyscraper. But Endell's description was not of the actual railroad building. What attracted his glance, desirous of visual poetry, was "the enclosing panel that was suspended laterally over the tracks," the large "glass apron." "Wonderful this Friedrich-Strasse railroad station, when one stands on the outer track above the Spree where one cannot see any of its architecture except the large expanse of the glass apron and the contrast to the maze of petty houses all about. Particularly beautiful when dusk conceals with its shadows this confused environment"—and even in this point Mies's charcoal perspective follows its literary example exactly—"and then the many small panels begin to reflect the sunset and the entire plane assumes a colorful, shimmering life."[51]

Endell's way of seeing arose out of that "novel aesthetic attitude," that "special aesthetic" that was the prerequisite for an artistic appreciation of construction.[52] Mies shared Endell's enthusiasm for the new construction methods and materials, both as to the intense aesthetic impression they made in space and to the play of light on their smooth surfaces. This play of light reflections, raised by Mies to a criterion of form-giving, was thematized as a new way of seeing by Endell. In his poetics of space and in Mies's glass visions, buildings were transposed into abstract, silent volumes that were called to life only by the effects of "fortuitous illumination, a beautiful distribution of shadows."[53]

Endell demonstrated the extent to which aesthetic fantasy can shift the principles of spatial apprehension from the material to the ideated and to the will to see. In his eyes, the powerful electric street lamps carved "gigantic vaults into the air" forming a space totally penetrated by light. Here man entered a "vault of light" that afforded a unique spatial experience: one found oneself in a "room" that was both limited and open, defined by "a transparent yet clearly perceived wall."[54] The modern explanation of space as given, for example, by Theo van Doesburg in 1925 affirms this sensual apprehension of space. Space is not perceived as a "measurable, limited surface" but rather in terms of "a concept of expansion that results from the relationship of one form-giving element to another."[55] The modern concept of space is ambivalent, for it is conceptualized in terms of opposites, or as Mondrian expressed it, it is a space that is "not enclosed but nevertheless limited."[56] The "open space formation" as Mies understood it, consisted of a novel type of architectonic space that is "harboring but not confining."[57] It conforms to the needs of modern man for both freedom and refuge. In the Tugendhat House, which stands in direct succession to the Barcelona Pavilion, Mies could realize this spatial idea in practically ideal purity. Here, a "space of a totally new type has been developed" that, according to Riezler in 1931, had "neither an immediately apprehensible unifying system nor any pronounced limitations."[58] Its peculiarity lay in its contradictoriness, which had been brought into such well-honed balance that one's apprehension of spatiality could orient itself to either openness or closedness. The secret of this interlocking of spatial concepts lay in the ambivalence of the respective archetypes. In the Tugendhat House Mies gave an interpretation of a house that was simultaneously cell and world, protective refuge yet open.

The wall-high windows, a "membrane"[59] that offered no resistance to the eye, connected the transparent microcosm of the interior with the expanse of landscape and sky. Space, although enclosed and self-contained, appeared to fuse with the universe.[60] It afforded tranquility and movement, static and dynamic, security and adventure, or permitted—in terms of the

"Glass curtain" on the Friedrichstrasse railroad station, Berlin.

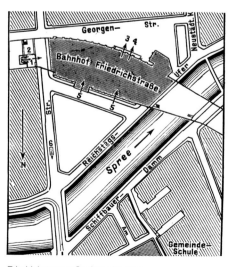

Friedrichstrasse Station, site plan.

Skyscraper project, Friedrichstrasse.

German Pavilion, Barcelona International Exposition, 1928–1929, entrance.

Apollonian and Dionysian that Ebeling employed to denote that "activated space"—both "absolute possibility for concentration" and "Dionysian fervor." Furthermore the Tugendhat House, the large glass panes of which could be lowered by the mere pressing of a button, fulfilled the need of a "serene, astrologically minded man" for "undiminished views and . . . the light from the nocturnal sky."[61]

The Miesian space offers man the possibility "of a true retreat," which, according to Ebeling, promises a new measure of freedom. The "wide, tranquil spaces" of the Tugendhat House, appreciated by its owner as a home to which he joyfully returned,[62] invite to contemplation, to "reveries of tranquility" (Bachelard).[63] To a space open to the span of the horizon corresponded an interior that was "severe and large, but in a manner that was expansive rather than oppressive."[64] Only the select preciousness of the materials in their extreme range from chrome to onyx and the opulence of the surfaces and colors[65] with which the interior was fitted out prevented one's losing oneself in infinity. The Tugendhat House was less a residence than an ideal example of the building art. In the poetics of its space, inside and outside, the tangible and the expansive combined in an intense spatial experience the rhythm of which found its resolution on one hand in a "fusion with the cosmos" (W. Riezler) but on the other hand also in a harmony with man, inviting him to take possession of space: "One must move in this space, its rhythm is like music."[66]

Tugendhat House, Brno, 1928–1930, entrance.

In this space prevailed "the spirit of technology" (W. Riezler); it spoke out of the nickel-clad posts, the mechanical installations, and the steel furniture, yet it did so here not in the sense of "that oft-lamented functionality but rather in the sense of a newfound freedom." The ultimate value and significance of this house as an ideal creation of the building art lay in this mastery of technical means: Mies proved here "that it is possible to reach for the realm of the spirit from the basis of what has up to now been a purely rational and functional concept of modern building. What has occasionally been questioned is here affirmed: the building art, for the first time in a long while, is again prepared to meet even the highest demands." As Walter Riezler stated in conclusion, in the space of the Tugendhat House the expression of a universal world feeling has been found that, "just as much as in philosophy, announces a new world image."[67]

The vantage point of modern man was explained by Mies in his 1928 lecture on "The Preconditions of Architectural Work," in which he spelled out the philosophical premises of his building art. The old order has lost its meaning for modern man, who embraces the new world and now "fights with its means." His work is "unrestricted" and lies no longer "in the shadow of conventions"; it "feels its way toward new possibilities" of life by way of experiment.[68] This is the result of the "changed situation" in which the existential problematic of a new type of living is reflected, a living that has severed itself from ties to the past, thereby gaining access to new possibili-

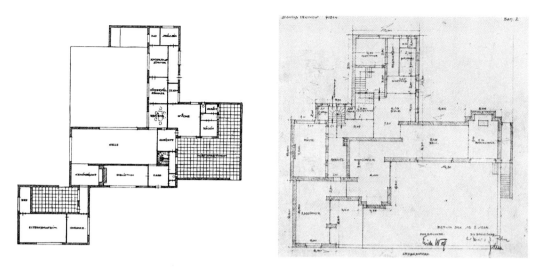

Left, Lessing House, Berlin, 1923; *right,* Wolf House, Guben, 1926.

Residential block in Stuttgart-Weissenhof, 1927, variable ground plans.

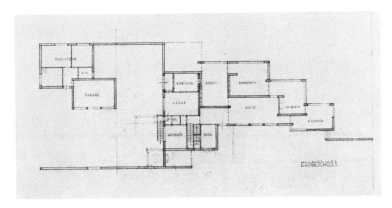

Esters House, Krefeld, 1927–1930.

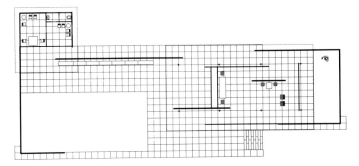

Barcelona Pavilion.

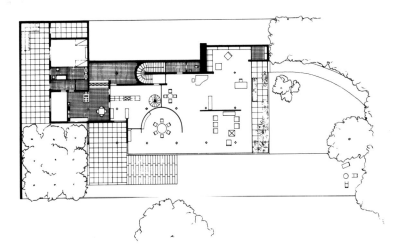

Tugendhat House.

Barcelona Pavilion, interior.

Tugendhat House, interior.

Barcelona Pavilion, exterior.

ties. However, modern man has also assumed the burden of a new responsibility insofar as he must now impart meaning and form to his own world.

The task facing the architect was therefore not primarily practical, technical, or formal in nature but philosophical. In the concluding words of his speech at the Vienna meeting of the Werkbund in 1930, Mies stated this conviction very clearly. The architect did not draw the consequences from the new mode of living and producing by a mere acceptance of mechanization, typification, and norms. It was much more important to demonstrate "how we assert ourselves toward these givens. It is here that the spiritual problems begin. What matters is not the what but only the how. That we produce goods and the means by which we produce them says nothing spiritually. Whether we build high or flat, with steel or with glass, says nothing as to the value of this way of building . . . But it is exactly this question of values that is decisive."[69]

As to the value of building, the responsibility of the architect does not exhaust itself in supplying adequate living space but must take into account a specific quality of life. The work of the master builder must begin by assigning to values "an order that permits free play for the unfolding of life."[70] Without this "genuine order," as Mies called it, "authentic life" is not possible, namely a life that—just like the Miesian space—is reclusive without hampering the "unfolding of the spirit."[71] It is not possible to articulate a critique of the then-prevailing functionalism more succinctly than Mies did in 1930: "For the meaning and justification of each epoch, even the new one, lies only in providing conditions under which the spirit can exist."[72]

Tugendhat House, exterior.

VI Architecture for the Search for Knowledge: The Double Way to Order

It is understood in all cultures that the spirit extrapolates an independent object through which the development of the subject from itself to itself takes its passage.

Georg Simmel, Philosophische Kultur, *1911*

Fulfill the law to gain freedom.

Ludwig Mies van der Rohe *(around 1950)*

"It began with Hölderlin and led very soon to Nietzsche, with the strange result that the Catholic cleric was considerably less distrustful and skeptical toward the phenomenon of Nietzsche than I, the Protestant with only a philosophical interest in Zarathustra and Dionysus." So reports Paul Fechter, commenting on his first meeting with Romano Guardini in the mid-twenties.

And in his book *An der Wende der Zeit* (At the Turning Point of Time), which devoted a whole chapter to Guardini, Fechter also reported on the second, accidental encounter he had with this professor of theology that took place in the studio of the wife of the painter Werner Scholz in Steglitz: "In this warm studio ambience the small figure of Professor Guardini arose from an easy chair as he welcomed us with a good and friendly smile that had an even more immediate and direct effect here than in the pulpit. Opposite to him, another guest had been seated approximately of the same height and just as slender, but more erect and tense than Guardini and of a somewhat sharper profile. It was the architect Mies van der Rohe . . ."[1]

Nietzsche, Guardini, Mies van der Rohe: these names, lining up almost coincidentally in Fechter's recollection, point to an imaginary axis that existed like an invisible spiritual order in the background. Romano Guardini was to play the decisive role in the clarification of Mies's building art, which sought to find itself in the search for a higher order. The conceptual ambivalence that hid in the words "building art" Mies had attempted to resolve in the twenties with his large-scale design projects: first there had been a flight forward into dramatic simplification under the sign of the primacy of construction and *Zeitwille*; toward the end of the decade there was an ideal creating of space in which material and construction, matter and idea, fused in a poetic equation into a new higher harmony, a "realm of the spirit" (W. Riezler) that appeared to announce a new "world image."

In the Barcelona Pavilion not only construction and material and thus the building as such, but even space itself had become symbol. Mies's building of the twenties spanned the architectonic range of possibilities from the extreme of the purely functional to the extreme of the purely representational. Mies appeared to have attained around 1930 that measure of "religious energy" (van Doesburg) that Walter Riezler registered in his discussion of the Tugendhat House with an audible sign of relief: the building art was "for the first time in a long while . . . again prepared to meet even the highest demands"—yes, "perhaps even the sacred one, provided one does not understand the sacred as the church presently understands it."[2]

Within the circumscribed spectrum Mies now attempted to redefine his position. The goal set in Stuttgart of leading building out of an "atmosphere of the unilateral and doctrinaire" (Mies) had its parallel in an architecture of thought that was equally opposed to all types of oversimplification. "Materialist and idealist. Unilaterally oriented and totally oriented. What can come of that?"[3]—a short note of Mies indicating that the architectural premise had been included in the wider horizon of ideological systems.

Many opportunities existed for encounters between Mies and Romano Guardini. Guardini, who had been called to the newly endowed chair for Philosophy of Religion and Catholic World Views at the University of Berlin in 1923, was also well known in the non-Catholic circles of the Berlin society of the mid-twenties. Mies might have encountered his name for the first time in the circle of friends around Alois Riehl. Possibly they met in November 1925 on the occasion of a series of lectures conducted at the Kunstgewerbeschule of Bremen. Here the names of Mies van der Rohe and Romano Guardini followed each other on the program.[4]

The first indications that Mies had met Guardini can already be detected in the beginning of 1927. And in the spring of 1928 the influence of Guardini becomes noticeable in the lecture "The Preconditions of Architectural Work," which gave an indication of how influential the acquaintance with the philosopher of religion, only one year older than Mies, was to become. Aside from sharing a common ideological basis, both men tended to conceptualize in terms of opposites.

Guardini had brought this dialectical thinking into a system that Mies could adapt without hesitation as it confirmed and legitimized his own contradictory positions. Thus Mies, who normally avoided public debates, entered with evident relief into a debate with Walter Riezler "On Form in Architecture." In the manuscript of his letter of January 1927, which is somewhat more expansive than the printed version, he performs a regular two-step of opposites: life and form, inside and outside, unformed and overformed, nothing or appearances, what had been or what had been thought, how and what, classical and Gothic, constructivist or functionalist. At the end came the resolution: "We are neither antiquity nor the Middle Ages, and life is neither static nor dynamic but includes both." Only a life "in its entire fullness"—so explains Mies without achieving greater clarity—can combine these opposites to arrive at real form.[5]

These words vividly recall a passage in a lecture given by Theo van Doesburg in 1922 in Berlin—"The Will to Style"—in which he interpreted the structure of life, in a very Nietzschean manner, as a "continuous evolution in life and art . . . that causes a reevaluation of all values," and in which life itself is viewed as a "battle between polarities." Doesburg had concluded in a very similar vein: "Neither an escape into the Middle Ages nor a reconstruction of Olympus, as advocated by art historians, can bring about a solution. . . . Neither feeling nor intellect alone can offer a solution to problems of art. . . . For life is not only static but also dynamic, not only constructive but also destructive; it is both simultaneously."[6]

Yet Mies did not speak with the words of Theo van Doesburg, of whom he did not think too much,[7] but with those of Romano Guardini. He had taken the arguments with which he countered Walter Riezler from Guardini's *Der Gegensatz. Versuche zu einer Philosophie des Lebendig-Konkreten* (Opposites: Attempt at a Philosophy of the Living and the Concrete) that had come out toward the end of 1925. In this work, Guardini immediately divided the "human existential condition" into a "first set of opposites that shall be called 'dynamic' and 'static,'" followed by others such as "structure and act," "duration and flux," "position and change." A very similar-sounding tentative conclusion was drawn that was so simple that one must restrain oneself not to call it banal: "Yes, life is experienced as something that comprises one as well as the other."[8]

"Every how is supported by a what. Only life intensity has form intensity" was the answer given by Mies to Walter Riezler as reason for his rejection of the latter's "form as goal"; and in saying this he may very well have had in mind a passage of Guardini's text that he had underlined: "Life is form, forming, form apprehension. Life intensity is form intensity. Yet it is precisely our time that stands in stark contrast to form. . . . Living form is always based on a 'what.' . . . It is not only the 'no' to form that is meant but something quite special, something that does not stand in contradiction to it, but in contrast . . . that 'something' that stands before each formal determination. . . . Life here is something that can only be expressed as simile; we will call it with a very trite word, 'fullness.' And the more profound life, the less specific is this 'fullness.' As fullness, life resists form."[9]

Guardini's dialectic, going back to Plato, German idealism, and the dialectic of the nineteenth and twentieth centuries, was also influenced by Schopenhauer, Nietzsche, Kierkegaard, Bergson, Simmel, Scheler, and Nicolai Hartmann;[10] it aimed at a unity that could not be apprehended either by the rational or by the intuitive faculty alone. By the same token, the building art could be seen as existing in a state of suspension that yielded neither to mathematical nor to artistic means unilaterally, but only assumed form, as Mies had it, out of the "entire fullness of life." Guardini's method had a certain constructive similarity to Mies's philosophy of building, insofar as polarity was viewed as a "basic model of experience"[11] corresponding to an elemental phenomenon of life. It represented the typicality of life, and thus constituted an elementary building block of reality, much as Mies needed for his concept of building, and one that he had thought to have found in construction. Guardini's attempt at a "philosophy of the living and the concrete" was a "rethinking from the inside" aimed at liberating thought from academic conventions and subjective limitations. Mies was guided by very similar thoughts in regard to building. Guardini wanted to see the fullness of reality unlocked not by abstract theorizing but by "rethinking concrete life," methodically, as "objective totality." "Life" is the crucial, central concept that functions as a corrective to thinking, for only in life are the opposites resolved.

Romano Guardini, at the end of the 1920s, at Castle Rothenfels. "We belong to the future. We must put ourselves into it, each one at his station. We must not plant ourselves against the new and attempt to retain a beautiful world, one that must perish. Nor must we try to build, with creative fantasy, a new one that claims to be immune to the ravages of becoming. We have to reformulate the nascent. But that we can only do if we honestly say yes to it; yet with incorruptible heart we have to retain our awareness of all that is destructive and inhuman in it. Our time is given to us as a soil on which we stand, and as a task that we have to master." Romano Guardini, *Briefe vom Comer See* (Mainz, 1927), p. 93.

Architecture for the Search for Knowledge:
The Double Way to Order

"Life is what matters" was the final argument Mies raised against Walter Riezler. The stress Guardini put on a philosophy of the living and the concrete was also echoed in these words of Mies: "We value not the result, but the starting point of the form-giving process. This in particular reveals whether form was derived from life or for its own sake."[12] And even more specific is an entry in Mies's notebook where the debate on form appears in its must succinct version "Fight with Riezler. Technical. We demand above all attitude. We want truth. Riezler beauty."[13]

What this "attitude" and "truth" represented can only be deduced by reverse logic. According to the statements, truth—much as life—must comprise opposites, a simultaneity of static and dynamic, and must be based on "living inwardness . . . on a what." The lesson of the interconnection between form and life that Mies learned from Guardini is easily reconstructible from his underlinings of passages. Beginning with the sentence "Fullness is not form," in which both categories represent a contrasting polarity, Guardini developed his thought in both directions. As "fullness of plastic and dynamic possibilities" life was only experienceable as a minimum of form and order. Where life went too far in the direction of fullness it led to chaos, "confusion," and existential "horror." If life went too far in the other direction in its search for order, creation, and form, then it entered upon "the second zone of polarity . . . the opposite extreme. . . . Pure form is no longer thinkable or possible; instead of evolving from the living, it is caricature: the formal. This is equivalent to death. Chaos is death, insofar as there is no attitude, no order . . . but schema is also death; frigidity and rigidity" (underlinings by Mies).[14]

This conflict of opposites was not resolvable by a redeeming formula. Life could not be thought of as a "synthesis of disparities" nor even as a whole the two sides of which are complementary "parts." It exists rather as an elemental form, a "bound duality" (underlined by Mies) that, "typical for human life," must be imagined as existing between two zones of death. The saying of Blaise Pascal that man is neither angel nor animal, and Friedrich Nietzsche's simile of man as a tightrope over an abyss, are discernible in Guardini's imagery.

Within that extreme delimitation, real life unfolds. In that respect it was—just like authentic building in the eyes of Mies—"an expression of spiritual decisions." Reality calls for an artfully designed order. Its principle of spiritual limitation requires that it be open toward the poles in order to attain fullness on one hand and a measure of definiteness on the other to secure existence against chaos. It was this "genuine order," as Mies called it, that was at issue: an order "with a reality content so large that authentic life can unfold in it."[15] Thus, too, "open space-form" realizes a "harboring but not a confining space" that secures life but allows room for the unfolding of the spirit, providing for twentieth-century man the ordered, if contrasting, reality of both freedom and retreat, expansiveness and restraint.

Guardini's dialectic brought two philosophical worlds in contact: the old world of the Platonic idea and the modern world of existential philosophy. Fundamental to his theory is his love of Plato, who could be equated with the religious. Next to it was the "tender love for life" that Guardini saw best expressed in Nietzsche's warning "It is dangerous and evil," for only that man who carries within himself the "power of adaptation" and who can face "each surprise of life with lightning speed by means of a new creative solution"[16] can, in the final analysis, survive.

As Hanna-Barbara Gerl so perceptively noted, "Nietzsche was, as so often, audible" behind Guardini,[17] who strove for a Platonic reevaluation of that Dionysian belief that, besides affirming its own existence, affirmed all of life. Guardini saw it as his task to revive Platonic thought *after* Kant and Nietzsche, after the declaration that "God is dead. We have killed him." Although he believed, along with Nietzsche that modern man can only find himself after jettisoning all the old symbols and deities, he also held that this new self-recollection, from which Siegfried Ebeling, too, had derived his ideas on space, had to go hand in hand with a fundamental experience of one's own limitations.

The new autonomy that resulted from the conquest over traditionalism must, according to Guardini, be itself overcome by the descendants of modernism: imbued with the spirit of a newfound freedom, man has to recommit himself to responsibility toward the whole. A new "unifying con-sciousness" has to supercede modern subjectivism: "Our task," so Mies underlined in Guardini's text, "is to progress further to a new, albeit critically tested unity."[18]

As Hanna-Barbara Gerl has it, who has traced the passages and aims of Guardini's though with utmost care, the "spiritual conquest of the future" should "lead to something even newer than the new time,"[19] namely an order that harnesses the forces of progress to guarantee life its requisite breathing space.

Thus Guardini called for something with which Mies was in profound agree-ment: another, new, but not unilateral modernism in which subjective forces were restrained by objective limits, but in which, conversely, the potentially threatening objective powers inherent in technology were subordinated to the subject, to man and his life. This constellation conformed very much to the position Mies had taken up since 1927, accepting the technological as a means of realization and also seeing it as a potential threat.

In this concept of a modernism conscious of the limitations of technology—a concept to which today in the crisis of modernism and postmodernism considerable actuality accrues—we find Mies decidedly in the shadow of Guardini. His writings[20]—and this deserves to be emphasized here again—were studied by Mies particularly in that time period that immediately pre-ceded the planning phase of the Barcelona Pavilion and the Tugendhat House.[21]

The great responsibility that rests on the shoulders of modern man is the need to establish a balance between ruling and serving, between freedom and order. What mattered, and Mies by his underlinings concurred, was to "reconnect the spontaneity of experience, the power of personality, the uniqueness of feeling, with discipline and attentiveness toward the objective world" and to lead a life "obedient to the objective order of reality . . . to the true nature of one's soul, to the objects, to the community, to the world, and to God."[22] This then was synonymous with a "proper attitude."

The following "sketch," arranged by Mies significantly under the title "programmatical points," renders in outline the constitutive polarities underlying Guardini's precepts: "Independence and adjustment to the communal. Space for personal development and subordination to the whole. Freedom and law; flux and order; ruling and serving; subjective and objective. Powerful totality. Meaningful, proper order. Appropriate, suitable attitude. From inside to outside and from outside to inside. Inner order instead of organization. Isolation of the physical by the spiritual. Contemplativeness and will to expression."[23]

In 1923 Guardini described the task facing the new period: "We have to build the new objectivity as men that have progressed through the late Middle Ages and through the present" (underlined by Mies); and the awareness of standing on the threshold of a new epoch he summarized in the sentence: "We stand at the turning point of two cultures."[24]

"We stand at the turning point of the times" was the motto chosen by Mies as central theme for his 1928 lecture "The Preconditions of Architectural Work,"[25] which attests, together with the corresponding entries in the notebook, to the influence exerted by Guardini.

Mies began his lecture by introducing a series of slides showing the "confusing and inadequate products of the present building art," that led from Oud, Gropius, Mendelsohn, by way of Poelzig, Höger, Tessenow, Fischer, Schmitthenner up to Schultze-Naumburg. Quite provocatively, in staccato as it were, Mies produced these photos in quick succession without any word of explanation:

Since these products may not instantly be recallable by everybody in full precision, and since words have lost their unambiguous meaning, I will clarify the present situation by means of a series of illustrations. . . . The choice of pictures does not constitute a value judgment, but only serves to clearly characterize the situation. Nor will I take a position in regard to these pictures, as I am convinced that the chaotic character of our building art will appear all by itself.

And the stony comment "That is today's building art" obtained its bitter aftertaste by such subsequent statements as "chaos" and "a sign of anarchy." Such a situation calls for a historical excursus. In order to show the meaning of the present situation in its historical dimension, Mies equated it with the "chaos" of "once upon a time," namely when the order of antiquity broke up into late antiquity.

That epoch also offered a suitable solution for the crisis. On the basis of the Platonic order, Augustine formulated "the medieval idea of order" that introduced a new epoch. In it, the antique spirit of "proportion exemplified and founded by Plato," in which Mies saw the noblest inheritance from antiquity, opened up a "totally new dimension."

Here was an exemplary—if not to say *the* exemplary—solution offered by history, namely how, by a recollection of the Platonic world of ideas, the problems of a period could be solved. That this orientation toward Plato was initiated by Guardini can practically be taken for granted. Antiquity had moved for Mies into a new perspective. The receipt accompanying the periodical *Die Antike,* purchased from Herder's bookstore on July 23, 1928, with the notice "enclosed journal contains: Jaeger, 'Plato's Position,'" shows the reason why Mies had ordered this publication from the bookseller: His interest had been aroused by a discussion of Werner Jaeger on "Plato's position in the structuring of Greek education."[26]

The particular exemplariness of the Middle Ages consisted for Mies in the idea of an order that gives man "a totally assured view of the meaning of life." The "healthy condition of that period of society" derived from an

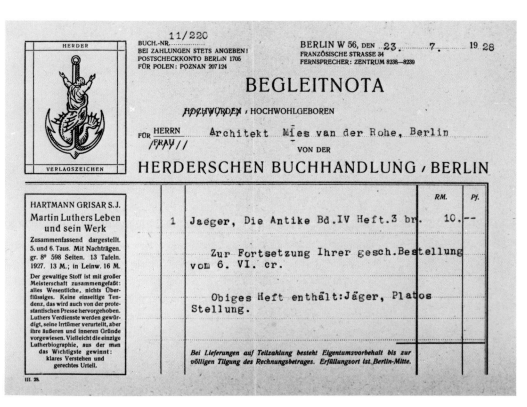

Mies's receipt for a copy of *Die Antike.*

"objectively correct sequence of spiritual life and use values. . . . Belief and science had not yet split apart." Paul Ludwig Landsberg's *Die Welt des Mittelalters und wir* (The World of the Middle Ages and Us) had recommended to Mies the "*ordo* as icon for the avant-garde."[27] Mies took over, almost verbatim, Landsberg's concept of the Middle Ages and the role of Augustine as great bringer of order,[28] a role in which Mies secretly might have wished to see himself.

The reference to the medieval thinkers Johannes Duns Scotus and William of Occam had also been taken by Mies from this text, to which he was to return in 1927–1928.[29] Aided by Landsberg and Guardini, both of whom stayed safely and namelessly in the background, Mies rendered a historical outline of the "process of disintegration" of the spiritual order that, beginning with Duns Scotus and William of Occam, introduced the modern age and led finally to the "victory of nominalism," as Mies explained in proper academically correct terminology—or rather cited tacitly.[30]

With the Renaissance, which moved even further from the antique sources of the Middle Ages, a new and fateful phase of history had begun: "More and more, spiritual life tends toward the will. The act of the autonomous individual becomes ever more important. People study nature. The control of nature became the longing of the period." Again Mies confronted his listeners with a name, this time that of the English statesman and philosopher Francis Bacon, scarcely a household name, who wanted to see the old method of finding truth in the spirit of Aristotle and the Scholastics replaced by experiments and the methodological observation on nature. Mies must have encountered this name in Friedrich Dessauer's *Philosophie der Technik* of 1927. Here he also found the headings for that part of his lecture that reached into the nineteenth century: "Middle Ages, show order. Harmony. Econom[y]. Renaissance. Personalities. Experiment. Art and science. Bacon. Influence on economy. Alienation because of profit. Bourgeoisie."[31]

These were the various stations of the fateful historical trajectory that was finally to end in chaos. Mies noted: "Question: What does mankind need, or how can I earn the most? Decisive is which question has primacy. . . . The idea of earnings had to lead to isolation. The idea of service leads to community."[32] The ultimate cause of those problems "that still lie before us today" arose out of an abuse of the newly gained spiritual freedom and power of self-determination. The "aggrandizement of the personality" and the "unbinding of the will to power" that began with the Renaissance had entered, with the "fateful alliance between iron and coal" and the subjugation of science by technology and economy, into a new phase of historical development. Supported by the progress of technology, which like an autonomous power broke through all barriers, man respected no limits:

Nothing seems impossible anymore. Thus begins the reign of technology. Everything succumbs to its impact. It detaches man from his restrictions,

Barcelona chair, 1929.

makes him freer and becomes his great helper, breaks down the isolation of geographical locations and bridges the largest distances. The world shrinks more and more, becomes surveyable and is investigated down to its remotest recesses. The characteristics of peoples become clear. Their social and economic structures are uncovered. World consciousness and a conscious awareness of mankind results. . . . Technology offers a thousand means to increase awareness. Nothing occurs anymore that is not observed. We survey ourselves and the world in which we stand. Consciousness is our very attitude.[33]

Ultimately this was not Mies but Romano Guardini talking. It was his description of the situation of mankind in the progressive industrial age that Mies—supported by his excerpts[34]—here rendered in essence.

But this was not the only place that showed that Mies, in the beginning of 1928, still stood under the powerful impact of the impressions received from Romano Guardini's *Briefe vom Comer See* (Letters from Lake Como) that had appeared toward the end of 1927. The visible traces already speak of the sense of involvement with which he read this book. His underlinings lose their usual restraint. Twice and occasionally three times he guides his pencil in rapid strokes up and down the margin of the page. The hand seems to register the inner excitement like a seismograph. Occasionally entire pages are marked up. Worse, Mies even scribbles, as he does nowhere else, across the typed text itself. In a large, generous ductus diagonally superimposed over the entire page, he gives his own title headings to the material: "Cultural Concept," "Attitude," "Perception," "Seniors."[35]

With these concepts the basic chords of an ideology were sounded in which the phenomena of the modern time signaled a cultural upheaval of epoch-making dimension. In his *Briefe vom Comer See,* Guardini had registered horror at the intrusion of the new into the old historical landscape of his northern Italian homeland: "Invasion by the machine of a land that hitherto had culture. I saw how death falls over a life of infinite beauty"—that is how Mies summarized this shocking experience in his notes.[36]

Yet at the terminal point of Guardini's contemplation, which dealt with the fundamental contrast between nature and culture and searched for the possibilities of cultural continuity under the new conditions—something that Mies in his notes traced step by step[37]—one finds by no means resignation. Guardini made it clear that it was not technology and its innate regularity that has to be viewed as the actual evil, but that it is the attitude man assumes toward these things that is decisive: "This new world is destructive . . . because the man that belongs to it is not yet here . . . it has not yet been conquered humanistically. It is an onrushing of unchained forces that are not yet curbed" (underlinings by Mies).[38]

Mies, in his lecture of 1928, unilaterally endorsed this diagnosis.[39] The detour into history, which was meant to lay bare "the structure of our time," terminated in a corresponding image of contemporary technological and scientific "achievements":

Technology follows its own laws and is not man-related. Economy becomes self-serving and calls forth new needs. Autonomous tendencies in all these forces assert themselves. Their meaning seems to be the attainment of a specific phase of development. But they assume a threatening predominance. Unchecked, they thunder along. Man is swept along as if in a whirlwind. Each individual attempts to brace himself against these forces singly. We stand at a turning point of time.

At this point, Mies returns to the initially rendered outline that showed the panorama of contemporary building: "You can now understand why the result in contemporary building art must be so confusing, as I have demonstrated. But even in this chaos, various types of structures are clearly discernible."

For Mies, three groups delineate themselves. The first group represents the belief "that even in our changed world, the means and methods of past epochs can be applied to solve the tasks of time. Their work is determined by the fear that invaluable treasures could be lost. And also by the belief that it is impossible, in the hard and clear atmosphere of technology and consciousness, that artistic and spiritual values can unfold. . . . They still believe in the vitality of the old order." Toward this group, in other places severely criticized as "men with the backward glance," Mies here demonstrated considerable tolerance: "We are not entitled to hold their achievements in low respect, even if we believe that the world to which they incline and in which they are rooted is inevitably sinking. We are obligated to appreciate their efforts, for they transmit values and insights that we must not lose sight of."

A second group that stood in the middle, still beholden to the old though it had opened itself up to the new, was only mentioned for the sake of completeness and was passed over as inconsequential, in a silent rebuke for its characterlessness.

For the third group, "the old habitual order" had become unbearable, it had lost its meaning and vitality: "It [this group] affirms the new world and fights with its means. It is feeling its way toward new possibilities of form-giving." This group corresponded in its attitude to the demands set by Guardini, who saw the advance signals of the new age primarily in works of architecture.[40] Not by romantic glances into the past, not by returns, reversals, or withholdings, "not even by mere changes or improvements" was the threat of chaos avertable, according to Guardini—"a chaos that will emerge as the result of our own doings." Only a deliberate "affirmation of our time" and "a new attitude" determined by a "new sense of relationships, of proportions and limits, of interchange . . . a totally new sensibility for nuances and gradations, a sensibility for projection and interconnections," could avert the danger.[41]

Guardini supplied the voice, occasionally by verbatim quotes, at other times by slightly altered citations, that is heard in Mies's moving finale:

Our time is not an external course on which we run. It has been given to us as a task that we have to master. . . . We have to affirm it, even if its forces still appear menacing to us. We have to become master of the unleashed forces and build them into a new order, an order . . . that is related to mankind. But that cannot happen from the technological problems themselves, but from living men. No matter how immense knowledge may be, how huge the economical apparatus, how powerful technology, all that is only raw material compared to life. We do not need less but more technology. We see in technology the possibility of freeing ourselves, the opportunity to help the masses. We do not need less science, but a science that is more spiritual; not less, but a more mature economic energy. All that will only become possible when man asserts himself in objective nature and relates it to himself.[42]

Even the concluding challenges, whose rhythmical, repetitious "It must be possible . . ." was meant to intensify the message, had been taken over from Guardini's *Briefe vom Comer See*. In typical juxtapositions, Mies announced: "It must be possible to heighten consciousness and yet keep it separate from the purely intellectual, . . . to solve the task of controlling nature and yet create simultaneously a new freedom, . . . to see elitism disappear and admit the fact of the masses, the fact that each of the many has a right to life and goods," and yet that this mass can "come to articulation from within itself."

These paired polarities fused into a confession of belief in which Mies cited his spiritual mentor Guardini, who in turn reiterated Nietzsche's thesis of men's gullibility. "It must be possible to let go of illusions, to see our existence sharply delineated and yet gain a new dimension, a dimension that arises out of the spirit."[43] And Mies concluded his lecture with the words: "But all that can only happen if we regain our belief in the creative powers, if we trust the power of life."

In these passages one can detect that "expression of a universal world feeling" that Walter Riezler sensed in the Miesian space in 1930. Guardini's theology and Mies's building art were interconnected by a philosophy in which—according to Riezler's remarks in regard to Miesian space—"a totally new world image" seemed to announce itself.[44] In it, justice was done to man's own temporal existence *and* the immutable laws of eternity to arrive at "a new order of value and of human existence."[45] Not something totally new, but a new totality stood at the heart of this philosophy. It opens its "membrane to the spirit of the epoch" (Jürgen Habermas) and has a sensitive feeler for timely processes, for aesthetic renovation and for major epochal changes, much as Guardini had diagnosed when he typified "consciousness" as the mentality of the new period. Modern man was characterized by a new relationship to himself. "Rhythmical culture of the body" (Guardini), new disciplines of research, and such sciences as psychology, traffic, and technology were all expressions of this process of coming into consciousness, along with the loss of "illusion" that goes hand in hand with it.[46]

In contrast to the old world order, this new, disillusioned, "sharply delineated" reality is immensely more complex and comprehensive. The plethora of individual appearances, the variety of interests and convictions must approach, in the dialectical philosophy of Guardini, a condition of chaos, a "death zone" that is symptomatic of the crisis of the present and its building. "Chaos in all areas, economic, social, spiritual"—so sounded the somber assessment of the existential threat to which Mies attached, silently, the anxious question that exceeded even the pessimism of Spengler: "Decline not only of the West but of the world"[47]

Modern subjectivism and mechanism was in need of a counterforce. The crisis of modern consciousness could only be stemmed by a new belief not only in man himself, but in an overarching absolute that challenges forth a new commitment to society. Contemporary subjectivism and the forces it unleashed could only be mastered by an ideology rooted outside the realm of the visible.[48] The passage has to lead beyond Nietzsche, the prototype of autonomy, to Plato, who thought in eternal and absolute terms, so that the ties to a spiritual, primordial order that alone contains the ultimate logic can be renewed. Sustaining values cannot be founded in individual existence with its limitations and finiteness or in the autonomy of the will but only in the objective laws of eternal being. This is the meaning of Mies's remark that the belief in the creative forces has to be regained.

The key to an "objective attitude" as demanded by Guardini was this "double way into the immanent." On it Mies erected the "organic order" of the building art, of which he was to talk in 1938. The "double way into the immanent" leads, as Mies noted in 1928, both beyond the "unique and special" and beyond "the permanent and universal": "We cannot go one way without also going the other. We find the immanent in the particular only if we are simultaneously open to its place in the universal."[49]

This openness to the universal referred to that new contact with the infinite advocated by Mies and Guardini that concerned itself with the problematic of being. Here was the "beginning of the humanism of this changed world," as Werner Jaeger affirmed in his 1929 essay "Die Geistige Gegenwart der Antike" (The Spiritual Presence of Antiquity) that Mies had obtained as a special printing, probably from the author himself. In it, Jaeger retraced the "line of development of our relationship to antiquity" that led back to Plato by way of Winckelmann, Goethe, Hölderlin, and Nietzsche, so that "with the help of the Greeks, we can find our way back to the whole." Especially a time that had lost confidence in its instincts appeared, according to Jaeger, predestined for a new, spiritual rather than formal-aesthetic confrontation with antiquity: "Plato has been revived like no other representative of antiquity."[50]

An "inner breadth," an "ability to believe in skepticism," as Guardini called it—this "infinity that emerges from the spirit" of which Mies spoke—should drive existence from "subjective constraints and arbitrariness" out into the larger perspective of "objective order," toward "a new self-discovery in the world" that, for Guardini's philosophy of religion and Mies's philosophy of architecture, is the proper goal of the human spirit.[51]

As Mies's February 1928 talk clearly proved, the dominance of Guardini's thought was so strong that the borders of identity frequently dissolved. The spiritual "preconditions of architectural work" had been largely determined by Guardini's presence in the background, and the question presents itself to what degree Guardini's intellectual presence also was influential for the results of Mies's architectural creation. Already the external circumstances seem to point to such an influence. The revamping of spiritual conditions that had begun in 1926 preceded a revolution of his architectonic reality that delineated itself very clearly in the programmatic building projects of Barcelona, Brno, and the Berlin Building Exposition. The new freedom and profundity with which space and volume were handled became fundamental for Mies's building art.

In particular in regard to the Barcelona Pavilion, the planning phase of which fell into the year 1928, the proximity of philosophy to architecture becomes difficult to ignore. This was a display structure the function of which was to point to itself as objective meaning. Regardless of the external impetus—the listing of the Spanish royal couple in the Golden Book—there were no concrete functions to be fulfilled that could have disturbed the impression of an ideal Platonic object. With this building Mies had the opportunity to deliver a similarly confessional testimony for a new, nonunilateral modernism, this time using the language of architecture. This seems indicated both by the closeness in time and the emotional tone that marked Mies's words in 1928, allowing us to construe the Barcelona Pavilion as a sort of spiritual "program." With this building Mies could deliver an architectonic example of that "totally new power . . . that new dynamic" that, according to Guardini, was called for so that the aspects of modern man's reality can be "seen in tandem."[52]

The metaphysical space of existence outlined by Guardini was "illuminated by the internal power of form-giving." In it a life unfolded in which man, "surrounded by greatness, by width," created his world in harmony with the absolute order of the world. The northern Italian cultural landscape of humanism delivered the prototype for this existence in which nature "without hesitation," all of itself, as it were, turned into "culture." Here the opposing orders of man and nature met and complemented each other to form a higher entity finding its expression in the harmonious relationship between landscape and architecture. Guardini's poetic descriptions of visits to Villa Pliniana near Lecco and Villa Giulia near San Giovanni on Lake Como had arisen out of a symbolic perception of space, the religious energy of which made the experience of those encounters with the Italian Renaissance villa a metaphor. "Do you not feel here nature and man's work wedded?" was the question Guardini asked his readers after completing his description of Villa Giulia and leading them into a sunlit arcadia that appeared to have been created solely so that man can move in it: "The entire layout so that man can stride through sunlight, over heights, in fully formed greatness."[53]

The spatial discipline of the northern Italian villa, emphatically described by Guardini, conveys the idea of an ideal existence to which he thought modern man should become receptive. It is not inappropriate to glance at the Barcelona Pavilion with Guardini's descriptions in mind and to ask whether Mies might not have been guided by quite similar motives when he placed this building, reduced to a minimum of restrictive materials, like a transparent gate symbolically in the way of the visitor to the world's fair.[54]

May one not assume that Mies wanted to reerect in a small way an analogous cultural landscape transposed into the modern present, a shape that was in a sense only built to be perambulated? Should not man here quite

Farnsworth House, 1945–1950.
"When one ties up at San Giovanni on the lakeshore, on a terrace on which a stonemason has now set up his shop, one sees a beautifully built stair climb up toward the land . . . toward the Villa Giulia. How delightful was this climbing and how indescribably wonderful the walking! Surrounded by greatness, by width, by sky and sun . . . all illuminated by the power of form-giving. . . . A large garden space opens up . . . within it, nothing . . . only space. But the villa of such simplicity that you marvel. . . . The entire layout so that man can stride through sunlight, over heights, in fully formed greatness." Romano Guardini on the Villa Giulia near San Giovanni, in *Briefe vom Comer See.*

deliberately be guided to another space so that he can perceive something of that "message from beyond, from the distance" (Guardini) and open his soul to it? And did not the description of the Italian villa lead Mies back to Schinkel's variation of the theme, and did not the critics, viewing Mies's pavilion and seeing Schinkel's Charlottenhof arise before their inner eyes, attest to a subliminal influence of Guardini's *Letters from Lake Como*? And is this newly awakened orientation toward Platonic thought not actually a continuation of a dialogue with classicism and the "spiritual presence of antiquity" that had already begun two decades earlier?

If one traces the statements, notes, and marginal markings of Mies, these questions can be answered affirmatively. Guardini's "double way into the immanent" led to a world internally shaped by variety and contrast, one that—much like Mies's space—can be described as open yet interrelated and "oriented." Two elements encounter each other in this space: the rational and the metaphysical, the limiting and the unlimiting. The visitor is sensitized to that "new infinity that arises out of the spirit" that Mies had expressed a longing for in his lecture of 1928. Here modern man could receive the sacrament of "inner expanse" that he so badly needed so he could "find himself in the universal expanse."[55]

The perambulation of the Pavilion was a symbolic act: the extraordinary spatial intensity gave the visitor the impression of having entered another world.[56] Enriched by the feeling of having gained, from the vantage point of this delimited interior, a new view of the outside world, he returned—elevated by an aesthetic vision of reality—back into that world out of which he had come.

Such a new intensity and symbolic experiencing is what Guardini hoped man would feel upon entering a church. His call "Man must again become able to think symbolically!"[57] aimed at such a renewed sensibility. Man should, in perambulating an ordered realm, become again a "seer" who can experience freshly what is expressed in things—in nature, in words, and in buildings—as "sacred signs" revealing the divine secret. With a remark in regard to the loss of symbolic value in architecture, and sounding very much like Guardini, Mies answered: "Steps, spaces. One has lost the meaning of this language, . . . one feels nothing anymore. . . . Who still feels anything of a wall, an opening? . . . We want to give meaning again to things."[58]

The Pavilion revealed an ideal world of opposites and a gradation of value. An order of becoming took up its position on the pedestal, the spiritual principles of which rested visibly on Platonic thinking. Plato's position in humanistic thought was transcribed by Mies into architectonic terms. The grid of slender pillars followed the geometrical net drawn by the seams of the travertine plates.[59] Their cruciform pattern demarcated the coordinates at which the concrete and the dematerialized orders interlock. The grid of pillars was not so much a statically required support system as a measured mediator of the infinite. In this order was placed a rhythmical sequence of wall panels that might answer to Siegfried Ebeling's demand for a Dionysian reevaluation of space. This new arrangement of space symbolically attests, in the freedom of its concepts, to that "spatial declaration of the changed situation" (Mies) in which the modern, self-contained individual finds himself.

The architectonics of the Pavilion demonstrate Guardini's "double way into the intrinsic" by idealizing in both directions: the pedestal conveys the belief in an ideal past rooted in the eternal; the artfully arranged dynamic balance of the freestanding wall panels of the Pavilion announce faith in an ideal future in which all opportunities stand open. Origin and utopia, myth and idea fused in Mies's spatial poetry.

The broad, strong wall panels of onyx and vert antique and the glass walls embody substance in an exemplary fashion. Out of them Mies erected an open, one is tempted to say neoplastic, cella that permitted, much as in classical space, a view over the pedestal, framed by the supports. This cell, by the abolition of limits, is transformed into a place of the universal, an order that lies beyond its confines. Much as in Guardini's philosophy, the subjective is affirmed but oriented to an objective order. The freedom gained by the new technological space dynamics has been reevaluated by Mies in the spirit of the infinite. Instead of erecting his walls with light-weight, prefabricated wall segments, which could have been fitted into the support structure—as would have been in keeping with such a temporary structure—Mies decided on onyx blocks that formed in their heaviness a gravitational counterweight to the grid of lightweight supports. Appearing in all its "natural" purity, this noble and valuable material shows in its structure a wealth of living forms and a temporal depth that could not have been exceeded by any historical building ornament or column order.

The steel supports also, to which Mies had given the profile of an even-armed cross, were related to an elemental form that could be viewed as the mystical symbol of all building. Encased in a garment of nickel, they remotely recalled Gothic pillars but also Greek columns with flutings. Furthermore, the shining skin imparted a dematerialized look that did not disrupt the unification of the space. The sky, the ultimate symbol of the yearning for infinity, was reflected on their polished surface.

Mies's "message of expanse" (Guardini) conveyed by architectural means the vision of the new ordering spirit that was the particular possibility innate in the time. "All possible freedom and yet such great profundity"[60]—this formula sized up for Mies the ideal existence, to the realization of which building had to make its contribution. To make conscious the possibilities residing in this freedom of movement in space and freedom of decision making, it was essential that the glance be reoriented to the absolute. Without that Platonic basis, this "encounter between the things and the soul," as Guardini had it, was not possible; without it the possibilities hid-

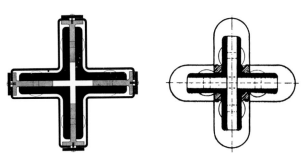

Cross section of the supports of the Barcelona Pavilion (*left*) and of the Tugendhat House (*right*).

den in the nature of things and in the nature of man could not unfold. In this place where the double ways into the immanent crossed, the creative principle is hidden that, while remaining itself secret, reveals itself in the form of things.[61]

Mies's building art rested on the belief in this possibility, supported by the longing and the hope that "in the hard and clear atmosphere of technology and consciousness, artistic and spiritual values could unfold."[62] That "It must be possible" that Mies had taken from Guardini pointed to the spiritual goal of his building, which aimed to throw a bridge over the abyss of contrasting worlds: "I felt that it should be possible," wrote Mies in 1965, looking back on his career, "to bring the old and the new forces of our civilization into harmony with each other. Each of my buildings was a demonstration of these thoughts, and a further step in my own search for clarity."[63] To give form to the invisible part of the visible world, namely the possible, was the task that connected the philosopher to the artist. In Barcelona Mies made experienceable by artistic means that metaphysical space that resides behind all empirical space, so that men who crossed this frame would feel the possibilities of a hidden life, both in themselves and in their epoch.

"This spiritual goal was a necessity, even if many see only the object and not the idea," wrote Wilhelm Lotz on the occasion of the Berlin Building Exposition in 1931 in defense of Mies's model house and his concept of the building art. "For Mies's houses are nothing less than a large goal-setting projected into the future. . . . Here man has, in a spiritual sense, become the measure of spatiality, here artistic shaping of space has been expressed in a novel sense. . . . Whoever asks here for the patron and views him really and physically as the type of a specific class, does not understand this exhibition, for the patron is simply the new man."[64]

Herbert Gericke, professor and director of the Academy of Rome in 1932, had held a competition for the design of his residence and invited Mies to participate; but he soon decided against a "real artistic architect" because "I did not want to engage in a spiritual fistfight with that person over the form

Gericke House on Wannsee, Berlin, design, 1930.

of a door latch, but needed a malleable personality who 'did what I wanted.'" Mies's reply of November 3, 1932, to Gericke makes it unmistakably clear that Mies viewed the renovation and development of the residence and the realization of new spatial ideas as the actual task of building. Not only the architect but also the patron was culturally committed to this societal task.

Dear Professor,
I can only answer your letter today since I have been in the last weeks too busy with the reconstruction of the Bauhaus and what I have to tell you would not serve any purpose at this time. I understand that you insist on owning a house as you conceive of it and as you desire it and I regret that this did not offer the opportunity to make a decisive step toward the development of the residence.

I do not want to deny that we are disappointed that you conceive of this question so utterly as private. From whom can we expect a readiness for cultural service if not from persons who are professionally committed to the cultural life of the nation?[65]

One must read between the lines that Mies was not concerned with the autonomy of the architectural will as opposed to the patron's, as Adolf Loos has rendered it in satirical vein in his murder parody "of a poor, rich man,"[66] but that the very continuity of culture in Germany was then threatened. In the harassment directed against modernism under the new economic and political conditions since 1930, each voice counted.

"We hope and fear nothing," declared Mies in October 1932 to a newspaper reporter who asked him, as director of the Dessau Bauhaus that had closed down in April, as to his plans for a reopening of the school in Berlin.[67] One could not express this situation more tersely or succinctly. The crisis of the Bauhaus was in its own way a comment on the demise of the Weimar Republic. On July 20, 1933, the Bauhaus Mies had installed in a Steglitz factory yard was also closed down by the new power clique.

For Mies not much was left to say. In October 1932, on the anniversary of the Werkbund in Berlin, he gave his last public speech in Germany. He asked his hearers not to give in to resignation and "to keep awake in the young Germans an attitude of the work ethic and of utopian boldness. . . . One must not allow oneself to be seduced into being inactive out of fear or acting immaturely and dilettantishly. Especially now one must remain loyal to oneself, remain steadfast and stand firm. One must insist on what one has recognized as important."[68]

In March 1933, a few weeks after Hitler assumed power, Mies recalled once more, in his unpublished contribution on the significance of glass, that "measure of freedom in spatial composition that we will not relinquish any more."[69] His last position before his emigration to the United States in August 1938 was published in the *Schildgenossen* in summer 1935. Here Mies explains briefly his unrealized project for the Hubbe House in Magdeburg, which has to be viewed as standing in close proximity to the courtyard house design of the thirties. His remark in regard to the spatial ("here also, besides freedom, the necessary seclusion") points to a retreat into privacy. The court is the place of an inner emigration that took place long before the actual one. The theme of the courtyard house that Mies posed for himself in the thirties took on symbolic content. The Miesian dream of "freedom and profundity" retired from life to an inner room, with which the longing for a "beautiful exchange of tranquil seclusion and open expanse"[70] now had to content itself.

"I know of no more beautiful effect than to be secluded on all sides, insulated against the turmoil of the world, and to see above, free, the sky. In the evening." With these words the young architect Friedrich Gilly, teacher of Karl Friedrich Schinkel, had expressed in 1797 a mood of retreat from a torn world. In the open cella of a temple that crowned the legendary design for the Friedrich Memorial, Gilly had given a home to Hölderlin's dream of a life that rests "as if on slender columns and rightful orders."[71]

But the way to the outside, too, corresponded to the logic of the "double way." There was no lack of attempts by Mies to come to terms with the new power structure, and the willingness to enter into compromises went further than he himself later on, when his words tended to become legend, was willing to admit.[72] The questionability of this adaptation is already foreshadowed in the design for the Reichsbank of 1933, the modified modernism of which emphasized absolute simplicity of form and detail as well as

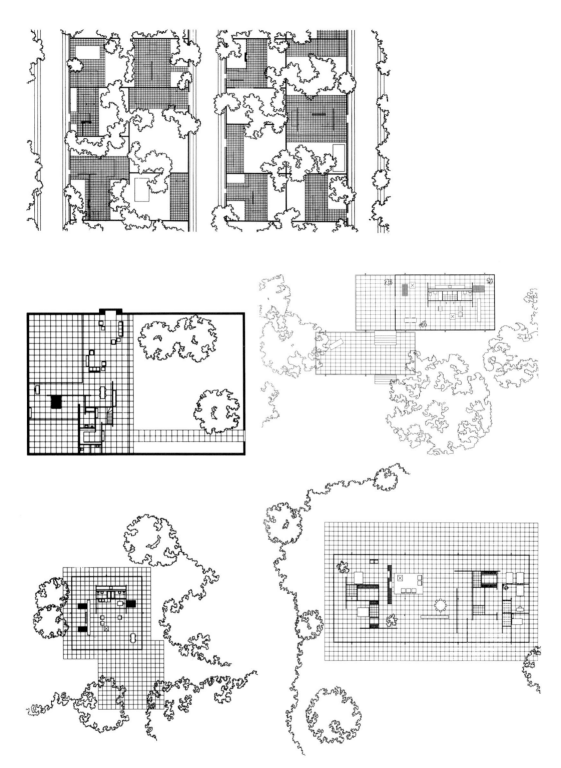

Top, courtyard houses, project, around 1931. *Center left,* house with three courts, project, around 1934 (office drawing of 1939). *Center right,* Farnsworth House, 1945–1950. *Bottom left,* Fifty-by-Fifty House, project, 1950. *Bottom right,* Caine House, project, 1950.

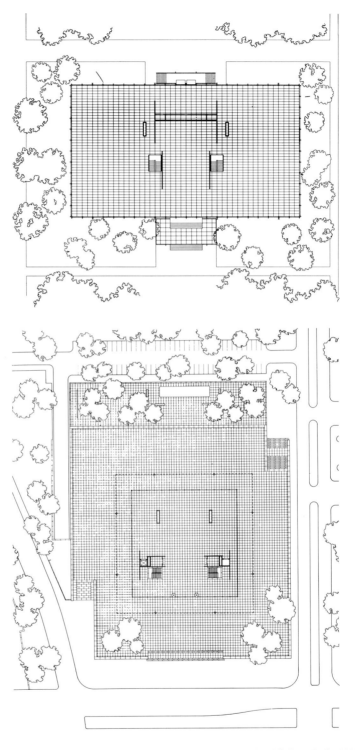

Top, Crown Hall, IIT, Chicago, 1950–1956; *bottom,* New National Gallery, Berlin, 1962–1967.

spatial generosity, but which also employed rigorous symmetry and massive blocks and thereby arrived at an oppressive monumentality. Mies also signed, on the urgings of the Propaganda Ministry, that declaration of devotion to the Führer that was published in the *Völkische Beobachter*, the official party publication of the NSDAP, as an "appeal of the cultural workers" on August 18, 1934—one day before the plebiscite on the fusion of the functions of Reichspräsident and Reichskanzler. Besides by Mies, this was signed, among others, by Ernst Barlach, Georg Kolbe, Emil Nolde, Wilhelm Furtwängler, Emil Fahrenkamp, and Paul Schultze-Naumburg.[73]

Mies took his leave of Europe in 1938 and took with him the insights gained in two decades of a simple but complete conceptual edifice. His inaugural speech as Director of Architecture at Armour Institute of Technology in Chicago, composed while he was still in Germany, marked the end of his European career. Nowhere else is the logic of the Miesian building art expressed more clearly and more emphatically. While more than architectural culture was being buried in Germany by the rhythm of marching columns, Mies outlined on a few pages his concept of order, according to which "the world of our creations" shall begin to "blossom from within."[74]

The Chicago inaugural speech can be viewed as a continuation of those thoughts that had started ten years earlier with the lecture on "The Preconditions of Architectural Work." Mies now transposed his dialectic, derived largely from his readings of Romano Guardini but also from Georg Simmel, Max Scheler, and Henri Bergson, into a commensurate order of the building art and a corresponding concept of teaching.

Without any noticeable assistance, based only on the security of his independent insight, Mies now formulated his thoughts. Even the immediacy of language, which breathes the poetic spirit of his precise architectural statements, shows that the "clear lawfulness of a spiritual order" Mies wanted to convey to his students had now been reached.

The order of the building art, which determined the method of his architectural teaching, was based on the principles of the philosophy of opposites and its notion of culture. By differentiating between practical aims, which guide man's "material life," and values, which make "spiritual existence" possible, Mies indicated its starting position: "Our practical aims determine the character of a civilization. Our values determine the height of our culture."[75]

A correlative interaction between these opposites was a primary condition for the building art:

Different as practical aims and values are, arising out of different planes, they are nevertheless closely connected. For to what else should our values be related if not to our aims in life? And where should these aims get their meaning if not through values? Both realms together are fundamental to human existence. . . . If this is true of all human activity where even the slightest question of value is involved, then it must be even more true in the field of architecture. In its simplest forms architecture is entirely rooted in practical considerations, but it can reach up through all degrees of value to the highest realm of spiritual existence, to the realm of the sensuously apprehensible, and to the sphere of pure art. Any teaching of architecture must recognize this situation.

The itinerary of building followed a path of insights "step by step" to find "what is possible, necessary, and significant," moving "from irresponsible opinion to responsible insight" to arrive at the "clear lawfulness of spiritual order." The stations the architect had to traverse with Mies in order to arrive at himself and the building art are autobiographically colored: "the disciplined path from materials through the practical aims of creative work" to the "sphere of pure art" delineates the architect's career and parallels Mies's own from the apprenticeship in the stone-cutting shop to the radical functionalism of the early twenties and right up to the ideal creations of 1929.

The dimension gained can be measured by comparing the statements. In 1938 Mies again guided his listeners to that familiar "healthy world" of primitive building. "Have you ever seen anything more perfect in terms of function and use of material?," Mies had asked in 1923 in regard to the leaf huts and the primitive skin and bone structure.[76] Now, however, the admiration also included an aesthetic interest in regard to these structures where "each axe stroke meant something and each chisel stroke made a real statement."

What feeling for material and what power of expression speaks in these buildings. What warmth they generate, and how beautiful they are! They sound like familiar songs. . . . Where do we find such wealth of structure? Where do we find more healthy energy and natural beauty? With what obvious clarity a beamed ceiling rests on these old stone walls, and with what sensitivity one cut a doorway through these walls.

These elementary images of existence created by "unknown masters" exemplified a clear understanding of material and a natural, symbolically saturated sensibility, and thus could stand as examples for the building of all ages. Here the two opposite realms of life, material life and spiritual existence formed an easy and universally valid alliance. Modern man, with modern materials and techniques at his disposal, had so far not been able to establish a commensurate bridge between object and subject so fundamental to the idea of culture. The availability of these means alone does not yet signify the presence of value. For this reason, so Mies implied, there is no justification in looking at primitive building with any feeling of superiority. "We expect nothing from materials in themselves, but only from the right use of them. Even the new materials give us no superiority. Each material is only worth what we make of it."[77]

Only the recognition of intrinsic possibilities could lead to the basics of real form-giving. Therefore one had to ask: "We want to know what [a building] can be, what it must be, and what it should not be." Besides an understanding of the nature of the materials and the nature of the purpose, a timely architecture must also inquire into "the spiritual position in which we stand" and must learn "the carrying and driving forces of our time." Only then can a critique of the givens of a time become a possibility: "We shall attempt to raise genuine questions—questions about the value and purpose of technology. We want to show that technology not only promises power and greatness, but also involves dangers; that good and evil apply even to it, and that man must make the right decision."

But each decision—so Mies leads the construction of his conceptual edifice toward its higher aim—terminates in a specific order: "Therefore we want to illuminate the possible orders and lay bare their principles." The fundamental division into mechanistic and idealistic order, hypothesized by Mies, brought his ideas of philosophy and the span of architectonic possibilities to their most common denominator: "The mechanistic principle of order," identified—much like the principle of "building" in 1923—with an overemphasis on "materialistic and functionalistic factors," had to be rejected because it does not satisfy "our feeling that means must be subsidiary to ends and our desire for dignity and value." The opposite, "idealistic principle of order," however—perhaps closer to the ideal structures of 1929–1932—could not be affirmed either, for in its "overemphasis on the ideal and the formal" it satisfies "neither our interest in truth and simplicity nor our practical sense."

Mies decided on the "organic principle of order" that aims at a higher unity of "meaningful and measurable parts." In this principle, which must under no circumstances be interpreted as a biological parallel, Romano Guardini's "philosophy of the living and concrete" found its equivalent. The "organic" referred to that share of the alive in which the opposites of matter and spirit, practical aims and value, technology and art realized themselves in their correlative existence. In it lay hidden the creative principle by means of which man can bring himself and things into concordance, producing beauty by means of the "proportions between things."[78] Concluding his speech of 1938 with Augustine, who had already served him as brilliant example in 1928 because he had, by injecting the principle of measure into chaos, transformed it into cosmos, Mies also pointed to the goal of "creating order out of the godforsaken confusion of our time":

But we want an order that gives to each thing its proper place, and we want to give each thing what is suitable to its nature. We would do this so perfectly that the world of our creations will blossom from within. More we do not want; more we cannot do. Nothing can unlock the aim and meaning of our work better than the profound words of St. Augustine: "Beauty is the radiance of Truth."

This *Summa theologica* of Mies's building art was to retain its meaning. To it nothing could be added, as the statement "Leitgedanken zur Erziehung in der Baukunst" (Principles for Education in the Building Art), published in 1965, demonstrates. The edifice of the building arts was complete and final, as can be seen from publications after 1938. Aside from autobiographical statements, introductions, welcoming speeches, and similar things, Mies was to refer only to one single topic: the relationship between technology and the building art.[79] Thought structure and occasional, only slightly varying citations show that Mies had returned to the same sources that had already supplied him before 1930, namely Friedrich Dessauer's *Philosophie der Technik* (1927), Rudolf Schwarz's *Wegweisung der Technik* (1929), and other writings from him in the *Schildgenossen*,[80] and, as a matter of course, Romano Guardini, all of whom stood by him in his new home.

According to Dessauer, technology is a "science of values" (underlined by Mies)[81] in which the opposing realms of necessity and freedom encounter each other. Technology serves as an educative force because it contributes toward an increase of conscious awareness; it not only opens up new facets of fulfillment but also obligates man to listen to its universal law. "The influence of technology on the soul,"[82] Mies noted in 1928, causes one to forgo "self-serving aims in one's work, moods, and vanities" and leads to an "encounter with an immanent plan"—a "participation in creation."

Friedrich Dessauer perceived the value of technology as educative as in it man faced an order that was not controlled by his own subjective expression: "For would it not be conceivable that man, by passing through the transcendent nature of technology, could establish the harmony between inside and outside, between psychic force and practical means? Why has this question been ignored? Why, if one thinks of culture and talks of technology, does one always mean drainage systems, microscopes, and steam machines?" (markings by Mies).[83]

Mies's philosophy of the building art responded to this question. He saw the technological, insofar as it finds its "fulfillment" in man, raised up from the realm of function to the realm of meaning and values, from where it was effortlessly transposable into the realm of culture, much as nature did in Guardini's Italian cultural landscape.

Only by traversing an objective order can man gain a specific "intrinsic value, called culture." Georg Simmel in his "Philosophie der Kultur"—an essay owned by Mies—saw the "objectivization of the subject and the subjectivization of the object" as that specific quality that constitutes the cultural process: "It is peculiar to the concept of culture that the spirit stipulates an independent object through which the development of the subject from itself to itself takes its passage." The metaphysical significance of this historical phenomenon "culture" consists in being as it were a

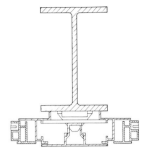 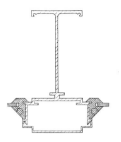 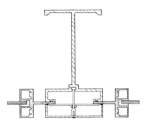

Left to right: 860 and 880 Lake Shore Drive Apartments, Chicago, 1948–1951; Pavilion Apartments, Colonnade Park, Newark, 1958–1960; One Charles Center, Baltimore, 1960–1963.

substitute for religion, as it renews the "incompletable, or, if completed, always again destroyed bridge between subject and object." According to Simmel, culture expresses that "longing for and anticipation of a transcendence of that rigid dualism" so that subject and object "as correlates that only find meaning in each other"[84] can be made to meet.

Beyond its significance in terms of culture, Mies perceived technology also as a "genuine historical movement . . . a world in itself." It was related to the architecture and could, in agreement with Simmel, be viewed as its correlate. Only out of this encounter between technology and the art of building could architecture arise as a "culture of building." "Our real hope is that they grow together, that someday the one be the expression of the other. Only then will we have an architecture worthy of its name: Architecture as a true symbol of our time."[85]

Even the historical cycle, the eternal return of that metaphysical bridgehead that demarcated Simmel's concept of culture inspired by Nietzsche, found its correlate in Mies. "With infinite slowness arises the great form the birth of which is the meaning of the epoch. . . . Not everything that happens takes place in full view. The decisive battles of the spirit are waged on invisible battlefields. The visible is only the final step of a historical form. Its fulfillment. Its true fulfillment. Then it breaks off. And a new world arises."[86]

The steel skeleton embodies and symbolizes that objective order by means of which the building art of this period should come to discover itself and transform technical order into culture. With his buildings, Mies laid the foundation of an objective culture along Simmel's lines, in which the technical and the spiritual values combine to a higher unity and resolve into "self-completion" (Simmel). In that sense, this understanding of the building art, which would integrate the new world of construction with the humanistic cosmos, corresponded to the "double way" of the "from itself" and the "to itself" and was "simultaneously radical and conservative: radical because it endorses the scientific dynamics of our time . . . conservative because it not only fulfills a purpose but also has a meaning, and because it does not

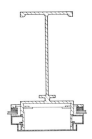
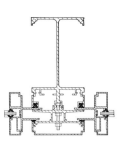
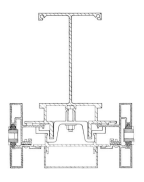

Left to right: 2400 Lakeview Apartments, Chicago, 1960–1963; Westmount Square, Montreal, 1964–1968; IBM tower, Chicago, 1966–1969.

merely subordinate itself to function but also is expressive. It is conservative because it is based on the eternal law of architecture: order, space, proportion."[87]

Mies was looking for a structure that could remain constant in a changing world. It should be the conveyor of meanings, even of the ultimate spiritual ones,[88] but it should nevertheless keep the door open for the *Zeitgeist* and establish "a real contact with the intrinsic nature of the epoch."[89] Viewed from this aspect of a philosophy of culture, Mies's work after 1938 turned from construction to structure. It stood for that unifying principle of order that contained not only the unity of construction and form, but also that of purpose and meaning.[90]

The universal that includes all possibilities opens up the possibility for a reconciliation of opposites.[91] In the subject-object equation that constitutes culture, Mies radically curbed the subjective element. The circumstance that the craze for power and the unrestrained will to rule engulfed the world a second time might have prodded him in that direction.

Simmel's theory of culture was now reduced by Mies to a single phrase: "Fulfill the law to gain freedom." The commensurate imperative "Serve rather than rule"[92] held out an ideal of ascetic containment. Modern man's problems, as described by Simmel, arose because he is surrounded by a host of cultural elements that "are not meaningless for him, but that ultimately are not meaningful either. As a mass, they are oppressive because they cannot be assimilated item by item, nor can they simply be rejected, because they belong potentially to the sphere of cultural development." Simmel characterized this situation by reversing St. Francis's motto of "Nihil habentes omnia possidentes [Those who have nothing have it all]"— in Simmel's version men of a wealthy and opulent culture were "omnia habentes, nihil possidentes."[93]

Suffering amid abundance is the symptom of our time: "And yet we have at our disposal a surprising wealth of technological possibilities. But perhaps it is just this wealth that prevents us from doing what is right. . . . The new freedom opened the door to a flood of things; maybe desirable, but without constructive value in themselves. . . . One pushed these things around, one surrounded one's life with machines and confused this organizing with building."[94]

"All possible freedom and yet such great profundity"—this motto stood over Mies's wish for simplification, over that "less is more" that should lead to "authentic form" and that is simultaneously "low and high."[95] The building master of the new epoch, much as Nietzsche's "genuine historian," must have that creative power that enables him to "remint the universally known into something never heard of before, and to express the universal so simply and profoundly that the simplicity is lost in the profundity and the profundity in the simplicity."[96] The process of dramatic simplification, already begun in 1922, found its completion in Mies's work after 1938. In Chicago, in the city of building engineers, his philosophy of the steel skeleton and his concept of the dematerialization of objective structure could be fully realized. In the support-free space—an engineering achievement that had already taken shape at the Paris World's Fair of 1889 and that was hard to surpass in expanse and size—the premises of Mies's structural concepts could find their full expression.

The reduction of the building to its most elementary constructive and space-forming components, ceiling, supports, and walls, and the emptying of space, all transforming the building into a neutral spatial container, as Ebeling had implied, all that could already be anticipated in 1922. The plans for the glass skyscrapers blended away the internal support structure from existential space and pointed to a space that Mies was to define more closely in his 1928 explanations for the design of the Adam department store. Space with maximum variability of use potential is best guaranteed "by an undivided expanse of the individual floor levels; for that reason," so Mies explained, "I have placed the supports of the building in the exterior walls."[97]

In the pavilion of the electrical industry at the world's fair at Barcelona, which remained practically unnoticed in the shadow of the spectacular Barcelona Pavilion, Mies had realized such a support-free space that gives the illusion of being open on all sides. The windowless cube was on the inside completely covered with plates onto which large-scale photos were projected. Combined, they gave the illusion of a three-dimensional panorama that seemed to open the space toward an imaginary horizon and made one forget its walls.

With technology, which was the subject of this space exhibit, a new rhythm had entered the world, a new expansiveness arising out of the dominance it afforded over time and space, but also a new density of life.[98] "Free movement in space, the most beautiful and exhilarating result of technology," deserved, as Rudolf Schwarz had pointed out in 1927, to be taken seriously as "a spiritual event."[99] Space, as developed by Mies, secured

Pavilion of the International Utilities and Heavy Equipment Industries at the International Exposition in Barcelona, 1929.

Assembly floor of the Martin Airplane Works, built by Albert Kahn.

Photomontage of a concert hall, project, 1942.

this freedom of movement by opening up construction. The possibilities afforded by this new spatial freedom were demonstrated by Mies in a 1942 photocollage that in its impact could be compared to the skyscraper design of 1922.[100] Mies boldly transformed the free-spanned space of the assembly floor of an airplane factory into an aesthetic object, thereby proving anew the thesis of an art promise innate in construction. Now the building withdrew to give way to space, reduced to the naked, engineered construction of a neutral frame that could be filled with changing contents. With a convincing spatial aesthetic vision—which could have gotten its functional problematic from the suggested use for a concert hall—Mies demonstrated with visual effectiveness his concept of the transformational potential of technology into culture that was outlined by the sentence: "Wherever technology reaches its real fulfillment, it transcends into architecture."[101] His visualization of the quality of space, which was connected to a constructive and conceptual determination of "architecture as frame," was brought to expression in that same year by another project that was also accompanied by a short explicative text. In the design for a "museum for a small city" the building itself was "conceived as one large area" that permitted the greatest possible flexibility. The precondition for this freedom was a principle consisting of only "three basic elements—a floor slab, columns and a roof plate."[102] The life lived by the art works in Mies's space had exemplary character and symbolic significance.

The freestanding human figure Mies liked to install as hypothesized inhabitant of his space serves to interpret room as "living space, location, where the personality is and is itself";[103] it gave to space that internal dimension of which Guardini had spoken. This room no longer should or could be a place where art was "interred," because it had lifted the "barrier" between the art work on the interior and the real outer world;[104] the experience of spatial freedom became an aesthetic event. Only in it could the "spiritual in man" find its "dignified expansive habitation."[105]

Simultaneous with his statements on the relationship between technology and architecture, Mies began around 1950, with the building of the Farnsworth House (1946–1951), a process of emptying space. The wall is reduced to a last symbolic relic on the interior to secure the irreducible minimum of spatial stability and functionality, for the sake of freedom of movement. This is analogous to the shift of the support structure from the inside to the outside, permitting a support-free interior and a general dissolving of the wall into glass, thereby opening up space to perception. Mies now continued almost ad absurdum along his indicated trajectory by means of an entire series of designs that reached from the small Fifty-by-Fifty House, the Caine House and Crown Hall to the gigantic proportions of the Chicago Convention Hall of 1953. Again, the intimate spiritual relationship with Rudolf Schwarz and Romano Guardini may deliver a key to understanding even this specific task. The preference for an empty, silent room may have had its ideological-religious impetus in the writings of Guardini

Corner detail of the Chemistry Building, IIT, Chicago, 1945–1946.

Crown Hall, IIT, 1950–1956.

National Theater, Mannheim, project, around 1952, photograph of model.

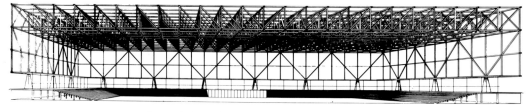

Convention Hall, Chicago, project, 1953.

Bacardi Office Building, Mexico City, 1957–1961, hall on ground floor.

and the church buildings of Rudolf Schwarz. Guardini described "fear of empty space and silence . . . as a fear of being alone with God and the forlorn standing in front of him," a confrontation man attempts to avoid: "That is why he always wants to have things, pictures, words, and sounds around himself."

Rudolf Schwarz, who claims that the idea of a large, pure, almost empty space is his idea,[106] created in his church structures, which were highly valued by Mies,[107] ascetic rooms in which Guardini's postulate assumed architectonic form: "We must again rediscover the emptiness of God's house, and the silence in his service; man is in need of it."[108]

"In the silence of the large rooms," of which Rudolf Schwarz had spoken, arises "not the longing to become lost, but the hope of finding oneself."[109] His *Wegweisung der Technik* gave a metaphysical dimension to the motto "back to construction," to which Mies rededicated himself in Chicago. The writings of Schwarz seem to point unequivocally to Mies's one-room buildings that refuse to predetermine function. In Schwarz's concluding sentences, Mies could practically feel called to systematically pursue an idea that constantly and serially seems to produce that type. "On the whole, one can courageously endorse the new 'serial tense' and enjoy its binding qualities. Yet, wherever one may take up position, the inevitable law of this form is: to gain distance, to learn to become world-transcendent. From the distance of a solitary room, one has to overcome the dangers inherent in this form. . . . It is certain that such a solitude, out of which one can truly gain the ability to transcend, must be searched for at great depths; and perhaps the final saving depth can only be reached by way of contemplation or—let us say, in order not to be misunderstood—by genuine religion."[110]

860 and 880 Lake Shore Drive Apartments, Chicago, 1948–1951.

Toronto Dominion Center, 1963–1969.

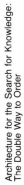

Karl Friedrich Schinkel, Roman baths in Potsdam, 1826.

Gallery of the Twentieth Century (New National Gallery), Berlin, 1962–1967.

Looked at this way, a simple, profoundly thought through structure such as the Farnsworth House can be called, with Rudolf Schwarz, a genuine "work" because it does not dissolve into function, for in it "something remains aloof, beyond time." The "silent form that escapes the flux" constitutes in the eyes of Schwarz a "type of classicism" in which "remoteness and service" balance each other.[111] These thoughts ultimately constitute the basic statements on the Farnsworth House, which as Mies himself said, "has never really been understood."[112]

The Farnsworth House pavilion is, much as Walter Genzner had said of the Barcelona Pavilion in 1929, "a place for contemplative lingering."[113] Here man could enter into a silent dialogue with the objective order of nature and, as can be assumed from the words of Mies, find himself at one with the great laws of creation: "Nature, too, shall live its own life. We must beware not to disrupt it with the color of our houses and interior fittings. Yet we should attempt to bring nature, houses, and human beings together into a higher unity. If you view nature through the glass walls of the Farnsworth House, it gains a more profound significance than if viewed from outside. That way more is said about nature—it becomes a part of a larger whole."[114]

Georg Simmel's definition of culture as "the great enterprise of spirit" that "creates itself as object in order to return, enriched by this creation, to itself,"[115] gives to the Miesian architecture its developmental logic. With his last building, the Gallery of the Twentieth Century in Berlin, later to be renamed the New National Gallery, Mies gave the Farnsworth House an urban counterpart.

Surrounded by the hectic town traffic, the glass exhibition pavilion, the wide-overhanging steel casement roof of which rests on T-beam columns— the architectural "order" of our day—sits on a monumental pedestal. This disposition, aloof and yet simultaneously intertwined with the urban context, intensifies that feeling of inner expanse characteristic of all Miesian space.

Secluded from the noisy turbulence of the city and yet visually connected to it, man is here thrown back upon himself and encounters his second nature, culture. Culture steps forward to meet him in double configuration, in the work of art and in the spirit of a built order, and even as the urban environment, in order to become—as Mies outlined as the aim of his art— "part of a larger whole." It is only to this goal much as to technology that Mies's frame architecture subordinates itself, so that its meaning can be found by an "educational perambulation."

"We wish to see *ourselves* translated into stone and plants, we want to take walks *in ourselves* when we stroll around these buildings and gardens." So Friedrich Nietzsche described the "architecture for the search for knowledge," in which Mies's space of the National Gallery seems to be anticipated. "One day, and probably soon, we need some recognition of

235

what above all is lacking in our big cities: quiet and wide, expansive places for reflection. Places with long, high-ceilinged cloisters . . . where no shouting or noise of carriages can reach . . . buildings and sites that would altogether give expression to the sublimity of thoughtfulness and of stepping aside."[116]

With this steel temple of the technological age Mies has given to the modern world such an expansive place of retreat, so that man may find himself and his epoch therein. As Romano Guardini expressed it in Nietzschean terms, such a room must not "deny the existence and activities of outside life," but must only facilitate a "repose . . . therein." The large double exclamation marks Mies had put in the margin of that passage in *Briefe vom Comer See* seem to indicate that Guardini has given him an important cue: "We surmise possibilities of recollection and inwardness in daily existence, in life, as it is today. I believe we come to the insight that technology, economy, and politics also call for such a stillness and inner fervor if they want to solve their tasks. He who stands in the world needs art, in himself and in a realm that is more profound than he is, to find support therein so that from that position he can seize the world."[117]

From this profundity arose Mies's expression: "This world and no other is offered to us. Here we must take our stand."[118]

Appendix
Manifestos, Texts, and Lectures

Mies around 1923.

I 1922–1927

1
Skyscrapers

Published without title in *Frühlicht*, 1, no. 4 (1922), pp. 122–124.

Only skyscrapers under construction reveal the bold constructive thoughts, and then the impression of the high-reaching steel skeletons is overpowering. With the raising of the walls, this impression is completely destroyed; the constructive thought, the necessary basis for artistic form-giving, is annihilated and frequently smothered by a meaningless and trivial jumble of forms. At very best one remains impressed by the sheer magnitude, and yet these buildings could have been more than just manifestations of our technical skill. This would mean, however, that one would have to give up the attempt to solve a new task with traditional forms; rather one should attempt to give form to the new task out of the nature of this task.

The novel constructive principle of these buildings comes clearly into view if one employs glass for the no longer load-bearing exterior walls. The use of glass, however, necessitates new approaches. In my design for the sky-scraper at the Friedrichstrasse railroad station in Berlin, intended for a triangular site, a prismatic form corresponding to the triangle appeared to offer the right solution for this building, and I angled the respective façade fronts slightly toward each other to avoid the danger of an effect of lifelessness that often occurs if one employs large glass panels. My experiments with a glass model helped me along the way and I soon recognized that by employing glass, it is not an effect of light and shadow one wants to achieve but a rich interplay of light reflections. That is what I strove for in the other design published here. At first glance the contour of the ground plan appears arbitrary, but in reality it is the result of many experiments on the glass model. The curves were determined by the need to illuminate the interior, the effect of the building mass in the urban context, and finally the play of the desired light reflection. Ground plan contours in which the curves were calculated from the point of view of light and shadow revealed themselves on the model, if glass was employed, as totally unsuitable. The only fixed points in the ground plan are the stairs and the elevator shafts.

All other subdivisions of the ground plan are to be adapted to the respective needs and executed in glass.

Glass Skyscraper, around 1922.

2
"Office Building"
Published in *G,* no. 1 (July 1923), p. 3.

Any aesthetic speculation
any doctrine } we reject
and any formalism

Building art is the spatially apprehended will of the epoch.
Alive. Changing. New.

Not the yesterday, not the tomorrow, only the today is formable.
Only this building creates.

Create form out of the nature of the task with the means of our time.

That is our work.

The office building is a building of work, of organization, of clarity, of economy. Bright wide workrooms, uncluttered, undivided, only articulated according to the organism of the firm. The greatest effect with the least expenditure of means.
The materials are concrete, iron, glass.
Ferroconcrete buildings are essentially skeleton structures.
Neither pastry nor tank turrets. Supporting girder construction with a nonsupporting wall. That means skin and bone structures.

The most practical distribution of the work stations determined room depth; it is 16 m. A double-shafted frame of 8 m span-width with 4 m long lateral cantilever brackets on either side was established as the most economical construction principle. The beam distance is 5 m. This post-and-beam system supports the ceiling panel, which, angled vertically upward at the end of the cantilever arms, becomes exterior skin and serves as back wall of the shelving, which was moved to the exterior walls in order to keep the interior uncluttered. Above the 2 m high shelving is a continuous band of fenestration reaching to the ceiling.

Berlin, May 1923

Office Building, 1923.

3
Office Building
Manuscript of August 2, 1923. This contribution for the *Deutsche Allgemeine Zeitung,* which is based on the manifesto "Office Building" published in G no. 1, was delivered too late by Mies and not published. In Museum of Modern Art, Manuscripts Folder 3.

It is no coincidence if today important architectural questions are discussed in the newspapers. The art and technical journals that were formerly focal points for artistic life have, due to their purely aesthetic viewpoints, failed to take note [of it—*crossed out*] of the development of the modern building art away from the aesthetic to the organic, from the formal to the constructive. The modern building art has, for a long time, refused to play a mere decorative role in our life. The creative building artists want to have nothing, nothing whatever, to do with the aesthetic traditions of past centuries. We leave this field without regret to the art historians. Their [the building artists'] work shall serve life. Life alone shall be their teacher. They reject any tutelage by art specialists; [the same applies to theory, aesthetic speculation, doctrine, and formalism.—*crossed out*] building art is for them neither theory nor aesthetic speculation nor doctrine, but spatially apprehended will of the epoch. Alive, changing, new. The character of our time must be conveyed by our building. We want to shape the form of our buildings out of the nature of the task, but with the means of our time.

The office building illustrated here is a building of work, of organization, of clarity, of economy. Bright wide workrooms, uncluttered, undivided, only articulated according to the organism of the firm. The greatest effect with the least expenditure of means. The materials are concrete, iron, glass. Ferroconcrete buildings are essentially skeleton structures. Neither pastry nor tank turrets. Supporting girder construction with a nonsupporting wall. That means skin and bone structures.

The most practical distribution of the work stations determined room depth; it is 16 m. A double-shafted frame of

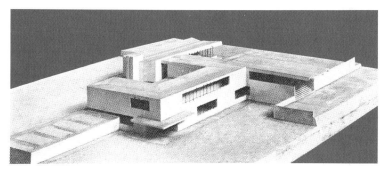

Concrete Country House, 1923, published with the article "Bauen" (Building).

8 m span-width with 4 m long lateral cantilever brackets on either side was established as the most economical construction principle. The beam distance is 5 m. This post-and-beam system supports the ceiling panel, which, angled vertically upward at the end of the cantilever arms, becomes exterior skin and serves as back wall of the shelving, which was moved to the exterior walls in order to keep the interior uncluttered. Above the 2 m high shelving is a continuous band of fenestration reaching to the ceiling.

4
"Building"

Published in G, no. 2 (September 1923), p. 1.

We know no forms, only building problems.
Form is not the goal but the result of our work.
There is no form in and for itself.
The truly formal is conditional, fused with the task, yes, the most elementary expression of its solution.
Form as goal is formalism; and that we reject. Nor do we strive for a style.
Even the will to style is formalism.
We have other worries.
It is our specific concern to liberate building activity [*Bauerei*] from aesthetic speculators and make building [*Bauen*] again what alone it should be, namely BAUEN.[1]

There have been repeated attempts to introduce ferroconcrete as a building material for apartment building construction. Mostly, however, ineptly. The advantages of this material have not been exploited nor its disadvantages avoided. One believes one has acknowledged the material sufficiently if one rounds off the corners of the house and of the individual rooms. The round corners are totally irrelevant for concrete and not even all that easy to execute. It will not do of course simply to translate a brick house into ferroconcrete. I see the main advantage of ferroconcrete in the possibility of considerable savings in material. In order to realize this in an apartment building, one must concentrate the supports and reinforcements in a few building locations. The disadvantage of ferroconcrete, as I see it, lies in its low insulating property and its poor sound absorption. This makes it necessary to provide additional insulation against exterior temperatures. The simplest way to remove the disadvantage of sound transfer seems to be to exclude everything that causes noise;

1.
Bauerei, as opposed to *Bauen,* carries a disdainful overtone; furthermore it alludes to *Bauer* (peasant).

here I have in mind rubber floors, sliding windows and doors, and similar installations: but then also spatial generosity in the ground plan.—Ferroconcrete demands the most precise planning before its execution; here the architect still has everything to learn from the shipbuilding engineer. With brick construction it is possible, even if not particularly advisable, to let the heating and installation crews loose on the house as soon as the roof is up; they will in the briefest time transform the house into a ruin. With ferroconcrete such a procedure is impossible. Here only disciplined work will achieve the desired result.

The model illustrated above demonstrates an attempt to solve the problem of a residential building in ferroconcrete. The main living section is supported by a four-shaft girder system. This construction system is encased in a thin concrete skin. This skin forms both walls and roof. The roof is slightly inclined from the exterior walls toward the center. The incline of the two roof planes forms a groove that permits the most simple imaginable roof drainage. All gutterwork is thereby omitted. I cut openings into the walls where I need them for view or illumination.

The preceding text (except for the first paragraph), under the heading "Concrete Residential Building," was sent on October 1, 1923, to the printer F. Koslowsky, Oranienburg, where *G* was printed. A note on the back of the manuscript (in the Library of Congress) reads:

It is mainly our concern to liberate all building activity [*Bauerei*] from aesthetic specialists. And make building [*Bauen*] again what it always has been. Building.

Barbarians have approached the problem with the least imaginable measure of boldness. Cupboards that look like skyscrapers models.

5
**"Solved Tasks:
A Challenge for Our Building Industry"**
This lecture was given at a public meeting of the Bund Deutscher Architekten (Association of German Architects), Brandenburg District (Berlin), on December 12, 1923, in the large auditorium of the Berlin Arts and Crafts Museum, Prinz-Albrecht-Strasse 8. The meeting had for its slogan: "How can we escape from the housing shortage? Building must be resumed!" Mies's lecture was published in *Die Bauwelt,* 14, no. 52 (1923), p. 719.

In the country it is a self-understood usage to plow under a plot overgrown by weeds without considering the few grains that had managed to survive. We, too, have no other choice *if we really strive for a new attitude toward building.*

You are all familiar with the condition of our buildings, and yet I wish to remind you of Kurfürstendamm and Dahlem, to bring to mind this total lunacy in stone. I have vainly attempted to understand the meaning of these buildings. They are neither comfortable, nor economical, nor functional, and yet they are supposed to be the home for the men of our time. One does not think very highly of us, if one really believes that these boxes can serve our life needs. There has been no attempt to comprehend and formulate these totally different needs elementarily. The inner needs were ignored, and one believed that one could get away with juggling historical allusions. These buildings are dishonest, stupid, and insulting.

We demand, by contrast, for the buildings of our time: *absolute truthfulness and rejection of all formal cheating.* Furthermore, we demand: that in the planning of apartment buildings the *organization of living* arrangements is given absolute priority. Rational economics have to be striven for, and the employment of technological means is a self-understood precondition. If we comply with these demands, then the apartment building of our epoch has found its form.

Since the rental apartment house is nothing but a number of individual apartments, the house organism here, too, forms itself out of their type and number. This determines the form of the apartment block.

I cannot show you any illustrations of new buildings that correspond to these demands. Because even the new attempts have not gone beyond formal matters.

To help you look beyond the historical and aesthetic junk heaps of Europe to the elementary and purposeful, I have assembled illustrations of buildings that lie outside the realm of the Greco-Roman culture. I have done this on purpose, because to me an axe stroke in Hildesheim is *closer* than a chisel stroke in Athens.

Wie retten wir uns aus der Wohnungsnot?
Es muß wieder gebaut werden!

Einladung
zur
öffentlichen Tagung
des Bundes Deutscher Architekten, Landesbezirk Brandenburg (Berlin) für
Mittwoch, den 12. Dezember 1923, abends 6½ Uhr
im Großen Hörsaal des Kunstgewerbemuseums,
Berlin, Prinz Albrecht-Str. 8.

Einleitende Ansprache und

Ehrenpräsidium: Geheimrat Professor **Dr. Cornelius Gurlitt**, Dresden,
1. Vorsitzender des Bundes Deutscher Architekten.

Vortrag des Herrn Städtebaudirektor der Stadt Berlin:

Baurat Karl Elkart,
über: Vorschläge zur Umgestaltung der Wohnungswirtschaft.

Korreferent: **Architekt B.D.A. E. Kraffert.**

Architekt B.D.A. Mies van der Rohe
über: Neue Wege im Wohnungsbau.

Anschließend Aussprache.

In grauenhafter Gestalt lastet die Wohnungsnot mit unübersehbaren sozialen Schäden auf unserem Volke. Alle Versuche, den bestehenden Wohnraum zu bewirtschaften und im Wege von Staatszuschüssen neuen Wohnraum zu schaffen, haben sich als nicht ausreichend erwiesen.

Die einzige Möglichkeit, Neubauten wieder herzustellen, scheitert an dem Mangel an Mitteln, die nur aufzubringen sind, wenn das private Kapital dem Wohnungsbau wieder zugeführt wird. Für das gesamte Volkswirtschaftsleben, nicht zuletzt für die Schaffung von Arbeitsgelegenheit, ist diese Frage von ungeheurer Bedeutung!

Der Bund Deutscher Architekten hält es für seine Pflicht, jetzt, wo es noch nicht zu spät ist, seinerseits mit allem Nachdruck für umgehende Maßnahmen einzutreten, und bittet Ew. Hochwohlgeboren, an dieser wichtigen Aussprache teilnehmen zu wollen. Insbesondere macht der Vorstand des Landesbezirk Brandenburg allen Kollegen das Erscheinen zur dringenden Pflicht.

Der Vorstand des Landesbezirks Brandenburg des B. D. A.
Straumer.

Lecture program of the Bund Deutscher Architekten.

I will now show you dwellings clearly formed in response to need and material.

Illustration 1 (an Indian tent).
This is the typical residence of a nomad. Light and transportable.

Illustration 2 (leaf hut).
This is the leaf hut of an Indian. Have you ever seen anything more perfect in terms of function and use of material? Is that not the best possible use of the jungle shadow?

Illustration 3 (Eskimo house).
Now I take you into night and ice. Moss and seal skins have here become building materials. Walrus ribs form the roof structure.

Illustration 4 (snow hut).
We go even farther north. The residence of a central Eskimo. Here is only snow and ice. And yet, man builds.

Illustration 5 (summer tent of an Eskimo).
This fellow even has a summer villa. The building material is skin and bones. From the stillness and loneliness of the north I bring you to warlike medieval Flanders.

Illustration 6 (castle of the counts of Flanders and Ghent).
Here the residence has become a fortress.

Illustration 7 (farm complex).
In the north German lowlands stands the house of the German farmer. His needs with respect to house, stable, and barn are all filled in this structure. All the pictures I have shown correspond in every way to the needs of the inhabitants. That is all we ask for ourselves. Only the means that are of our time. Since there are no buildings that are equally responsive to the needs of modern man, I can only show you a structure from a related field that is of modern sensibility and fills those conditions that I also long for and strive for in our houses.

Illustration 8 (the *Imperator*).
Here you see a floating apartment building, created according to the needs and means of our time. Now I must ask again: have you ever seen anything more perfect in terms of responsiveness to purpose and use of material? We would be enviable if we had buildings on dry land that would suit our needs equally well. Only when we experience the needs and means of our time so elementarily will we obtain a new building attitude. It is the purpose of my short speech to awaken an awareness of these matters.

Dunoyer de Segonzac

BAUKUNST UND ZEITWILLE!
Von
MIES VAN DER ROHE

6
"Building Art and the Will of the Epoch!"
Published in *Der Querschnitt*, 4, no. 1 (1924), pp. 31–32.

It is not the architectural achievement of earlier times that makes their buildings appear so significant to us, but the circumstance that the antique temples, the Roman basilicas, and also the cathedrals of the Middle Ages were not the work of individual personalities but the creations of entire epochs. Who asks, when viewing such buildings, for names, and what would the accidental personality of their builders mean? These buildings are by their very nature totally impersonal. They are pure representatives of the will of the epoch. This is their significance. Only so could they become symbols of their time.

The building art is always the spatially apprehended will of the epoch, nothing else. Only when this simple truth is clearly recognized can the struggle for the principles of a new building art be conducted purposefully and effectively. Until then it must remain a chaos of confusing forces. For this reason the question as to the nature of the building art is of decisive importance. One will have to understand that all building art arises out of its own epoch and can only manifest itself in addressing vital tasks with the means of its own time. It has never been otherwise.

For this reason it is a futile endeavor to use contents and forms of earlier building periods today. Even the strongest artistic talent will then fail. We find again and again that excellent building masters fail because their work does not serve the will of the epoch. In the final analysis, they remain dilettantes despite their great talent, for the élan with which one undertakes the wrong thing is irrelevant. It is the essential that matters. One cannot walk forward while looking backward, and one cannot be the instrument of the will of the epoch if one lives in the past. Remote observers fall into the same old fallacy when they make the epoch responsible for such tragic cases.

The entire striving of our epoch is directed toward the secular. The efforts of the mystics will remain episodes. Although our understanding of life has become more profound, we will not build cathedrals. Even the grand gesture of the romantics is meaningless for us, for we sense behind it the formal emptiness. Our time is unpathetic, we do not value the great gesture but rationality and reality.

The demands of the time for realism and functionality have to be filled. If that is done with generosity, then the buildings of our time will demonstrate the generosity our time is capable of, and only a fool would maintain that it is without greatness.

Questions of a general nature are of central interest. The individual becomes less and less important; his fate no longer interests us. The decisive achievements in all fields are objective in nature and their originators are for the most part unknown. It is here that the great anonymous trait of our time comes into view. Our engineering buildings are typical examples. Gigantic dams, large industrial complexes, and important bridges arise with great natural ease without their builders becoming known. These structures show also the technical means we will have to employ in the future.

If one compares the ponderous weight of Roman aqueducts with the spider-thin power system of a contemporary crane, or bulky vault constructions with the dashing weightlessness of new ferroconcrete structures, then one gets an inkling how our form and expression differ from those of earlier times. Industrial production methods, too, will exert their influence. The claim that these are only functional structures is irrelevant.

If one rejects all romantic viewpoints, one recognizes that the masonry structures of antiquity, the brick and concrete constructions of the Romans, and the medieval cathedrals were incredibly bold engineering feats, and one can be certain that the first Gothic buildings were perceived, in their Romanesque environment, as foreign bodies.

Our utilitarian structures will only grow into the art of building when, by filling their purpose, they become instruments of the will of the epoch.

The manuscript of February 7, 1924 (collection of Dirk Lohan, Chicago), extends beyond the printed version of the essay as follows:

The purpose of a building is its actual meaning. The buildings of all epochs served purposes, and quite real ones. These purposes were, however, different in type and character. The purpose was always decisive for the building [and characterized it—*crossed out*]. It determined the sacred or profane form.

Our historical schooling has dulled our outlook for these things, that is why we always confuse effect with cause. This accounts for the belief that buildings exist for the sake of architecture. Even the ritualistic language of temples and cathedrals is the result of a purpose. This is the case and not the other way around. Each time, the purpose changes the language, and the same holds true for the means, material, and technique.

People who lack a feeling for the essential [and whose profession it is to concern themselves with antiquities— *crossed out*] always attempt to set up the results of old epochs as examples for our time and recommend the old work methods as means for artistic success. Both are wrong; we cannot use either. We need no examples. Those suggesting handicraft methods in our time prove that they have no inkling of the interrelationships of the new time. Even handicrafts are only a work method and a form of economics, nothing more.

[And here again it is the historians who recommend an outdated form, always the same mistake. Here, too, they mistake form for essence.—*crossed out*] One always believes handcrafting is better and one attributes an innate ethical value to it. But it is never the work method but the work itself that has value.

As I was born into an old family of stonemasons, I am very familiar with hand craftsmanship, and not only as an aesthetic onlooker. My receptiveness to the beauty of handwork does not prevent me from recognizing that handicrafts as a form of economic production are lost. The few real craftsmen still alive in Germany are rarities whose work can be acquired only by very rich people. What really matters is something totally different. Our needs have assumed such proportions that they can no longer be met with the methods of craftsmanship. This spells the end of the crafts: we cannot save them any more, but we can perfect the industrial methods to the point where we obtain results comparable to medieval craftsmanship. Whoever has the courage to maintain that we can still exist without industry must bring the proof for that. The need for even a single machine abolishes handicrafts as an economic form.

Let us keep in mind that all these theories about hand craftsmanship have been composed by aesthetes under the beam of an electric lamp. They enter upon their propaganda mission on paper that has been produced by machines, printed by machines, and bound by machines.

If one would devote only one percent greater care to improving the bad binding of the book, [one would have done a greater service to humanity—*crossed out*] one would recognize by that example what immense capabilities industrial production methods afford. To bring this to mind is our task. Since we stand only in the beginning phase of industrial development, we cannot compare the initial imperfections and hesitancies to a highly mature culture of craftsmanship.

That eternal preoccupation with the past is our undoing. It prevents us from accomplishing the task at hand out of which alone a vital building art can arise. Old contents and forms, old means and work methods, have for us only historical value. Life confronts us daily with new challenges; they are more important than the entire historical rubbish. They call for creative people, people who look forward, who are unafraid to solve each task without prejudice from the bottom on up, and who do not dwell excessively on the results. The result is simply a by-product. Each task represents a new challenge and leads to new results. We do not solve formal problems but building problems, and the form is not the goal but the result of our work. That is the essence of our striving; and this viewpoint still separates us from many. Even from most of the modern building masters. But it unites us with all the disciplines of modern life.

Much as the concept of building is, for us, not tied to old contents and forms, so it is also not connected to specific materials. We are very familiar with the charm of stones and bricks. But that does not prevent us nowadays from taking glass and concrete, glass and metal, into consideration as fully equivalent materials. In many cases, these materials correspond best to present-day purposes.

[Steel serves today in skyscrapers as structural skeleton, and ferroconcrete has proven itself in many cases as an excellent building material. If one already constructs a building with steel, it is hard to see why one should then encase it with massive stone walls and give it the appearance of a tower. Even from the point of view of fire safety, this cannot be justified. It is a similar nonsense to wrap a ferroconcrete structure in a mantle. In both cases more ideas instead of more materials would lead to the goal.— *crossed out*]

The purposes of our tasks are for the most part very simple and clear. One only has to recognize them and formulate them, then they will lead of themselves to significant building solutions. Skyscrapers, office buildings, and commercial structures practically call forth clear, comprehensive solutions, and these can only be crippled because one repeatedly attempts to adapt these buildings to outdated attitudes and forms.

The same applies to residential building. Here, too, certain house and room concepts lead to impossible results. Instead of simply developing a residence to suit its purpose, namely organizing the activity of living, one views it as an object that demonstrates to the world how far its owner has progressed in the realm of aesthetics.

A residence must only serve for living. The site, the exposure to the sun, the program of rooms, and the building materials are the essential factors for the design of a residence. The building is to be formed in response to these conditions. Old familiar pictures may disappear, but in their place residences will arise that are functional in all respects. The world did not become poorer when the stagecoach was replaced by the automobile.

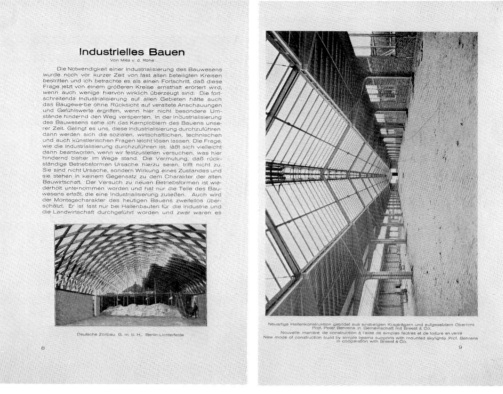

Two pages of *G*, no. 3.

7
"Industrial Building"
Published in *G*, no. 3 (June 1924), pp. 8–13. The essay had been published earlier in April 1924 in *Der Neubau*, 6, no. 7 (1924), p. 77, under the title: "Industrialization of Residential Building—A Question of Materials." The following sentence preceded the text: "The article 'Industrialization of Residential Building' that appeared in issue 5 discusses the great complex of problems associated with the new building, the social, economic, technical, and also artistic nature of which is still totally misunderstood."

Just a short time ago the need to industrialize the building trades was denied by almost all affected circles, and I consider it already a step forward that this question can now be discussed seriously in a larger circle, even if only a few are really convinced. The progress of industrialization taking place in all areas would also have taken place in the building trades without concern for antiquated attitudes and convictions, if very specific circumstances had not here barred the way. I hold that the industrialization of building constitutes the core problem of our time. If we are successful in carrying out this industrialization, then the social, economic, technical, and even artistic questions will solve themselves. The question how this industrialization is to be achieved can perhaps best be answered if we point out what has prevented it so far. The belief that obsolete operational practices stand in the way is not true.

248

They are not the cause but the result of a situation, and they do not stand in opposition to the old building trades. The attempt to modernize operational methods in the construction trades has often been made, but it has only succeeded in those branches that permitted of industrialization. Furthermore, the assembly character of today's building is no doubt overestimated. The entire frame structure and the interior finishing have been executed by the same methods since time immemorial and are of pure handicraft nature. This character cannot be changed by economic forces or work methods, particularly as it guarantees the survival of the small firms. As the new building practices have shown, one can, of course, save materials and wages by using larger and other stone formats, but that does not in any way alter the handicraft character of building; and one still has to point out that brickwork has undeniable advantages over the new building methods. What matters is not so much a rationalization of existing work methods, but a fundamental reorganization of the building trades.

As long as we use essentially the same materials, we will not change the character of building, and this character, as I have already pointed out, determines the method of construction. The industrialization of the building trades is a matter of materials. That is why the demand for new building materials is the first prerequisite. Technology must and will succeed in finding a building material that can be produced technologically, that can be processed industrially, that is firm, weather-resistant, and sound and temperature insulating. It will have to be a lightweight material, the processing of which not only permits but actually demands industrialization. The industrial production of all parts can only be carried out systematically by factory processes, and the work on the building site will then be exclusively of an assembly type, bringing about an incredible reduction of building time. This will bring with it a significant reduction of building costs. The new architectural endeavors, too, will then find their real challenge. It is clear to me that this will bring with it the destruction of the building trades as we know them, but he who regrets that the house of the future will no longer be erected by artisans must keep in mind that the automobile, too, is no longer built by the wheelwright.

8
Lecture

The place, date, and occasion of this lecture are not known. Unpublished manuscript of June 19, 1924 (collection of Dirk Lohan, Chicago). The largest part of the text is based on sections of the manuscript "Building Art and the Will of the Epoch" of February 7, 1924: even in the last third of the lecture, in which slides are used for illustration, there is very little new material, but Mies repeats his sparse comments on the Friedrichstrasse skyscraper and on the Office Building. For the first and only time he gives a short explanation of his Brick Country House design.

Ladies and Gentlemen!

Never have the building trades been more talked about than today, and never has one been further removed from understanding the nature of building. For this reason the question as to the nature of the building art is today of decisive importance. For only when it has been clearly understood can the struggle for the principles of a new building art be conducted purposefully and effectively. Until then it must remain a chaos of confusing forces. One will have to understand that building art as spatial expression is spiritually connected to its times and can only manifest itself in addressing vital tasks with the means of its own time.

It has never been otherwise. For this reason it is a futile endeavor to use contents and forms of earlier periods today. . . . [followed by "Building Art and the Will of the Epoch!," paragraph 3] . . . one cannot walk forward while looking backward, and one cannot be the instrument of the will of the epoch if one lives in the past.

The structure of our period is fundamentally different from that of earlier epochs. That applies to both its spiritual and its material aspects. But these determine our work. The striving of our epoch is directed toward the secular. The efforts of the mystics will remain episodes. . . . [followed by "Building Art and the Will of the Epoch!," paragraphs 4, 5, and 6] . . . Our engineering buildings are typical examples. Gigantic dams, large industrial complexes, and important bridges arise with great natural ease without their builders becoming known. These structures show also the technical means we will have to employ in the future.

The objection that these are only functional structures is irrelevant. The function of a building is its actual meaning. . . . [followed by the material included in the unpublished manuscript of February 7, 1924] . . . The world did not become poorer when the stagecoach was replaced by the automobile.

Now I will explain to you by a few examples what we mean by elementary form-giving.

Taut.

This is the plan for the expansion of the city of Magdeburg designed by the much-reviled Bruno Taut. In this plan one does not find anything fantastic or arbitrary. It has been designed in response to the landscape, the traffic, and with respect for the people that have to live and work there. This plan has obtained its significant and characteristic form just because form was not striven for.

Häring.

This is the plan for a farm estate. It is a nursery under intensive management and is directed by a modern farmer who conducts his operation according to scientific methods with the help of the latest technical innovations. This method of operation determined the projected layout. This design comes from the Berlin architect Hugo Häring.

I would have liked to show to you further works of other architects designed elementarily, but due to the rarity of such works and the short time at my disposal, this was not possible. Excuse me, therefore, if I demonstrate to you in the case of my own work the influence of material and technology on building.

Friedrichstrasse.

The building site was triangular; I have attempted to make full use of it. The depth of the lot forced me to split up the fronts so that the inner core obtains light. Since I consider it senseless to drape the steel skeleton of the building with stone fronts, I have given the building a skin of glass. The objection has been raised that the glass wall does not adequately insulate against exterior temperatures.

These fears are exaggerated. Buildings with large glass fronts already exist and it has not come to my attention that the large glass planes are considered disadvantageous. Furthermore we have today Rudeglass, a material that, on account of its vacuum layer, possesses considerable insulating capacity.

This is another design for a skyscraper. Here it has been objected that it is not formed but remains restricted to the schematic concept. This reproach is typical. It arises out of another manner of thinking in which one still, even if with modern architectonic concepts . . . [sentence incomplete in manuscript]. What is overlooked is that the schematic is implied by the task and therefore finds its expression in the form-giving. This is the ground plan for the building just shown. Here, too, I have attempted to approach the core of the building from the outside. This caused the deep recesses. Since my work with the problems of glass structures has taught me the dangers of too-large planes, I have here chosen polygonal curves for the ground plan in order to obtain a rich play of light reflections.

This is the design for a Concrete Office Building.

Ferroconcrete buildings are essentially skeleton structures. Supporting girder construction with a nonsupporting wall. That means skin and bone structures. The most practical distribution of the work stations determined room depth; it is 16 m. A double-shafted frame of 8 m span-width with 4 m long cantilever brackets on either side was established as the most economical construction principle. The beam distance is 5 m. This post-and-beam system supports the ceiling panel, which, angled upward at the perimeter, becomes exterior skin and serves as back wall for the shelving, which was moved to the exterior walls in order to keep the interior uncluttered. Above the 2 m high shelving is a continuous band of fenestration reaching to the ceiling.

This picture illustrates the attempt to solve the problem of a residential building in ferroconcrete.

The main living section is supported by a four-shaft girder system. This construction system is encased in a thin concrete skin. This skin forms both walls and roof. The roof is slightly inclined from the exterior walls toward the center. The incline of the two roof planes forms a groove that permits the most simple imaginable roof drainage. All gutterwork it thereby omitted. I cut openings into the walls where I need them for view or illumination.

This house, to be executed in brick, shows you the direct opposite of the previous illustration as to the influence of material in form-giving. In the ground plan of this house, I have abandoned the usual concept of enclosed rooms and striven for a series of spatial effects rather than a row of individual rooms. The wall loses its enclosing character and serves only to articulate the house organism.

Conclusion.

The actual value of the works shown to you I see not so much in the degree of achievement, as in the particular manner of form-giving. Nothing illuminates more clearly the situation in which we find ourselves than the fact that Ford's book could trigger such a strong reaction here in Germany. What Ford wants is simple and illuminating. His factories show mechanization in dizzying perfection. We agree with the direction Ford has taken, but we reject the plane on which he moves. Mechanization can never be goal, it must remain means. Means toward a spiritual purpose.

While we want to stand with both feet firmly on the ground, we want to reach with our head to the clouds.

9
Review of Paul Tropp,
Entwicklung und Aufbau der Miete
Published in *Die Baugilde*, 6, no. 5 (1924), p. 56.

Paul Tropp presents, under the title *Entwicklung und Aufbau der Miete* (Development and Organization of Rent),
the results of his investigation into the apartment economy
with great detail and clarity. For the first time, our apartment economy is expertly illuminated. Tropp shows how
it is and how it could be. He discusses existing apartment
and tax economies, incomes and rents, service on capital,
maintenance and repair costs, and ground rents and
draws expert conclusions from his objective observations.
One welcomes this text as it appears at the very moment
when the biggest efforts are being made to stimulate the
building economy and put it on a sound basis. As Tropp's
book makes a valuable contribution in this direction, I
recommend it warmly to all interested circles.

10
Letter to *Die Form*
Published in *Die Form,* 1, no. 7 (1926), p. 179.

Die Form carried in volume 5 an article on "American
Building Art" by Lewis Mumford, with an editorial that
claimed that this article is more informative as to the state
of American architecture than the exhibition "Neue Amerikanische Architektur" that took place not long ago in the
Academy of Arts.

In reading Mumford's article I found that the exhibition was
a particularly apt illustration of Mumford's beliefs. That
speaks for the exhibition. The objection has been
expressed in the Berlin press that the exhibition was not
organized according to a specific plan but that only outstanding achievements of American architecture were presented. I consider it an advantage that this exhibition did
not adhere to a specific and narrow program, but allowed
the visitor to form his own judgment as to the American
building art.

However interesting it may be to learn how you yourself,
how Mendelsohn, Paulsen, or Rading appraise America,
it appeared to me necessary and desirable that each arrive
at his own picture of the present state of the American
building art, and this, as I see it, constituted the value of
the Berlin exhibition.

11
Lecture
Place, date, and occasion unknown. Unpublished manuscript, first version of March 17, 1926, two further versions undated; in the collection of Dirk Lohan, Chicago.

Ladies and Gentlemen!

Never has building been more talked about than today, and never have we been further removed from understanding the nature of building. For this reason the question as to the nature of the building art is today of decisive importance. For only when it has been clearly understood can the struggle for the principles of a new building art be conducted purposefully and effectively. Until then it must remain a chaos of confusing forces. One will have to understand that building art is always the spatial execution of spiritual decisions, that it is tied to its times and can only manifest itself in addressing vital tasks with the means of its own time. It has never been otherwise.

For this reason it is a futile endeavor to use contents and forms of earlier epochs today. Even the strongest artistic talent will then fail. We find therefore again and again that even excellent building masters fail because their work does not serve the spirit of the epoch. In the final analysis they remain dilettantes despite their talent, for the élan with which one does the *wrong thing* is irrelevant.

It is the essential that matters. One cannot walk forward while looking backward, and one cannot be the instrument of the will of the epoch if one lives in the past.

[*Handwritten addition:*] However interesting it may be to trace the intellectual impulses of an art period and illuminate its formal problems, the spiritual forces of a period can here also be effective. Building art is not the implementation of specific formal problems, however much these may be contained in it.

The structure of our period is fundamentally different from that of earlier epochs. This applies to both its spiritual and its material conditions. But this is what determines our work. With or against our will. It is astonishing how little this simple fact is understood. One affirms modern life in thousands of ways. One uses all technical innovations. One is enthusiastic over new inventions and one never hesitates a moment to apply the boldest invention if economic advantages derive from it. But one refuses to draw consequences for the building arts from these changes in living conditions. There are many reasons for this. One has specific preconceptions about what the building art is and one believes in the eternal value of what has so far been. This should not astonish us, for it is also the mistake perpetuated in our schools.

What is astonishing, however, is the total lack of historical understanding connected with this love for historical things. One misconstrues the real interdependence of things, both what concerns the new and what concerns the old. Everything that has so far been was closely connected with life, out of which it arose, and a change of things always was brought about by a change of life. Even Plato recognized the changes of forms in state and society and saw these changes as transformations in the soul of the populace that forms state and society, while the soul in turn is influenced in a myriad of ways by the forms of life that surrounds it.

Each culture arises out of the landscape and its economic givens. Only in this connection can one even understand the term culture. Only one who understands the consequences of the need for irrigation of the lower Nile valley and its influence on societal structure can fully comprehend the nature of Egyptian culture. Ignorance of the economic basis and the social structure of the Greeks led to a complete misunderstanding of antiquity. Nordic culture, too, is the result of very specific economic conditions without which it would either have failed to develop or would have developed differently. Transformations within cultures, too, depend on transformations of their economic structures. These can succumb to political influences, much as they in turn can influence them. They change the living conditions of a particular people, and this in turn leads to a change of formal expression.

It is, of course, wrong to assume that an economic change in a society is automatically followed by a change in ideology. The change of the ideological superstructure takes place often very much later and much slower than the changes in the societal ground. The exterior shell of things, the crystallization of life processes, remains standing even then and exerts its influence long after its kernel has been hollowed out. Even where one no longer comprehends their meaning, one still adheres to the forms; one continues to devalue them, one alienates them even further from their original meaning. What once was highest expression of vital forces gradually deteriorates into a senseless banality unless [a full-blooded generation—*crossed out*] power and grandeur can be summoned to impart new expression to the changed life content.

We ourselves are witnesses to such a tragedy. The sins committed in this respect today exceed the imagination. It is regrettable if an individual does not fathom these interconnections and therefore does wrong things. But if new things are impeded officially, it is our duty to fight this obstruction with all our ability, as it arises out of an indifference toward spiritual things and a complete misunderstanding of the past. Those who assume the right to interfere in the lives of individuals and the community in a regulatory way should first of all acquire adequate knowledge of things and their interconnections. Only superior abilities and real mastery entitles one to authority.

Neither sentimentality nor brutal force are suitable predispositions for that. The force of life will one day push aside this farce and create its own form all the quicker. Nothing is more stupid than to assume that our will is adequate to change the situation under which we live, in this or that direction. Neither a populace nor an individual can attain its aim immediately. Only what lies in the direction of our life's goals can find fulfillment.

Before I hold forth on the modern movement and its principles (or its fundamentals), I will explicate with a few examples what building, quite in spite of various theories, has always been and to what preconditions it has always been subject. This will facilitate our understanding of the new considerably. Two large building domains lie before us as we survey the development of building. One realm concerns building for life in a general sense, the other is intimately connected with specific spiritual atmospheres that we perceive as characteristic cultures.

The buildings of the first type are completely intertwined with the ground out of which they arose; they and they alone are in truth native. They grew out of the primal material of the landscape. No one invented them, but they grew in the true sense of the word out of the needs of the inhabitants, and they reflect the rhythm and character of the landscape in which they are imbedded. These features are typical for all farmhouses regardless of where on earth they may be found. The difference of their layout is the consequence of different racial characteristics. But with their living quarters, stables, and barns, they correspond in all aspects to the requirements of their inhabitants. The illustrations that I show you will make clearer than all words to what degree human building forms express the character of their arrangements.

Illustration 1
I leave open whether the single-farm settlement that we find in the area west of the Weser on the lower Rhine up to the coast of Holland and Flanders is the primitive form of Germanic settlement or whether here Saar-Frankish influences prevail.

Illustration 2
They are built without directional preference and order in an open field, surrounded by wall and ditch, near a spring or wooded area, in the middle of their work fields and removed from the highway.

Illustration 3
The farmer lives as a free man on free soil, depending on no one, growing what he needs for his own life and that of his family. Only field paths connect the individual farms to each other.

Illustration 4
The splitting up of families may have reduced operational means and brought with it cluster settlements to compensate for reduced defense capabilities and to extend help in times of need. But even now each builds with the old independence wherever he feels like it and where he finds soil offering adequate support potential.

Illustration 5
The Germanic cluster villages, too, do not follow a set pattern but arise spontaneously in their relationship to the landscape. Although denser, the houses stand about without pattern.

Illustration 6
Traffic of any type was not required. Much as formerly the individual farmstead, so now the individual village is self-supporting. Only field paths connect the villages with each other.

Illustration 7
These village formations come from the Germanic-Slavic border area and are planned with defense possibilities in mind. The areas between the individual farmsteads can easily be blocked in case of attack.

Illustration 8
This settlement type is held to be the original Germanic village form. Here the old characteristic field divisions are still visible.

Illustration 9
This village complex is without doubt of colonial origin. The common is the center of village life. It is the place for the wagons and for pronouncing judgments, the feast and meeting place. The common exercises a certain influence on the formation of the village. The buildings orient themselves in respect to the common in a free, natural order. By and by handicrafts and trade emerge. Both gain in importance. Agricultural work decreases gradually. Traffic grows. The street gains in importance and finally forms the backbone of the village settlement. While once, when Romanesque churches were built, entire villages became depopulated to escape from decades of forced labor in the praise of God and in the service of the church, one now searches out the shadow of fortified churches and castles for protection against attacks. In exchange for the promised protection one had to participate in defense and

perform services of other types. Even though some farmers attempted to settle in such protected locations, they were mainly inhabited by craftsmen and tradesmen.

Illustration 10

With the resulting growth it was in the communal interest to secure also the areas lying outside the castle or church district with walls.

Illustration 11

Gradually cities grew in which crafts and trade could develop undisturbed. The enclosures and the limited size of these early urban formations forced the inhabitants to live very closely together, but it also forced them for the sake of survival to regulate production and consumption. This was entrusted to the individual trades. The guilds arose. It is evident that life behind protective city walls combined with a shared economy brought with it an incredible communal sense. This in turn intensified religious feeling. A highly developed crafts system and the high point of the German cities coincided with the unrestricted secular power of the church in Europe, both finding their expression in the medieval township with its dominating cathedral.

Illustration 12

The churches also changed their shape. First they lay in the open landscape and were for a long time fortified; and they, too, have only gradually, under the protection of the fortified town, attained the full freedom of their form. For a long time the guilds were able to control production and consumption. But increasingly they had to ward off the forces of accumulating merchant capital. They lost more and more ground and finally succumbed in this struggle, leaving the way open for the development of trade. This brought in its wake true prosperity and with it the power of the cities. The cities founded schools and universities, often in competition with the church. With the invention of the printing art, the crafts came in contact with a realm of high spiritual aspirations and the cause of the reformation obtained substantial support. They obtained rights of all types, their own administration and defense system. The ornate guildhalls and town halls are the expression of a proud awareness of power. Increasingly secularization set in and with it the great ascendency of the German bourgeoisie.

Illustration 13

The invention of gunpowder decreased the value of city walls. One changes over to protect the land by means of fortified strongholds.

Illustration 14

The political development leads to the formation of prin-

cipalities. This change, too, is expressed in the development of the German cities.

Illustration 15

Now the domiciles of the princes influence building development. Courtly life finds its clear expression in them. Furthermore, the newly created residential towns clearly show the stratification of political life.

Illustration 16

The once proud citizens have become vassals. Their residences border the access routes to the castle and bear the physiognomy of liveried servants. It was the specific merit of Protestantism to have put science in the service of technology and economics. One now made scientific experiments. This, together with an attitude oriented toward reason already in ascendency since the Middle Ages, and the onset of capitalism that found nourishment in the existing nations, led to the development of industrial methods. Traffic, formerly tied to land and waterways, expanded immensely after the invention of the steam engine. From now on industry, and along with it trade, was no longer bound by restrictions. The tempo of life increased in manifold ways. The population expanded rapidly. Customs barriers fell so that the interior economy of the country could develop freely. The mechanization of the country progressed further. The unified German empire achieved world power status. International traffic and international trade determine life from now on. Metropolises of immense proportions develop. The speed of development permits no reflection.

Illustration 17

One builds street upon street in endless sequence. Industry experiences unexampled expansion. A new technology arises with unforeseen possibilities. Bold constructions never seen before are invented. [Here, too, one knows no limits.—*crossed out*]

Illustration 18

Traffic takes on immense dimensions and interferes in the organism of our cities with fierce brutality.

Illustration 19

Gigantic industrial complexes arise, yes, entire industrial cities.

Illustration 20

The machine has long since become master of production. That is generally the prewar situation. Even though the speed of this development was reduced by the outbreak of war, its direction is unchanged. On the contrary, the situation quickens. If one formerly managed loosely for a thousand reasons, one now has just as many reasons to carry out the sharpest calculations. The degree to which life before the war was already tied to the economy only became clear to us in the postwar years. Now there is only economy. It dominates everything, politics and life.

Ladies and gentlemen, I did not plan to hold forth on the history of economic or building development, but wanted only to show to what degree building is intertwined with living and the degree to which transformations in life find their expression in the transformations of our building forms.

The situation in which we find ourselves today is in no way comparable to that of earlier epochs. It is totally new and it will know how to express this in an equally new building form. I have already pointed out earlier that economic changes in a society are by no means instantly and automatically followed by changes in ideology, but take a much longer time to develop. It should therefore not surprise us that despite fundamental changes in the structure of our existence, the exterior form of our life has not yet been able to create its new expression. This transformation will take place only very gradually, by and by. The urgency of life will increasingly articulate itself and push away the old, long-obsolete forms.

Illustration 21

It is well known that certain technical requirements lead to new forms with powerful expressive qualities. But one must not confuse this with spiritual expression. It is beauty of a technical kind. Technical forms are the product of a technical, not a spiritual will. The degree to which a new technology influences the construction of a building can be seen in this picture.

Illustration 22

That it makes no sense to drape a building with masses of stones is quite obvious.

Illustration 23

These forms, too, are only possible by means of a new technology.

Illustration 24

How a new type of technical thinking can lead to new constructions can be seen in this wooden hall.

Illustration 25

Ferroconcrete facilitates wide-span and overhanging constructions.

Illustration 26

This type of a girder system leads to a totally new form of building and therefore to a new external appearance. That the vital force of life cannot be held back by administrative regulations is shown in this picture.

Illustration 27

Here the influence of building code restrictions is noticeable in the stepped gradations. Restrictions have never called forms into life. But in our administered world this defect, too, is understandable. In reality, only creative forces can truly give form.

If now a whole number of modern building masters embark upon the attempt to give new expression to changed life conditions, this must not be viewed as arbitrariness or whimsy. Le Corbusier has occupied himself with the form problem of the metropolis.

Illustration 28

He is of the opinion that the city of the future cannot do without skyscrapers, rather they appear to him an appropriate means to control increasing traffic congestion. He arranges them in groups, puts an airport in their middle, and connects them with a subway. Since he leaves the lower floors open, traffic flow can take place unimpeded.

Illustration 29

Apartment buildings, too, exceed the height attained formerly and surround gardens and parks.

Illustration 30

In continuation of the work of Haussmann, Le Corbusier suggested rebuilding the antiquated medieval quarters of Paris.

Illustration 31

Here, too, he suggests the skyscrapers.

Illustration 32

The plans of Le Corbusier can only be understood from the Parisian point of view.

Illustration 33

Paris is, on account of its historical development, a city of representation.

German city building goes along different tracks. Academic theory still attempts to understand medieval city planning; one cannot forget the charm of these cities. But in the meantime life goes on and makes brutal demands without regard to the arbitrary longings of individuals. Traffic poses problems. The senseless separation of working and living quarters leads, particularly in the large cities, to an insupportable increase in the cost of living. Entire residential quarters in industrial areas are being torn down to make room for industry. Further difficulties arise out of the present distribution of administrative districts. Each district is administered without regard to the whole. That this lack of planning will in the short or long run stifle the economic and industrial development, yes, stop it altogether, gradually seems to be sinking in. Sociological con-

Lieber Herr Doktor!

Ich wende mich nicht gegen die Form, da Leben immer Form hat, sondern nur gegen die Form als Ziel und zwar tue ich das aus einer Reihe von Erfahrungen heraus und der dadurch gewonnenen Einsicht. Form als Ziel mündet immer in Formalismus, denn dieses Streben richtet sich nicht auf ein Innen, sondern auf ein Aussen. Aber nur ein lebendiges Innen hat ein lebendiges Aussen. Alles Wie wird getragen von einem Was. Nur Lebensintensität hat Formintensität. Das Ungeformte ist nicht schlechter als das Übergeformte. Das Eine ist Nichts, das andere ist Schein. Wirkliche Form setzt wirkliches Leben voraus, kein gewesenes und auch kein gedachtes. Deshalb ist die Frage Klassik oder Gotik eben so unernst, wie die Frage konstruktivistisch oder funktionalistisch. Wir sind weder Antike noch Mittelalter und Leben ist nicht Statik oder Dynamik, sondern umschliesst beides. Nur ein richtig angesetzter und durchgeführter Gestaltungsprocess führt zum Ziel. Sie werten das Resultat und wir den Ansatz des Gestaltungsprocesses.

So gewiss der Gestaltungsprocess nur in seinem Resultat sichtbar wird, so gewiss führt nur ein richtig angesetzter und durchgeführter zu einem Resultat. Ist es nicht die Wichtigste, vielleicht einzigste Aufgabe Deshalb scheint es mir wichtiger statt zu werten, die geistige Situation in der wir stehen, aufzuhellen, sichtbar zu machen, ihre Strömungen zu ordnen und dadurch zu führen.

Ist es nicht wichtiger, als zu werten, die geistige Situation aufzuhellen, in der wir stehen, aufzuhellen, sichtbar zu machen, zu ordnen.

Sollten wir nicht, statt zu werten, die geistige Situation, in der wir stehen, aufhellen, sichtbar machen, ihre Strömungen ordnen und dadurch zu führen.

WERKBUNDKOMMISSION
BEIM MESSAMT FRANKFURT AM MAIN

Manuscript of a letter to Walter Riezler: "I am not addressing myself against form, only against form as goal. . . ."

siderations are gaining influence in city planning. The value of the siting theory in urban planning has begun to be recognized. Industry must be housed where it finds the most advantageous conditions. That these difficulties are particularly evident in the industrial districts of Rhineland-Westphalia, the most industrialized economic center, and that here the call for relief is loudest, is understandable. With the creation of the Ruhr Settlement Association, 325 city administrations were united under one urban planning concept. This offered the opportunity to establish a unified economic plan, independent of individual administrative districts. This economic plan is simply the planned arrangement of working and residential zones, of railroad, agricultural, and recreational zones. Only on the basis of this allocation does one determine the traffic installations. Thus traffic installations do not determine but follow a specifically planned development, or to say it in other words, traffic planning follows economic development.

Thus the dominance of economic power over us begins to exercise its determinative influence in the most important areas in the planning of cities. Only the implementation of such thoughts will lead to an organic form for our cities. Only on such a basis can the industrial, residential, commercial, and administrative centers unfold freely according to their particular nature. Only thus can the changed structure of our life find its corresponding expression. [Only here can building art arise that, I repeat, is always the spatial execution of spiritual decisions.— crossed out]

[Handwritten postscript:] Only here can the spiritual capabilities of our time become effective. Building art is not the realization of specific formal problems, no matter how much they may be contained therein. But it is always, I repeat, the spatial execution of spiritual decisions.

12

Letters to *Die Form*

Mies addressed Walter Riezler, editor of the periodical *Die Form* supported by the Deutsche Werkbund, in two now famous letters, attacking the name of the periodical. The short exchange between Riezler and Mies concerning the concept of form was carried on publicly in *Die Form*.

"Regarding the New Volume"
Published in *Die Form*, 2, no. 1 (1927), p. 1.

Dear Dr. Riezler:

May I make a suggestion to you at the moment in which you take on the editorship of the journal of the Deutsche Werkbund? Give another title to the journal. Some neutral title pointing to the Werkbund.

You may ask what I have against the present title?

Do you not think that the title *Die Form* makes too great a claim?

A claim that obliges? That would not yet constitute a danger; but does it not oblige in the wrong direction?

Do we not guide the attention away from the essential?

Is form really an aim?

Is it not rather the result of the form-giving process?

Is it not the process that is essential?

Does not a small change in preconditions bring about another result?

Another form?

That is why I would prefer to march without a flag. Think about my suggestion.

Yours, Mies van der Rohe

"On Form in Architecture"
Published in *Die Form*, 2, no. 2 (1927), p. 59.

I am not addressing myself against form, only against form as goal.

And I do that on the basis of a number of experiences and the insights gained from them.

Form as goal results always in formalism.

For this effort does not aim toward something internal but toward an external.

But only a vital inside has a vital outside.

Only life intensity has form intensity.

Every how is supported by a what.

The unformed is not worse than the overformed.

One is nothing, the other illusion.

Authentic form presupposes authentic life.

But not one that has been nor one that has been thought.

Therein lies the criterion.

We value not the result but the starting point of the form-giving process.

This in particular reveals whether form was derived from life or for its own sake.

This is why the form-giving process appears to me so important.

Life is what matters.

In its entire fullness, in its spiritual and concrete interconnection.

Is it not one of the most important tasks of the Werkbund to illuminate the spiritual and concrete situation in which we find ourselves, make it visible, order its currents, and thereby direct it? Should one not leave all else to the creative forces?

The manuscript of the letter to Riezler "On Form in Architecture" (in Museum of Modern Art, Manuscripts Folder 6) is identical with the printed version up to the sentences "Authentic form presupposes authentic life. But not one that has been, nor one that has been thought. Therein lies the criterion." The manuscript goes beyond it in the following manner:

[This is why the question of classical or Gothic is as irrelevant as the question of constructivist of functionalist. We are neither antiquity nor the Middle Ages, and life is neither static nor dynamic but includes both.—*crossed out*]

Only a properly initiated and executed process of form-giving leads to the [aim—*crossed out*] result. You value results, we value the point of departure. As certainly as a form-giving process is only recognizable by its result, so one that has been initiated properly will lead to a result. Is that not the most important, perhaps only task? That is why I think it is more important to illuminate, make visible, and direct the currents of the spiritual situation in which we stand than to evaluate it.

Added on the back:

We want to open ourselves to life and seize it. Life is what matters in all the fullness of its spiritual and concrete relations.

We do not value the result but the starting point of the form-giving process. It in particular reveals whether form was arrived at from the direction of life or for its own sake. That is why the form-giving process appears to me so important. Life is what matters. In all the fullness of its spiritual and concrete interconnections.

Is it not the most important, perhaps only, task of the Werkbund to illuminate and make visible the spiritual and concrete situation in which we stand, order its currents and thus direct them? Should one not leave all else to the creative force?

Stuttgart-Weissenhof housing settlement, 1927.

13
**Foreword to the Official Catalog of the Stuttgart
Werkbund Exhibition "Die Wohnung"**
The exhibition "Die Wohnung" (Housing) ran from July 23 to
October 9, 1927; the catalog was published by the exhibition
directorate (Stuttgart, 1927).

The problems associated with the new housing are rooted
in the changed material, social, and spiritual structure of
our time; only from this vantage point can the problems
be understood.

The degree of structural change determines the character
and extent of the problem. They are not subject to any
arbitrary forces. They cannot be solved with slogans, nor
can they be argued away with slogans.

The problem of rationalization and typification is only part
of the problem. Rationalization and typification are only
the means, they must never be the goal. The problem of
the new housing is basically a spiritual problem, and the
struggle for new housing is only an element of the larger
struggle for new forms of living.

Mies's residential block at the Weissenhofsiedlung.

14

Foreword to *Bau und Wohnung*

The book *Bau und Wohnung* (Building and Housing) was published by the Deutsche Werkbund (Stuttgart, 1927).

It is not entirely useless to specifically emphasize today that the problem of the new housing is a problem of the building art, in spite of its technical and economic aspects. It is a complex problem and therefore can only be solved by creative forces rather than by calculation or organization. Based on this belief I thought it necessary, in spite of such current slogans as "rationalization" and "typification," to respond to the challenge posed in Stuttgart by raising tasks out of an atmosphere of the unilateral and the doctrinaire. I have attempted to illuminate the problem comprehensibly and have, for that reason, invited the respective representatives of the modern movement to take up positions in regard to the housing problem.

In order to permit each one as much freedom as possible to execute his ideas, I have set neither guidelines nor given programmatic orientation. And in establishing my plan arrangement it was important to me to avoid everything schematic and rule out everything that could constitute a restriction to free work processes.

"Concerning My Block"

In *Bau und Wohnung*, p. 77.

Economic reasons today necessitate rationalization and typification in the construction of apartment buildings. The increasing differentiation of our housing needs, however, demands on the other side an ever greater freedom of usage. In the future it will become necessary to do justice to both claims. For this purpose the skeleton structure is the most suitable system of construction. It makes a rational production possible and yet permits total freedom of disposition in the interior. If one limits oneself to the predetermination of kitchen and bath locations on account of the required installations, and if one divides the other space by movable walls, I feel that all legitimate living purposes can be accommodated.

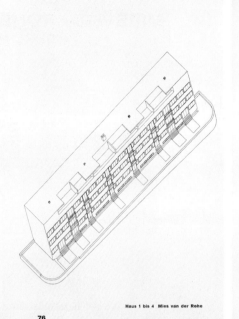

Haus 1 bis 4 Mies van der Rohe

76

MIES VAN DER ROHE
BERLIN

Zu meinem Block

Wirtschaftliche Gründe fordern heute beim Bau von Mietwohnungen Rationalisierung und Typisierung ihrer Herstellung. Diese immer steigende Differenzierung unserer Wohnbedürfnisse aber fordert auf der andern Seite größte Freiheit in der Benützungsart. Es wird in Zukunft notwendig sein, beiden Tendenzen gerecht zu werden. Der Skelettbau ist hierzu das geeignetste Konstruktionssystem. Er ermöglicht eine rationelle Herstellung und läßt der inneren Raumaufteilung jede Freiheit. Beschränkt man sich darauf, lediglich Küche und Bad ihrer Installation wegen als konstante Räume auszubilden und entschließt man sich dann noch, die übrige Wohnfläche mit verstellbaren Wänden aufzuteilen, so glaube ich, daß mit diesen Mitteln jedem berechtigten Wohnanspruch genügt werden kann.

Mies v d Rohe

77

Das konstruktive System ist ein Eisenskelettbau, dessen Gefache mit halbsteinstarken Wänden ausgefüllt sind und die an den Außenwänden gegen Temperaturschwankungen mit 4 cm starken Torfplatten belegt und mit einem Putzträger überspannt wurden.
Die Trennwände zwischen den einzelnen Wohnungen, wie auch die Treppenhauswände wurden gegen Schall mit 2 cm starken Torfplatten geschützt.
Für die massiven Decken wurde folgende Ausführung vorgeschrieben: Steineisendecken nach dem System Kleine, hierauf eine 2 cm starke Sandschüttung mit Gipsestrich als Unterlage für den Linoleumbelag.
Als Putzträger wurden Tektonplatten vorgeschrieben, die an zwischen den Eisenträgern eingespannten Holzriegeln befestigt wurden.

84

Für die Terrassen wurde eine Bichnache Dichtung vorgesehen.
Das Dach besteht aus einer Massivdecke, die mit einer doppelten Lage Ruberoid gedeckt wurde.
Für den gauzen Block ist eine zentrale Warmwasserheizungs- und Warmwasserbereitungsanlage vorgesehen. Sämtliche Rohrleitungen liegen frei vor der Wand, die Lichtleitungen unter dem Putz.
Die Außenflächen des Gebäudes sind mit Zementmörtel verputzt.
Die Fenster sind als Rekordfenster so konstruiert, daß sich die Flügel im geöffneten Zustande aufeinanderlegen lassen.

85

Four pages from *Bau und Wohnung* (1927).

15

Introductory Remarks to the Special Issue
"Werkbundausstellung: Die Wohnung"

Die Form, 2, no. 9 (1927), p. 257. This special issue was devoted to the Deutsche Werkbund exhibition "Die Wohnung" (Housing).

In the summer of 1925, on the occasion of the meeting of the Deutsche Werkbund in Bremen, the request made by the Württemberg Work Collective of the Deutsche Werkbund to deal with the housing problem at an exhibition in Stuttgart was accepted and I was entrusted with the implementation of this task.

On July 29, 1926, the Stuttgart City Council accepted this proposal and our building plans were approved. In mid-November 1926, the "Verein Werkbund—Ausstellung die Wohnung" (Werkbund Association for the Exhibition on Housing) was founded and by March 1, 1927, ground was broken for the excavations at Weissenhof.

In taking on this assignment I knew that we had to realize it in contradiction to commonly held expectations, since the complex character of the problem was clear to all who have occupied themselves seriously with the housing problem.

The battle cry "rationalization and typification," along with the call for the economizing of the housing industry, represent only parts of the problem, for, although important, they have significance only if seen in right proportions. Next to them, or rather above them, stands the spatial problem that can only be solved by creativity rather than by calculation or organization. I have therefore not given out guidelines but have limited myself to solicit the cooperation of those whose work leads me to expect interesting contributions to the housing question. The exhibition was conceived from the beginning as experimental and thus has its value quite independent of the results achieved.

Each participating architect has investigated the new materials available in the marketplace for their applicability, and each one has made the choice as to his construction according to his responsibility. The state of the building technology has set the limits to our efforts.

The organizational problem cannot be solved without the cooperation of the building trades. This was completely impossible in Stuttgart as we had no authority over the letting-out of contracts. This also deprived us of exercising control over the quality of execution. We were really independent only in regard to spatial problems, which means questions in respect to the actual building art.

Residential block of the Weissenhofsiedlung, interiors.

Lecture
Given at the "Immermannbund" in Düsseldorf. Unpublished manuscript of March 14, 1927, in the collection of Dirk Lohan, Chicago.

Even the building arts movement has its test of loyalty. It is the struggle for the flat roof. Here also one accuses the opponents of being reactionary, the advocates of being under the influence of alien influences. This battle is conducted with a seriousness as if it concerned the survival of the building art. In reality it is only a battle for external elements, even though it is conducted by bearers of resounding names. It has no significance in our struggle for the basis of a new building art.

That struggle takes place on an altogether different plane and is only part of the greater struggle for new forms of living, not, as the academicians believe, the whimsy of a small clique. It is a struggle that concerns changed living and working conditions, a new technology and new materials. A changed world wants its own form. Not formal trends but the mastery of real relations stands in the center of our efforts.

For us, neither the lack of spirituality on the part of the intellectuals nor the historicizing games of a tired society are meaningful. The desire of financial and economical leaders to simulate in their workplaces the life forms of medieval merchant princes does not close our eyes to the fact that it is their work in particular that has the greatest influence on the transformation of our life. Nor are we surprised that one still decks out theaters and movie houses with the trimmings of the period of Pompadour and that nowadays people still prefer bad imitations of pleasure palaces for their residences. Everywhere one notes the same striving to legitimize oneself. This behavior is typical of the beginning phases of great social upheavals. But one should not justify this rubbish and masquerade by claiming it serves the needs of the masses.

The masses do not appear to us quite as characterless as the mass-production clothiers see them. Especially the masses demonstrate clear, strong impulses for living, and a great urge toward functionality and an undistorted affirmation of life. The forces residing in them will become effective and will make themselves heard.

Because the building art is only vital when it is supported by life in all is fullness, the leaders of the modern movement attempt to recognize the spiritual and material forces of our period, investigate them and draw, without prejudice, the consequences. For only where the building art leans on the material forces of a period can it bring about the spatial execution of its spiritual decisions. But that is its actual meaning and it has never been otherwise.

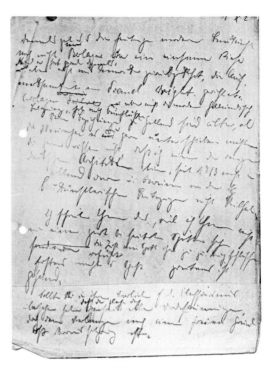

Draft of a letter, around 1927.

17
Draft of a Letter
In Museum of Modern Art, Manuscripts Folder 2.

[*page 1*]
At that time the modern art of building did not yet exist. [Only—*crossed out*] Berlage was a solitary giant and, having returned from America, had just drawn attention to Frank L. Wright. Berlage [was my leader—*crossed out*], but not the modern Dutch achievement, has influenced me. My relationship to Holland is older than opinions [only—*crossed out*] make it out.

The gentlemen do not know that I am one of the few German architects [who] have not been in Holland since 1913 and therefore can have no part in the building art achievements. I write this to you because I see [in] you not only a well-equipped mocker [but—*crossed out*]. The delight in mockery causes mistakes. First of all it is fun and secondly it is healthy.

Should you have overlooked in your preference for classicism that the flat roof, beyond all roof fashions, is nevertheless a prerequisite of the free ground plan?

[*page 2*]
The situation is such that a hot battle has erupted over the flat roof. That is exactly like round or fat butterballs: calculating natures work off their excess energies by rationalizing. Overtime work.

The actual movement, far away from this battlefield, is struggling for new insights and . . . [*illegible*] works like science. Only that the new results will gain ascendancy one day and the battle will be decided.

This battle within the building art will not only be conducted in the professional circle and decided there but is part of a larger dispute in all areas.

Tradition:
If only today's generation would assume real and positive attitudes toward today's life and its tasks, and not follow a false [forgotten and locked—*crossed out*] tradition: the real tasks as instruments of intellectual development.

The masses [are] by no means as characterless as the mass-production clothiers maintain, but we feel particularly in them the strongest impulses for living.

Today's society feels itself obligated to hold on to an antiquated, ridiculous tradition, and [that it—*crossed out*] we understand of course that the individual does not want to fall outside of this norm.

Building art is the spatial process of intellectual decisions.

[*page 3*]
We are furthermore aware, that . . . [*illegible*] the remark about the masses is inadequate, for [they are in—*crossed out*] who seriously wants to believe that they are really so lacking in character as the mass-production clothiers [see them—*crossed out*] maintain. We feel particularly in them the strongest life impulses for living and a strong urge toward functionality. Is it not precisely a criterion, what a person feels in respect to the masses?

Banality:
Is it not the duty of each generation to assume a positive attitude toward life, rather than remain caught up in dusty thinking? Was that not once the most lively expression [of a life-determ—*crossed out*] of the times?

Is it not a shame to what degree large challenges are passed up? (Is not life what we make of it?)

Is it really economically justifiable to hand over real tasks to mass-production clothiers and allow oneself to be satisfied with solutions that are already antiquated before they are completed?

We are aware that the time has great potential but that it cannot be made visible as long as clothiers' attitudes and field marshals' conceits are in control.

Does one not trip over the discrepancies in the behavior of . . . [*illegible*] leading heads in all other intellectual areas?

Has one forgotten that the building art always was the spatial process of spiritual decisions?

[*page 4*]
Why do you believe the Dutch have had this influence over me? I do not really value that building art so much.

II Notebook (1927–1928)

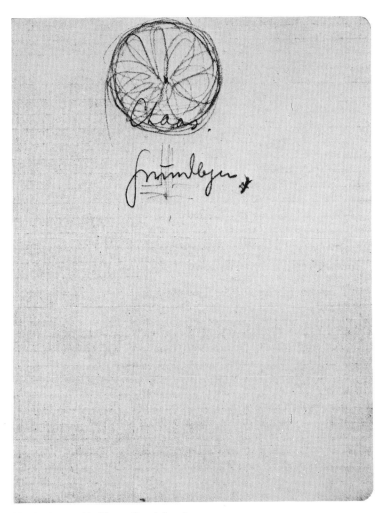

Notebook, page 13, "Chaos. Foundations."

Editorial Preface

The notebook of Mies, preserved at the Mies van der Rohe Archive of the Museum of Modern Art in New York, is a collection of loose pages (80 pages, 14.9 × 11.5 cm) of handwritten notes (pencil). Presumably on account of its peculiarities combined with a lack of legibility and identifiability, it has been so far unevaluated and unpublished.

Aside from the problem of deciphering the handwriting, the evaluation of the notebook is made difficult by the question of the original sequence of the unnumbered pages. Furthermore, the often telegram-like reduction of the style is little conducive to reconstruction. On account of certain numbers in front of or behind notes it appears that many entries constitute excerpts from books. Only in a few cases, however, do we find indications as to specific authors or book titles. Even here, Mies's predisposition to a reduction to the utmost minimum is in evidence. For example the word "Como" stands not necessarily for the city by that name, but the book *Briefe vom Comer See* (Letters from Lake Como) by Romano Guardini. Another work, Friedrich Dessauer's *Philosphie der Technik,* was so familiar to Mies that he failed to identify his excerpts with either author or book notation and simply indicated the page numbers.

Understanding and legibility of Mies's notes are restricted in many respects. Basically the texts have not been quoted verbatim but have been reduced to what appeared to him as their most essential aspects, whereby his own words and those of the authors quoted fuse. Mies's typical comprehension of the essential reveals itself only if one takes the trouble to compare his notes to the texts they refer to.

It also has to be added that Mies tended to enrich the excerpts by his own thoughts and associations to which the reading had stimulated him. For example he recites literally the following sentence out of Romano Guardini's *Liturgische Bildung,* p. 42, concerning the Taylorism of the industrial age: "The purposes started their dominance, the formulas and methods"—to which he added: "There are people who would like to make a Ford factory out of nature." Another example illuminates the assimilation of the readings by way of analogies. In the text *Von heiligen Zeichen,* Guardini quotes Pope Pius IX (pp. 11–12): "Give the meaning back to the words"— an admonishment Mies applied to the arts by adding "the handling of forms." And Guardini's call for a religious renovation of life, "We want to give things their meaning again," is affirmed by Mies with the analogy to architecture: "Who still feels anything of a wall, an opening?" (See notebook pages 61, 62.)

An arrangement of the legacy according to criteria of legibility seemed to make sense. So parts that appeared to relate to lectures were separated from the rest of the excerpts unless they were otherwise identified. Some overlapping was unavoidable. To increase legibility, punctuation marks have been added. Additions are indicated by square brackets.

To facilitate the comparison of Mies's excerpts with the respective passages from the books, citations by page number and abbreviated title have been given in footnotes. Similarly, Mies's additions have been noted here insofar as they arise out of the readings. Not reproduced here are five pages of the notebook that contain only lists of architects' names.

The dating of the notes is only partially assured by Mies's entry "17.III.28. Diary" (notebook page 33). The earliest entries are from the final months of the year 1927. This is indicated by certain notes in regard to experiences connected with the Weissenhofsiedlung in Stuttgart (see page 8); references also point to the French journal *Le Génie Civil,* number 18, of October 29, 1927 (see page 31). On the other hand the lecture held in February 1928, "Die Voraussetzungen baukünstlerischen Schaffens" (The Preconditions of Architectural Work), makes clear that Mies here made use of his excerpts. The publication year of books noted down in the notebook also limits the time frame of the remarks.

Romano Guardini's *Briefe vom Comer See,* printed according to the imprint on September 3, 1927, came out in the last months of 1927. Friedrich Dessauer's *Philosophie der Technik* similarly appeared in 1927, and also Leopold Ziegler's study *Zwischen Mensch und Wirtschaft.* Mies's interest in other writings of Romano Guardini, particularly his *Liturgische Bildung* (1923) and *Von heiligen Zeichen* (1922), was seemingly awakened after Mies had read *Briefe vom Comer See.* References to these earlier works are, however, occasionally mixed with those to the 1927 volume, so that an earlier date than 1927 can be excluded.

Most of the notes probably do not go beyond 1928, even though that cannot be stated categorically. One cannot rule out that the existing pages are only part of a larger notebook or perhaps parts of several notebooks of like format. The entry "Cassel. A damn frugality. Regretfully also in this enlightment. Fuchs" and "Do not standardize everything. Only where it makes sense. Why tie one's hand voluntarily" (page 8) might concern the Rothenberg housing settlement in Kassel, the layout of which was made by Otto Haesler in the summer of 1929 in a rigid rowhouse manner according to the example of Dammerstock. In 1930–1931 the first building segment of Kassel-Rothenberg was erected.

1

Notes for Lectures

Page 1

Lecture

How senseless economy

becomes when it only wants economy

is shown by the efforts of

the Steelwork Association

with those steel houses.

Instead of spiritualized economy;

that would not be less,

but more important.

Page 2

Lecture

In all epochs

life was built;

What has our life?

———

Man and technology.

Gigantic (masses.)

form. In the gigantic

the differentiated

for the masses or against the

steel arm.

To internalize

the masslike.

To spiritualize the technological.

The means of the new technology,

new technical materials.

Page 3

Lecture

It is wrong of Le Corbusier

to mingle his attitude

with that of pure classicism.[1]

———

Middle Ages[2]

67.76.90 Hoffmann

on technology and spatial art, building art

counts for the same.

92.98

Vom Ewigen im Menschen

[Max] Scheler, [Leipzig, 1919]

1
This comment probably also comes from Mies's reading of Guardini. In Guardini's *Liturgische Bildung* (Rothenfels, 1923), Mies underlined the following passage on p. 74 that might have stimulated his remark on Le Corbusier: "This is the attitude demonstrated by Hefele in his *Gesetz der Form* with such convincing power. However, in reply one has to stress: What he talks about is not 'the Catholic,' for the Catholic encompasses also the subjective energies, not just the valuable, the right thing generally. Above all it was wrong to equate this attitude and Catholicism with the romantic-classical attitude."

2
Probably relates to Paul Ludwig Landsberg, *Die Welt des Mittelalters und wir* (Bonn, 1922).

Page 4

Lecture

The battle against the new

need not necessarily arise out of

an attachment to the old,

and we believe freely

that at bottom,

it is a battle against reason.

Man wants to salvage

the transrational.

Question,

whether that is possible

in that way.

Como 38

Page 5

Lecture

Dahlem Dadaism.

———

Technology everywhere, also

in the spiritual. Como.

Page 6

Lecture

One speaks of the victory

of the new building art. I must say

that this is entirely out of the question.

We have barely started.

In only a very few places is

the new land visible. What is victorious

is perhaps a new formalism.

We can only talk of a new building art when

[the battle—crossed out] new

life forms have been formed.

———

Untermann

———

[Ernst] Mach, Erkenntnis + Irrtum.

Leipzig 1905.

Notebook, page 6.

Page 7

Lecture

The art lovers and the intellectuals

stand too remote from real life

to draw meaningful conclusions out of it

for forming an attitude.

———

Guardini. Faith is

supernatural

awareness of reality.

Hearing is life in

invisible realities.[3]

———

Page 8

Lecture

To come up against limits.

Stuttgart. Limit-testing.

Limits set by the

economic situation

of society

are insurmountable!

———

Cassel. A damn frugality.

Regretfully also in this

enlightenment!

Fuchs.[4]

———

Do not standardize everything.

Only where it makes sense.

———

Why tie one's hand voluntarily.

———

Page 9

Lecture. Service. B.T.

Purposeful, not the same

as [functional—crossed out]

deliberate setting of goals.

———

Credit question as to old houses.

Contrast to the rest of their actions

that only aim for reasonable activities.

———

Form smashing

through structural change

and through economic demands.

3
Romano Guardini, *Von heiligen Zeichen* (Würzburg, 1922), p. 13, underlined by Mies: "Faith is supernatural awareness of reality. Faith is life in invisible realities. Do we have such faith?"

4
Mies refers here to Eduard Fuchs, who had published his multivolume illustrated cultural history in 1912, a standard work of which Mies had a copy. Fuchs lived in the Perls House, to which Mies erected an addition in 1926. It was Fuchs who asked Mies to make a design for the Rosa Luxemburg–Karl Liebknecht memorial. For further details see Franz Schulze, *Mies van der Rohe: A Critical Biography* (Chicago, 1985), pp. 124ff.

Page 10

Lecture

Call for the strong man.

Non-commissioned officer

———

economical, social, spiritual.

———

Economic situation

of society.

———

Is the confusion

of our suburbs

not more than just anarchy?

Does not a differentiation

hide behind it? [5]

Page 11

Lecture

Everything is in the service of utility.

One even justifies artistic things and preferences

[with] utility.

———

Old art appears to us unreachable

and really was always so.

Art can only arise out of the soil

of our economic structure.

———

The absence of style

is viewed as absence of culture.

That explains nothing.

Absence of style is

in reality anarchy. Anarchy in

economic realms corresponds to

anarchy in the artistic,

for it, too, is expression

of differentiation.

Continued.

5
Compare Mies's position in his lecture of December 12, 1923, "Gelöste Aufgaben" (see Appendix I, 5): "You are all familiar with the condition of our buildings, and yet I wish to remind you of Kurfürstendamm and Dahlem, to bring to mind this total lunacy in stone."

Page 12

Continued

*The call for style,
for culture, is lunacy and the
last remains of a legacy
of a confused unspiritual epoch
Tropp.*[6]

*Lecture
Any attempt
to solve building art problems
by calculating means
must fail.*

———

*Paynet [?] Rings [?] p. 96
Against the dominance of technology,
for serving. Technology as means
to freedom.*

———

Page 13

*Chaos.
Foundations*

Page 14

*Lecture
Decline not only of the West
but of the world.*

———

*[Is there no—crossed out]
Therefore conservators and
historical preservationists. Tomorrow
cultural preservation parks.*[7]

Page 15

*Lecture
The demand for equalization of
living quarters is based on economic
equalization.
The social equalization of the masses
does not cancel the differentiation
of soul. Therefore a dwelling
cannot merely be made
from an economic angle.*

37.

6
Probably refers to Paul Tropp, whose *Entwicklung und Aufbau der Miete* was reviewed by Mies in *Die Baugilde,* 6, no. 5 (1924), p. 56 (see Appendix I, 9).

7
Presumably Rudolf Schwarz, *Wegweisung der Technik* (Potsdam, 1929), taken from the following passage: "The 'historical preservation' movement . . .—in the broadest sense—wants to preserve the old homestead, where it exists, or rebuild it where it has disappeared. It addresses thereby the entire panorama of the problem, without, however, meeting it creatively. . . . Besides that, it aims at a preservation of soul side by side with temporal reality, like a preservation park in which old vegetation and dying peoples find their old-age home. . . . The gesture of the conservator remains defensive, compromise and retreat." Quoted from Maria Schwarz and Ulrich Conrads, *Rudolf Schwarz. Wegweisung der Technik und andere Schriften zum neuen Bauen 1926–1961* (Brunswick and Wiesbaden, 1979), p. 41.

Page 16

Lecture

In regard to the new, also,
the attitude is not the same.
Here also, it is the inner attitude
of man that counts.

Page 17

Lecture

Immense work. Already
reduced from 8 to 6 hours.[8]
Food for thought.

———

Parallel to the intensification
of tools and methods
usable in spiritual realms.
Higher performance from
each beginning, higher achievement
from all means.

Page 18

Primitive oversolicitousness
tends toward the decorative. Sullivan
toward the spiritual.
A spiritual person does not want more
than he can use.[9]
Regulation of oversolicitousness
through technology. Highest effect
rules out the decorative.
Chile House is like
primitive technology. Quantity
instead of quality.

———

Woman at work, then and now.
Unfolding of beauty,
directly.

———

Business advertising with light

8
Compare Leopold Ziegler, *Zwischen Menschen und Wirtschaft* (Darmstadt, 1927), pp. 50f.

9
Compare Siegfried Ebeling, *Der Raum als Membran* (Dessau, 1926), p. 16: "It is the symptom of a dying culture that a populace produces more than it can use, that it whips its spirit harder than is good for it, that it anticipates needs that it itself does not have."

Page 19

Fritz Klatt, Schöpferische
Pause [*Creative Pause*], Jena [19]21

———

The last twenty years
have brought an upsetting of scientific thinking,
[that for—crossed out] the
significance of which for the future
cannot yet be measured.

Page 20

New demands:
Connections with real life.
New man. Form
Relationship to surroundings.
Not rejection but
[affirmation—crossed out] mastery.

Page 21

Masses.
Here we stand.
Mastery through organization
of the future.
Differentiation
and new attitude
[new task—crossed out]
Attempt at solution:
mechanical
economic,
[ideological—crossed out] spiritual
new building art.
Different directions.

Page 22

Lecture
The apartment is a use item.
May one ask for what? [Obviously—crossed out]
May one ask to what it relates?
Obviously only to physical existence. [that—crossed out]
So that all may proceed smoothly.
And yet man also has the needs of
his soul, which can never be satisfied
by merely making sure that he does not
get stuck in his walls.

Notebook, page 22.

Even the strongest organizational achievements

do not exceed ordering.

One can only organize the existing.

Chaos

in all areas,

economic,

social,

spiritual.

The creative

Beauty is the radiance of truth

Answer of the inner to the outer.

To bring technology in relationship

to men.

To achieve a new position

[illegible]

Economics.

Contemplation.

Logos before ethos.

Silence. Silence.

City building.

Fight with Riezler. Technical.

We demand above all attitude.

We want truth.

Riezler, beauty.

———

The nature of the technical is

determined in its fulfillment.[10]

———

The technical is alien to ornament.[11]

Technology as educator.

———

He who builds a factory as if it were a temple

lies and disfigures

the landscape.

10

Underlining by Mies in Friedrich Dessauer, *Philosophie der Technik* (Bonn, 1927), p. 137: "The nature of the technical is determined in its *fulfillment.* If a watch is unfulfilled, if it does not run, then it is meaningless, essentially not a watch, even though it may contain all the parts. And if only a final quality is missing in this watch, something in its entelechtical order maybe, and all else stands ready, then it is not a watch, but a silly heap of unfulfilled form. Its essence springs into being when the last precondition of its idea is adequately close to the ultimate."

11

Underlinings by Mies in Dessauer, *Philosophie der Technik,* pp. 141, 142: "One thing is quite sure. In the fundamental process of invention the aesthetic plays no role. It has no root either in the conception of the circumscribed problem or in the sphere of natural lawfulness. But it is similarly certain that the completed technical product can evoke aesthetic experiences. . . . The technological is alien to ornament. Its beauty is enclosed in itself. . . . The ability of technical objects to elicit aesthetic feelings seems to have its roots in the same ultimate ground out of which the autonomous value arises. This ultimate ground is the spiritual penetration of form in intuition of purpose. When meaning triggers through, shines through, when matter becomes glowing, transparent, from the invading spirit, when this spirit is rhythm of moving limbs, distribution of mass, color and form, so that the manifold becomes subordinate to a final unity, then the technical object contains the objective root for the aesthetic experience. The articulation of the rooms of a house, the color and its gradations, are also contained in the ground. For the technical aim of building is not the house but dwelling, just as the goal of machine making is not a locomotive but its ride."

To recognize ordering laws,
not to establish them.[12]
theories functionalism

Intensive and extensive

Technik 12.[13]
Something must
join the elements,
the creative.

Guardini, attitude toward things.

Suprematism.

Building huts.
Monk's Latin.

Building without culture
Commerce without culture.

Lack of schools,
Spiritual schooling for building.
Nowadays connections arise again.
Engineer-like building.

The belief of engineers
is, to realize
secure walls [?].

Today. Unfolding of technology.
Unfolding of economy.
Fusion of the technical,
the commercial [with]
the financial speculation.

Notebook, page 27.

12
Underlinings by Mies of a passage in Dessauer, *Philosophie der Technik,* pp. 148, 149, that could also be read as a description of Mies's work method which oriented itself on the example of engineering. Dessauer talks about an "autonomous imperative for the realization of the idea" that could possess man, practically burn him. Mies underlined: "Inventors of all degrees . . . feel themselves as implementers of this task; so they are locked into an order. This order is found anew wherever technology is accomplished. . . . In this order the inventor is free only once, in the beginning, when he isolates and delimits precisely the task he wants to solve. From then on he is the instrument of this task, without freedom. Now his spirit encounters, with its total force, a strict order of things per se. It is so strong and so powerful that against it each desire and everything arbitrary totally breaks. . . . In the crucible of problem solving the human spirit is recast according to the imperturbable order that it encounters in its spiritual struggle. This struggle therefore is not an overcoming, but a getting overwhelmed, a service-ready self-sacrifice, a giving-oneself-up, a subjugation of extreme consequence, more strict than the rule of any order could be. This is the encounter of the inventor: one who is larger than he is steps up to him and it is out of him alone that the fulfillment comes."

13
Refers to Dessauer, *Philosophie der Technik,* p. 12.

Page 29

New forms through
new orders,
limits.

———

The methodically thorough research,
penetration of nature, economics,
technology corresponds to the [?] of building,
then comes a new order of things; and out of that a new
building art.

———

To make
be out of should,
out of skills a task.

———

Nowadays effects everywhere.

Page 30

Conscious technology.
Against Gothic.
Technology. Consciousness.

———

Middle Ages.
81

———

Sailboat as technology [14]

———

To make conscious.

———

Concert hall

———

We want to do with composure
whatever it is we have to do.

Page 31
Le Génie Civil
N.18.29.10 [19]27. [15]

[14]
Compare Romano Guardini, *Briefe vom Comer See* (Mainz, 1927), p. 18.

[15]
Refers to the journal *Le Génie Civil, Revue Générale Hebdomadaire des Industries Françaises et Étrangères,* Paris. In the indicated issue number 18, 1927, on pages 421 to 427 a concert hall is introduced ("La Nouvelle Salle de Concert Pleyel à Paris") that has a special acoustical ceiling in ferroconcrete. In his lecture "Die Voraussetzungen baukünstlerischen Schaffens" of February 1928 (see Appendix III, 1), Mies showed a slide of a "concert hall for 3,000 persons in Paris": "Scientific effort for the understanding of acoustical laws is being applied and begins to exert its influence on the planning of large halls."

Page 32

V.O.2.

The nonferrous metals.

The Middle Ages
had no stadium.

Influence of purpose
on order,
modifying.

Page 33

Exhibition
Havel room layout.
Garden restaurant,
Shopping street.
Hotel Boarding House,
Tree Nursery

17.III.28 Diary

Wutenow 2

Page 34

Lecture
Main theme.
Seizing hold of the
technical world by
means of the building art.
Impact of the technical
world on our life and
spatial execution
of the changed situation.
Technik. 7 [16]
Influence of technology
on the soul.
Complete rununciation of
one's own aims in the work,
of whimsies,
or vanity.
Encounter with an
immanent plan. Participation
in the creation.
8 [17]

[16]
Mies noted here the themes that appeared important to him from the synopsis of chapter 2, "Mensch und Technik," in Dessauer, *Philosophie der Technik,* pp. 7, 8.

[17]
Refers to ibid., p. 8.

Page 35

Lecture

Not only self-revelation

but also service.

Misunderstanding between

client and creator,

materialist and

idealist.

Unilaterally oriented

and totally oriented.

What can come of that?

52 searched-for art

107

We are questioned by the Sphinx [18]

and life and death depends on

whether we find an answer. [108—crossed out]

Page 36

Lecture

Each culture

feels in itself also

the forces of its decline.

———

Liturgische Bildung

52. [19]

Each period has its mission and

its value and pays for its

achievement

always with a defect

in another direction.

———

Page 37

Chaos.

Sinking away of the old world.

Consciousness,

World of technology.

Man, technology,

Creative,

Social.

Economical

Organizational.

18
See Guardini, *Briefe vom Comer See,* p. 10.

19
Guardini, *Liturgische Bildung,* p. 52.

2

Excerpts

Excerpts from Romano Guardini, *Briefe vom Comer See* (Mainz, 1927)

Page 38

To find an answer, the living part of being, not only of thinking.[20]

———

Much is contained in a question. It wants to know the meaning of what is going on. The answer confronts us with a decision, and I do not know what in all that will be stronger: the events and their inescapable force or insight and surpassing work.[21]

[verso]

In the singing contour line of the landscape a factory[22] *that tears it all up. Proportion and rhythm.*

Page 39

Invasion by the machine of a land that hitherto had culture.

I saw how death falls over a life of infinite beauty.

The world of natural humanity, of humanely dwelled-in nature, perishes.

A world is arising in which "man" in this special sense can no longer live.[23]

20
Briefe vom Comer See, p. 9: "We talked of so many things; of one's own life and of what happens in the overall, the general, what fuses together. There I tried to articulate a question that I felt everywhere. [Mies's underlinings begin] I had felt it for a long time, how it presses forward stronger and stronger, and I knew that much depends for our lives on whether we find the answer, the living part of being, not only of thinking."

21
Ibid., pp. 9, 10; quoted almost verbatim.

22
Ibid., p. 13.

23
For the excerpts on this page, see *Briefe vom Comer See,* pp. 11–14: "How can I tell it to you? . . . I saw the machine invade a land that hitherto had culture. I saw how death came over a life of infinite beauty and felt: That is not only an external loss. . . . When I drove through the valleys of Brianza, from Milan to Lake Como, copious, diligently cared for, enclosed by harsh mountains, all forms powerful and broad, I did not want to believe my eyes. Everywhere inhabited land. Valleys and mountainsides covered with villages and small towns. The entire nature transformed by man . . . full of well-being . . . and nature here is such that it fuses into culture with ease. . . . I cannot express how human this nature is and how one feels in it the possibility of being human in a quite clear and yet inexhaustibly profound sense.

"But now I saw suddenly in the singing contour line of a small city the crude box of a factory! Saw how . . . next to the high campanile a chimney stood suddenly and all was torn. It was awful. You will have to take a bit of trouble to understand that. Up there in the north we are used to it. . . . But here it was different! Here a humanized form had still been alive. Here was still a nature humanely dwelled in. And now I saw the destruction break in. . . . The world of natural humanity, of humanely dwelled-in nature, perishes! I cannot tell you what sadness that is. . . . Here I understood Hölderlin! I felt it clearly, a world is arising in which 'man'—in this special sense—cannot live any more. A world somehow inhuman."

Page 40

There is a totally untouched nature,
and the longing for it
is itself a cultural result.
Nature is truly affecting
only when it begins
to be dwelled in; when culture
begins in it.
Piece by piece nature is formed.
Man creates in it
his own world, not
only out of a
natural need, but
with deliberate purpose,
serving spiritual
ideas.[24]

Page 41

Old world—organic culture.
Piece by piece of
untouched nature is formed.
Man creates his own world within it,
according to his own set purposes,
serving spiritual ideas.
To make serviceable
by adaptation;
visible world:
everything relates to that.[25]

Page 42

Human world
distances itself
necessarily from nature,
in "a sphere of culture."
In this cultural world lives man,
in pure nature the animal.
To be human means
to be spiritualized.[26]

A maximum of
spirit-drenched culture,
yet always close to nature,
so that natural forces
may circulate in it.[27]

Notebook, page 42.

24
Ibid., pp. 15, 16.

25
Ibid., p. 16: "Piece by piece, nature is formed. Man creates his own world within it, according to thoughts, dominated not only by natural needs but by set purposes, serving spiritual ideas; as an ecology that relates to him.

26
Ibid., p. 16.

27
Ibid., p. 17.

Sailboat,

built since Roman times.

Primordial formal legacy.

Fulfillment of the law.

Balanced attitude.

Correct relationship of

man to natural forces.[28]

———

Culture, spiritual work.

Can only be created

by overcoming, by overcoming

nature. But yet close to nature,

in harmony with it.[29]

Motorboat, lake steamer

Masterwork of technology,

insensitive to wind and weather,

nature has no more power

over it.[30]

Experienced nearness to nature

is being lost.

The first appearance of humane

culture is being lost.[31]

Nature has been overcome,

ruled out.[32]

Fire   origin

candle   elect. light

Plow   motor plow.[33]

Smith   factory

Carriage and animal   automobile.[34]

From that [world] of the

German Middle Ages

to the onset of the

technological age,

the same can be said.[35]

———

The language of newspapers, of

the books, the city building types.

Houses, furnishings

of mankind. So I see the hand-formed,

the one-of-a-kind disappear.

Everything becomes impersonal.

28
Ibid., pp. 17f, underlined by Mies: "Nevertheless, all spiritual work seems to presuppose a sort of ascetism; a sort of furrowing, dissolving, deconcretization of nature. Only then can man erect his work.

"So it seems that all culture from the start contains elements alien to nature; something unreal, artificial. That increases until a certain limit is reached: a maximum of culture permeated by spirit. It is distanced from nature … yet it remains near enough, flexible enough, that this culture stays 'natural' and natural juices circulate in it.

"I will search for an example so that what I have said will not remain empty. Take a sailboat. . . . I do not know what historians think, but it seemed plausible to me when someone told me that these boats have been the same since Roman times. Here is a primordial formal legacy. Can you feel what a wonderful cultural fact that is, when man with bowed and fitted wood and stretched linen makes himself master of wind and water? . . . Permeated by spirituality, this totally formed movement with which man harnesses the forces of nature! Certainly, he has paid for it with a loss. Man is no longer fitted into the realm of wind and water like bird or fish. The Dionysian abandonment has taken place. I read once how fishermen of the South Seas throw themselves, riding a board, into the surf, for play, for fun! What an incredible ecstasy of intoxication must overcome man in such fusion with nature? As if he were a water creature or part of the wave! Man has distanced himself from nature. He has resigned; . . . he has 'overcome.'. . . This is how culture, the work of the spirit, comes about."

29
Mies on ibid., pp. 18, 19.

30
Ibid., p. 19.

31
Ibid., p. 20.

32
Ibid., p. 21.

33
Ibid., p. 22.

34
Ibid., p. 23.

35
Ibid., p. 25: "Here, in this world [the world of the northern Italian culturescape], I feel everywhere personally addressed—one could of course say the same of the German Middle Ages or the time following it, up to the onset of the technological age. Physical entities stand here; I live in their midst and have a vital relationship with them. Tools, houses, streets, cities, all are like personalities, family practices, customs, feasts. . . . Each stands, complete in itself." Diagonally across this is written in Mies's large script: "Culture concept."

All culture is bought at the
expense of a living reality.
In all cultures the problem consisted of surpassing
the transient individual
case to arrive at the special.
And from that never-recurring special
to the comprehensive, the general.[36]
Man wants to progress
from this always new
uniqueness, to which he
would sooner or later
have to succumb,
to an overall connection,
an attitude that is right for
many, if not for all cases.

in order thus to control
the entire reality
surrounding him.
A double way leads into
the immanent.
Beyond both the unique and special
and the permanent and universal.[37]
We cannot go one way
without also going the other.
We find the immanent
in the particular only
if we are simultaneously open
to its place in the universal.
And there, we can see
it rightly only
if we also perceive it
in its never-to-return
uniqueness.[38]

36
Ibid., p. 26.

37
Ibid., p. 27.

38
Ibid., p. 28.

Page 48

Responding to the particular
is from the start different
from sinking into the existing.[39]

Culture arises, if man
can penetrate from the merely
concurrent to the meaningful,
the immanent.
That can only occur by an act
that stretches toward
both poles—even if in each
single instant and man one direction
prevails and is able to
impart a particular form to it.[40]

Page 49

All culture has from the start
an abstract trait.
But when modern conceptual
thinking began, and in
action the modern technology,
this trait gained definite
preponderance.
For the most part,
it determined
our behavior toward
the world and therefore
our attitude and
thence our being.[41]

Page 50

Consciousness is part
of culture, is perhaps
its prime prerequisite;
the basis from which it rises.[42]

Culture presupposes a distance
from immediate reality.
Only from the realm of consciousness
can the creative and form-giving hold on the world
be set free.[43]

There was in the Middle Ages
and there was in the subsequent centuries,
aside from actual science, a profound and
sensitive awareness of men
about themselves.[44]

[39] Ibid.

[40] Ibid.

[41] Ibid., p. 31.

[42] Ibid., p. 32.

[43] Ibid., pp. 32, 33.

[44] Ibid., p. 33.

284

Sharp glances penetrated
to one's inner self,
bright luminous words were spoken
opening profound
interconnections. And yet
if I compare the general
attitude of that
culture with ours,
an immense consciousness
overcomes me.[45]

Historical knowledge.
Piece by piece
our past is excavated.
By ever-sharper methods are the

traces of the past determined.
Connections retrieved.[46]
Ever more comprehensively
the past of mankind
in all the fullness of its [?] details
and its relationships
enters our consciousness.
And we order ourselves
ever more knowledgeably
into this context.
Ourselves within our times
and our times in the
context of all times.[47]

45
Ibid.

46
Ibid.

47
Ibid., p. 34.

Page 53

The space.

Country after country

is explored.

Asia enters our

consciousness in its

historical context.

Mount Everest, the throne

of the gods; and the earth

is fitted into

its astronomical context.[48]

The characteristics of nations

become [known—crossed out] clear.

Appear in relationship

to the European whole,

and that again

to larger units.[49]

Page 54

A world consciousness,

a consciousness of mankind

appears of itself to

delineate itself

in its first contours.

Statistics as means

of raising consciousness.

Steps. Investigations

of all types uncover inner connections

and lead one phenomenon

back to a previous one.

And we ourselves.

Physiological, anatomical,

morphological researches

explore the life of the body.[50]

antike hätte es als Hybris gescheut. Erst jener Mensch, dem solche Gottverbindung den Sinn für das Unbedingte gegeben; dem die Parabeln vom Schatz im Acker, und von der kostbaren Perle, und die Lehre vom Verlierenmüssen des Lebens nahe gebracht haben, daß etwas ist, für das alles hingegeben werden muß — er war überhaupt erst zu einer solchen Entschlossenheit fürs Letzte fähig, wie sie die neuere Wissenschaft beherrscht, die Wahrheit will, und sollte darüber das Leben unmöglich werden; wie sie in der Technik lebt, die das Werk will, und sollte durch solche Umformung der Welt alles Menschendasein in Frage geraten. Erst ein Mensch, dem der christliche Glaube an das ewige Leben die tiefe Sicherheit gegeben hat, daß sein Wesen unzerstörbar ist, hatte die Zuversicht, die zu solchem Unternehmen gehört. Aber freilich, jene Kräfte haben sich aus der Hand der lebendigen Persönlichkeit gelöst — oder sollen wir sagen: Diese hat sie nicht halten können? hat sie fahren lassen? — und so verfielen sie der Dämonie der Zahl, der Maschine, des Herrschaftswillens . . .

Wir haben in wesensgerechter Arbeit das Neue zu durchdringen, um es zu meistern. Wir müssen Herr werden über die entfesselten Kräfte und sie zu einer neuen Ordnung bauen, die auf den Menschen bezogen ist. Das kann aber letztlich nicht von den technischen Problemen selbst her ge-

95

Markings of Mies in Romano Guardini, *Briefe vom Comer See* (1927).

48
Ibid.

49
Ibid., p. 35.

50
Ibid.

Increased awareness of the body

by rhythmical culture.[51]

Psychoanalysis has brought

a new realm of the living soul

into our field of view and revealed

deep connections.

How the soul

has become conscious

thereby.[52]

Technique of making conscious,

the newspaper.

There are no more

unobserved events.

We perceive this as normal.[53]

Lecture

Becoming conscious

The understanding of

all relationships

Letters from Lake Como, 35/36

Arrive at consciousness by

taking apart, going into detail

[*the coming-into-consciousness*—crossed out]

an image-like, luminous

awareness of a living

whole.[54] [*That is why*

detail and—crossed out]

All was here with consciousness.

We have consciousness as

attitude, as atmosphere.[55]

42/43/49/50/63 Middle Ages 78

Awareness as

atmosphere.

Becoming conscious of the unconscious, read up.[56]

All life must be founded

in an unconscious.

But can life also

become conscious and remain alive?

Awareness becomes attitude.

Basic trait of our cultural life.[57]

We survey ourselves and the world

in which we stand.[58]

51
Ibid.

52
Ibid., p. 36.

53
Ibid., p. 37.

54
Ibid., pp. 35, 36.

55
Ibid., p. 38.

56
Ibid.

57
Ibid., p. 41.

58
Ibid., pp. 41–43: "Finally I wrote about the awareness of our time. . . . It appeared significant to me that an attitude of awareness has become the basic trait of our cultural life. . . . We survey ourselves and the world in which we stand. In our political situation something has occurred that is new and decisive as opposed to former times: the world becomes surveyable. . . . Now we feel the fact that we live in a no longer expandable space. Perhaps there was once a protostage of this awareness. What was called by late antiquity *Oikumene,* the 'total space of the inhabited world,' seems to lie in this direction. . . . Now Oikumene has finally arrived: the awareness of a no longer expandable space for dwelling, living, and work. Earth becomes surveyed. There are no more possibilities of escape, no more reserves.

"This gives rise to totally new poltical problems. . . . Our entire external human existence seems to be subject to what one could call pressure at the margins, because escape into adjoining areas is no longer possible. . . . Now the questions as to 'relationships' become very urgent. . . . Totally new problems are posed, a new attitude and art are called for to master them. . . . The time for a naive Europeanism is past."

Page 58

*Totally new problems
are posed, a new attitude
and art are called for
to master them.*

Page 59

Lecture

*To feel and acknowledge
differences. Large, delicate—etc.
104. Today's art
108.   "   "59*

*Yes, perhaps even sanctity,
extreme realism. More
than everything natural.
Formed body is expression
for how the soul maintains
itself toward the surroundings
and how it masters them.*

Excerpts from Romano Guardini, *Liturgische Bildung*
(Rothenfels, 1923), and *Von heiligen Zeichen*
(Würzburg, 1922)

Page 60

Liturgische Bildung 42

———

*The purposes began their domination,
the formulas and methods.
There are people who would
like to make
a Ford factory of nature. 43,44*[60]

Page 61

*Give meaning back
to the words.
Handling of forms.*

Notebook, page 63.

59
Ibid., pp. 104, 108. The following lines are Mies's addition.

60
The last sentence is Mies's addition. He underlined in Guardini, *Liturgische Bildung,* pp. 43, 44: "We want to become
essential. But that means, for us, to become human. And
essentially human shall be the relationships and actions of life,
the ways of the community, of work, and of joyfulness. Everywhere shall be an 'anima' that is 'forma corporis.'. . . The same
will, however, wants to approach things also. Formulas and
concepts blocked our view of reality. We no longer thought in
living images; signs, assemblies of detached signs, stood in
for things much like paper money means value without being
it. . . . Now the will wants to see things again, not concepts. . . .
Our task is to confront the entire hard but ever so fruitful
conflict with the real world in all its autonomous fullness and
power. As task, to stand in reverence before the *Eigen-Sinn*
of things. [A play on words: *eigen Sinn* is "their own meaning,"
but *Eigensinn* also means "stubbornness."] . . . This constitutes the task of truly creative symbol formation: that man
should not force things, but that in revealing himself in them,
he should simultaneously unlock the immanent in them. Much
as it is the nature of art that, by means of it in a purpose-free
and pure configuration, man should reveal the innermost being
of his soul, but should do so in revealing what resides in the
object—that is the mystery of the symbol: icon of expressive
man and immanence of thing speak of each other in turn."

Page 62

We want to give meaning again

to things.

Who [still has nowadays—crossed out] still feels anything

of a wall, an opening.

Guardini page 41+.[61]

We want to give sense

again to things.

Liberate them

out of frozen forms—formalism—

and protect them against

oversimplification.

Page 63

Lecture

Instead of organic connections

Organization.

———

Steps, spaces.

One has lost

the meaning of this language,

(Von heiligen Zeichen)

one feels nothing anymore.[62]

———

The creative.

The nature of the thing outside

and the answer of man on

the inside: both combined,

he pronounced them with the name.[63]

61

Underlinings by Mies in Guardini, *Von heiligen Zeichen,* pp. 12, 13: "'Give meaning back to words!' How profoundly this admonition affects our soul today. Yes, to give meaning back to words and also to the forms and actions of life. That is the task of youth." Underlinings by Mies in pp. 40, 41: "Words are names. And to speak is the high art of relating to the names of things; with the essence of things and the essence of one's own soul in its divinely ordained harmony. . . . But language with its names is no longer a numinous communication with the essence of things, no longer an encounter between object and soul. It is not even longing for a lost paradise, but a busy clacking of word coins, like a counting machine that counts change without knowing it." The following sentences in the notebook are Mies's comment.

62

In the chapter "Stufen" (Steps), ibid., pp. 34–35, Guardini describes the spatial sensation associated with climbing steps. In this chapter the echo of Nietzsche's Zarathustra topography is particularly evident, in which the low was equivalent with the bad, the small, and the high was equivalent with the noble and the strong ("Life wants to climb and in climbing transcend itself"); compare also Peter Behrens, "We want to be elevated, not cheated," quoted in chapter III above. Mies's remark that the "meaning of this language" has been lost refers to this symbolical experience of space. Guardini writes: "Especially the most self-understood things, the everyday actions, contain the profoundest. In the simplest lies the biggest secret. For example, there are the steps. Innumerable times you have climbed them. But have you noticed what went on inside you? For something goes on inside of us when we climb. . . . A profound secret reveals itself. It is one of those processes that originate in the matrix of our humanity, puzzling, one cannot solve it with reason and yet all understand it. . . . When we climb up stairs, it is not only the foot that climbs, but our entire being. Spiritually, too, we climb. And if we do it attentively, then we sense something of those heights where everything is large and complete: that is the heaven in which God resides. . . ."

63

Guardini, *Von heiligen Zeichen,* p. 39.

Excerpts from Friedrich Dessauer, *Philosophie der Technik*
(Bonn, 1927)

Page 64

Invention of objects

and processes (methods)[64]

———

Establish the number of hobbyists.

Each man is technician.[65]

———

To simplify the household

is a technical problem;

not the housewife

but the technician will solve it.

———

Technology + economy as transformers

of our existence.

Bavarian (illegible)

Page 65

Technik. 78

Concretization of the idea to an object.

Mass object.[66]

Transition from building art

to building economy.

The actual work field of

organizers.

———

77/79

Socrates "Skill is based on

knowledge"[67]

———

Limits of realizability in materials,

in the state of technology

in need

———

Abuse of technology

does not speak against technology.[68]

———

90. Technology and architecture.[69]

64
Dessauer, *Philosophie der Technik,* p. 14: "The aim of technical work is not always an object. It can also be a procedure, a 'process' such as the obtaining of liquid fuel out of coal. Ford made numerous inventions in building his automobiles but his greatest concerned the method of production itself. The difference between inventing objects and inventing processes is technically unimportant, but depends on a change of the teleological elements."

65
Perhaps related to ibid., p. 17: "A large treasure is hidden in the pedagogical power of a technical education. This treasure has not yet been raised for the public. A reserve army stands available of people that have learned, like few others, to work without egoism." The following sentences in the notebook are Mies's addition.

66
Ibid., p. 78. The following lines are Mies's addition.

67
Underlinings by Mies in ibid., pp. 75, 79: "One can practically say with Natorp the *Socratic law of technology,* that skill is based on knowledge." The following sentence in the notebook is Mies's addition.

68
Ibid., p. 86: "Is there a field that does not employ technology? That has little to do with technology per se. What is contained in this great phenomenon of technology, including its ethical dimension, is one thing; what man does with it is quite another. Have men not also abused religion, justice, everything, in short? The will to power employs all means; even before the gates of technology, man's freedom of action is not commanded to halt."

69
Ibid., p. 90: "Not only inventions that help to move weights have made architecture possible; architecture is itself imprinted by the state of technology. The lines of the Greek temples, of the Romanesque and Gothic building styles are technological lines, animated so to speak by the forces of pressure and tensions."

It is always the need that

brings things into being?

But beyond that, often in

anticipation, new things are formed by fantasy

that are not identical with momentary

needs, yes, that even

stand in contradiction.

———

98 Culture and technology [70]

———

Service as interconnectedness

instead of individual act. Effect on everything.

Housing. Participation

of all on everything

is the consequence.

99 [71]

———

Bacon? Middle Ages [72]

100

Relationship of external means

to inner means.

Once too little, now too much.

———

101 Culture 102/103 [73]

Notebook, page 66.

70
Ibid., p. 98.

71
Ibid., p. 99.

72
Ibid., pp. 98ff., refers to Francis Bacon's utopian fiction *Nova Atlantis,* in which an island is described whose population has attained happiness by a developed technology and freedom of means. In his 1928 lecture "Die Voraussetzungen baukünstlerischen Schaffens" (see Appendix III, 1), in which Dessauer's ideas are reflected, Mies refers to Bacon. Dessauer summarized Bacon's teaching: "Technological redemption, technological means alone do not make happy, do not make noble, but they are significant elements toward ennobling happiness, cultural factors" (*Philosophie der Technik,* p. 101, marked by Mies).

73
Ibid., pp. 101–103, excerpts from Mies's underlinings: "The level of the battle propositions in human life, the level of man's interests, show the degree of his culture. To raise this field from the lowly, the instinctive-chaotic, to the rarefied, well-ordered, free, that is the meaning of the world 'culture.' For culture means 'ennobling care.'. . . For, finally, culture means striving for unity. One finds it in a coherence between experience, consciousness, existence; away from the realm of the primitive 'being for oneself, thinking for oneself, caring for oneself,' toward a mystical matrix in unity. . . . Means alone, of course, do not make man happy. But would it not be conceivable that man, by passing through the transcendent nature of technology, could establish the harmony between inside and outside, between psychic force and practical means? Why has this question been ignored? Why, if one thinks of culture and talks of technology, does one always mean drainage systems, microscopes, and steam engines?"

Page 67

Chaos

Old world—organic culture.

How does that come about?

Preconditions.

Economic,

social,

[cultural—crossed out] intellectual = order, culture

Middle Ages,

show order.

Harmony.

Econom[y]. Renaissance

Personalities.

Experiment.

Art + Science

Bacon.

Influence on economy.

Alienation because of profit

Bourgeoisie.[74]

Page 68

104. Culture. Society.[75]

106. 107.

———

Spiritual reasons of

social reorganization 107

———

112. Realization of culture

by populations instead of

by individual classes.[76]

———

114. Interweaving of people.

Influence on external attitude.[77]

Spans [illegible] separate the

property

of landholdings.

Work not for individuals,

but for millions of unknown,[78]

thence the nonsense of

individual direction.

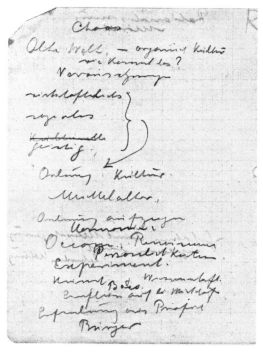

Notebook, page 67.

74
See ibid., pp. 103–111.

75
Ibid., p. 104.

76
Ibid., p. 112.

77
Ibid., p. 114, marked by Mies in margin with three lines: "This fundamental change arising out of technology means an interweaving of people and a step from the narrow realm of self and its environment toward others, toward the masses." The following sentence in the notebook is Mies's addition.

78
Ibid., p. 115: "The change indicates an expansion of the sphere of effectiveness of the individual. He does not work for one, or five, but for hundreds, thousands, millions. [Underlined by Mies:] And he does not work for people he knows, but for the unknown, for the nameless, for the no longer personal." The following lines in the notebook are Mies's addition.

Page 69

121

Objection by commercial interests,
this will not be sold. Products that
contradict the immanent, sell.
That is why one manufactures.[79]

———

Economic planning and housing policies
failed.[80]
Houses do not correspond
to the level of technology and
the rhythm of Life.

———

Only philosophical understanding
reveals the true ordering principles
of our service and thence
the value and dignity of our existence.
Not the abolition of
commercial gain, but its control.
One has dignity if one
fulfills a human mission
knowingly.[81]

79
Mies on ibid., p. 121.

80
Compare ibid., p. 125: "Under the name of 'economic planning' one attempted, after the German collapse, to bring about a distribution of goods by replacing the economy of unorganized individuals by one in which profits alone were not determinative, but need. Engineer W. Rathenau, and especially Wichard von Moellendorf and Rudolf Wissell, a mechanical engineer arising out of the working class, were its fathers. [Underlined by Mies:] Technology is the native soil of this thought. It failed not because it was wrong, but because one was not yet ready for it. A planned economy is the consequence of technical thought about service. Indeed the just distribution of earthly goods according to need is the result of technically organized services. But one cannot enforce by either law or organization what was accomplished by the striving for profit of a generation raised under the concept of an economic egoism. We need the economic egoism to break the ground. Planned economy can one day distribute goods justly, once production is fully mature."

81
Ibid., p. 127.

Page 70

Question:

What does mankind need,

or how can I earn the most?

It is decisive which

question has primacy.[82]

---

130 Ministry of technology

Ministry of building art.[83]

---

132 read

Technology groups the new society.

—Ties all together,

creates a new order according

to service instead of earnings.[84]

The idea of earnings

had to lead to isolation.

The idea of service

leads to community.

132[85]

Excerpts from Leopold Ziegler, *Zwischen Mensch und Wirtschaft* (Darmstadt, 1927)

Page 71

Guardini.

On the value of talent.

Ziegler 157, 159, 160, 161

Need and necessity

52.–53.

Nature proceeds from relatively

unorganized unity to highly

organized unity, goes therefore

in all ways from

whole to whole

and differentiates only

to reorganize on a higher level.[86]

Notebook, page 70.

82
Ibid., p. 130.

83
Dessauer's suggestion of installing a "Ministry of Technology" might have arisen out of the striving for quality products to which Mies, in the Werkbund and otherwise, was committed. Dessauer, p. 130: "The Ministry of Technology would have to ask in innumerable details: how in Germany do we obtain the best products for our needs. One would also have to strive for the most perfect solution for this plurality. . . ."

84
Mies on Dessauer, p. 132.

85
Ibid., underlined by Mies: "The legalization of the free economy, the impregnation of life with the concept of earnings, had to lead to an ideal of isolated destiny. The idea of technical service leads to the ideal of a common destiny.

86
Ziegler, *Zwischen Mensch und Wirtschaft*, pp. 52, 53.

Page 72

All capitalistic economy is

organized economy, that is,

a type of production that,

by planned dismembering

and assembling, dividing and

putting together of the work process,

aims for greater effectiveness than

would be possible without

such ordering.[87]

45 and 46 important Ziegler.

_____

Rathenau:

The creation of an organic

economy is what we need.

Ziegler 51[88]

53 on top

53 on bottom

To take and give in one breath.[89]

Page 73

To differentiate and to integrate,

dissociate without associating.[90]

For the building art, expansion

instead of Dahlem. Corbusier

instead of Schulze Naumburg.

Building meant for the masses

can only be effective

and live itself out on a large scale.

Ziegler 64 on top

Saying of Marx, very good,[91] *67 very good, 81,*

112–115.[92]

87
Ibid., p. 45.

88
Ibid., p. 51.

89
Ibid., p. 53.

90
Ibid. The following lines in the notebook are Mies's addition.

91
Mies refers here to a paragraph in which Ziegler, in his search for an "organic economic form," discusses Marxist economics. The passage of which Mies writes "saying of Marx, very good," indicated as "64 on top," reads: "Just as the savage must wrestle with nature to satisfy his needs, to maintain his life and to reproduce, so must the civilized man, and he must do that under all forms of social organization and under all possible modes of production. . . . Freedom in this area can only exist so far as societal man, the associated producers, regulate their material exchange with nature rationally, bring it under their societal control, in order not to be ruled by its blind power. . . . But there always remains a realm of necessity. Only beyond that begins . . . the true realm of freedom, which, however, only blooms forth if it is erected with the realm of necessity as its basis." Mies shows a comparable idea of freedom as an understanding of necessity in his concept of the building art, the technical necessities of which must be mastered so that "the world of our creations will blossom from within. We want no more; we can do no more." (See his inaugural address at Armour Institute of Technology; Appendix III, 14.)

92
Ziegler, *Zwischen Menschen und Wirtschaft*, p. 81: "The initiated emancipation of the fourth estate, the event of the age and not preventable by any power on earth, leads either to the absorption of the proletariat into the organic economy, or it leads to the chaos of social revolution. There is no third possibility. Either Abbe and his ideological relatives Rathenau and Ford—or Marx and Lenin!" Pages 112–115 express themselves in flowery terms as to the phenomenon of this stage, "where the citizen transforms himself to mousy bourgeois, or where, in the language of Marx, he becomes exploiter of society's work force and turns profit thief" (p. 113).

Page 74

Lecture.

Ziegler 233

Impractical work

is unsocial.

———

Mensch und Wirtschaft. 23

It has again come to pass

that a historical impulse must by necessity

activate its counter-impulse, if it does not

want to wear itself out.[93]

———

[In the final analysis we must

rise up against an economy and technology,

that—crossed out]

23. on bottom

29. on bottom Death.[94]

Page 75

Riehl tombstone.

Ziegler 149

Against use-objects

150 very [important—crossed out] right,

optimal products.[95]

However the functionalists

may rationalize their work,

it is all the same to us

provided we can say yes

to their achievements.

93
Ibid., p. 23.

94
Ibid., p. 23: ". . . the deliberate rebellion against an economy that claims to be *causa sui* and thereby wants to make one forget the circumstance that the earth has been entrusted to the human species as domicile and workplace rather than as an object of commercial speculation. And just as the land reform of George, Damaschke, and Oppenheimer places the inalienable world beyond the laws of merchandise, so socialism in the historically valid stance of Marx fights against the abusive habits of delivering human labor to the same laws of merchandise." Ibid., p. 29: "Such a realization of socialism is implied when Henry Ford expressly announced in *The Great Today, the Greater Tomorrow*: 'Labor is no merchandise'" (a reference to Henry Ford, *Today and Tomorrow* [Garden City, 1926]).

95
Ibid., pp. 149f.: "What motivates the imagination and stimulates desire are mainly goods that differentiate themselves from others by the claim that each in its own way is the best of its kind. It is not the most necessary nor the most functional or most comfortable that is viewed as the best and most excellent. In short, we encounter here a mythologically styled instinct that functions like a powerful human sacral system oriented toward desirable goods of optimal rank, optimal value. I need not emphasize here the role played by optimal products in mythological tradition. We all remember the winged sandals, the seven-mile boots, the magic hood, the bag of fortune . . . all of which embody the optima of their type and heighten the human capabilities of their happy owners beyond all natural measure."

III 1928–1938

Mies and Le Corbusier in Stuttgart-Weissenhof, 1927.

1

"The Preconditions of Architectural Work"

Lecture held at the end of February 1928 in the Staatliche Kunstbibliothek Berlin; also on March 5, 1928, at the invitation of the Arbeitsgemeinschaft für Frauenbestrebung (Work Association for the Women's Movement) of the Museumsverein and the Kunstgewerbeschule Stettin in the auditorium of the Marienstiftsgymnasium in Stettin; as well as on March 7 at the invitation of the Frankfurter Gesellschaft für Handel, Industrie und Wissenschaft (Frankfurt Society for Trade, Industry and Science) in Frankfurt am Main. Unpublished manuscript in the collection of Dirk Lohan, Chicago.

Ladies and Gentlemen!

The building art is for me not a subject for clever speculation. I do not expect anything from theories and specific systems. But particularly nothing from an aesthetic attitude that merely touches the surface. The building art can only be unlocked from a spiritual center and can only be understood as a living process.

The building art is man's spatial dialogue with his environment and demonstrates how he asserts himself therein and how he masters it. For this reason, the building art is not merely a technical problem nor a problem of organization or economy. The building art is in reality always the spatial execution of spiritual decisions. It is bound to its times and manifests itself only in addressing vital tasks with the means of its times. A knowledge of the times, its tasks, and its means is the necessary precondition of work in the building art.

It is not a lack of talent but a lack of clarity in regard to these relationships that seems to me to be the cause of the confusing and inadequate products of the present building art. Since these products may not instantly be recallable by everybody in full precision, and since words have lost their unambiguous meaning, I will clarify the present situation by means of a series of illustrations and conduct my investigation on this basis. It goes without saying that I will only show works that deserve to be taken seriously. The choice of pictures does not constitute a value judgment, but only serves to clearly characterize the situation. Nor will I take a position in regard to these pictures, as I am convinced that the chaotic character of our building art will appear all by itself.

(Pictures)

That is today's building art. We all have reason to infer corresponding causes from this result.

Chaos is always a sign of anarchy. Anarchy is always a movement without order. Movement without central direction. Chaos occurred before. When the order of antiquity degenerated into late antiquity. But out of this chaos a new order arose, the order of the Middle Ages. On the basis of the Platonic theory of ideas, Augustine formulated the basic ideas of medieval belief. In the medieval idea of order lived, even if in a totally new dimension, that spirit of proportion exemplified and proven by Plato. The noblest legacy of antiquity.

The idea of order controlled the spiritual life of the Middle Ages and it realized itself in its society, most of all in its social ideas. Society was, on account of the feudal system, immensely static. The classes were not only an economic, but above all a daily and spiritual fact. Honor and duty, law and solidarity in all social things were inseparable. The order of rank corresponded to the objectively correct order of spiritual life values and economic values. This natural arrangement of classes was the basis for the health of the society of that time. The life of medieval man was determined through and through by a totally secured understanding of the meaning of life.

(Picture: Strassburg)

Everything points to a spiritual aim. Insight stands before deed. Belief and knowledge have not yet stepped apart. This idea of order is the point of departure for the change we want to demonstrate.

The deterioration of the medieval form of life was preceded by a deterioration of its spiritual structure. The process of disintegration began with the attempt by Duns Scotus to stake out a separate territory and law for knowledge.

In overstepping the concept of almightiness William of Occam destroyed the idea of order, leaving behind only empty *nomina*. The victory of nominalism signals the victory of a spirit turned toward reality long before it ever expressed itself in reality itself. This spirit was antimedieval. With it the Renaissance begins. While it reaches back to the antique sources of the Middle Ages, it deals with them more freely and spontaneously and already harbors the tendency to decay. Whereas man in the Middle Ages was committed, internally and externally, to the community, now takes place the great detachment of the individual, who conceives himself entitled to advance his talents and develop his forces.

This development became the basis for spiritual freedom, for the will to think autonomously and search independently. The result was a contrast between *Bildung* and *Unbildung*. [Not translatable by a single word. It has connotations of "formed" and "unformed," "cultivated" and "uncultivated," "learned" and "unlearned."] This contrast, which was to give a new form to the social situation of Europe, brought with it those problems that still lie before us today.

This lack of *Bildung* is the cause for the excessive aggrandizement of the personality, an unbinding of the will to power, and of unrestrained arbitrariness. More and more, spiritual life tends toward the will. The act of the autonomous individual becomes ever more important. People study nature. The control of nature became the longing of the period.

Its immense potential was recognized. The English statesman and philosopher Francis Bacon spoke out against pure science, against science for the sake of science, recognizing its practical potential and demanding that it serve life. He put knowledge in the service of culture and introduced method and experimental science. We stand at the beginning of something new.

In the same century began the fateful alliance between iron and coal. Science enters into the service of technology and economy, acquires a certain degree of understanding of the forces of nature and invades its domain. Steam, electricity, and chemical energy are detached from their natural contexts. Their rational laws are understood and their effectiveness is unleashed.

Man develops a corresponding attitude in which will and capability undertake rational work. Carried along by this will, the powers of nature, heretofore isolated, come into play. Will freely sets its aims, places them in the service of use, and wrests performance from conquered nature. Nothing seems impossible anymore. Thus begins the reign of technology. Everything succumbs to its impact. It detaches man from his restrictions, makes him freer and becomes his great helper, breaks down the isolation of geographical locations and bridges the largest distances. The world shrinks more and more, becomes surveyable and is investigated down to its remotest recesses. The characteristics of peoples become clear.

Their social and economic structures are uncovered. World consciousness and a conscious awareness of mankind results. Man, too, moves into the circle of consciousness. Physiological and psychological understanding becomes universal and determines the conduct of life.

Technology offers a thousand means to increase awareness. Nothing occurs anymore that is not observed. We survey ourselves and the world in which we stand. Consciousness is our very attitude.

Simultaneously and interconnected with this development a huge population increase takes place.

(Picture: Berlin Stadium)
Masses form, posing totally new problems of an economic and social nature.

(Picture: Krupp)
Technology is the means to their solution.

(Picture: Leipzig)
Traffic develops.

(Picture: New York)
Traffic serves economy. Economy becomes the great distributor, interferes in all domains, forces man into its service.

(Picture: New York Street)
Economy begins to rule. Everything stands in the service of use. Profitability becomes law. Technology forces economic attitudes, transforms material into power, quantity into quality. The most effective use of power is consciously brought about.

Ladies and Gentlemen!
It seemed to me necessary to trace the course of development, even if in large jumps, for it alone leads to a comprehension of the condition of our time. We have laid bare the structure of our period and have established that our givens are consciousness, economy, technology, and the fact of the masses. The effect of this structural change can be demonstrated by the following examples:

(Picture: viaduct, Acoustic Paris)
Scientific effort for the understanding of acoustical laws is being applied and begins to exert its influence on the planning of large halls. This picture shows a concert hall in Paris for 3,000 people.

(Picture: [design of] Hannes Meyer)
And this picture shows the design of the League of Nations Palace and a cross section through the large auditorium.

(Picture: lamp, lamp rays)
Another effect of scientific work is evident in this picture. It is the demonstration of the light rays based on the Paulsen lamp.

(Picture: lamp)
This purely technical-scientific work leads to this result. This lamp is not the result of a design, but of construction.

These are amazing achievements; all these are results of will, of rigorous discipline. Technology follows its own laws and is not man-related. Economy becomes self-serving and calls forth new needs. Autonomous tendencies in all these forces assert themselves. Their meaning seems to be the attainment of a specific phase of development. But they assume a threatening predominance. Unchecked, they thunder along. Man is swept along as if in a whirlwind. Each individual attempts to brace himself against these forces singly. We stand at a turning point of time. The degree and the intensity of this experience are determined by the attitude of the individual. This explains the chaotic appearance of these phenomena, the multiplicity of currents.

You can now understand why the result in the building art must be so confusing, as I have demonstrated. But even in this chaos, various types of structures are clearly discernible. You saw that one group subscribes to the belief that even in our changed world, the means and methods of past epochs can be applied to solve the tasks of our time. Their work is determined by the fear that invaluable treasures could be lost. And also by the belief that it is impossible, in the hard and clear atmosphere of technology and consciousness, that artistic and spiritual values can unfold. We are not entitled to hold their achievements in low respect, even if we believe that the world to which they incline and in which they are rooted is inevitably sinking. We are obligated to appreciate their efforts, for they transmit values and insights that we must not lose sight of. They still believe in the vitality of the old order.

A few stand in the middle, still committed to the old, yet alert to the new. For the other group, the old habitual order has lost its meaning and vitality. One cannot suffer it any more. This group affirms the new world and fights with its means. It is feeling its way toward new possibilities of form-giving. It experiments, is unrestricted in its work and stands no longer under the protection of conventions.

In the beginning of my lecture I pointed out that the building art is always bound to its own time and can manifest itself only in vital tasks and by the means of its own period. I have attempted to trace the changes of our time and make visible the forces at work in it. Our time is not an external course on which we run. It has been given to us as a task that we have to master. We see its immense power and its will. The determination with which it stands ready to fight.

We have to affirm it, even if its forces still appear menacing to us. We have to become master of the unleashed forces and build them into a new order, an order that permits free play for the unfolding of life. Yes, but an order also that is related to mankind.

But that cannot happen from the technological problems themselves, but only from living men. No matter how immense knowledge may be, how huge the economic apparatus, how powerful technology, all that is only the raw material compared to life.

We do not need less but more technology. We see in technology the possibility of freeing ourselves, the opportunity to help the masses. We do not need less science, but a science that is more spiritual; not less, but a more mature economic energy. All that will only become possible when man asserts himself in objective nature and relates it to himself.

It must be possible to heighten consciousness and yet keep it separate from the purely intellectual. It must be possible to let go of illusions, see our existence sharply defined, and yet gain a new infinity, an infinity that springs from the spirit.

It must be possible to solve the task of controlling nature and yet create simultaneously a new freedom.

It must be possible to see elitism disappear and admit the fact of the masses, the fact that each of the many has a right to life and goods. Mass must not be a cliché for us. It must come to articulation from within itself, for only that way can the forces residing in it be made serviceable for all.

The way leads from the extensive to the intensive. But all that can only happen if we regain our belief in the creative powers, if we trust the power of life.

Addendum: press reports on the lecture
"The Preconditions of Architectural Work"

Deutsche Tageszeitung of February 29, 1928:
"The Preconditions of Architectural Work:
Lecture by Mies van der Rohe."

The art of building can only be understood as a life process and its understanding has to emanate from the soul. As Mies van der Rohe explained in his lecture in the Staatliche Kunstbibliothek, it is an expression of man's ability to assert himself in respect to his surroundings and master them. The lecturer admitted that the building art surrounding us nowadays is in a chaotic condition, caused by changing times. Chaotic conditions in earlier historical periods had corresponded to the collapse of world views, as for example during the decline of antiquity and also the disintegration of the medieval beliefs that had emotionally secured men of that period. It was, however, not the Renaissance that liberated the individual from his chains, but rather the onset of our epoch with its teaming up of coal and iron that brought profound changes. Technology and economy began their rule by taking the forces of nature, carefully calculated, into their service.

To demonstrate the various attitudes of many well-known artists whose works deserve to be taken as important, and to show what their suggestion for the solution of our period is, Mies marched many slides of different building types past us. Höger, Pölzig, Oud, Gropius, Mendelsohn, along with Theodor Fischer, Schmitthenner, Tessenow, Schulze-Naumburg—to name only a few. The lecturer restricted himself to explanations without taking a personal stand on them. Remarkable, however, were his statements summarizing the slide demonstration.

He pointed to the three concurrent directions of today's building art. One group still believes today that it can solve the tasks of our epoch with the means of earlier times; their motivation is the fear of the loss of an invaluable legacy. Mies van der Rohe emphasized that no one is entitled to hold their work in low esteem even though he may himself believe that the world they are rooted in is sinking. There are indeed values we must not lose. Another group stands in the middle, connected to the old, but open-minded toward the new. But for the third group, the old order has lost all meaning and vitality; they stand on the side of the new world and are still now engaged in a battle for the means it takes to express it; they grope, still experimentally, for new types of form-giving. A juxtaposition that demonstrates the excellent neutral, suprapersonal attitude of Mies van der Rohe, the second chairman of the Deutsche Werkbund.

The speaker does not ask for an abolition of technology, but for an expanded, more mature technology and economy, allied and serviceable to the building art. Only that way can the needs of the masses be adequately satisfied. This, however, requires that the total endeavor not be subject to hackneyed solutions but remain nuanced. Without expressing any skepticism, with joyful optimism, the speaker confessed commitment to the tasks of the time and faith in the creative forces that will liberate us from illusions and formulate things according to their innate qualities.

Berliner Börsenkurier of March 1, 1928: **"New Building"**
The architect Mies van der Rohe, years ago, had a vision; he designed on paper a wonderful skyscraper for the Friedrichstrasse railroad station. This plan of the architect, who visualized the execution for this first real Berlin skyscraper totally in ferroconcrete and glass, only progressed to a plastic architectural model. This model, photographed and reproduced in all magazines in the world, pictures a nonexisting vision of the Berlin cityscape. The beautiful vision of Mies will never be realized, it will remain a paper plan, a book drama. Yet the Berlin art world has high hopes for the future of this architect, although a housing settlement built by him in the Afrikanische Strasse had not nearly as much success as the skyscraper. As guest speaker at the Staatliche Kunstbibliothek, Mies was supposed to speak on the "Preconditions of Architectural Work," but his lecture was only a sketch to this theme. One heard some aphorisms on building, some well-known facts, and even the slides did not show anything that was new.
Stn.

Berliner Tageblatt of March 2, 1928: **"New Building"**
The Berlin building master Mies van der Rohe lectured in the framework of a lecture series "New Building" at the Staatliche Kunstbibliothek on the preconditions of architectural work. In short epigrammatic sentences, in symbolic imagery, supported by instructively employed picture slides of various modern building styles, he heightened the receptiveness of the audience for his presentation of the process of a meaningful transpersonal building process that has been occurring since antiquity. The tendency: clearly apparent his desire for comprehensiveness and matter-of-fact presentation. His demand for a nuanced differentiation of spirituality without loss of universality, his demand for material quality without giving up quantity. Sublimation without loss of volume, these are the themes advanced by him. This luxury consumption in ever larger format is to deliver the basics for the new building style and new art forms in general. But Mies van der Rohe has often spoken up in fields in which he should have kept silent; in spite of his knowledge of the causal relationships in history, he projects "illusions" into the future that are no more than the expression of his imagination.

Berliner Börsen-Zeitung of March 2, 1928:
"The Preconditions of Architectural Work"
Mies van der Rohe is one of our most progressive architects and powerfully stimulative.

He talked recently at the Staatliche Kunstbibliothek's lecture series "New Building" on "The Preconditions of Architectural Work." It evolved that the creative artist Mies van der Rohe has far more ideas than the lecturer Mies van der Rohe. That is beneficial for the building art of today, but less so for the audience of lectures. Nevertheless, the lecture was marked by conceptual clarity and compelling proof. (He explicated the nature of the powers that drive our times and drove earlier

Mies with students in the Dessau Bauhaus, around 1930.

At the opening of the Barcelona Pavilion, 1929.

Mies on the building site of the Berlin Bauhaus, 1932.

times in respect to the building art.) What one missed was the convincing amplitude of explicative detail. He contented himself with describing the spiritual attitude prevailing among today's building artists and demonstrating three groups of presently active architects by means of examples, giving only the names of each respective architect by way of explanation. He divided them into three groups: one looks to the past in creating the new (Schulze-Naumburg, Schmitthenner, Bonatz), the second does not deny the ties to the past, but remains open-minded toward the new (Tessenow, Fahrenkamp), and the third looks for totally new rules (Taut, Mendelsohn, May). Van der Rohe believes that only the latter understand the signs of the times. The spiritual attitude of the architect is seen as determined by consciousness, technology, and the masses. Only out of this can a building art arise in the spirit of our times, honest, hard, and stark. To us, however, this direction still appears all too hard and constructivist-playful. We hope it is a necessary transition to pure and simultaneously graceful forms.

(Other reviews: "Neue Ordnung im Bauen," in *Vossische Zeitung* of March 1, 1928; "Vom baukünstlerischen Schaffen," in *General-Anzeiger für Stettin und die Provinz Pommern,* 80, no. 66, of March 6, 1928.)

2
"We Stand at the Turning Point of Time:
Building Art as the Expression of Spiritual Decisions"

Published in *Innendekoration,* 39, no. 6 (1928), p. 262.

Building art is not the object of clever speculation, it is in reality only understandable as a *life process,* it is an expression of man's ability to assert himself and master his surroundings. A knowledge of the time, its tasks and means, are necessary prerequisites for the work of the building artist, the *building art is always the spatial expression of spiritual decisions.*

Traffic increases. The world shrinks more and more, it comes more and more into view right into the remotest recesses. World consciousness and consciousness of mankind are the results.

Economy begins to rule, everything is in its service. Profitability becomes law. Technology brings economical attitudes with it, transforms material into power, quantity into quality. Technology presupposes knowledge of natural laws and works with their forces. The most effective use of power is deliberately introduced. We stand at the turning point of time.

3
"On the Theme: Exhibitions"

Published in *Die Form,* 3, no. 4 (1928), p. 121.

Exhibitions are instruments of economic and cultural work. They must be handled with care.

An exhibition depends both as to type and effect on the basic problem it sets. The history of the great exhibitions has shown that only those exhibitions were successful that dealt with current problems and that employed means corresponding to their goals.

The period of representative exhibitions with profitability is past. Decisive for us is the productive achievement of an exhibition, and its value can only be demonstrated by its cultural impact.

Economic, technological, and cultural preconditions have changed fundamentally. Technology and economy face totally new problems. It is of crucial importance that they be correctly recognized and that meaningful solutions be found; not only for economy and technology but for our entire social and cultural life.

If the German economy, and beyond that the European, wants to maintain its position, it must recognize its specific task and act on it. Its way goes from quantity to quality, from the extensive to the intensive.

On this itinerary, economy and technology encounter the important forces of spiritual and cultural life.

We stand in the middle of a transformation, a transformation that will change the world.

To point to this transformation and further it, that will be the task of the upcoming exhibitions. Only if they succeed in illuminating this transformation suddenly and forcefully will they achieve a productive effect. Only if the central problem of our time—the intensification of life—becomes the content of the exhibition will they find meaning and justification.

They must be demonstrations of leading forces and bring about a revolution of our thinking.

4

The Adam Building

Draft of a letter on the 1928 project for the Adam department store. Manuscript in Museum of Modern Art, Later German Projects, Folder 1. The design was introduced in *Das Kunstblatt,* 14, no. 3 (1930), pp. 111–113.

Berlin, July 2, 1928

Firm S. Adam, Berlin W., Leipziger Strasse 27.

Yesterday my project was delivered to your office at Leipziger Strasse 121. I take the liberty to present briefly the thoughts that determined the project. The variability you want is best served by an undivided expanse of the individual floor levels; for that reason I have placed the supports in the exterior walls. Your request that the building be divisible both horizontally and vertically to accommodate the workshops you need make three staircases necessary. The secondary staircase for the workshops I have arranged so that it is accessible from the Friedrichstrasse as well as from the Leipziger Strasse. Right and left of it are the two freight elevators so that each can be used from either part of the building. In the stairwells, the toilets for the employees are accessible from the landings. Each of the two main staircases is easily reached from the Friedrichstrasse and Leipziger Strasse respectively. In these stairwells are the elevators for building visitors and the elevators for internal use. Next to the stairwells are the toilets for managers or customers.

You have indicated in your requirements that in general a building with vertical articulation would conform to your tastes. May I say in all frankness that in my opinion a building has nothing to do with taste but must be the logical result of all requirements that result from its purpose. Only if these are established can one speak of the intrinsic forming of a building. You need layered floor levels with clear, uncluttered spaces. Furthermore you need much light. You need publicity and more publicity.

We stand at the beginning of new developments. Your building must not appear obsolete in 2–3 years; it must last for years to come, an important never-failing instrument in your hands. All this requires not only from the architect but also from the client a good dose of boldness. I therefore suggest to you making the skin of your building of glass and stainless steel, with the bottom floor of transparent glass, the others of opaque glass. Walls of opaque glass give the rooms a wonderfully mild but bright and even illumination. In the evening it represents a powerful body of light and you have no difficulties in affixing advertising. You can do as you like, regardless whether you write on it "For the Summer Vacation," "For Winter Sports," or "Four Bargain Days." Such a brightly lit advertising on an evenly illuminated background will have a fairy-tale effect.

For the back walls of the display windows, too, I would recommend colored mirror glass, and that in mouse-gray. Your building should bear the character of your business and should fit in with sailboats and automobiles, or, expressed differently, with the modern time and with people that embody it.

Respectfully

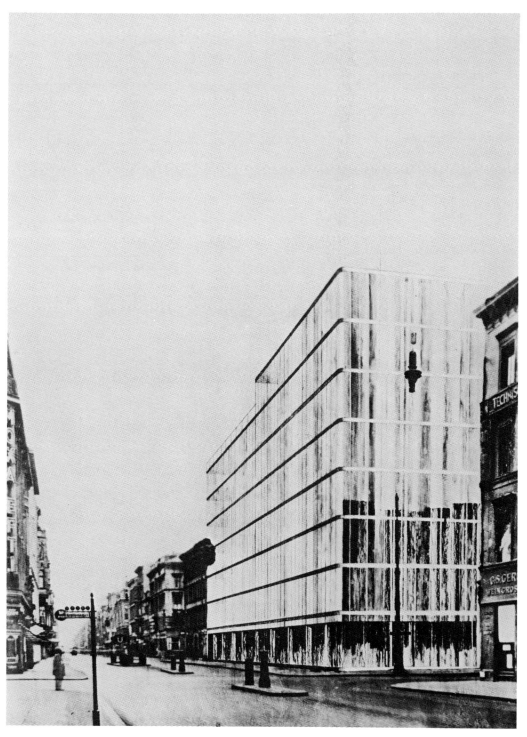

Project for the Adam department store, Berlin, 1928.

5
"Build Beautifully and Practically!
Stop This Cold Functionality"

Publication of a survey ("Representative architects address a timely theme: Will the modern building style be decorative again?") in the *Duisburger Generalanzeiger,* 49 (Sunday, January 26, 1930), p. 2, in which the architects Hugo Häring, Bruno Taut, and Rolf Sklarek also expressed themselves.

There is not the slightest doubt that in today's architecture the artistic is being short-changed. I believe that sometime in the future we will have to come to a decision whether architecture should be merely practical or also beautiful. How this decision will turn out cannot be predicted with any degree of certainty.

What appears totally evident to me is that with our changed requirements and with the new means made available by technology, we will arrive at a new type of beauty. That we will ever again befriend "beauty per se," however, I find unlikely. But how does a medieval sentence so nicely say it? "Beauty is the radiance of truth!" Yes, in the final analysis beauty is coupled to truth, it does not float around in the air but is attached to things and irrevocably connected to the forms of the real world. Real truth therefore will only be attained by those who work with a mind open to reality.

The old architecture was not as function-proclaiming as ours. But in spite of "beauty" it was tied to the conditions and to the forms of existence and appearance of its times and was in that sense reality-bound.

It is fundamentally wrong to assume that the problem of the modern architecture has been recognized as soon as one admits the need for a rational solution. This belief, today taken as self-evident, is only a precondition. If one wants to produce beautiful objects or beautiful houses, one must first of all be able to produce them in the most economical, that is, the most practical way. This verity, as banal as it is, is today often heralded as the ultimate goal, whereas in reality it is not an artistic nor a building aim but simply a necessary precondition, a basis.

It is a natural, human characteristic to consider not only the purposeful but also to search out and love beauty. Due to the powerful advance of technology this self-evident awareness seems to be somewhat repressed. It often appears as if our time would content itself with technical perfection. But this will not remain so. Our time has enormously many means for form-giving at its disposal. It just has not yet learned to master them—perhaps because the mastery of the means, the technical difficulties alone, already requires so much energy that nothing is left over to apply these means also in a form-giving way.

What we consider today as impractical, what we would therefore no longer build today, are simple forms that have lost their meaning. But what we call practical today does not stand in opposition to what was always and at all times practical—namely meaningful. Only what has become meaningless should and must be thrown overboard, but we must not in blind reversal reject the concept of the beautiful for our times.

And what finally is beauty? Certainly nothing that can be calculated or measured. It is always something imponderable, something that lies in between things.

Beauty in architecture, just as necessary and just as desired as in former times, can only be attained if in building we have more than the immediate purpose in mind.

6
"On the Meaning and Task of Criticism"
This contribution appeared in a series of reports on art criticism held on occasion of a meeting of the Association of Art Critics in April 1930. *Das Kunstblatt* published minutes of the individual reports under the title "Artists on Art Criticism" (*Kunstblatt*, 14, no. 6 [1930], p. 178).

Do not fear that I will add to the long chain of reproaches and attacks. Are misjudgments not a matter of course?

Is criticism then so easy? Is real criticism not just as rare as real art? I would like, therefore, to direct your attention to the basic preconditions of any criticism, because I believe that without adequate clarity on that issue real criticism cannot be practiced and demands will be made of criticism that it is unable to fulfill.

Criticism is the testing of an achievement in regard to its meaning and value. In order to test an achievement it is necessary to assume an attitude toward the object to be tested, get a handle on it. This is not so easy. Art works have a life of their own. They are not accessible to all. For them to speak, one must approach them in the way they demand. This constitutes the obligation of the critic.

Another obligation of criticism concerns the gradation of values. Here criticism finds its measuring scale. Real criticism is ultimately service to value.

There is an eight-page handwritten manuscript for the lecture on art criticism, unpublished, in Museum of Modern Art, Manuscripts Folder 4.

[*page 1*]
Ethics should point to the purposes for the sake of which all means exist, particularly the highest, absolute purposes that cannot be understood as means for something else.

Usefulness is a general category of praxis, the relationship of means to purpose. It is therefore senseless to make utilitarianism out of utility. It makes the means into an end, the dependent into the principle, a self-evident irrelevance into the content of life.

For each value content a value meaning must be individually awakened. Situations, too, are something unique, that occur only once and do not return.

[*page 2*]
First basic question. What should we be?
Second basic question. What is valuable in life, yes, in the world as such?

What I am to do I can only determine when I see what is valuable in life. And I can only see what is valuable when I feel this seeing itself as valuable action, as assignment, as an inner duty.

[*page 3*]
Ladies and Gentlemen. Do not fear that I will add to the long chain of [desires—*crossed out*] complaints and attacks. I would like to direct your attention to [the fundamentals of the matter, because I believe that complete clarity on that issue—*crossed out*] [the] basic preconditions of any type of criticism, which includes art criticism, and I believe that without adequate clarity on that issue real criticism cannot be practiced and furthermore demands may be made on criticism that it is unable to fulfill. [By—*crossed out*] Criticism [one understands—*crossed out*] is the testing of an achievement in regard to its meaning and value. [But the testing of an achievement in regard to its meaning and value presupposes that one has a good handle on the object to be tested, that one assumes an attitude toward it.—*crossed out*]

[*page 4*]
But the testing of an achievement in regard to its meaning and value presupposes that one gets a handle on the object to be tested and assumes an attitude toward it. That is not so easy but again dependent on certain rules. [The nature of things is not the same—*crossed out*] Good will and upright thinking alone, while certainly very valuable, are not sufficient. [For the things are not identical but differ intrinsically, they are as they are, different according to type or rank of their dignity.—*crossed out*] Things have their own life and a dignity arising out of their intrinsic nature.

[*page 5*]
The things are not the same, but different not only according to their intrinsic nature, but also according to the type and rank of their dignity. There is a hierarchy of things, and they are not readily accessible but only if, in stepping in front of them, one is as they demand and assumes a position that relates to them.

To the hierarchy of objects corresponds a hierarchy of levels of perception on which the perceiver stands and on which he must stand if he wants to relate to the object. There is an awareness attitude assigned to each object. [that stands with it on the same rank.—*crossed out*]

[*page 6*]
They are not the same but different. Different not only in respect to their intrinsic nature but also according to the type and rank of their dignity. [They do not respond to all, but only to those who are as they demand, and assume the position that corresponds to them.—*crossed out*] Things also are subject to a hierarchy. So it is that each object has a corresponding awareness attitude that stands with it on the same level of rank.

Much as there is a hierarchy of objects, there is a hierarchy of awareness attitudes.

[page 7]

These are irrevocable facts [and binding for any criticism—*crossed out*]. A further obligation lies in the hierarchy of values itself. [One cannot measure spiritual achievements according to a scale of values that has been taken over from the realm of utility, something that is all too often done today.—*crossed out*] Here criticism finds its means of evaluation [Real criticism is service to value—*crossed out*] and real criticism is service to value.

[page 8]

By criticism one understands, I assume even today, the testing of an achievement in regard to its meaning and the value of what is offered. Separation of the valuable from the valueless.

7

"The New Time"

Concluding words of a speech given at the Viennese meeting of the Deutsche Werkbund, June 22–26, 1930. Published in *Die Form,* 5, no. 15 (1930), p. 406; reprinted in *Die Form,* 7, no. 10 (1932), p. 306.

The new time is a fact; it exists whether we say yes or no to it. But it is neither better nor worse than any other time. It is a pure given and in itself undifferentiated. That is why I will not stop long to describe the new time and to point to its relationships and lay bare its support structure. Similarly, we do not want to overestimate mechanization, typification, and standardization. Even the changed economic and social conditions we will accept as facts.

All these things go their fateful, value-blind way. What is decisive is only how we assert ourselves toward these givens. It is here that the spiritual problems begin.

What matters is not the what but only the how. That we produce goods and the means by which we produce them says nothing spiritually. Whether we build high or flat, with steel or with glass, says nothing as to the value of this way of building. Whether one aims for centralization or decentralization in urban planning is a practical question, not one of values. But it is exactly this question of values that is decisive.

We must set new values and point out ultimate goals in order to gain new criteria. For the meaning and justification of each epoch, even the new one, lie only in providing conditions under which the spirit can exist.

Manuscript of the speech in the collection of Dirk Lohan, Chicago:

Ladies and Gentlemen!

I would like to begin with a practical question, namely with the question as to the organizational structure of the exhibition. This question appears to me of particular importance in regard to an international exhibition, for only the right choice of the organizational basis permits us to perform our work.

So far it has been the practice at international exhibitions to set the theme in terms of nationalities. This means that the specific conditions of the individual countries were emphasized. This principle led to constant repetition and to confusion; it did, however, afford an easier and more relaxed execution on account of the financing available on a national basis and the decentralization of responsibility.

Another solution would be to go a step further. One could strive for a transnational approach to intellectual issues, but could make economic contributions along national lines. This would, however, lead to a fragmentation of the exhibition, for it implies the ordering of one segment of the exhibition according to ideal, the other according to economic points of view. This approach also appears to me unsuitable for Cologne, as it deprives us of the necessary orientation for the industrial sector.

What is called for is a transnational treatment of all problems, the economic ones included; this requires preparation and execution by international committees. Only thus can the emphasis on the theme be guaranteed and transnational economic aims be approached. All this, of course, leads to a much more complex organization, for it calls for an expansion of responsibility and demands common financing. It will not be easy to achieve this aim. But here we put all our confidence in Professor Jäckh, who will create the basis for this new type of exhibition.

As to the three groups that I am supposed to elaborate on, I cannot yet submit practical suggestions. That lies in the nature of the matter. Real tasks can only be taken into view when it has been established at what time the exhibition will take place, for each situation is unique and calls for a special point of view. I will, however, briefly express myself as to my attitude in regard to the problems brought up:

The new time is a fact; it exists whether we say yes or no to it. . . . [*The rest of the manuscript is identical with the printed text.*]

8
Program for the Berlin Building Exposition
Restating of the building program arranged by Mies van der Rohe for the 1931 Berlin Building Exposition. Prepared 1930; published in *Die Form*, 6, no. 7 (1931), p. 242.

The dwelling of our time does not yet exist. But changed living conditions demand its realization.

The precondition for this realization is the clear definition of actual dwelling needs. This will be the main purpose of the exhibition.

A further task will be to demonstrate the means required for the satisfaction of the dwelling needs.

Only that way can we combat the present discrepancy between real dwelling needs and wrong dwelling expectations, between genuine demand and inadequate supply.

To overcome that is a burning economic necessity and a precondition for cultural reconstruction.

Model House at the Berlin Building Exposition, 1931.

9
Radio Address

Manuscript of August 17, 1931, in the collection of Dirk Lohan, Chicago.

It may appear strange to discuss artistic building in times of economic depression. And yet I want to use the few minutes that are available to speak of this.

The call for economical methods and functionality in the new building is not the result of the economic distress in which the world finds itself today. It is much older than the worldwide economic crisis and has quite different reasons. Yet this economic depression encourages to a very great degree the direction toward economical and functional building.

Insofar as economics and functionalism constitute preconditions for the new building, the present situation will exercise a considerable influence on the development of building.

There is, however, a danger connected with this development. It could contribute to further spreading the misconception prevalent in many circles that the new building is merely a question of function and economy, and thus cause serious damage to the development of the building art.

Because this belief is wrong. No matter how much function and economics are preconditions for new building, the ultimate problems are of an artistic nature. No matter how much function and economics determine our building, they say very little as to its artistic value.

They do not prevent it, however. The artistic appears in step with the structure of purpose and function, or rather, it realizes itself in that structure. But not in the sense of adding to it; rather, in the sense of giving form to it.

The artistic expresses itself in the proportions of things, often even in the proportions between things. Essentially it is something immaterial, something spiritual. And thus independent of the material conditions of a period. It is a wealth that even a materially poor period need not renounce, indeed must not renounce. We do not want to add to the material loss a cultural one.

The need for simplicity need not be equivalent to cultural deprivation as long as we attempt to lock in as much beauty as possible.

10
Speech on the Occasion of the Anniversary Meeting of the Deutsche Werkbund (1932)

The speech was given in October 1932 in Berlin. Manuscript in the collection of Dirk Lohan, Chicago.

One speaks much these days of a new Germany. Who wants to doubt the need to rearrange the German space. The new arrangement also applies to our work, and it is our hope that genuine arrangements will be found with a reality content so large that authentic life can unfold in them: but life that—vitally secured—permits space for the unfolding of the spirit. Then, so we hope, the German soil will again carry human features.

Even in the days of our need we remain firmly convinced that the value of our existence lies only and exclusively in offering the spirit in the most comprehensive sense the possibility for realization.

Draft manuscript of the lecture to the anniversary meeting of the Deutsche Werkbund in October 1932 in Berlin, unpublished hand- and typewritten draft, in Museum of Modern Art, Manuscripts Folder 5, page D. 1. 2—D. 1. 11.

[page 1]
Ladies and Gentlemen.
You have been introduced to the work of the Werkbund up to now. There also have been hopes expressed as to the future of the Werkbund work. I will explain in a few short words how we visualize such work.

[The Werkbund will be, in the great transformation of our way of life—crossed out. In the great transformation of our form of life, the Werkbund will—crossed out. In the great reformulation of our existence, gives our—crossed out]

[page 2]
One speaks now of a new Germany. [We hope it will not only be new—crossed out] We also are profoundly convinced that it [will be—crossed out] is necessary to recognize the German space. It is our hope that genuine arrangements may unfold [it is our hope.—crossed out].

[page 3]
Form-giving work for all that serves spiritual progress and the benefit of mankind; in young Germans an attitude of work ethics to keep awake bold utopian thought.

[page 4]
I do not consider it right to put in the foreground questions that deal with the reform of economic life. It is obvious that one will not have to take a position on that. These questions are especially controversial, [but] may not have the weight that one attributes to them. [There are clearly—crossed out] A tendency of our time is clearly bent on

setting limits to economics and subjecting them to stricter controls. The concept of the apartment is totally unclear. In fact the apartment must be defined from the point of view of man. The question of the [praxis—*crossed out*] basic forms of houses, whether small house, large house—surely there are intermediate forms.

[*page 5*]
Also we will concern ourselves with the metropolis, as we do not believe that it can of itself bring forth the right form. It appears necessary to issue rules.

[*page 6*]
[We want the great—*crossed out*] We too want to investigate the potential residing in the German space and its landscapes. We want to expand the question of the formal form-giving of the products of craftsmanship and industry to a critique of the production of goods, for here not only the how but also the what becomes crucial.

[Furthermore school policy—*crossed out*] Furthermore [the question—*crossed out*] we are interested in the question of school policy, insofar as it relates to questions of work, form, and art.

The second way.

One must know that the world is formed and that this form matters.

[*page 7*]
We want to confine ourselves to work in those fields in which we are recognized as specialists. This work must be conducted in a thorough manner with underlying problems solved by the best experts.

We will investigate the entire field of settlement housing. Village and metropolis.

[*page 8*]
Given this basic orientation, individual fields will be worked on by diverse work groups. We will deal with the question of settlement, the question of education, the question of products, not unilaterally but from all points of view.

First criticism, then clarification, then reconstruction.

[*handwritten addition:*] Poverty is no deprivation.

[*page 9*]
The Werkbund suffers like everything else under the confusion and insecurity of the present situation, all feel this turbulence and unrest and suffer from it. One gropes in the dark, one fears to speak up, one wants to see things ripened and matured. One must not allow oneself to be seduced into doing nothing, out of fear of doing the wrong thing or acting immature and dilettantish.

Especially now to remain loyal to oneself, to remain constant and firm. Insist [on] what one has rightly recognized as essential.

We refuse to approach things and questions only from the outside, [which] can bring about only organization, only the formal, only quick solutions. We are concerned with a deepening of the work process that should bring us to the unquestionable kernel of the problems.

The Werkbund cannot, must not go with the times.

[*handwritten addition:*] The Werkbund can only concern itself with the contents of things, always the how.

[*page 10*]
Respect for things and material. Unselfish service.

11

"Expressways as an Artistic Problem"

Published in *Die Autobahn,* organ of HAFRABA (Haupt-Aus-schuss für den Reichs-Autobahn-Bau) e. V. Frankfurt am Main, 5, no. 10 (1932), p. 1; reprinted in *Pariser Zeitung,* the organ for European cooperation, 7, no. 44 (1932), p. 1.

Is there even such a thing as an artistic problem in expressways? Such a question is not without meaning in regard to a configuration that is so overwhelmingly economic and technical in nature.

And yet this question must be affirmed if we keep in mind that the expressways, as the most important traffic routes of the future, will not only cut through landscapes with their stations, intersections, overpasses, and valley spans but will also, in those areas where they lie embedded in the landscape, unlock new landscapes as we drive through them. Here, too—even if in a more passive vein, more as consequence—questions of form-giving arise. These formal questions are of a particular type, but nevertheless essential.

That economic and technical reasons determine the routing of expressways is self-understood. But beyond that, much can be done to protect the peculiarity and the particular character of a landscape. Yes, one could even hold that the laying-out of traffic ribbons, beyond the obligation to protect farming interests, can even, under certain circumstances, entail the obligation to heighten the landscape.

Certainly such questions can only be dealt with very circumspectly and only in cooperation with district and village administrations. Our time can no longer afford the recklessness of the previous century that erected technical structures without regard to the farm economy.

Mr. Becker, the *Landesoberbaurat* [regional planning officer] has made suggestions (Hafraba Circular no. 7 for 1930) on plantings along expressways. These suggestions arise apparently out of a desire to fit the traffic ribbons organically into the landscape. This striving goes so far as to extend even to the traffic signals. It appears to me doubtful, however, that the proposed means are suitable in each special case to achieve the goal.

For example the obelisk-like treatment of the border plantings seems to me rather to lead to an emphasis of the road within the landscape, instead of a fitting in. From the point of view of the expressway, this arrangement of border plantings cuts through the landscape image where it should fuse with it. And this cutting apart is heightened in a fast-driven car to a disagreeable chopping up of the landscape. Also I do not believe that the suggested sig-naling of curves and overpasses by means of individual trees or groups of trees can be accomplished, because it would presuppose that all terrain adjoining the route would have to be kept free of trees. Here, other means must be searched for.

When we talked above of the preservation of the landscape, in which, by the way, village views should also be included, it was taken for granted that the usual highway advertising should under no circumstances be permitted. Commercial interests, however, may not be willing to renounce advertising rights in regard to the traffic network of the future, and possibly cannot even do without them. This would mean that a way would have to be found that permits legitimate economic interests to find opportunity, without, however, allowing a rampant spread of advertising to take place. I could conceive that groups of advertisements could be clustered to indicate danger zones, or that the installations of advertisements be restricted to the circumference of cities and furthermore that all advertising be subject to a central control. This agency should, however, not operate with fixed rules, but do justice to ongoing change and fluctuating conditions; otherwise a pedantic rigidity and bureaucracy will set in, destructive to advertising and destroying what may specifically be artistic and valuable in it. It would be more a matter of attitude than of regulations, more an artistic sense than restrictive measures. All in all, more form-giving than administration.

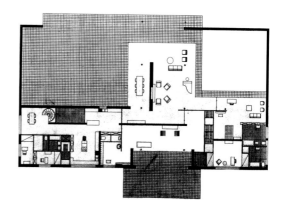

12

"What Would Concrete, What Would Steel Be without Mirror Glass?"
Contribution to a prospectus of the Verein Deutscher Spiegel-glas-Fabriken (Association of German Mirrorglass Factories) of March 13, 1933, not printed. Manuscript in Library of Congress.

The space-toppling power of both would be undermined, yes, even canceled; would remain empty promise. The glass skin, the glass walls alone permit the skeleton structure its unambiguous constructive appearance and secure its architectonic possibilities. Not only in the large functional structures. Although there, on the basis of function and necessity, a development sets in that needs no more justification, the full unfolding of which, however, will not occur there but in the realm of residential buildings. Here, in greater freedom without immediate obligation to narrow functionality, the artistic value of these technical means could be proven.

They are genuine building elements and the instruments of a new building art. They permit a measure of freedom in spatial composition that we will not relinquish any more. Only now can we articulate space freely, open it up and connect it to the landscape. Now it becomes clear again what a wall is, what an opening, what is floor and what ceiling. Simplicity of construction, clarity of tectonic means, and purity of material reflect the luminosity of original beauty.

A different version in the first draft of the manuscript, in the Library of Congress:

They are genuine building elements from which a new, richer building art can arise. They permit a measure of freedom in spatial composition that we will not relinquish any more. Only now can we articulate space, open it up and connect it to the landscape, thereby filling the spatial needs of modern man. Simplicity of construction, clarity of tectonic means, and purity of material shall be the bearers of a new beauty.

13

"The H. House, Magdeburg"
Published in *Die Schildgenossen*, 14, no. 6 (1935), between pp. 514 and 515; original manuscript dating from August 7, 1935, in Library of Congress.

The house was to be built on the Elbe island in Magdeburg, under old beautiful trees with a far-reaching view over the Elbe. It was an unusually beautiful place for building. Only the exposure presented problems. The beautiful view was to the east; to the south the view was dull, almost disturbing. This defect would have had to be corrected by the building plan.

For that reason I have enlarged the living quarters by a garden court surrounded by a wall and so locked out this view while allowing full sunshine. Toward the river the house is entirely open and melts into the landscape. Thereby I not only entered into the situation but obtained a beautiful alternation of quiet seclusion and open spaces.

This articulation also corresponds to the dwelling needs of the client, who, although living alone in the house, wanted to cultivate a relaxed social life and hospitality. This also is reflected by the interior arrangement. Here also, the required privacy combined with the freedom of open room forms.

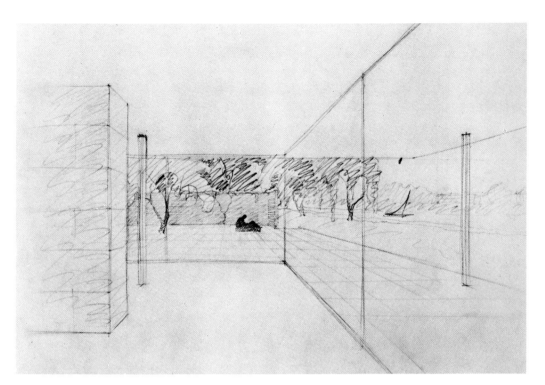

Project for the Hubbe House, Magdeburg, 1935, plan and sketches.

14

Inaugural Address as Director of Architecture at Armour Institute of Technology

Delivered on the occasion of a testimonial dinner at Palmer House, Chicago, November 20, 1938. Manuscript in the Library of Congress; a translation was published in Philip Johnson, *Mies van der Rohe* (New York, 1947), pp. 191–195.

All education must begin with the practical side of life. If one wants to address real education, however, one must transcend this to mold the personality, leading to an improvement of mankind.

The first aim should be to equip the student for practical life. It gives him the proper knowledge and skills. The second aim addresses the development of personality. It enables him to make the right use of this knowledge and skill.

Thus true education is concerned not only with practical goals but also with values. By our goals we are bound to the specific structure of our epoch.

Our values, on the other hand, are rooted in the spiritual nature of man. Our practical aims determine the character of our civilization. Our values determine the height of our culture.

Different as practical aims and values are, arising out of different planes, they are nevertheless closely connected.

For to what else should our values be related if not to our aims in life? And where should these goals get their meaning if not through values?

Both realms together are fundamental to human existence. Our aims assure us of our material life, our values make possible our spiritual existence.

If this is true of all human activity where even the slightest question of value is involved, then it must be more true in the field of architecture.

In its simplest form architecture is entirely rooted in practical considerations, but it can reach up through all degrees of value to the highest realm of spiritual existence, into the realm of the sensuously apprehendable, and into the sphere of pure art.

Any teaching of architecture must recognize this situation if we are to succeed in our efforts.

It must fit the system to this reality.

It must explain these relations and interrelations.

We must make clear, step by step, what is possible, necessary, and significant.

If teaching has any purpose at all, it is to implant knowledge and responsibility.

Education must lead us from irresponsible opinion to responsible insight.

It must lead us from chance and arbitrariness to the clear lawfulness of a spiritual order.

Therefore let us guide our students over the disciplined path from materials through the practical aims of creative work.

Let us lead them into the healthy world of primitive buildings, where each axe stroke meant something and each chisel stroke made a real statement.

Where can we find greater clarity in structural connections than in the wooden buildings of old?

Where else can we find such unity of material, construction, and form?

Here the wisdom of whole generations is stored.

What feeling for material and what power of expression speaks in these buildings.

What warmth they generate, and how beautiful they are! They sound like familiar songs.

And buildings of stone as well: what natural feeling they express!

What a clear understanding of the material. What certainty in its use. What sense they had of what one could and could not do in stone. Where do we find such wealth of structure? Where do we find more healthy energy and natural beauty? With what obvious clarity a beamed ceiling rests on these old stone walls, and with what sensitivity one cut a doorway through these walls.

Where else should young architects grow up than in the fresh air of a healthy world, and where else should they learn to deal simply and astutely with the world than from these unknown masters?

The brick is another teacher. How sensible is this small handy shape, so useful for every purpose.

What logic in its bonding, what liveliness in the play of patterns.

What richness in the simplest wall surface. But what discipline this material imposes.

Thus each material has its specific characteristics that one must get to know in order to work with it.

This is no less true of steel and concrete. We expect nothing from materials in themselves, but only from the right use of them.

Even the new materials give us no superiority. Each material is only worth what we make of it.

In the same way that we learn about materials, we learn about our goals.

We want to analyze them clearly. We want to know what they contain and what distinguishes a building for living in from other kinds of buildings.

We want to know what it can be, what it must be, and what is should not be.

We want, therefore, to learn its essence.

We shall examine one by one every function of a building, work out its character, and make it a basis for design.

Just as we acquainted ourselves with materials and just as we must understand the nature of our goals, we must also learn abut the spiritual position in which we stand.

No cultural activity is possible otherwise; for also in these matters we must know what is, because we are dependent on the spirit of our time.

Therefore we must come to understand the carrying and driving forces of our time. We must analyze their structure from the points of view of the material, the functional, and the spiritual.

We must make clear in what respects our epoch is similar to earlier ones and in what respects it differs.

At this point the problem of technology arises for the students.

We shall attempt to raise genuine questions—questions about the value and purpose of technology.

We want to show that technology not only promises power and greatness, but also involves dangers;

that good and evil apply to it also, and that man must make the right decision.

Every decision leads to a specific kind of order.

Therefore we want to illuminate the possible orders and lay bare their principles.

Let us recognize that the mechanistic principle of order overemphasizes the materialistic and functionalistic factors.

It fails to satisfy our feeling that means must be subsidiary to ends and our desire for dignity and value.

The idealistic principle of order, however, with its over-emphasis on the ideal and the formal, satisfies neither our interest in truth and simplicity nor our practical sense.

So we shall emphasize the organic principle of order that makes the parts meaningful and measurable while determining their relationship to the whole.

And on this we shall have to make a decision.

The long path from material through purpose to creative work has only a single goal:

to create order out of the godforsaken confusion of our time.

But we want an order that gives to each thing its proper place, and we want to give each thing what is suitable to its nature.

We would do this so perfectly that the world of our creations will blossom from within.

More we do not want; more we cannot do.

Nothing can unlock the aim and meaning of our work better than the profound words of St. Augustine:

"Beauty is the radiance of Truth."

IV 1939–1969

Mies around 1950.

1

"A Tribute to Frank Lloyd Wright"

Text for an unpublished catalog of the Frank Lloyd Wright exhibition at the Museum of Modern Art, 1940. Mies's text was published in the *College Art Journal,* 6, no. 1 (1946), pp. 41–42.

Mies with Frank Lloyd Wright at Taliesin, 1937.

Toward the beginning of the twentieth century, the great revival of architecture in Europe, instigated by William Morris, began to grow over-refined and gradually to lose its force. Distinct signs of exhaustion became manifest. The attempt to revive architecture from the standpoint of form was apparently doomed. Even the greatest efforts of artists could not overcome the patent lack of any usable convention. Then, however, these efforts were limited to the subjective. But the authentic approach to architecture must always be the objective. Accordingly, the only valid solutions at that time were in cases such as industrial building, where objective limitations made subjective license impossible. Peter Behrens' significant creations for the electrical industry are a vivid illustration. But in all other problems of architectural creation, the architect ventured into the dangerous realm of the historical; to some of these men the revival of classic forms seemed reasonable, and in the field of monumental architecture, even imperative.

Of course this was not true of all early twentieth century architecture. Van de Velde and Berlage, especially, remained steadfastly loyal to their own ideals. Once a way of thinking had been accepted as essential, Van de Velde's intellectual integrity and Berlage's sincerity and almost religious faith in his ideal allowed no compromise. For these reasons the former won our highest respect, the latter our special veneration and love.

Nevertheless, we young architects found ourselves in painful inner conflict. We were ready to pledge ourselves to an idea. But the potential vitality of the architectural idea of this period had, by that time, been lost.

This, then, was the situation in 1910.

At this moment, so critical for us, there came to Berlin the exhibition of the work of Frank Lloyd Wright. This comprehensive display and the extensive publication of his works enabled us really to become acquainted with the achievement of this architect. The encounter was destined to prove of great significance to the development of architecture in Europe.

The work of this great master revealed an architectural world of unexpected force and clarity of language, and also a disconcerting richness of form. Here finally was a master-builder drawing upon the veritable fountainhead of architecture, who with true originality lifted his architectural creations into the light. Here, again, at last, genuine organic architecture flowered.

The more deeply we studied Wright's creations, the greater became our admiration for his incomparable talent, for the boldness of his conceptions, and for his independence in thought and action. The dynamic impulse emanating from his work invigorated a whole generation. His influence was strongly felt even when it was not actually visible.

After this first encounter, we followed the development of this rare man with eager hearts. We watched with astonishment the exuberant unfolding of the gifts of one who had been endowed by nature with the most splendid talents. In his undiminishing power he resembles a giant tree in a wide landscape, which, year after year, ever attains a more noble crown.

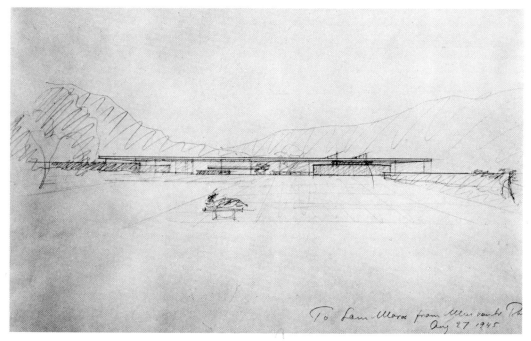

Museum for a Small City, 1943.

2

"Museum for a Small City"
Published in *Architectural Forum,* 78, no. 5 (1943), pp. 84–
85.

The museum for the small city should not emulate its metropolitan counterparts. The value of such a museum depends upon the quality of its works of art and the manner in which they are exhibited.

The first problem is to establish the museum as a center for the enjoyment, not the interment of art. In this project the barrier between the art work and the living community is erased by a garden approach for the display of sculpture. Interior sculptures enjoy an equal spatial freedom, because the open plan permits them to be seen against the surrounding hills. The architectural space, thus achieved, becomes a defining rather than a confining space. A work such as Picasso's *Guernica* has been difficult to place in the usual museum gallery. Here it can be shown to greatest advantage and become an element in space against a changing background.

The building, conceived as one large area, allows every flexibility in use. The structural type permitting this is the steel frame. This construction permits the erection of a building with only three basic elements—a floor slab, columns and a roof plate. The floor and paved terraces would be of stone.

Under the same roof, but separated from the exhibit space would be the offices of administration. These would have their own toilet and storage facilities in a basement under the office area.

Small pictures would be exhibited on free-standing walls. The entire building space would be available for larger groups, encouraging a more representative use of the museum than is customary today, and creating a noble background for the civic and cultural life of the whole community.

Two openings in the roof plate (3 and 7) admit light into an inner court (7) and into an open passage (3) through one end of the building. Outer walls (4) and those of the inner court are of glass. On the exterior, free-standing walls of stone would define outer courts (1) and terraces (10). Offices (2) and wardrobes would be free standing. A shallow recessed area (5) is provided, around the edge of which small groups could sit for informal discussions. The auditorium (8) is defined by free-standing walls providing facilities for lectures, concerts and intimate formal discussions. The form of these walls and the shell hung above the stage would be dictated by the acoustics. The floor of the auditorium is recessed in steps of seat height, using each step as a continuous bench. Number (6) is the print department. Above it is a space for special exhibits. Number (9) is a pool.

Museum for a Small City, illustration of interior room.

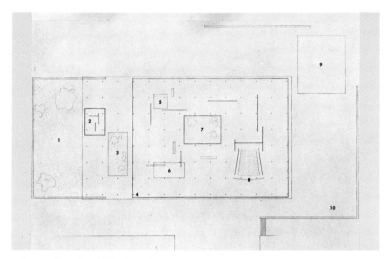

Museum for a Small City, floor plan.

3
Introduction to Ludwig Hilberseimer,
The New City: Principles of Planning (Chicago, 1944)

"Reason is the first principle of all human work." Consciously or unconsciously L. Hilberseimer follows this principle and makes it the basis of his work in the complicated field of city planning. He examines the city with unwavering objectivity, investigates each part of it and determines for each part its rightful place in the whole. Thus he brings all the elements of the city into clear, logical order. He avoids imposing upon them arbitrary ideas of any character whatsoever.

He knows that cities must serve life, that their validity is to be measured in terms of life, and that they must be planned for living. He understands that the forms of cities are the expression of existing modes of living, that they are inextricably bound up with these, and that they, with these, are subject to change. He realizes that the material

and spiritual conditions of the problem are given, that he can exercise no influence on these factors in themselves, that they are rooted in the past and will be determined by objective tendencies for the future.

He also knows that the existence of many and diverse factors presupposes the existence of some order which gives meaning to these and which acts as a medium in which they can grow and unfold. City planning means for the author, therefore, the ordering of things in themselves and in their relationships with each other. One should not confuse the principles with their application. City planning is, in essence, a work of order; and order means—according to St. Augustine—"The disposition of equal and unequal things, attributing to each its place."

Erich Mendelsohn, Walter Peterhans, Ludwig Hilberseimer,
and Mies in Chicago, around 1940.

4

"Architecture and Technology"
Published in *Arts and Architecture,* 67, no. 10 (1950), p. 30.

Technology is rooted in the past.
It dominates the present and tends into the future.
It is a real historical movement—
one of the great movements which shape and
represent their epoch.
It can be compared only with the Classic
discovery of man as a person,
the Roman will to power,
and the religious movement of the Middle Ages.
Technology is far more than a method,
it is a world in itself.
As a method it is superior in almost every respect.
But only where it is left to itself as in
the construction of machinery, or as in the
gigantic structures of engineering, there
technology reveals its true nature.
There it is evident that it is not only a useful means,
that it is something, something in itself,
something that has a meaning and a powerful form—
so powerful in fact, that it is not easy to name it.
Is that still technology or is it architecture?
And that may be the reason why some people
are convinced that architecture will be outmoded
and replaced by technology.
Such a conviction is not based on clear thinking.
The opposite happens.
Wherever technology reaches its real fulfillment,
it transcends into architecture.
It is true that architecture depends on facts,
but its real field of activity is in the realm
of the significance.
I hope you will understand that architecture
has nothing to do with the inventions of forms.

It is not a playground for children, young or old.
Architecture is the real battleground of the spirit.
Architecture wrote the history of the epochs
and gave them their names.
Architecture depends on its time.
It is the crystallization of its inner structure,
the slow unfolding of its form.
That is the reason why technology and architecture
are so closely related.
Our real hope is that they grow together,
that someday the one be the expression of
the other.
Only then will we have an architecture worthy
of its name:
Architecture as a true symbol of our time.

5

Lecture

Chicago, occasion and date unknown. Nineteen sheets of unpublished lecture manuscript, in Library of Congress. Heading on cover sheet: "Manuscript of one important address Mies gave here in German."

[page 1]

Ladies and Gentlemen!

The attempt to revitalize the building art from the direction of form has failed. A century's worth of effort has been wasted and leads into the void. That heroic revolution of extremely talented men at the turn of the century had the time span of a fashion. The invention of forms is obviously not the task of the building art. Building art is more and different. Its excellent name already makes it clear that building is its natural content and art its completion.

[page 2]

Building, where it became great, was almost always indebted to construction, and construction was almost always the conveyor of its spatial form. Romantic and Gothic demonstrate that in brilliant clarity. Here as there structure expresses the meaning, expresses it down to the last remnant of spiritual value. But if that is so, then it must follow that the revitalization of the building art can only come from construction and not by means of arbitrarily assembled motifs.

[page 3]

But construction, that loyal safekeeper of an epoch's spirit, had rejected all that was arbitrary and created an objective basis for new developments. And so it has happened here also. The few authentic structures of our period exhibit construction as a component of building. Building and meaning are one. The manner of building is decisive and of testimonial significance.

[page 4]

Construction not only determines form but is form itself. Where authentic construction encounters authentic contents, authentic works result; works genuine and intrinsic. And they are necessary. Necessary in themselves and also as members of a genuine order. One can only order what is already ordered in itself. Order is more than organization. Organization is the determination of function.

[page 5]

Order, however, imparts meaning. If we would give to each thing what intrinsically belongs to it, then all things would easily fall into their proper place; only there they could really be what they are and there they would fully realize themselves. The chaos in which we live would give way to order and the world would again become meaningful and beautiful.

[page 6]

But that means to let go of the self-will and do the necessary. To articulate and realize the timely and not prevent what wants to and must become.

[page 7]

In other words: serve rather than rule. Only those who know how hard it is to do even simple things properly can respect the immensity of this task. It means to persevere humbly, renounce effects, and do what is necessary and right with loyalty.

[page 8]

Only yesterday one spoke of the eternal forms of art, today one speaks of its dynamic change. Neither is right. Building art is beholden neither to the day nor to eternity, but to the epoch. Only a historical movement offers it space for living and allows it to fulfill itself. Building art is the expression of what historically transpires. Authentic expression of an inner movement.

[page 9]

Fulfillment and expression of something immanent. This may also be the reason why the nineteenth century failed. Unsuspected and deep beneath all the confused attempts of that time ran the quiet current of change, fed by forces of a world that was intrinsically already different, and a jungle of new forms broke out. Unusual and of wild power. The world of technical forms; large and forceful.

[page 10]

Genuine forms of a genuine world. Everything else that occurred looked, next to that, pale and marginal. Technology promises both power and grandeur, a dangerous promise for man who has been created for neither one nor the other. Those who are truly responsible feel depressed and respond to this promise by searching for the dignity and value of technology.

[page 11]

Is the world as it presents itself bearable for man?
More: is it worthy of man or too lowly?
Does it offer room for the highest form of human dignity?
Can it be shaped so as to be worthwhile to live in?

[page 12]

And finally: Is the world noble enough to respond to man's duty to erect a high and magnanimous order? These are questions of immense weight. One can quickly affirm them and quickly negate them, and one has done that.

[page 13]

To the careful, however, beyond all prejudices and misjudgments, technology appears as a world which is what it is, specific and narrow, dependent on the panorama of

---

its own time just as any other building art, and precluding a host of possibilities.

[page 14]

There is no reason to overestimate this form. But it is, like all other authentic forms, both deep and high. Called to the one, attempting the other. A real world.—If that is true, then technology, too, must change into building art to complete itself. It would be a building art that inherits the Gothic legacy. It is our greatest hope.

[page 15]

But none of this comes by itself. History does not come about by itself. [addition in the original manuscript: History must be done.] And historical measurements are shorter than many realize. Only thirty life spans separate us from the Acropolis. And the breathing span of the Middle Ages was too short for it to complete its cathedrals. [addition in the original manuscript: We have all reason to be wide awake and not sleep away our time.]

[page 16]

Furthermore, the technological age is not as young as it may appear. Whitehead transferred the hour of its birth into the seventeenth century. That may be. The ultimate reasons for what occurs today may be found in the discussions of lonely monks behind quiet, Romanesque monastery walls.

[page 17]

With infinite slowness arises the great form the birth of which is the meaning of the epoch. [But a reconciliatory forgiving kindness of history permits great things to die in their greatness and spares them from old age—crossed out]. Not everything that happens takes place in full view. The decisive battles of the spirit are waged on invisible battlefields.

[page 18]

The visible is only the final step of a historical form. Its fulfillment. Its true fulfillment. Then it breaks off. And a new world arises.

[page 19]

What I have said is the ground on which I stand; that which I believe and the justification of my deeds. Convictions are necessary, but in the realm of one's work they have only limited significance. In the final analysis it is the performance that matters. [crossed out addition in the original manuscript: That is what Goethe meant when he said: Create artist, do not talk.]

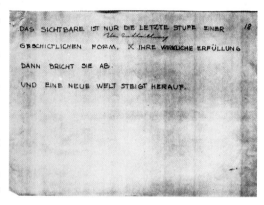

Pages of a lecture manuscript, Chicago (undated).

6
Miscellaneous—Notes to Lectures
These notes relate to the themes of technology and the building art and might have been made for statements on those or other topics. The notes reproduced here are excerpts from approximately 130 pages of notes, previously unpublished, from a notebook block in loose form, undated (around 1950), in Library of Congress, "Drafts and Speeches."

To reestablish the meaning of things.

To develop things in a new way from the perspective of mankind.

To think through the service of those things from the beginning.

That is determinative. What is important, therefore, is not only goal-orientedness but also the mandate and values. In the search for the respective correspondence there opens again a new hierarchy of values determining everything, from the small to the large.

Form that has an effect instead of effective form.

Growth of form; from the origin slowly rising to the last stage of design where form manifests itself. Form as experienced because it grows out of meaning; therefore full of meaning and also meaningful.

Technology
Tradition of doing
historical formalism
modern formalism
Appearance of new contents
Need for new solutions
New materials
New techniques
Reciprocal (complementary) influence

All possible freedom and yet such great profundity, but that seems to be harder for us than [it] was at any prior time.
And yet we have at our disposal a surprising wealth of technological possibilities.
But perhaps it is just this wealth that prevents us from doing what is right.
Perhaps building is the outcome of a simple deed.
Of a simple work process and of a clear building structure.
We even believe that this is how it is.
And we find this belief demonstrated in many old and a few modern buildings.

He who wants a building art must decide. He must subordinate himself to the great objective demands of the epoch. Give constructive form to them. (Nothing more and nothing less.) Building was always linked to a simple deed, but this deed has to hit the nail on the head. Only in this sense can one understand Berlage's saying BUILDING IS SERVING.

[on Viollet-le-Duc]
For over a century one has attempted, by thought and deed, to come to a closer understanding of the nature of the building art. In retrospect it becomes clear that all attempts to renew the building art from the formal direction have failed. Wherever important things occurred, they were of a constructive, not of a formal nature. This is doubtless the reason for the conviction that construction has to be the basis of the building art. These thoughts are by no means new. They are in fact as old as the movement of new building itself.

V.L.D. [Viollet-le-Duc] already, in tracking down the causes of the deterioration of the building art, understood with rare penetration the actual basics of the building art and explained them in his *Entretiens sur l'architecture* that appeared in the sixties. For him, the building art was the honest fulfillment of purpose and material and the constructive means of the epoch. Even then he recognized the double nature of work in the building art; the dependence on all purposes and the execution with all means.

He called for an attitude of honesty in regard to one as well as to the other.

Form was already then to him the result of genuine processes and not, as with his contemporaries, something independent, a question of a new art. "TOUTE FORME, QUI N'EST PAS ORDONNÉ PAR LA STRUCTURE DOIT ETRE REPOUSSÉ." [All form that is not decreed by structure must be rejected.] This sentence stood at the beginning, not at the end of a long movement. These thoughts leave nothing to be desired as to clarity. They are insights gained by familiarity with the great structures of the past and refer directly to the building art. And there they are valid.

[on handicrafts and industry]
The great movement introduced by William Morris was essentially an arts and crafts movement, something it has remained, in all its shadings, until today. Its ultimate goal was dwelling and it was succesful in achieving its liberation. But in the course of this development, handicrafts have not risen to the level of a building art, as is so often stated. Rather, building was more and more interpreted as handicraft. But wherever real building arose, in industry and commerce, function was the ultimate form-giver and technology furnished the constructive means.

Here and not on the Mathildenhöhe the new language was first heard. Of course one can interpret these things differently. But he who wants a building art must decide. He must subordinate himself to the great objective demands of the epoch and realize them constructively. Only in this sense can we understand Berlage's saying "building is serving."

[on the situation of modern architecture]
Let us not deceive ourselves. Many modern buildings will not stand the test of time. They may conform to all the general rules of the building art except the most fundamental one of "building" [*Bauen*]; and it is this last demand that will seal their fate.

One of the greatest hurdles in the application of the new-found freedom is the loss of security of action, building action. This building action is more and more being replaced by machines. The new freedom opened the door to a flood of things; maybe desirable, but without constructive value in themselves. But these things were accepted as they offered themselves and one employed them as well as one could. One pushed these things around, surrounded one's life with machines and confused this organizing with building.

Chapel of the Illinois Institute of Technology, 1952.

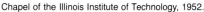

[on Karl Friedrich Schinkel]

Karl Friedrich Schinkel, the greatest building master of classicism, represents the end of an old and the beginning of a new time. With the Altes Museum he built a waning time. With his boring Gothic churches he was the forerunner of an unspeakably kitchy century, but with the Building Academy he introduced a new epoch. Apparently his students failed to understand this work. [Maybe it was hard to understand—*crossed out*] They persisted in the classical style and failed to notice that times had changed.

[on building art]

The purpose of building art is permanence. Building art is not, as many think, at the mercy of sudden changes, nor is it bound to the great eternal course of infinity, but only and exclusively to its epoch. Today the building represents more an appliance than a monument.

Building is giving form to reality.

Fulfill the law to gain freedom. Thus room would be created for personal values, for unique things. Not the interesting and unique, but the self-understood and valid is the real theme of the building art. For this reason we do not ask what this or that master has expounded on but what he has contributed to the growth of history. Do what is expected: apply what is self-evident, and realize what is about to reveal itself.

Order is more than organization. Organization is purposeful. Order is meaningful, and this is what it shares with the building art. Both reach far beyond function, and aim in the final analysis for values.

This world and no other is offered to us.
Here we must take our stand.
We have every reason to assume that, when technology develops into building art, great things will come about.

7
Statement on the Design of the Carr Chapel, Illinois Institute of Technology
Published in *Arts and Architecture,* 70, no. 1 (1953), p. 19.

I chose an intensive rather than an extensive form to express my conception, simply and honestly, of what a sacred building should be. By that I mean a church or chapel should identify itself, rather than rely upon the spiritual associations of a traditional fashion in architecture, such as the Gothic. But the same motives of respect and nobility are present in both instances.

I know there are those who may take exception to the chapel, but it was designed for the students and staff at the school. They will understand it.

Architecture should be concerned with the epoch, not the day. The chapel will not grow old . . . it is of noble character, constructed of good materials, and has beautiful proportions . . . it is done as things should be done today, taking advantage of our technological means. The men who did the Gothic churches achieved the best they could with their means.

Too often we think of architecture in terms of the spectacular. There is nothing spectacular about this chapel; it was not meant to be spectacular. It was meant to be simple; and, in fact, it is simple. But in its simplicity it is not primitive, but noble, and in its smallness it is great—in fact, monumental. I would not have built the chapel differently if I had had a million dollars to do it.

8

"Walter Gropius"

Speech given by Mies van der Rohe in the Blackstone Hotel in Chicago on May 18, 1953, on occasion of the seventieth birthday of Walter Gropius; published in Sigfried Giedion, *Walter Gropius. Mensch und Werk* (Stuttgart, 1954), pp. 20–22.

I do not know whether Gropius recalls that we—the office staff of the great German architect Peter Behrens—organized a birthday party for him forty-three years ago in the back room of a cheap suburban Berlin restaurant. I for my part remember this feast very well. We had very enjoyable hours together. Never again have I seen Gropius so happy and I believe that this birthday celebration belonged to the happiest hours of his life. At that time he had no inkling that one day he would have to carry the heavy burden of fame.

Gropius, who was a few years older than most of us, left the office of Peter Behrens and became independent. He built a factory of steel, glass, and brick. It is still in use today. This building was so excellent that he became with one stroke one of the leading European architects.

A few years later he erected a building complex for the Cologne Exhibition—office buildings and machinery halls—in an even more radical manner. With this work he proved that his first work was no accident.

Subsequently the world war put a stop to all work for four long years. After the war Gropius took over the Weimar Academy that had been directed before the war by the great Belgian architect van de Velde. It is never easy to succeed a great man; but Gropius took this task upon himself. He reorganized the Weimar Academy from bottom on up and called it the Bauhaus.

The Bauhaus was not an institute with a clear problem, it was an idea, and Gropius himself articulated this idea quite precisely.

He said: "Art and technology—a new entity!" He wanted the Bauhaus to be all-inclusive, from painting, sculpture, theater, yes, even ballet and weaving to photography—in short everything from a coffee cup to city planning.

For art he gained the Russian Kandinsky, the German Klee, and the American Feininger as co-workers—artists that were for that time very radical. Today we know that they belong to the art masters of our age.

In 1923 Gropius wanted to show and represent his work and his idea in a larger framework. A Bauhaus Week was organized in Weimar, and during these days many visitors came from all over Europe to look at his work and express their respect and appreciation.

As I said before: The Bauhaus was an idea, and I believe that the influence the Bauhaus had in the world was due to the fact that it was an idea. Such a resonance one cannot obtain with organization alone nor with propaganda. Only an idea has the forcefulness to spread to such an extent.

In the year 1926, after moving the Bauhaus to Dessau and erecting its own facilities for it, Gropius became interested in industrialization. He recognized the necessity for standardization and prefabrication. I was happy that in Stuttgart I was able to support him so that he could demonstrate his ideas on industrialization, standardization, and prefabrication. At that time he built two houses that were the most interesting houses of the exhibition.

Later, upon leaving the Bauhaus, Gropius became interested in the social aspects of apartment building. He became the most important member of the state-owned Research Institute for Apartment Building in Germany and he built large apartment complexes in various locations in Germany. Along with Le Corbusier, he was one of the most important members of the International Congress for New Building, CIAM, which had membership organizations in almost all countries.

When the Nazis came, Gropius went to England. There he worked together with friends for many years and was subsequently called to Harvard. I believe his work from that point on is known to most of you. Gropius has trained and educated a large number of students. Many of them today have leading positions in large architectural offices. I need not mention that Gropius is one of the greatest architects of our age. Simultaneously he is the greatest educator in our field—that, too, we all know. But what I want to stress and what you may not be aware of is that he was always a courageous fighter in the never-ending struggle for the new idea.

9
Foreword to Rudolf Schwarz, *The Church Incarnate*

The Church Incarnate (Chicago, 1958) was the English version of Schwarz's *Vom Bau der Kirche* (Würzburg, 1938), which had a foreword by Romano Guardini.

This book was written in Germany's darkest hour, but it throws light for the first time on the question of church building, and illuminates the whole problem of architecture itself.

Rudolf Schwarz, the great German church builder, is one of the most profound thinkers of our time. His book, in spite of its clarity, is not easy reading—but he who will take the trouble to study it carefully will gain real insight into the problems discussed. I have read it over and over again, and I know its power of clarification. I believe it should be read not only by those concerned with church building but by anyone sincerely interested in architecture. Yet is is not only a great book on architecture, indeed, it is one of the truly great books—one of those which have the power to transform our thinking.

I have always felt it should be translated into English. Now, thanks to Cynthia Harris, it can be studied by anyone in the English speaking world.

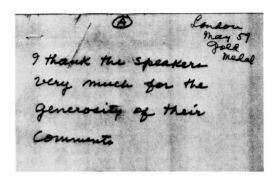

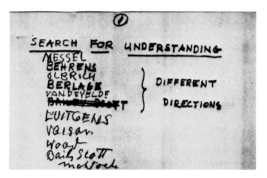

Speech on the occasion of receiving the gold medal of the Royal Institute of British Architects(1959): arrangement of the "standard speech" on library cards.

10

Notes for a Talk on the Occasion of Receiving the Gold Medal of the Royal Institute of British Architects

Ideas for Mies's acceptance speech, given in London in May 1959. Manuscript notes in English on catalog cards, in the Library of Congress. The following acceptance speeches were composed on this model, in almost identical words: on the occasion of receiving the Bundesverdienstkreuz from the ambassador of the German Federal Republic, Baron von Lupich, speech given in the Arts Club of Chicago on April 2, 1959 (manuscript in Library of Congress); on receiving the gold medal of the American Institute of Architects, speech given in San Francisco in April 1960 (manuscript in Library of Congress); on receiving the gold medal of the American Academy of Arts and Letters and the National Institute of Arts and Letters, speech given on May 22, 1963 (published in *Proceedings of the American Academy of Arts and Letters,* New York, 1964, pp. 331f). Translated excerpts of this Miesian standard speech were published in *Bauen und Wohnen,* 15, no. 11 (1960), p. 391, under the title "Wohin gehen wir nun?" [Where Do We Go from Here?] (see below) and also as the foreword to Werner Blaser, *Mies van der Rohe. Die Kunst der Struktur* (Zurich and Stuttgart, 1965), pp. 5–6 (see below).

(A)

I thank the speakers very much for the generosity of their comments

(B)

—I wish to thank Her Majesty, the Queen, for the great honor she has bestowed on me.

—and I thank sincerely the Council of the R.I.B.A. for proposing my name for her approval.

(I)

Search for understanding

Messel

Behrens ⎫
Olbrich ⎬ different directions
Berlage ⎭

van de Velde

Luitgens

Voison

Wood

Baily Scott

(2)

learned most from old buildings

(3)

Architecture must belong to its own time.

—But what is our time [?]

—What is its structure, its essence?

—What are the sustaining and driving forces?

(4)

—What is civilization?

—What is culture?

—What is the relation between the two?

(5)

In this peculiar year—1926

—Schwarz—

—Max Scheeler—

—Whitehead—

(6)

There is a truth relation.

But what is truth?

—Thomas: *adaequatio rei et intellectus*

—Augustine: Beauty is the radiance of truth

(7)

Slowness

Architecture as the expression of the slow unfolding of an epoch.

An epoch is a slow process.

(8)

Ending: Ulrich von Hutten

[*unnumbered*]

Tell about—3000 books

—sent me 300 to Chicago

—I could return 270

The glance back at order: Mies on the Acropolis, 1959. "I had no conventional architectural education. I worked under a few good architects; I read a few good books—and that's about it" (Mies, 1965).

11

"Where Do We Go from Here?"

Published in *Bauen und Wohnen,* 15, no. 11 (1960), p. 391.

Teaching and work have convinced me of the importance of clarity in deed and thought. Without clarity there is no understanding. Without understanding there can be no orientation—only confusion.

Sometimes confusion holds even great men in its grip—as it was around 1900. As Wright, Berlage, Behrens, Olbrich, Loos, and van de Velde worked, all did so in different directions.

I was often asked by students, architects, and interested lay people: "Where do we go from here?" It is of course not necessary or possible to invent a new architecture each Monday morning.

We are not at the end but at the beginning of a new epoch. This epoch is being determined by a new spirit and driven by new technological, sociological, and economic forces, and they will come up with tools and new materials. For this reason we will also have a new architecture.

But the future does not come about by itself. Only if we do our work properly can we create a good foundation for our future. In all these years I have learned more and more that architecture is not just a playing with forms. I have understood the close connection between architecture and civilization. I have understood that architecture must develop out of the supportive and dynamic forces of civilization and that in its best examples it expresses the innermost structure of its epoch.

The building of civilization is not simple, since the past, the present, and the future have a share in it. It is difficult to define and difficult to understand. What belongs to the past cannot be changed any more. The present must be affirmed and mastered. But the future stands open—open for the creative thought and the creative deed.

It is against this background that architecture arises. Consequently, architecture should only stand in contact with the most significant elements of civilization. Only a relationship that touches on the innermost nature of the epoch is authentic. I call this relationship a truth relationship. Truth in the sense of Thomas Aquinas: as *adaequatio intellectus et rei,* as congruence of thought and thing. Or as a philosopher would express it in today's language: truth means facts.

Only such a relationship can comprise the multiple nature of civilization. Only thus can architecture be part of the development of civilization. And only thus can it express the slow unfolding of its form.

This was and will be the task of architecture. Surely this is a difficult task. But Spinoza has taught us that great things are never simple. They are as difficult as they are rare.

12

Thank-you Speech on the Voice of America on the Occasion of His Seventy-fifth Birthday, 1961
Manuscript in the collection of Dirk Lohan, Chicago.

I gladly use the opportunity to thank my German friends for their friendly commemoration of my seventy-fifth birthday. On this day I think not only of my friends but also of my hometown of Aachen, within whose walls I spent my youth. And then of the city of Berlin, where I lived and worked for a quarter of a century. This city of the great building masters Schlüter, Knobelsdorff, and Schinkel, in which I found in Bruno Paul and Behrens my first great teachers. Then of the shared work in the community of the German Werkbund.

I also think of the rich and grand times in the twenties, which contributed so much to our western culture and which ended with the battle for the Bauhaus.

All this was of great importance to me and my subsequent work in America. All this I never cease to appreciate.

[in English:] To my English-speaking friends I like to say that we are not at the end but at the beginning of a new epoch and that I like to say with Ulrich von Hutten: It is the dawn of a new day and it is a joy to live.

13

"Rudolf Schwarz"
Contribution for the catalog of the Rudolf Schwarz memorial exhibition in Cologne (*Gedächtnisausstellung des BDA Köln, gefördert von der Akademie der Künste Berlin* [Heidelberg, 1963], p. 5).

Chicago, April 14, 1963

Rudolf Schwarz was a great building master in the full sense of the word. His entire life—not only his activities but his incomparably profound thinking—was a constant effort to achieve clarity, meaning, and order. Rudolf Schwarz was a thinking building master, and building art was for him a form-giving, meaning-imparting ordering.

Whatever challenges in life confronted him, whether giving meaningful organization to a training school or an academy, or the planning of new villages or entire landscapes, or the exquisite plan for the rebuilding of Cologne and particularly its many beautiful churches, his thinking penetrated the task and set about its ordering work.

Basic to his accomplishments were his thoughts—carefully unfolded—in his wonderful writings.

Thought and work prove the unique greatness of a dead friend.

Eulogy for Le Corbusier
A one-page, typewritten text in English, in the Library of Congress. (Le Corbusier died on August 27, 1965.)

Everyone recognizes by now that Le Corbusier was a great Architect and Artist, a real innovator. Ever since 1910, when I first knew him, he has reminded me of the great Renaissance artists, who built, painted, and sculptured all at the same time. To me his deepest significance lies in the fact he was a true liberator in the fields of architecture and city planning. Only the future can reveal how those who have been liberated will use the freedom opened up to them by his courage and imagination. Any liberation can result in a new confusion, a new Baroque, or in what we can hope for, from those who will follow Le Corbusier—an essential expression of our civilization.
Mies van der Rohe

"Peterhans's Seminar for Visual Training at the Architecture Department of IIT"
Published in Werner Blaser, *Mies van der Rohe. Lehre und Schule* (Basel and Stuttgart, 1977), pp. 34, 35.

Chicago, February 5, 1965

When friends and students of Walter Peterhans decided to publish a selection of drawings for the seminar for visual training that he had established at the Illinois Institute of Technology, I was asked, on account of the responsibilities that I had in the beginning of this course, to write an introduction for this publication. When I took over the Bauhaus in Dessau in 1930 Walter Peterhans was in charge of the photography department. It was there that I became acquainted with his conscientious work with the students and the immense discipline he taught and expected of them. He was not only a first-rate photographer, but a strong personality with a broad education in many fields, especially in mathematics, history, and philosophy.

Later, when I became director of the architecture department at the Illinois Institute of Technology in Chicago, I asked Ludwig Hilberseimer, a leading theoretician in urban planning, and Walter Peterhans to become members of the faculty and to work out in close cooperation with me a new teaching program for young students.

Confronted with the problem of having to change a school that consisted of pupils in various levels of development, namely from first year to graduation, it was obvious that the only possible starting point was the level of the first study year. As students progressed step by step, a curriculum conforming to our ideas could then gradually be developed.

I am convinced that a beginner with proper training and guidance can become a good drawer in one year. I asked Peterhans to work out lectures for this purpose so that in the graduating class we would wind up with students that would conform to our expectations. He was totally successful in this. The teaching program worked out by him became the basis for clean, clear, precise work—precondition for the subsequent training.

Somewhat later I made the surprising discovery that the students, while seeming to understand what I told them about the significance of proportions, did not develop any sensibilities for them in their exercises. It became clear to me that their eyes simply failed to register proportions. The problem was discussed with Peterhans and we decided to introduce a new course with the special aim of exercising visual perceptions and helping to bring the sense of proportion to maturity. It was meant to be a

Mies at Armour Institute of Technology (James Speyer at left, George Danforth at right).

continuation of the basic studies but was to be taught only at the beginning of the second year. To achieve this, Peterhans developed a course that he called visual training. The result of it was a total change of attitude in the students. Everything awkward and disorderly disappeared from their work; they learned to leave out all superfluous lines and a real understanding of proportion developed. Although particularly talented students often came up with drawings that could have enriched the collections of museums, it was never the purpose of this course to create art works, but merely to train the eye.

16

"Building Art of Our Time (My Professional Career)"

Foreword to Werner Blaser, *Mies van der Rohe. Die Kunst der Struktur* (Zurich and Stuttgart, 1965, new edition 1973), pp. 5–6.

My conscious professional career began around 1910. The Jugendstil and Art Nouveau had come and gone. Representative buildings stood more or less under the influence of Palladio or Schinkel. The great achievements of that period, however, were to be found among industrial buildings and purely technological structures. It was actually a confused time and nobody could or would answer the question as to the nature of the building art. Perhaps the time was not yet ripe for an answer. At any rate, I posed this question and was determined to find an answer to it.

It became increasingly evident only after the war, in the twenties, how much technical developments had begun to influence many aspects of our lives. We began to realize that technology was a civilizing force that could not be ignored.

Out in the field of building, the evolving technology furnished new materials and work methods that stood very often in stark contrast to our traditional concepts of the building art. Nevertheless, I saw the possibility of developing a building art with the help of these novel means. I felt that it should be possible to bring the old and the new forces of our civilization into harmony with each other. Each of my buildings was a demonstration of these thoughts and a further step in my own search for clarity.

I became increasingly convinced that these new scientific and technical developments constituted the actual preconditions for the building art of our time. I have never lost this conviction. Now as then I believe that the building art has nothing or little to do with the invention of interesting forms or personal predispositions.

True building art is always objective and expresses the inner structure of the epoch out of which it arises.

17
"Principles for Education in the Building Art"
Published in Werner Blaser, *Mies van der Rohe. Die Kunst der Struktur* (Zurich and Stuttgart, 1965, new edition 1973), pp. 50–51.

The architecture department aims, by means of its building program, to teach the required knowledges and skills to architectural students; through its pedagogical methods, however, it aims at forming the students so that they can apply the acquired knowledges and skills in the proper way. The theory therefore aims at the function, while the pedagogic training aims at values. For it is the meaning of education to train and teach accountability. It must add the binding force of insight to the casualness of opinion and must lead from the realm of the accidental and arbitrary to the lucid laws of a spiritual order. Building art in its simplest forms is still rooted in purpose, but it reaches through the whole scale of value into the highest realms of spiritual being, into the sphere of pure art.

All teaching of building must be based on this understanding. Step by step, it must make intelligible what is possible, necessary, and meaningful. This is why the individual fields of instruction have to be interconnected so that they result on each level in an organic order and the student always works with the entire field of building and all that relates to it in full view.

Aside from scientific instructions, the students must first of all learn how to draw in order to master this skill and to train eye and hand. Practice should instill in them a sense for proportions, structure, form, and material and make their relationship and expressive possibilities clear. Then students should become acquainted with materials and the construction of simple wood, stone, and tile buildings; after that with the constructive uses of iron and ferroconcrete. Simultaneously they should be made acquainted with the meaningful interrelationships of these building elements and their immediate formal characteristics.

Each material, whether natural or artificial, possesses specific characteristics that one must know if one wants to work with it. New materials and new constructions, too, are not necessarily signs of superiority. What matters is the right application. Each material is only worth what we make of it. Subsequent to an understanding of materials and constructions comes the purpose. It must be clearly analyzed and its contents understood. It must be demonstrated in which respect one building task differs from another; what constitutes its intrinsic nature.

An introduction to the problems of urban planning should teach its principles and the relationship of all buildings to each other and to the entire urban organism.

And finally, as synthesis of the entire program, follows the introduction to the artistic principles of building, to the nature of the artistic, the manner and application of its means and its applicability in building.

Together with this course of study, the spiritual nature of the epoch on which we depend should also be illuminated. We should investigate to what extent our epoch conforms with earlier ones and in which material and spiritual aspects it differs. For this reason the buildings of the past are to be studied and a vivid demonstration of them given. Not only to gain an architectural appreciation of their magnificence and significance but also to demonstrate that they are bound to an unrepeatable historical situation and thus present a challenge to us to bring forth our own creative achievements.

18
"Walter Gropius (1883–1969)"
This eulogy for Walter Gropius (died on July 5, 1969) appeared on August 1, 1969, in *Deutsche Bauzeitung,* 103, no. 12 (1969), p. 597. On August 17, Mies van der Rohe died at the age of eighty-three in Chicago.

It was by grace of fate that Walter Gropius, so near to his life's end, was permitted to be present in Stuttgart at the opening of the exhibition honoring the fiftieth anniversary of the Bauhaus—the school that he had founded and that represented one of the most vital educational ideas of our epoch.

When I glance back over these sixty years during which I knew him as one of the leading architects of our time and as its greatest educator, I am deeply impressed by the generosity of his spiritual stance.

The powers of conflict in this century have been mighty; disorder, competitive strife, specialization, materialism. All this never discouraged Gropius from searching for both unity and multiplicity; he never abandoned his conviction that cooperation is more fruitful than rivalry; he never hesitated in the fearless pursuit of his aim to coordinate the efforts of the many and integrate them. He had the rare gift to bring people together. I said years ago that he was always a courageous fighter in the never-ending struggle for new ideas.

He participated in this battle right up to the end of his long and creative life.

These are, in my view, Gropius's most noble legacies to us all.

Christian Norberg-Schulz:
A Talk with Mies van der Rohe

Published in *Baukunst und Werkform,* 11, no. 11 (1958), pp. 615–618.

Mies van der Rohe is known as a man of few words. Unlike Le Corbusier, Wright, and Gropius, he has never defended his ideas in speech or text; his name only became familiar after the war. But the man behind the name remains as unknown as ever. As a replacement, so to speak, one has attempted to weave legends around him. The opponents of his architecture have discovered that he must be cold and without feelings, a formalist and logician who treats buildings like severe geometry. His adherents perceive him as a distant godhead floating above everything, divulging to his subalterns fundamental truths in the form of short aphorisms in professional journals. These aphorisms contain a certain mystical poetry reminiscent of the medieval mystic Meister Eckhart.

His office in Chicago is full of models of all sizes, very beautiful models of entire buildings, but also of individual corners and details. It is the same in the design rooms of his department at the Institute of Technology. The students work like professional metalworkers and construct detailed skeletons of large proportions. Everything points more to "building" than to the drawing of "paper architecture." The main thing is the model, and the drawings are nothing but tools for the building site. The Institute of Technology constantly gets bigger. Mies is the planner. That way the students have a regular building practice during their courses of study.

"As you see, we are primarily interested in clear construction" said Mies.

"But is it not the variable ground plan that is typical for your school?" I asked somewhat surprised, for most of those writing on Mies emphasize the so-called variable ground plan.

"The variable ground plan and a clear construction cannot be viewed separately. Clear construction is the basis for a free ground plan. If no clear-cut structure results we lose all interest. We begin by asking ourselves what it is that we have to build: an open hall or a conventional construction type—then we work ourselves through this chosen type down to the smallest detail before we begin to solve the problem of the ground plan. If you solve the ground plan or the room sequence first, everything gets blocked and a clear construction becomes impossible."

"What do you understand by 'clear construction'?"

"We say specifically: clear, because we want a methodical construction in step with today's demands for standardization."

"Could one say that such a methodical construction should also serve to hold the building formally together?"

"Yes, the structure is the backbone of the whole and makes the variable ground plan possible. Without this backbone, the ground plan would not be free, but chaotically blocked."

Mies then began to explain two of his most important projects, Crown Hall and the Mannheim Theater. Both are large halls formed of roofs and walls suspended from a gigantic steel structure. Crown Hall has two floor levels, one of which is half underground. It houses the workshop of the Institute of Design, while Mies's own Department of Architecture is housed in the upper hall. Malicious tongues have it that Mies has arranged this because he does not esteem the pedagogical methods of the Institute of Design and wishes—quite literally—to keep it down.

"We do not like the word 'design.' It means everything and nothing. Many believe they can do it all: fashion a comb and build a railroad station. The result: nothing is done well. We are only concerned with building. We prefer 'building' to 'architecture'; and the best results belong in the realm of the 'building art.' Many schools get lost in sociology and design; the result is that they forget to build. The building art begins with the *careful* fitting of two bricks. Our teaching aims at training the eye and the hand. In the first year we teach our students to draw exactly and carefully, in the second year technology, and in the third the elements of planning, such as kitchens, bathrooms, bedrooms, closets, etc."

Crown Hall and the Mannheim Theater are symmetrical; I asked Mies why so many of his buildings are symmetrical and whether symmetry is important.

"Why should buildings not be symmetrical? With most buildings on this campus it is quite natural that the steps are on both sides, the auditorium or the entrance hall in the middle. That is how buildings become symmetrical, namely when it is natural. But aside from that we put not the slightest value on symmetry."

Another remarkable similarity between the two buildings is the exterior construction. "Why do you always repeat the same construction principle instead of experimenting with new possibilities?"

"If we wanted to invent something new every day we would get nowhere. It costs nothing to invent interesting forms, yet it requires much additional effort to work something through. I frequently employ an example of Viollet-le-Duc in my teaching. He has shown that the three hundred years it took to develop the Gothic cathedral were above all due to a working through and improving of the same construction type. We limit ourselves to the construction that is possible at the moment and attempt to clarify it in all details. In this way we want to lay a basis for future development."

Apparently Mies is very fond of the Mannheim Theater: he describes it in all details. He emphasizes that the complicated ground plans conformed to the demands of the competition program. It called for two stages that—having identical technical installations—can be played on independently of each other.

While Mies worked on some projects for months and years, this building was designed within a few weeks of hectic work, in the winter of 1952–53. Students who helped him recounted how he would sit for hours in front of the large model, in his dark suit "as if for a wedding," the inevitable cigar in his hand.

"As you see, the entire building is a single large room. We believe that this is the most economical and most practical way of building today. The purposes for which a building is used are constantly changing and we cannot afford to tear down the building each time. That is why we have revised Sullivan's formula 'form follows function' and construct a practical and economical space into which we fit the functions. In the Mannheim building, stage and auditorium are independent of the steel construction. The large auditorium juts out from its concrete base much like a hand from the wrist."

There were still many things to ask; Mies suggested continuing the conversation in his apartment over a glass. He lives in an old-fashioned apartment. The large living room has two white walls, the furniture is simple, cubist and black. On the walls glow large pictures by Paul Klee. The maid serves on a low Chinese table, as if she wanted to arrange a Miesian ground plan.

"One is surprised that you collect Klee pictures; one thinks that does not fit your building."

"I hope to make my buildings neutral frames in which man and artworks can carry on their own lives. To do that one needs a respectful attitude toward things."

"If you view your buildings as neutral frames, what role does nature play with respect to the buildings?"

"Nature, too, shall live its own life. We must beware not to disrupt it with the color of our houses and interior fittings. Yet we should attempt to bring nature, houses, and human beings together into a higher unity. If you view nature through the glass walls of the Farnsworth House, it gains a more profound significance than if viewed from outside. This way more is said about nature—it becomes a part of a larger whole."

"I have noticed that you rarely make a normal corner in your buildings but that you let one wall be the corner and separate it from the other wall."

"The reason for that is that a normal corner formation appears massive, something that is difficult to combine with a variable ground plan. The free ground plan is a new concept and has its own 'grammar'—just like a language. Many believe that the variable ground plan implies total freedom. That is a misunderstanding. It demands just as much discipline and intelligence from the architect as the conventional ground plan; it demands, for example, that enclosed elements, and they are always needed, be separated from the outside walls—as in the Farnsworth House. Only that way can a free space be obtained."

"Many criticize you for adhering to the right angle. In a project of the thirties, though, you employed, together with a free ground plan, curved walls."

"I have nothing against acute angles or curves provided they are done well. Up to now I have never seen anybody who has truly mastered them. The architects of the baroque mastered these things—but they represented the last stage of a long development."

Our conversation ended late at night. Mies van der Rohe is not the man of the legends. He is a warm-hearted and friendly man, who demands only one thing from his co-workers: the same humble attitude toward things that he himself has.

Mies in his apartment in Chicago.

Notes

Introduction

1
Mies van der Rohe, "Wir stehen in der Wende der Zeit. Baukunst als Ausdruck geistiger Entscheidung" (We Stand at the Turning Point of Time: Building Art as the Expression of Spiritual Decisions), *Innendekoration,* 39 (1928), p. 262.

2
Mies van der Rohe, "Die neue Zeit" (The New Time), *Die Form,* 5 (1930), p. 406.

3
Mies van der Rohe, "Wir stehen in der Wende der Zeit," p. 262.

4
Peter Blake, *The Master Builders* (New York, 1976), p. 183.

5
Mies van der Rohe, "Was wäre Beton, was Stahl ohne Spiegelglas?" (What Would Concrete, What Would Steel Be without Mirror Glass), contribution to a prospectus of the Verein Deutscher Spiegelglas-Fabriken of March 13, 1933, not printed; manuscript in the Library of Congress.

6
Mies van der Rohe, "Haus H., Magdeburg" (The H. House, Magdeburg), *Die Schildgenossen,* 14 (1935), p. 514.

7
Mies van der Rohe, "Museum for a Small City," *Architectural Forum,* 78, no. 5 (1943), p. 84.

8
Undated manuscript, probably about 1950, in the Library of Congress (see Appendix IV, 6).

9
Manuscript for a lecture, in Library of Congress (see Appendix IV, 5), p. 11.

10
Philip Johnson, *Mies van der Rohe* (New York, 1947; third, revised edition, New York, 1978; Max Bill, *Ludwig Mies van der Rohe* (Milan, 1955); Arthur Drexler, *Ludwig Mies van der Rohe* (New York, 1960); Peter Blake, "Mies van der Rohe and the Mastery of Structure," in *The Master Builders*; Werner Blaser, *Mies van der Rohe. Die Kunst der Struktur* (Zurich and Stuttgart, 1965; revised edition as *Mies van der Rohe,* Zurich, 1973); James Speyer, *Mies van der Rohe* (Chicago, 1968) (catalog of the exhibition at the Art Institute of Chicago); Martin Pawley, *Mies van der Rohe* (New York, 1970); Peter Carter, *Mies van der Rohe at Work* (New York, 1974); Lorenzo Papi, *Ludwig Mies van der Rohe* (Florence, 1974); David Spaeth, *Mies van der Rohe* (New York, 1985).

11
Ludwig Hilberseimer, *Mies van der Rohe* (Chicago, 1956).

12
Werner Blaser, *Mies van der Rohe. Die Kunst der Struktur,* pp. 20–21.

13
Wolf Tegethoff, *Mies van der Rohe. Die Villen und Landhausprojekte* (Krefeld and Essen, 1981), pp. 42ff.

14
Johnson, *Mies van der Rohe,* p. 49.

15
Robert Venturi, *Complexity and Contradiction in Architecture* (New York, 1966), p. 23.

16
Sibyl Moholy-Nagy, "Has 'Less Is More' Become 'Less Is Nothing?,'" in *Four Great Makers of Modern Architecture* (New York, 1963), pp. 118–123.

17
Venturi, *Complexity and Contradiction,* p. 27.

18
Ibid., p. 26.

19
"I believe this is the clearest building we ever created and the one that best expresses our philosophy." Mies van der Rohe as quoted in Peter Carter, "Mies van der Rohe," *Bauen und Wohnen,* 16 (1961), p. 241.

20
Stanley Tigerman, *Versus: An American Architect's Alternatives* (New York, 1982), p. 27. See also his "Letter to Mies" (1978), ibid., pp. 29, 30.

21
Justus Bier, "Kann man im Haus Tugendhat wohnen?," *Die Form,* 6 (1931), pp. 392f.

22
Joseph Rykwert, "Mies van der Rohe," *Burlington Magazine,* 91 (1949), pp. 268f.

23
Joseph A. Barry, "Report on the American Battle between Good and Bad Modern Houses," *House Beautiful,* 95 (1953), pp. 172f., 266, 270–273.

24
Julius Posener, "Absolute Architektur," *Neue Rundschau,* 84, no. 1 (1973), pp. 79–95; in the context of this evaluation see also the critique of Mies by Giovanni Klaus Koenig, "Gropius or Mies?," *Casabella,* 33, no. 342 (1968), pp. 34–39. For a totally different evaluation of the National Gallery see Tilmann Buddensieg, "Ordnungsprinzip im Tumult der städtischen Umwelt," *Frankfurter Allgemeine Zeitung,* no. 159 (July 14, 1982), p. 19.

25
Lewis Mumford, on the occasion of Mies's receiving the gold medal of the Royal Institute of British Architects, quoted in Reyner Banham, "Mies van der Rohe on Trial: Almost Nothing Is Too Much," *Architectural Review,* 132 (1962), p. 125. James Marston Fitch, "Mies van der Rohe and the Platonic Varieties," in *Four Great Makers of Modern Architecture,* p. 163, responded to the confusion of functional and idealistic viewpoints of Mies's critics with the following metaphor: "To acclaim Mies for the monumental purity of his forms, and yet to deplore their malfunction in some pragmatic detail, is rather like praising the sea for being blue, while chiding it for being salty, or admiring the tiger for the beauty of his coat while urging him to become a vegetarian."

26
Philip Johnson, "The Seven Crutches of Modern Architecture," *Perspecta,* 3 (1955), pp. 40–44.

27
Reyner Banham, "Mies van der Rohe on Trial," p. 125.

28
Richard Padovan, "Mies van der Rohe Reinterpreted," *UIA International Architect,* issue 3 (1984), p. 39.

29
"They seemed less factorylike, more classical; the Barcelona Pavillon had marble, and the Schinkel-Persius thing was already in my mind. . . ." Philip Johnson in 1977 viewing the buildings of Mies in retrospect, in Johnson, *Mies van der Rohe,* third edition (1978), p. 205.

30
Padovan, "Mies van der Rohe Reinterpreted," p. 39.

31
Bruno Zevi, *Poetica dell' architettura neoplastica* (Milan, 1953).

32
Padovan, "Mies van der Rohe Reinterpreted," p. 39.

33
Post-Modern Classicism: The New Synthesis, ed. Charles Jencks (London, 1980, *Architectural Design* Profile); *Free Style Classicism: The Wider Tradition,* ed. Charles Jencks (London, 1982, *Architectural Design* Profile 39).

34
See Jencks, *Post-Modern Classicism,* p. 5.

35
Colin Rowe, *The Mathematics of the Ideal Villa and other Essays* (Cambridge, Mass., 1976). See especially the essay "Neo-'Classicism' and Modern Architecture," which traces the "Space Time Palladian" in the work of Mies van der Rohe.

36
Aldo Rossi and Paolo Portoghesi, "An Interview by Antonio de Bonis," *Architectural Design,* 52, nos. 1–2 (1982), p. 14.

37
Aldo Rossi, *A Scientific Autobiography* (Cambridge, Mass., 1981), p. 74: "Mies, on the other hand, is the only one who knew how to make architecture and furniture which transcend time and function."

38
Padovan, "Mies van der Rohe Reinterpreted," p. 42.

39
David A. Spaeth, *Ludwig Mies van der Rohe: An Annotated Bibliography and Chronology* (New York, 1979).

40
Tegethoff, *Mies van der Rohe. Die Villen und Landhausprojekte.* Exhaustive and critical review by Christian Wolsdorf, in *Kunstchronik,* 37 (1984), pp. 399ff.

41
The Propylean Art History may serve as proof of this. The volume on twentieth-century art edited by Giulio Carlo Argan includes in its documentation of programs and manifestos to modern building three texts by Mies van der Rohe: "Industrielles Bauen" (1924), "Über die Form in der Architektur" (1927), and "Die Neue Zeit" (1930).

42
Ludwig Mies van der Rohe. Escritos, Diálogos y Discursos, introduction by James Marton Fitch (Murcia, 1981, Coleccion de Arquitectura I).

43
Papi, *Mies van der Rohe,* p. 40.

44
"Mies van der Rohe: Ich mache niemals ein Bild," interview in *Die Bauwelt,* 53 (1962), p. 885.

45
Ludwig Wittgenstein, *Tractatus Logio-Philosophicus,* translated by D. F. Pears and B. F. McGuinness (New York, 1961), p. 171.

46
Blake, *The Master Builders,* p. 206.

47
Peter Serenyi, "Spinoza, Hegel and Mies: The Meaning of the New National Gallery in Berlin," *Journal of the Society of Architectural Historians,* 30 (1971), p. 240.

48
Mies van der Rohe, "Baukunst und Zeitwille!" (Building Art and the Will of the Epoch!), *Der Querschnitt,* 4, no. 1 (1924), p. 31.

49
Carter, "Mies van der Rohe," pp. 229ff.

50
Mies van der Rohe, inaugural address as Director of Architecture at Armour Institute of Technology, 1938, manuscript in the Library of Congress (see Appendix III, 14).

51
Mies van der Rohe, "Baukunst unserer Zeit" (Building Art of Our Time), in Werner Blaser, *Mies van der Rohe. Die Kunst der Struktur* (Zurich and Stuttgart, 1965), p. 5.

52
Sergius Ruegenberg, "Ein Fünfzigjähriger," *Die Bauwelt,* 27 (1936), p. 346.

I The Double Work Field: Architect as Author

1
Mies van der Rohe in a letter to Jennings Wood, May 3, 1963, in the Library of Congress.

2
For the period between 1918 and 1922, the records in New York and Chicago show no sources of any interest that would throw light on the important projects of that period. The personal correspondence stored in the manuscript division of the Library of Congress in Washington, D.C., offers only occasional glimpses that enrich existing sources. The recent biography of Franz Schulze, *Mies van der Rohe: A Critical Biography* (Chicago and London, 1985), which offers a detailed Mies vita based on all available sources, affirms this lacuna.

3
On the Riehl House, see Anton Jaumann, "Vom künstlerischen Nachwuchs," *Innendekoration,* 21 (1910), pp. 266–274; and anonymous, "Architect Ludwig Mies," *Moderne Bauformen,* 9 (1910), pp. 42–48. On the competition design for the Bismarck memorial, see Max Schmidt, *Das Bismarck-Nationaldenkmal auf der Elisenhöhe bei Bingerbrück (Hundert Entwürfe aus dem Wettbewerb)* (Düsseldorf, 1911); Max Dessauer and Hermann Muthesius, *Das Bismarck-Denkmal. Eine Erörterung des Wettbewerbs* (Jena, 1912).

4

"Then there was a competition announced in the old town hall of Berlin. They relegated my design to some dark corner because they thought it was a sort of joke." *Mies in Berlin,* phonograph record, Bauwelt Archiv I, 1966. See also Ulrich Conrads, "'Ich mache niemals ein Bild. . .'. Ludwig Mies van der Rohe—Baumeister einer strukturellen Architektur," *Jahrbuch Preussischer Kulturbesitz,* 8 (1968), p. 60. On the competition see [Friedrich Paulsen], "Ideenwettbewerb Hochhaus Friedrichstrasse," *2. Sonderheft der Stadtbaukunst alter und neuer Zeit* (Berlin, 1922).

5

The only commissions that can be established from Mies's work catalog for the time span 1919 to 1926 are orders for four single-family residences, all of which employed the simplified language of prewar classicism: the Eichstädt House (1920–1922); Kempner House (1921); Feldmann House (1921–1922); and Mosler House (1924–1926). He also had the remodeling of the Urbig House (1924–1925). These houses have so far found no adequate attention in the historiography of the work of Mies van der Rohe. Wolf Tegethoff, in *Mies van der Rohe. Die Villen und Landhausprojekte* (Krefeld and Essen, 1981), regretfully omitted them from his work on the villas and landhouse projects and thereby impaired the comprehensiveness of his analyses. In the course of my research I was able to locate the so far unknown plans for the Kempner House and Feldmann House. The Feldmann House, of which up to then only the name was known, still stands— even if in considerably altered form—in Erdener Street in Berlin-Wilmersdorf.

6

Carl Gottfried, "Hochhäuser," *Qualität. Internationale Propaganda für Qualitätserzeugnisse,* 3 final issue 5 (August 1922/ March 1923), pp. 63–66. That this design has retained its modernity is proven by contemporary skyscraper architecture, which has turned away from the simple boxlike shapes and attempts to open up the volumes by interstices and the displacement of volumes. Compare the remark by Philip Johnson in 1973 that Mies's 1921 skyscraper project is "astoundingly" modern. (Heinrich Klotz and John W. Cook, *Architektur im Widerspruch. Bauen in den USA von Mies van der Rohe bis Andy Warhol* [Zurich, 1974], p. 52.) Rem Kolhaas has paid homage to this design of Mies in his contribution to the IBA competition for Kochstrasse/Friedrichstrasse, West Berlin, 1980–1981. In the site plan, Mies's skyscraper design is shown as an existing component of the urban topography. See illustration 318 in Heinrich Klotz (ed.), *Revision der Moderne. Postmoderne Architektur 1960–1980* (Munich, 1984). The change that has taken place in commercial metropolitan architecture can be illuminated by the remark Mies made on the back of his manuscript to "Building": "Cupboards that look like skyscrapers models." Mies's former pupil Philip Johnson, with his AT&T skyscraper in New York (1979)—a key structure of postmodernism that calls to mind a superdimensional Chippendale sideboard—has as it were taken up this aperçu of Mies under a different prefix.

7

Gottfried, "Hochhäuser," pp. 63f.

8

Bruno Taut, "Nieder den Seriosismus!," *Frühlicht,* no. 1 (January 1920), p. 1.

9

In this connection compare the little-noted article by Peter Behrens, "Das Ethos und die Umlagerung der künstlerischen Probleme," in *Der Leuchter, Jahrbuch der Schule der Weis-*

heit, ed. Graf H. Keyserling (Darmstadt, 1920), pp. 315–340, which describes an extraordinary change of viewpoint.

10

Mies van der Rohe, "Aphorismen" (1955), in Werner Blaser, *Mies van der Rohe, Lehre und Schule* (Basel and Stuttgart, 1977), p. 96.

11

Museum of Modern Art, Manuscripts Folder 1 (see Appendix II, p. 16).

12

"As was to be expected, this design, too, is without fault and excellent, for the artist has absolutely solved the difficult task of bringing the large roof into a harmonious relationship with the building. The colors with the blue-green slate roof and the brick-red walls, effectively interrupted by the white-framed windows, will harmonize well with nature. . . . The street façade is conceived without any decoration, as a result of which the house will have the effect of a façade . . . on the lakeside, too, it does not fit into the neighborhood. Here, too, there is no hint of articulation, so that it appears bland." Protest letter of the Potsdam surveyor's office. The building was approved under the condition that the house be animated by a variety of colored stones and that the foundation be hidden by a hedge. According to Renate Petras, "Drei Arbeiten Mies van der Rohes, in Potsdam-Babelsberg," *Architektur der DDR,* 23, no. 2 (1974), pp. 120f.

13

Mies van der Rohe, "Baukunst und Zeitwille!" (Building Art and the Will of the Epoch!), *Der Querschnitt,* 4, no. 1 (1924), pp. 31–32.

14

The lack of conviction expressionism had undergone is already evident in earlier *Frühlicht* issues. Adolf Behne, who had defended expressionist art in 1920 against the accusation of being unreal ("We work for the future. We are not concerned with the present!"), showed in issue 2 of 1921 pronounced sympathies for Oud, Hilberseimer, and Le Corbusier in his article "Architekten" and criticized the "cult of the fantastic." We find in issue 4 of 1922, besides the article of Mies, also J. J. P. Oud's programmatical article "Über die zukünftige Baukunst und ihre architektonischen Möglichkeiten," to which Behne's article referred.

15

G. F. Hartlaub, letter to Alfred Barr, Jr., July 1929, quoted in Kenneth Frampton, *Modern Architecture, A Critical History* (London, 1980), p. 130; art critic Hartlaub was organizer of the exhibition "Neue Sachlichkeit, Deutsche Malerei seit dem Expressionismus" that took place in the Kunsthalle Mannheim in 1925. On the concept of "Neue Sachlichkeit" see Frampton, ibid., p. 130.

16

While Mies's design was largely ignored, the design of Hans Scharoun found a purchaser. Compare [Paulsen], "Ideenwettbewerb Hochhaus Friedrichstrasse."

17

"Among things essential to the theme of the new form-giving, the *rational nature of new form-giving* takes priority. For it is above all *rationality* that modern man is concerned with." Piet Mondrian, "Die neue Gestaltung in der Malerei," *De Stijl,* 2, nos. 1–12 (1918), reprinted in Hagen Bächler and Herbert Letsch (eds.), *De Stijl. Schriften und Manifeste zu einem theoretischen Konzept ästhetischer Umweltgestaltung* (Leipzig and Weimar, 1984), p. 89.

18
Theo van Doesburg, *Grundbegriffe der neuen gestaltenden Kunst* (Frankfurt, 1925; reprinted Mainz, 1966), p. 5. It is stated in the foreword that the manuscript was completed in 1917 and translated 1921–1922 by Max Burchartz during van Doesburg's stay in Weimar. Compare p. 9: "The modern artist does not want a mediator. He wants to address the audience directly with his work. If the public fails to understand it, it is his own task to explain it."

19
Ibid., p. 4 (foreword).

20
G, no. 3 (July 1924) showed a charcoal drawing by Mies of the skyscraper as the title page. According to the masthead, Mies was one of the editors of *G*, nos. 2 and 3. That his contributions to *G* were not limited to areas concerned with building is proven by Hans Prinzhorn's article "Gestaltung und Gesundheit" in *G*, no. 3, p. 42. Prinzhorn, occupied with the theme "picture-making of the mentally disturbed," began his article with: "Dear M.v.d.R.! Your wish that I inform you as to whether my studies on the picture-making of the mentally disturbed resulted in something fruitful for you, I can only meet partially . . ."

21
Masthead of *G*, no. 3 (June 1924).

22
Letter to Mies from the *Frankfurter Zeitung* of July 17, 1925, in the Library of Congress.

23
Hans Richter, *Begegnungen von Dada bis heute. Briefe, Dokumente, Erinnerungen* (Cologne, 1973), p. 54. "After I had used up an arbitrarily estimated sum for the first two issues, Mies helped out. . . . He had a gigantic drawing board, about four meters long, that rested on two solid supports in his workroom. On top of this drawing board towered several hundredweights of books and journals . . . Between bookshelf and supports Mies kept a supply of dollar bills with which, at that time, he could easily have purchased the entire elegant street Am Karlsbad. 'Nobody,' so he assured me, 'can lift up this board' to get at this, for the time, fabulous treasure. He raised up the board, braced it against his shoulder, and we could, with a few dollar bills, finance our most luxurious number 3." Werner Graeff, "Concerning the So-called G Group," *Art Journal*, 23 (1963), p. 281, reported on the financing of the printing costs: "So, in 1924, Mies, whose income, though meager, was still bigger than that of any of us, had to buy the type for the entire issue." Mies, the propagandist of the skeleton building method, wanted to have *G* in skeleton script type. This printing type, used to denote steel supports and also used in other industries, was in the early twenties not common in the printing trade. In order to be able to print *G*, no. 3, in skeleton script, Mies is reported to have bought up all typecasts of this script available in Berlin (oral statement of Sergius Ruegenberg, 1985).

24
Helga Kliemann, *Die Novembergruppe* (Berlin, 1969), p. 41: "Various hubs formed. A certain circle congregated around Mies van der Rohe, who was president of the Novembergruppe from 1923 to 1925, for lectures and discussions." On ibid., pp. 64ff. there is a reproduction of the new regulations of 1925 that lists Mies as first president. Compare also Willi Wolfradt's statement on the exhibition of the Novembergruppe: "From this results the transition to the building forms of the circle of the Novembergruppe (decisive were Mies van der

Rohe and Arthur Korn)" (*Das Kunstblatt*, 8, no. 7 [1924], p. 221). Compare Tegethoff, *Mies van der Rohe. Die Villen und Landhausprojekte*, p. 41, n12.

25
Compare Graeff, "Concerning the So-called G Group," pp. 281ff.

26
Compare the biographical timetable in Hansjürgen Bulkowski (ed.), *Theo van Doesburg. Das andere Gesicht. Gedichte, Prosa, Manifeste, Roman, 1913 bis 1928* (Munich, 1983), p. 217.

27
See Werner Graeff, "Concerning the So-called G Group": "If one were to take the most active collaborators of *G* as the 'G Group,' these, taken in alphabetic order, would be, according to my recollection: Hans Arp, Theo van Doesburg, Werner Graeff, Raoul Hausmann, Ludwig Hilberseimer, El Lissitzky, Mies van der Rohe, Hans Richter, Kurt Schwitters. One could add to these, perhaps C. van Eesteren, Naum Gabo and Man Ray."

28
Compare Tegethoff, *Mies van der Rohe. Die Villen und Landhausprojekte*, p. 20.

29
From the exchange of letters between Mies and van Doesburg it appears that the sale of *G* in Holland and the printing in Paris (where van Doesburg had taken up residence in May 1923) was considered. In his letter to Mies of August 14, 1925 (in the Library of Congress), Doesburg reports that he had received many requests for subscriptions and that a publisher in Holland declared himself willing to assume the representation of *G*; furthermore, the mention of a printing cost subsidy of *G* in Paris is mentioned.

30
Compare Theo van Doesburg's "Antikunstvereinsmanifest" of 1921 in which, by means of a phonetic wordplay on "pure logic and guitar," aim is taken at the cubists: "All this rattling and carrying on over 'Die Sitzende' and 'Stilleben,' the entire Kant-Hegel-Fichte-Schopenhauer-Bolland-Spinoza has no other purpose than to blow oneself up with words and vanity." In van Doesburg, *Das andere Gesicht*, p. 102.

31
Compare *De Stijl*, 6, nos. 3–4 (1924), following p. 57, as well as 6, nos. 6–7 (1924) in front of p. 72. Further mention of *G* is in 6, no. 8 (1924), p. 114, as well as in 7, nos. 5–6 (1926–1927), p. 47. Works by Mies van der Rohe are, strangely enough, only introduced to the *Stijl* reader in the last issue of *De Stijl*, 8, nos. 5–6 (1928), pp. 123–126, and this only in the form of a few illustrations on occasion of the Werkbund Exhibition in Stuttgart-Weissenhof of 1927.

32
G, no. 3 (June 1924), p. 58. References to the periodical *De Stijl* in *G*, no. 1 (July 1923), p. 4, and no. 2 (September 1923), p. 4.

33
In regard to the exhibitions of the Novembergruppe, see Kliemann, *Die Novembergruppe*, pp. 22ff. According to this account, Theo van Doesburg, Vilmos Huszár, Gerrit Thomas Rietveld, Cornelis van Eesteren, J. J. P. Oud, and Mart Stam "were represented more than once in the Novembergruppe exhibitions" (p. 24). In 1926 Hendrik Berlage exhibited with the Novembergruppe; the Malevich show at the Grosse Berliner

Kunstausstellung was also made possible by the November-gruppe (ibid).

34
Mies to Hermann von Wedderkop, Cologne (editor of *Der Querschnitt*), January 18, 1924, in the Library of Congress. *Der Querschnitt,* founded by the art dealer Alfred Flechteim, also counted during the editorship of von Wedderkop (from 1924) among the most important art periodicals of the twenties.

35
Rudolf Schwarz, letter of May 1, 1919, to Werner Becker, quoted in Hanna-Barbara Gerl, *Romano Guardini, 1885–1968, Leben und Werk* (Mainz, 1985), p. 195.

36
Letter to Mies from F. Paulsen of *Die Bauwelt,* Verlag Ullstein, Berlin, November 27, 1925 (in the Library of Congress), regarding a promised essay: ". . . Mr. Safranski is in great embarrassment because you have not yet mailed him the essay you promised him."

37
The publication of "Bürohaus" in the *Deutsche Allgemeine Zeitung* was prevented by the text arriving too late. See correspondence with the *Deutsche Allgemeine Zeitung* of July 18 and August 8, 1923, in the Library of Congress.

38
Letter of Mies to the Verein Deutscher Spiegelglas-Fabriken, Cologne, March 13, 1933, in the Library of Congress. The planned pamphlet *Das Fenster,* to which, besides Mies, Gropius, Mendelsohn, and Schneck were supposed to contribute articles, was not realized (see Appendix III, 12).

39
Hermann von Wedderkop, Cologne, to Mies, February 19, 1924, in the Library of Congress.

40
Mies to Hermann von Wedderkop, Cologne, on February 22, 1924, in the Library of Congress: "Dear Mr. Wedderkop, I received your card of February 18, 1924, and will add today a second part to my article that will deal with the new house, just as you desire. I hope thereby to approach the agreed-upon 4 pages of *Querschnitt.* Since I am no writer writing is hard for me; in the same time I could have completed a design. . . ." Mies's article "Baukunst und Zeitwille!" appeared without that addition in *Der Querschnitt,* 4, no. 1 (1924), 31f. Two illustrations from Werner Lindner, *Die Ingenieurbauten in ihrer guten Gestaltung* (Berlin, 1923) and Mies's design for a "Bürohaus aus Beton, Eisen, Glas," as well as a photomontage of the Friedrichstrasse skyscraper, were added on pp. 25, 33f., 49.

41
Walter Gropius, Dessau, September 29, 1925, to Mies, in the Library of Congress.

42
Letter of Dr. Hans Prinzhorn of May 6, 1925, to Mies, in the Library of Congress.

43
Mies van der Rohe, letter of March 1, 1926, to Dr. Hans Heyse, Breslau, in the Library of Congress. Mies further stated in this letter: "It was catastrophic that I had no slides and therefore had to express myself abstractly. In such a situation even architects do not understand each other." Students of the Bremen Kunstgewerbeschule expressed their thanks to Mies for the lecture in a letter of December 11, 1925: "The logic of your exposition in respect to the organic building method that arrives at formal values by fulfilling the requirements of function has met with our full comprehension and we want to express our thanks to you for this stimulation." Mies replied in a letter of December 14, 1925: "I would like to thank you and your friends for the kind words you addressed to me. I was especially glad that, without knowing it, I was able to provide young people with a stimulation for their future work." For the program of the lecture series, see correspondence with Dr. Salander, Bremen, in the Library of Congress.

44
"Die Voraussetzungen baukünstlerischen Schaffens, anonymous review in the *Berliner Börsen-Zeitung,* March 2, 1928. (For the complete review see Appendix III, 1.)

45
Mies van der Rohe, "Über Sinn und Aufgabe der Kritik" (On the Meaning and Task of Criticism), in *Das Kunstblatt,* 14 (1930), p. 178.

46
Mies van der Rohe, "Über die Form in der Architecktur" (On Form in Architecture), in *Die Form,* 2 (1927), p. 59.

47
Mies van der Rohe, "Die Neue Zeit" (The New Time), in *Die Form,* 5 (1930), p. 406.

48
Mies van der Rohe, inaugural address as Director of Architecture at Armour Institute of Technology (see Appendix III, 14).

49
Mies van der Rohe, "Wir stehen in der Wende der Zeit. Baukunst als Ausdruck geistiger Entscheidung" (We Stand at the Turning Point of Time: Building Art as the Expression of Spiritual Decisions), *Innendekoration,* 39 (1928), p. 262.

50
Mies van der Rohe, "Gelöste Aufgaben. Eine Forderung an unser Bauwesen" (Solved Tasks: A Challenge for Our Building Industry), *Bauwelt,* 14 (1923), p. 719.

51
Mies van der Rohe, "Wir stehen in der Wende der Zeit," p. 262.

52
Mies van der Rohe, "Bauen" (Building), *G,* no. 2 (July 1923), p. 1.

53
Mies van der Rohe, lecture, Chicago, occasion and date unknown (around 1950), manuscript in the Library of Congress: "Convictions are necessary, but in the realm of one's work they have only a limited significance. In the final analysis it is the performance that matters. [*addition in the original manuscript:* That is what Goethe meant when he said: Create, artist, do not talk.]" (See Appendix IV, 5, p. 19.)

54
Mondrian, "Die Neue Gestaltung in der Malerei" (1917–1918), p. 87.

55
Ibid., p. 88.

56
Ibid., pp. 88f.

57

One of the few possibilities for Mies to meet Mondrian was in summer 1923 on occasion of the Bauhaus Week, to which Mondrian made a contribution. Ludwig Hilberseimer, *Berliner Architektur der 20er Jahre* (Berlin, 1967), p. 24, states that Mondrian did not himself go to Berlin but that his work was known to "all those interested in the arts" by the effort of Theo van Doesburg.

58

See Tegethoff, *Mies van der Rohe. Die Villen und Landhausprojekte*, pp. 50f.

59

Hans M. Wingler (ed.), *Piet Mondrian, Neue Gestaltung. Neoplastizismus. Nieuwe Beelding* (Eschwege, 1925 [Bauhausbuch 5]; reprint, Mainz, 1974), p. 69.

II Philosophy as Patron

1 The View into the Intrinsic

1

Mies van der Rohe, "Baukunst unserer Zeit" (Building Art of Our Time), in Werner Blaser, *Mies van der Rohe. Die Kunst der Struktur* (Zurich and Stuttgart, 1965), pp. 5f.

2

J. J. P. Oud, "Über die zukünftige Baukunst und ihre architektonischen Möglichkeiten," *Frühlicht,* 1, no. 4 (1922), p. 199.

3

Mies van der Rohe, inaugural address at the Armour Institute of Technology (see Appendix III, 14).

4

Mies van der Rohe, "Wohin gehen wir nun?" (Where Do We Go from Here?), *Bauen und Wohnen,* 15 (1960), p. 391.

5

Mies van der Rohe, "Baukunst und Zeitwille!" (Building Art and the Will of the Epoch!), *Der Querschnitt,* 4, no. 1 (1924), pp. 31f.

6

Leon Battista Alberti, *Zehn Bücher über die Baukunst,* ed. Max Theuer (Vienna and Leipzig, 1912). Compare also other works on Alberti of this time period: Irene Behn, *Leon Battista Alberti als Kunstphilosoph* (Strassburg, 1911); Willi Flemming, *Die Begründung der modernen Ästhetik und Kunstwissenschaft durch Leon Battista Alberti* (Berlin and Leipzig, 1916).

7

Among Mies's books stored at the Mies van der Rohe Collection of the University of Illinois at Chicago, Special Collections Department, the following are listed: Heinrich Wölfflin, *Die klassische Kunst* (Munich, 1908); Wölfflin, *Kunstgeschichtliche Grundbegriffe* (Munich, 1917); Wölfflin, *Renaissance und Barock* (Munich, 1908); Wilhelm Worringer, *Formprobleme der Gotik* (Munich, 1920); Alois Riegl, *Die Entstehung der Barockkunst in Rom* (Vienna, 1908); Riegl, *Stilfragen* (Berlin, 1893). It should be noted that it cannot be established at which time the individual books were acquired, so that, with a few exceptions, one does not know which books Mies already owned before 1938, which books he brought with him upon immigration, and which books were acquired subsequently in second-hand bookstores.

8

Mies van der Rohe in "Gespräch mit Peter Carter," *Bauen und Wohnen,* 16 (1961), pp. 230ff.

9

"I recall that as a boy in my hometown, I saw many old buildings. Only a few of them were of any significance. For the most part they were very simple and very clear. I was impressed by the severity of these buildings, because they did not belong to any specific period. They had already stood for over a thousand years and were still impressive, and nothing could change that fact. All stylistic trends had bypassed them, but they still stood. They had lost nothing and were still as good as at the time in which they were built. They were medieval buildings without specific character but they were indeed 'built.'" Mies van der Rohe in ibid., pp. 229f. Especially stimulating in this connection is Kurt Forster, "Mies van der Rohes Seagram Building," in Tilmann Buddensieg and Henning Rogge (eds.), *Die nützlichen Künste. Gestaltende Technik und Bildende Kunst seit der Industriellen Revolution* (Berlin, 1979), pp. 359–369. In his analysis of the Seagram Building, Forster attempts to draw an analogy to late Gothic wall architecture and makes the beautiful comparison between the door panel motif of the Carolingian bronze door of the Hubertus Chapel, which Mies as pupil of the Cathedral School of Aachen had to pass, and the façade grid of the Seagram Building.

10

Adolf Loos, "Architektur" (1909), in Adolf Loos, *Trotzdem. 1900–1930* (Innsbruck, 1931), p. 101.

11

Draft manuscript of the lecture to the anniversary meeting of the Deutsche Werkbund in October 1932, in Museum of Modern Art, Manuscripts Folder 5, page D.1.10 (see Appendix III, 10).

12

"One day I was assigned a drawing table at Schneider's, I was cleaning it out when I came across a copy of *Die Zukunft,* a journal published by Maximilian Harden, plus an essay on one of Laplace's theories. I read both of them and both of them went quite over my head. But I couldn't help being interested. So every week thereafter, I got hold of *Die Zukunft* and read it as carefully as I could. That's when I think I started paying attention to spiritual things. Philosophy. And culture." Excerpt from the documentary film *Mies van der Rohe* (1979), quoted by Franz Schulze, *Mies van der Rohe: A Critical Biography* (Chicago and London, 1985), pp. 17f.

13

Compare Doris Schmidt, "Gläserne Wände für den Blick auf die Welt: Zum Tode Mies van der Rohes," *Süddeutsche Zeitung,* no. 198 (August 19, 1969), p. 11, quoted by Wolfgang Fried, "Ludwig Mies van der Rohe. Das Europäische Werk 1907–1937" (dissertation, Bonn, 1976), p. 60.

14

C. A. Werner, "Um Deutschlands Zukunft," *Berliner Zeitung,* 2 (1946), cited by Jürgen Krause, *"Märtyrer" und "Prophet." Studien zum Nietzsche-Kult in der bildenden Kunst der Jahrhundertwende* (Berlin and New York, 1984), p. 91.

15

Henry van de Velde did the renovation and enlargement of the Nietzsche archives in Weimar and the 1911 design of the Nietzsche Temple and the stadium of Weimar. See Krause, *"Märtyrer" und "Prophet."*

16
Turin also had a cultic value for the Nietzsche adherents of 1900, because Nietzsche had lived in this city for several years up to his collapse in 1889, as this was "the first place in which I am possible." For his Turin letters, see *Werke in drei Bänden,* ed. Karl Schlechta (Munich, 1966), vol. 3, pp. 1282–1352, where Nietzsche sketched the urbanity of the Italian town with its arcades and piazzas. His Turin impressions obtain new importance in regard to the metropolis of the late nineteenth century insofar as a new sensibility toward the city is here implied, as was later most impressively expressed by August Endell in *Die Schönheit der grossen Stadt* (Stuttgart, 1908). Advance excerpts of this book appeared in 1908 in *Die Zukunft.* Endell, who had turned to applied arts and to architecture after studying philosophy, had been introduced to the Weimar Nietzsche circle by his cousin Kurt Breysig. Compare Krause, *"Märtryr" und "Prophet,"* pp. 167, 177. For a possible influence of Endell's book on Mies, see part V, chapter 3, below.

17
Julius Meier-Graefe, "Peter Behrens—Düsseldorf," *Dekorative Kunst,* 8 (1910), pp. 381f., reports of his encounter with Behrens: "His hobby, at that time, was Egypt. When we met again in Turin where he had made the solid entrance hall with the no less solid fountain figures, he talked of Ramses II like he would discuss the work of an admired older colleague."

18
Philip Johnson, referring to the Berlin years, as quoted in Heinrich Klotz and John W. Cook, *Architektur im Widerspruch* (Zurich, 1973), p. 57: "Mies! He would never have admitted it, but he was a passionate anti-intellectual. He said, 'I have just read,' so I looked around his library, and found that it was not true—he had anyway only three books. Not a one had been taken from the shelf in all these years." In contrast to that see Hans Richter, *Begegnungen von Dada bis heute. Briefe, Dokumente, Erinnerungen* (Cologne, 1973), p. 54: "Mies . . . had . . . a huge drawing board. . . . On this drawing board were heaped several hundredweights of books and journals. . . ." According to Doris Schmidt, "Gläserne Wände für den Blick auf die Welt," the philosopher Alois Riehl was, on occasion of a visit to Mies, amazed at the well-stocked and well-ordered philosophical library that Mies said he had assembled from the footnotes of a standard philosophical work. Mies mentioned several times that he had 3,000 books in Germany, 300 of which he had brought with him to America, of which he was able to send back 270. But he could not have discovered the remaining 30 if he had not read the 3,000; compare "Six Students Talk with Mies" (interview of February 13, 1952), in *Master Builder* (student publication of the School of Design, North Carolina State College), 2, no. 3 (1952), pp. 21ff.; and Werner Blaser, *Mies van der Rohe. Lehre und Schule* (Basel and Stuttgart, 1977), pp. 283f., with excerpts of book titles from Mies's library. By my count, the works bequeathed to the library of the University of Illinois at Chicago (circa 620 titles), those held privately by Dirk Lohan, Chicago (circa 100 titles), and those held by Georgia Mies van der Rohe, New York (circa 60 titles) add up to some 800 volumes.

19
Museum of Modern Art, Manuscripts Folder 1 (Mies's notebook, p. 69; see Appendix II).

20
Mies van der Rohe in "Gespräch mit Peter Carter," pp. 229ff.

21
Marcus Vitruvius Pollio, *On Architecture,* trans. Frank Granger (London, 1931), pp. 12/13.

22
Walter Gropius, *Apollo in the Democracy* (New York, 1968), p. 171. In 1918 Gropius also excerpted the preceding passage of Vitruvius concerning philosophy. Compare Karin Wilhelm, *Walter Gropius. Industriearchitekt* (Wiesbaden, 1983), p. 129.

23
Mies van der Rohe, "Ich mache niemals ein Bild," *Bauwelt,* 53 (1962), p. 884.

24
Carl Boetticher, *Die Tektonik der Hellenen* (vol. 1, Potsdam, 1844; vol. 2, Potsdam, 1852). According to Boetticher the intrinsic form was determined by necessity; art forms that were meant to raise the materials to the level of an ideal identity were characterized by expressing function while simultaneously giving to function a higher level. Art was to Boetticher not directly linked with structure, but was understood as an addition that realizes itself as decoration and therefore legitimizes eclecticism. Gottfried Semper in *Der Stil* (vol. 1, Frankfurt, 1860; vol. 2, Munich, 1863) attempted to found a new "practical aesthetic," in which intrinsic form and art form exist in a relationship of dialectical interdependence.

25
Adolf Loos, significantly, entitled his essay on the Deutsche Werkbund (1908) "Die Überflüssigen"; in Loos, *Trotzdem,* pp. 72ff. For Loos, the nineteenth century deserved "a large chapter in the history of mankind" because it had achieved the "heroic deed" of having brought about "the clean division between art and industry." It is in this sense that one has to understand the often quoted caustic remark of Karl Kraus: "From the city in which I live I demand: asphalt, sewers, door keys, heat, hot water. I am contented by myself," in *Auswahl aus dem Werk* (Munich, 1978), p. 48.

26
Mies van der Rohe, "Aphorismen" (1955), in Werner Blaser, *Mies van der Rohe, Lehre und Schule* (Basel and Stuttgart, 1977), p. 96.

2 From Accident to Order: The Way to Building

1
See *Der Grosse Brockhaus* (Wiesbaden, 1956); *Wer ist wer?* (Berlin, 1914), p. 1372; 1922 edition, p. 1286; 1928 edition, p. 1270. Alois Riehl had come to attention through his main work *Der philosophische Kritizismus und seine Bedeutung für die positive Wissenschaft* (3 vols., 1876–1887) and through his studies on Plato, Immanuel Kant, Giordano Bruno, and Friedrich Nietzsche, which, together with his main work, were republished in 1925 after his death the previous year. See Alois Riehl, *Philosophische Studien aus vier Jahrzehnten* (Leipzig, 1925), and the *Festschrift für Alois Riehl, von Freunden und Schülern zu seinem siebzigsten Geburtstag dargebracht* (Halle, 1914).

2
"One day Mrs. Riehl, the wife of my future patron, came to look for a young man who could help her design a birdbath, one of those flat bowls . . . for later, they [the Riehls] intended to build a house, but they were so idealistic. They did not want an experienced architect but a young person. . . . I had a conversation with Mrs. Riehl and she asked: 'What have you already built?' I said, 'Nothing!' Whereupon she replied: 'That won't do, we don't want to be guinea pigs.' 'Yes,' I said. 'I can build a house. I have never built one independently. But I have done it. Just think about it, if one would say to me "Have you

ever done this before?" until I am sixty or so.' At that she laughed and said she would get me to meet her husband. Just that night she had an invitation, a dinner party, in her house and I was invited. I will never forget that. First of all Ohlig's assistant told me at noon that I would have to wear tails; I did not even know what tails were. 'Hurry up and buy them. One can get them everywhere, perhaps can even borrow them.' At any rate, I had to borrow all over Bruno Paul's office, to get enough money together to buy a coat with tails. Then of course I had no idea what kind of tie to wear with it and wore a flashy yellow one or some such foolish thing. In the evening I went to the house and there was a couple with me in the elevator. All very elegantly dressed in evening wear and with medals. I was thinking they are certainly going where I am going, let them get out first. Right! Then the door was opened and I almost fainted. I saw how the man and his wife zipped over the parquet as if on ice skates where I was afraid to break my neck. The host dashed from person to person to welcome them. It was very funny. After dinner the *Geheimrat* asked me into his library. We went there, and he asked me all sorts of questions that I can no longer recall. Then he said: 'Let's not keep the other guests waiting,' and we went back into the salon. And to his wife he said: 'He will build our house!' But I must make a correction here. Mrs. Riehl was shocked, she did not trust her spouse, the *Geheimrat,* and she asked me if I could meet her the next day. . . . When I was talking to her, I said: 'I work for Bruno Paul, and he wants me to build him a tennis pavilion or a clubhouse. Why don't you ask him what he thinks of me!' Bruno Paul later told me that she had said: 'You know, this Mies is a genius, but he is too young. He has no experience.' Bruno Paul suggested that I build the house together with his office. I said no. He asked me how I had the guts to say no. He did not understand that. I imagine I wanted to build it myself. And I received the commission. When the house was finished, Bruno Paul asked me whether I would let him have some photos of the Riehl House for an exhibition of his students, former and present, to show what they are doing. And in the course of a tour one morning he said to somebody, 'You see, that house has only one fault, and that is that I have not built it' . . . [Lohan: Were the Riehls then very satisfied with you?] Oh, sure. They were a bit surprised that it cost more than anticipated. But that is clear, it always tends to cost more." Mies van der Rohe in "Gespräch mit Dirk Lohan" (unpublished transcript, Museum of Modern Art).

3
Ibid.: "Mrs. Riehl also gave us money, namely to Popp [Josef Popp was Ohlig's assistant and had designed the bird fountains for Mrs. Riehl; Popp wrote the first monograph on Bruno Paul that appeared in 1916 in Munich] and me so that we could go to Italy for six weeks. That was the first Italian trip. . . . We were to go to Munich. There was an exhibition, I don't recall exactly, where Riemerschmid had fabricated some house with interiors that we were to look at, because Mrs. Riehl liked that. But in the main she sent us to become more mature. It was a very interesting journey. For my taste, Popp went into too many museums to look at pictures. Not that I did not understand it, but I stayed away now and then to look at the city. That was wonderful."

4
Eduard Spranger, "Alois Riehl" (obituary), *Der Tag,* no. 282 (November 23, 1924), p. 2.

5
Notebook of 1927–1928 (Museum of Modern Art, Manuscripts Folder 1; see Appendix II), entry on page 75: "Riehl tombstone." The design for the tombstone is not in Mies's papers.

6
Announcement for the honoring of Alois Riehl and printed congratulatory address (in the Library of Congress); among others the following are mentioned: Elisabeth Förster-Nietzsche, Edmund Husserl, Werner Jaeger, Eduard Spranger, Wolf Graf von Baudissin.

7
Among Mies's patrons were Professor Herbert Gericke, director of the German Academy in Rome (house design, 1932), the painters Emil Nolde and Walter Dexel (projects of 1929 and 1925), industrialist Erich Wolf (project for Guben House, 1925), and banker Ernst Eliat (project of 1925). For the projects for these patrons, see Wolf Tegethoff, *Mies van der Rohe. Die Villen und Landhausprojekte* (Krefeld and Essen, 1981).

8
See "Gespräch mit Dirk Lohan." Jaeger edited *Die Antike. Zeitschrift für Kunst und Kultur des klassischen Altertums;* his studies of Plato particularly attracted Mies's attention in 1928. (See chapter VI, below.)

9
See Franz Schulze, *Mies van der Rohe: A Critical Biography* (Chicago and London, 1985), p. 71. A copy of Wölfflin's *Die klassische Kunst* (Munich, 1905) with the handwritten entry "November 1909 von H.W.," which probably had belonged to Ada, is also in Mies's library. Mies also owned Wölfflin's *Renaissance und Barock* (3d ed., Munich, 1908) as well as *Kunstgeschichtliche Grundbegriffe* (2d ed., Munich, 1917).

10
Paul Mebes, *Um 1800. Architektur und Handwerk im letzten Jahrhundert ihrer Entwicklung* (Munich, 1908).

11
Anonymous, "Architekt Ludwig Mies. Villa des Herrn Geheimer Regierungsrat Prof. Dr. Riehl in Neu-Babelsberg," *Moderne Bauformen,* 9 (1910), pp. 20–24.

12
Anton Jaumann, "Vom künstlerischen Nachwuchs," *Innendekoration,* 21 (1910), pp. 265–274.

13
See note 2 above, describing the circumstances that led to the commission for the Riehl House: "When I was talking to her, I said: 'I work for Bruno Paul, and he wants me to build him a tennis pavilion or a clubhouse.'" An exact dating of the clubhouse (destroyed) has not been established. It was first publicized in *Deutsche Kunst und Dekoration,* 25 (1909–10), illustrations pp. 214ff.; Sonja Günther dates the structure (the locality of which has not been established) as "approximately 1908–09" in her "Werkverzeichnis Bruno Paul," *Stadt, Monatshefte für Wohnungs- und Städtebau,* 29, no. 10 (1982), p. 56. It cannot be established from present sources whether the design for the tennis pavilion immediately preceded the design of the Riehl House or whether both projects arose simultaneously.

14
For the relationship of the Wiegand House to the Werner House, see my investigation in Wolfram Hoepfner and Fritz Neumeyer, *Das Haus Wiegand von Peter Behrens in Berlin-Dahlem* (Mainz, 1979), pp. 52ff.

15
See the thorough analysis of the Barcelona Pavilion by Wolf Tegethoff (*Mies van der Rohe. Die Villen und Landhausprojekte,* particularly pp. 85ff.).

16

Mies van der Rohe, "Was wäre Beton, was Stahl ohne Spiegelglas? (What Would Concrete, What Would Steel Be without Mirror Glass?)," contribution to a prospectus of the Verein Deutscher Spiegelglas-Fabriken of March 13, 1933, first version (manuscript in Museum of Modern Art), quoted by Tegethoff, *Mies van der Rohe. Die Villen und Landhausprojekte,* pp. 66f.

17

See Jaumann, "Vom künstlerischen Nachwuchs." Renate Petras, "Drei Arbeiten Mies van der Rohes in Potsdam-Babelsberg," *Architektur der DDR,* 23, no. 2 (1974), p. 121, reports that the inscription "Klösterli" remained until recently on the cement coat of the stone wall surrounding the property.

18

While Mies built the Riehl House, Bruno Paul designed ship interiors for the steamers *Kronprinzessin Cecilie* (1908), *Derfflinger* (German packet steamer, 1907), *Prinz Friedrich Wilhelm* (1908), and *George Washington* (1908). For further information on the work of Bruno Paul see *Die Stadt. Monatsschrift für Wohnungs- und Städtebau,* 29, no. 10 (1982).

19

Rudolf Fahrner (ed.), *Paul Thiersch, Leben und Werk* (Berlin, 1970), p. 27. Paul Thiersch was the son of the well-known building researcher August Thiersch. In 1906 Paul Thiersch left the construction office of Heinrich Schweitzer in Berlin, joined the Düsseldorf atelier of Peter Behrens for half a year, and was employed after his return by Bruno Paul as office manager. "After I had completed the house, Thiersch, of whom we had heard recently, came. Thiersch had been with Behrens and then had become office manager for Bruno Paul, and he told me that Behrens had asked him to let him know when they had good people there and send them to him. He told me: 'You should really go there, he is a first-rate man.' That is how I came to Behrens." Mies in "Gespräch mit Dirk Lohan."

3 The "Great Form" and the "Will to Style"

1

Peter Behrens, *Feste des Lebens und der Kunst. Eine Betrachtung des Theaters als höchsten Kultursymbols* (Leipzig, 1900), quoted by Fritz Hoeber, *Peter Behrens* (Munich, 1913), p. 223.

2

August Schmarsow, *Das Wesen der architektonischen Schöpfung* (Leipzig, 1894), *Barock und Rokoko* (Leipzig, 1897), *Grundbegriffe der Kunstwissenschaft* (Berlin, 1905); Alois Riegl, *Stilfragen* (Berlin, 1893), *Die spätrömische Kunstindustrie* (Leipzig, 1902); Heinrich Wölfflin, *Renaissance und Barock* (Munich, 1899); building on these and other writings: *Kunstgeschichtliche Grundbegriffe. Das Problem der Stilentwicklung in der neueren Zeit* (Munich, 1915).

3

Peter Behrens, *Ein Dokument Deutscher Kunst. Die Ausstellung der Künstlerkolonie in Darmstadt 1901* (Munich, 1901), quoted by Hoeber, *Peter Behrens,* p. 224.

4

See Tilmann Buddensieg, "Riegl, Behrens, Rathenau," *Kunstchronik,* 23 (1970), pp. 228f.

5

Peter Behrens, "Über die Kunst auf der Bühne," *Frankfurter Zeitung,* 54, no. 78 (March 20, 1910), quoted by Hoeber, *Peter Behrens,* p. 226.

6

Wilhelm Worringer, "Abstraktion und Einfühlung. Ein Beitrag zur Stilpsychologie" (dissertation, Neuwied, 1907; published as a book, Munich, 1908).

7

Peter Behrens, "Was ist monumentale Kunst?," from a lecture published in *Kunstgewerbeblatt,* 20, no. 3 (1908), pp. 46, 48.

8

Compare Hoeber, *Peter Behrens,* p. 2.

9

Ibid., p. 62. On account of its geometrical marble incrustation on the façade—which soon had to be removed due to construction flaws—the crematorium in Hagen intensely recalls San Miniato al Monte in Florence, which showed a late Roman wall concept and was therefore held to be an example of renewal under the aegis of the antique and exercised considerable influence on the churches of the early Renaissance (for example those of Alberti). In that respect, the analogy had been chosen deliberately by Behrens.

10

Das Tonhaus und das Krematorium in Hagen in Westfalen von Peter Behrens (Berlin, 1906).

11

Rudolf Fahrner, *Paul Thiersch. Leben und Werk* (Berlin, 1970), p. 27.

12

Max Creutz, "Das Krematorium von Peter Behrens in Hagen in Westfalen," *Kunstgewerbeblatt,* 20, no. 3 (1908), pp. 41f. Compare in this connection the article of Wilhelm Niemeyer, "Peter Behrens und die Raumaesthetik seiner Kunst" in *Dekorative Kunst,* 10 (1907), pp. 137–148.

13

Hoeber, *Peter Behrens,* p. 64: "The magnificent architectonic cadence of the road up to the columbarium situated on top of the hill is entirely conceived in the mood of an approaching mourning procession and has a profoundly religious impact. . . ."

14

Hoeber (ibid.) continues as follows: ". . . a feeling that the artist already attempted to explain in the catalog to the Darmstadt House in which he wrote: 'The rhythmical movement of climbing imparts to us the inner idea of an elevation to Something.'"

15

Friedrich Ahlers-Hestermann, *Stilwende, Aufbruch der Jugend um 1900* (Berlin, 1941), p. 81, introduces this concept on the basis of Behrens's Darmstadt House on the Mathildenhöhe. On this house and the relationship of Behrens to Nietzsche see Tilmann Buddensieg, "Das Wohnhaus als Kultbau. Zum Darmstädter Haus von Behrens," in *Peter Behrens und Nürnberg. Geschmackswandel in Deutschland; Historismus, Jugendstil und die Anfänge der Industriereform* (Munich, 1980), pp. 37–48. I owe considerable stimulation to Buddensieg's investigation, which lays bare, in exemplary fashion, a previously overlooked but significant vein of tradition leading to modernism. See also Paul Fechter, "Nietzsches Bildwelt und der Jugendstil" (1935), in Jost Hermand (ed.), *Jugendstil* (Darmstadt, 1971), pp. 347–357.

16
Friedrich Nietzsche, *Also sprach Zarathustra,* in *Werke in Drei Bänden,* ed. Karl Schlechta, vol. 2 (Munich, 1921), pp. 290, 359.

17
Peter Behrens, "Über die Kunst auf der Bühne," quoted in Hoeber, *Peter Behrens,* p. 226.

18
Peter Behrens, "Was ist monumentale Kunst?," p. 48.

19
After the First World War, Heinrich Wölfflin, along with Thomas Mann and Hugo von Hofmannsthal, was active in the directorship of the Munich Nietzsche Society. Basic to the study of Nietzsche's influence on the art of around 1900 is Jürgen Krause, *"Märtyrer" und "Prophet." Studien zum Nietzsche-Kult in der bildenden Kunst der Jahrhundertwende* (Berlin and New York, 1984).

20
Heinrich Wölfflin, *Die klassische Kunst,* quoted from Hubert Faensen's edition of Wölfflin's *Kunstgeschichtliche Grundbegriffe* (Dresden, 1983), p. 403.

21
Peter Behrens, "Was ist monumentale Kunst?," p. 46.

22
Compare Friedrich Nietzsche, *Die Geburt der Tragödie,* in *Werke,* vol. 1, p. 37.

23
Peter Behrens, "Was ist monumentale Kunst?," p. 48. Behrens's fascination with Nietzsche is not only proven by this text. The cheerful pride of the "Let it be thus" ascribed to a youth that not simply carries its generation to the tomb but creates a new generation ("Vom Nutzen und Nachteil der Historie," in *Werke,* vol. 1, p. 265) speaks in Behrens's *Feste des Lebens und der Kunst:* "We have become serious. We take our life importantly, we put a high value on work. . . . We feel we have accomplished something for practical life that has never been there before and that cannot be lost, and this feeling elevates our mood. . . . It is a laughing from the heart. . . . We have understood our epoch, our new powers, our needs. . . . With our powers we can afford something additional that will make us greater and cause us to have higher needs, and these, too, we will satisfy energetically and beautifully. For this reason we will have a new style, our own style throughout, in all that we create."

24
"Die Ausstellung der Darmstädter Künstlerkolonie," quoted in Hoeber, *Peter Behrens,* p. 232.

25
See Karl Scheffler, "Peter Behrens," *Die Zukunft,* 16 (1907), pp. 240–276.

26
Friedrich Nietzsche, *Die Geburt der Tragödie,* in *Werke,* vol. 1, p. 134.

27
J. J. P. Oud, "Über die zukünftige Baukunst und ihre architektonischen Möglichkeiten," *Frühlicht,* 1, no. 4 (1922), p. 199.

28
Theo van Doesburg, "Der Wille zum Stil" (lecture held in Jena and Weimar, 1922) in *De Stijl* (1922), no. 2–3, pp. 23–41, quoted in Hagen Bächler and Herbert Letsch (eds.), *De Stijl.*

Schriften und Manifeste zu einem theoretischen Konzept ästhetischer Umweltgestaltung (Leipzig and Weimar, 1984), p. 178.

29
Goerd Peschken, *Karl Friedrich Schinkel. Das Architektonische Lehrbuch* (Munich and Berlin, 1979). For the relationship of architecture and nature see Eva Börsch-Supan, "Architektur und Landschaft," in *Karl Friedrich Schinkel. Werke und Wirkungen,* exhibition catalog (Berlin, 1981), pp. 48–64.

30
Van Doesburg, "Der Wille zum Stil," in Bächler and Letsch, *De Stijl,* p. 173.

31
Friedrich Nietzsche, *Also sprach Zarathustra,* in *Werke,* vol. 2, p. 394.

32
Mies van der Rohe, "Bauen," *G,* no. 2 (September 1923), p. 1.

33
Eduard Spranger, "Alois Riehl" (obituary), *Der Tag,* no. 282 (November 23, 1924), p. 2. Spranger reported of his visit of condolence to the Riehl House in Neubabelsberg: "Outside in the garden, according to the eternal laws of the changing seasons, slumber the once blooming hedges and garden beds, and above the high terrace the eye beheld the serious traits of the landscape of the Prussian mark in the November fog."

34
Rudolf Schwarz, Mies's close friend, characterized Mies in his 1961 birthday address "An Mies van der Rohe," which revealed a profound understanding of Mies's building philosophy, as an apostle of that "voluntary service": "In your buildings has been preserved the ancient wisdom that life never succeeds more than when it is embedded in the great law of a strong objective form that protects its vulnerability, and that human life is carried on most humanely when it is conducted against the open horizon of that great lawfulness. Not where life is told how it should act spontaneously, and where the soft enclosure of spontaneity is preplanned, but where it is simply set under the open firmament of a great law, will it awaken to its profoundest insights and bravest deeds and risk its tender game; it awakens to its real freedom—not that supposed to consist in a rejection of all obligations and the pursuit of arbitrary and accidental whims, but that other much older one that is unspeakably more noble and to which it is a privilege to be tied to a large extent. . . . You have done your share and for that we are thankful—that the message of this beatific necessity has been preserved and has been salvaged for our art over and above that terrible danger that would have subjected our work to the lowest necessity, where the deployment of mechanical forces was held to constitute the only freedom for today's men, and that other danger that stems from the shallow, the swollen, the immature, and the arbitrary conglomeration. . . . So you have fitted your work into the great tradition that beckons from the past and that surely was more humane than ours and to which you confessed yourself to be voluntarily committed." In Maria Schwarz and Ulrich Conrads (eds.), *Rudolf Schwarz, Wegweisung der Technik und andere Schriften zum Neuen Bauen 1926–1961* (Brunswick and Wiesbaden, 1979), pp. 191f.

35
Mies van der Rohe, notebook of 1928 (Museum of Modern Art, Manuscripts Folder 1), p. 35 (see Appendix II).

36
Manuscript for the lecture "Über Sinn und Aufgabe der Kritik" (On the Meaning and Task of Criticism), in Museum of Modern Art, Manuscripts Folder 4.

37
Max Scheler, *Vom Umsturz der Werte* (Leipzig, 1923), vol. 1, p. 23.

38
Friedrich Nietzsche, *Also sprach Zarathustra,* in *Werke,* vol. 2, p. 290.

39
Mies in Berlin, phonograph record, Bauwelt Archiv 1, 1966.

40
Peter Behrens, *Feste des Lebens und der Kunst,* quoted in Hoeber, *Peter Behrens,* p. 223.

41
See Krause, *"Märtyrer" und "Prophet."* See also Buddensieg, "Das Wohnhaus als Kultbau." On the axis Nietzsche-Behrens-Le Corbusier, see Fritz Neumeyer, "Im Schatten des mechanischen Haines. Versuchsanordnungen zur Metropole," in Karl Schwarz (ed.), *Die Zukunft der Metropolen: Paris, London, New York, Berlin,* vol. 1 (Berlin, 1984), pp. 273–282.

42
Spranger, "Alois Riehl," points out that Riehl's work on Nietzsche was the first monograph published on Nietzsche. Before Riehl, the Danish literary critic Georg Brandes, who gave lectures on Nietzsche at the University of Copenhagen and is generally viewed as the "discoverer" of Nietzsche, had dedicated an essay to Nietzsche in *Mensch und Werke* (2d ed., Frankfurt, 1895) that had been published under the title "Aristokratischer Radicalismus" in the *Neue Rundschau,* 1, no. 2 (1890), pp. 52–89. On the importance of Riehl see also Alfredo Guzzoni (ed.), *90 Jahre philosophische Nietzsche-Rezeption* (Königstein, 1979), p. viii.

43
Alois Riehl, "Schopenhauer und Nietzsche—zur Frage des Pessimismus," in *Zur Einführung in die Philosophie der Gegenwart* (Leipzig, 1903; 3d ed., 1908), pp. 234–250, reprinted in Guzzoni, *90 Jahre philosophische Nietzsche-Rezeption,* pp. 16–24. A chapter on Socrates from Riehl's *Philosophie der Gegenwart* appeared in *Die Zukunft,* 9 (1902), pp. 198ff., with the note: "From the finely stimulating lectures that will appear in November under the title 'Zur Einführung in die Philosophie der Gegenwart.'"

44
Jürgen Habermas, *Der philosophische Diskurs der Moderne. Zwölf Vorlesungen* (Frankfurt, 1985), discussing the dialectic between modernism and postmodernism and the intertwining of myth and enlightenment, assigns to Nietzsche the function of a turnstile that marks the "entrance to postmodernism." (Chapter 4, pp. 104ff.) In this context see Karl Heinz Bohrer (ed.), *Mythos und Moderne* (Frankfurt, 1983).

45
Riehl's *Philosophie der Gegenwart* (3d ed., Leipzig, 1908), in the possession of Dirk Lohan, Chicago, shows the entry "Ada Mies." The underlinings, though, show the unmistakable hand of Mies. Whether Mies had his own volume of this book cannot be determined. Of all the other works of Riehl named here, none are found among the books left by Mies.

46
Alois Riehl, *Nietzsche als Künstler und Denker* (1897; Stuttgart, 1909), p. 107. On Mies's readings of Nietzsche see below, chapter IV.1, note 31.

47
Eduard Spranger, "Lebensformen," in *Festschrift für Alois Riehl, von Freunden und Schülern zu seinem 70. Geburtstag dargebracht* (Halle, 1914), pp. 492f. Mies owned Spranger's book *Lebensformen* in the third edition (Halle, 1922). There are numerous markings by Mies in the extant copy.

48
Mies van der Rohe, unpublished lecture manuscript of March 14, 1927, in the collection of Dirk Lohan, Chicago (see Appendix I, 16).

49
Mies van der Rohe, "Die Voraussetzungen baukünstlerischen Schaffens" (The Preconditions of Architectural Work), unpublished lecture manuscript of 1928, in the collection of Dirk Lohan, Chicago.

50
Riehl, *Nietzsche als Künstler und Denker,* p. 54.

51
Nietzsche, *Die Geburt der Tragödie,* in *Werke,* vol. 1, p. 131.

52
See Gert Sautermeister, "Zur Grundlegung des Ästhetizismus bei Nietzsche. Dialektik, Metaphysik und Politik in der *Geburt der Tragödie,*" in Christa Bürger, Peter Bürger, and Jochen Schulte-Sasse (eds.), *Naturalismus/Ästhetizismus* (Frankfurt, 1979), pp. 224—243.

53
Nietzsche, *Die Geburt der Tragödie,* in *Werke,* vol. 1, p. 90.

54
Mies van der Rohe, "Baukunst und Zeitwille!" (Building Art and the Will of the Epoch!), *Der Querschnitt,* 4, no. 1 (1924), pp. 31f.

III The Ambivalence of Concepts: Construction or Interpretation of Reality? Berlage or Behrens? Hegel or Nietzsche?

1
"Peter Behrens had a marvelous feeling for form. This was his main interest, and it is this feeling for form that I learned from him to know and appreciate." Mies van der Rohe in "Gespräch mit Peter Carter," *Bauen und Wohnen,* 16 (1961), p. 231.

2
Mies van der Rohe, "A Tribute to Frank Lloyd Wright," *College Art Journal,* 6, no. 1 (1946), pp. 41, 42. Also compare Mies's handwritten note: "But wherever real building arose, in industry and commerce, function was the ultimate form-giver and technology furnished the constructive means. Here and not on the Mathildenhöhe the new language was first heard." (Manuscript in Library of Congress; see Appendix VI, 6.)

3
Mies van der Rohe, "A Tribute to Frank Lloyd Wright." Also compare Mies van der Rohe, "Wohin gehen wir nun?" (Where Do We Go from Here?), *Bauen und Wohnen,* 15 (1960), p.

391: "Sometimes confusion holds even great men in its grip—as it was around 1900. As Wright, Berlage, Behrens, Olbrich, Loos, and van de Velde worked, all did so in different directions."

4
Mies van der Rohe, "Baukunst unserer Zeit" (Building Art of Our Time), in Werner Blaser, *Mies van der Rohe. Die Kunst der Struktur* (Zurich and Stuttgart, 1965), p. 5: "Representative buildings stood more or less under the influence of Palladio or Schinkel. The great achievements of that period, however, were to be found among industrial buildings and purely technological structures. It was actually a confused time and nobody could or would answer the question as to the nature of the building art."

5
Mies van der Rohe in "Gespräch mit Peter Carter," p. 242.

6
Ibid., p. 231.

7
Mies van der Rohe, "A Tribute to Frank Lloyd Wright," p. 42.

8
Mies in Berlin, phonograph record, Bauwelt Archiv I, 1966.

9
Ibid.: "The stock market building made a grandiose impression, and Behrens was of the opinion that everything of Berlage's was passé, and I told him: 'I just hope you are not wrong!' He looked at me furiously [laugh] . . . he would have liked to box my ears." In contrast to this, see Peter Behrens, "Sachlichkeit und Gesetz," in *Die Pyramide,* 14 (1928), pp. 92–95, where Behrens praised Berlage's stock market building as "modern even today and pioneering for the future."

10
H. P. Berlage, *Gedanken über den Stil in der Baukunst* (Leipzig, 1905), p. 8. On the significance of Berlage see Pieter Singelenberg, *H. P. Berlage. Idea and Style. The Quest for Modern Architecture* (Utrecht, 1972); Manfred Bock, *Anfänge einer neuen Architektur. Berlages Beitrag zur architektonischen Kultur der Niederlande im ausgehenden 19. Jahrhundert* (Wiesbaden, 1983).

11
Gottfried Semper, *Der Stil in den technischen und tektonischen Künsten,* vol. 1 (Frankfurt am Main, 1860), p. viii, quoted in Berlage, *Gedanken,* p. 26.

12
Berlage, *Gedanken,* pp. 27ff.

13
Ibid., pp. 33, 47, 48, 51.

14
Ibid., p. 48: "For who ever asks the name of the first building master of a medieval cathedral or the name of an Egyptian architect?" Mies van der Rohe, "Baukunst und Zeitwille!" (Building Art and the Will of the Epoch!), *Der Querschnitt,* 4, no. 1 (1924), p. 31: "And also the cathedrals of the Middle Ages were not the work of individual personalities but the creations of entire epochs. Who asks, when viewing such buildings, for names, and what would the accidental personality of their builders mean?"

15
Berlage, *Gedanken,* pp. 5, 6.

16
Mies van der Rohe, "Gelöste Aufgaben. Eine Forderung an unser Bauwesen" (Solved Tasks: A Challenge for Our Building Industry), *Bauwelt,* 14 (1924), p. 719. Compare for example Bruno Taut, "Nieder den Seriosismus" (1920): "Damn this self-aggrandizement! Funeral stones and cemetery enclosures opposite four-storied knickknack stores and barter dens! Smash these Doric, Ionic, and Corinthian limestone columns, tear down these puppet jokes!" Quoted in Ulrich Conrads, *Programme und Manifeste zur Architektur des 20. Jahrhunderts* (Berlin, 1964), p. 54. "We are repelled by our houses," says Le Corbusier in *Vers une architecture* (1922).

17
Mies van der Rohe, "Gelöste Aufgaben."

18
Berlage, *Gedanken,* pp. 11, 23.

19
Ibid., p. 13.

20
H. P. Berlage, *Grundlagen und Entwicklung der Architektur* (Berlin, 1908), p. 108.

21
Friedrich Nietzsche, *Thus Spake Zarathustra,* translated by Thomas Common, in *The Complete Works of Friedrich Nietzsche,* ed. Oscar Levy, vol. 11 (New York, 1911), p. 217.

22
Georg Wilhelm Friedrich Hegel, *Aesthetics,* translated by T. M. Knox (Oxford, 1975), vol. 1, p. 101.

23
See Singelenberg, *H. P. Berlage,* esp. chapter 13, "The Influence of Hegel and Schopenhauer."

24
Berlage, *Grundlagen,* pp. 117, 113, 117.

25
Ibid., pp. 14, 39, 9.

26
Undated manuscript, presumably around 1950, in Library of Congress (see Appendix IV, 6).

27
Mies van der Rohe, "Wohin gehen wir nun?," p. 391. "Only a relationship that touches on the innermost nature of the epoch is authentic. I call this relationship a truth relationship. Truth in the sense of Thomas Aquinas: as *adaequatio intellectus et rei,* as congruence of thought and thing."

28
Undated manuscript (see Appendix IV, 6).

29
Berlage, *Grundlagen,* pp. 86, 91f.

30
Ibid., p. 89.

31
Manuscript for a lecture (Chicago, occasion and date unknown), p. 14 (see Appendix IV, 5).

32
Berlage, *Grundlagen,* p. 93.

33
Ibid., p. 77.

34
Hegel, *Aesthetics,* vol. 1, p. 103.

35
Berlage, *Grundlagen,* p. 88.

36
Ibid., p. 89. Berlage condemned Semper presumably because Semper rejected the Gothic style on account of its aesthetic indecisiveness. It is interesting that Berlage and Semper used similar lines of argument, although from different points of view, insofar as they accused each other of inconsequentiality, one from the point of view of construction, the other from that of appearance.

37
Franz Schulze, "'I Really Always Wanted to Know about Truth,'" *Chicago News,* April 27, 1968.

38
Berlage, *Grundlagen,* p. 68.

39
Museum of Modern Art, Manuscripts Folder 1 (Mies's notebook, p. 26; see Appendix II).

40
Sergius Ruegenberg, who was working in Mies's office in 1925–1926 and 1928–1931, recalls that Mies proudly recounted that he had contributed the window design of the long western side of the Turbine Factory (S. Ruegenberg, personal communication).

41
Berlage, *Grundlagen,* p. 88.

42
See the letter of Behrens to Mies, May 5, 1924, in the Library of Congress.

43
Mies in Berlin, phonograph record, Bauwelt Archiv I, 1966.

44
"When I came as a young man to Berlin and looked around, I was interested in Schinkel because Schinkel was the most important architect in Berlin. There were several others, but Schinkel was the most important man. His buildings were an excellent example of classicism—the best I know. And certainly I became interested in that. I studied him carefully and came under his influence. That could have happened to anybody. I think Schinkel had wonderful constructions, excellent proportions, and good detailing." See Peter Blake, "A Conversation with Mies," in *Four Great Makers of Modern Architecture* (New York, 1963), p. 94. In "Conversation with Dirk Lohan" (manuscript in the Museum of Modern Art), Mies indicates that he only discovered Schinkel through Behrens. Before he had been interested in Messel. "In the center of town was Wertheim, the large department store. It had a façade, wonderful. That Messel was simply marvelous, like Palladio. He could imitate Gothic exquisitely. Schinkel one could always look at by going to the Altes Museum."

45
"Around 1910, Schinkel was still really the greatest representative in Berlin. His Altes Museum in Berlin was a beautiful building—you could learn everything in architecture from it—and I tried to do that." "Architect of the Clear and Reasonable: Mies van der Rohe Considered and Interviewed by Graeme Shankland," *The Listener,* 15 (October 1959), p. 622.

46
Undated manuscript (see Appendix IV, 6).

47
Philip Johnson, "Karl Friedrich Schinkel im zwanzigsten Jahrhundert" (1961), in *Festreden. Schinkel zu Ehren 1846–1980,* chosen and introduced by Julius Posener (Berlin, 1981), pp. 314–328. Compare Henry Russell Hitchcock, "Architecture chronicle—Berlin," *Hound and Horn,* 5, no. 1 (1931), pp. 94–97; Agnoldomenico Pica, "Mies a Berlino," *Domus,* no. 478 (1969), pp. 1–7; Jacques Paul, "German Neo-Classicism and the Modern Movement," *Architectural Review,* 152 (1972), pp. 176–180. Compare also Hugo Häring, "vom neuen bauen" (1952), in Jürgen Joedicke (ed.), *das andere bauen* (Stuttgart, 1982), p. 89: "Mies van der rohe finally carried the gracious theme of the greeks a step further and thereby guided it toward its end. The greeks had started to create their works according to laws of harmony that sounded in the celestial spheres, the reflections of which were held to appear in geometrical harmony. Thereby they created a big theme for occidental culture. But the work of mies van der rohe lets us know that this way into the domain of architecture also leads out of it."

48
Paul Westheim, "Mies van der Rohe: Entwicklung eines Architekten," *Das Kunstblatt,* 11, no. 2 (1927), pp. 55–62. Rpt. as "Mies van der Rohe: Charaktervoll bauen," in Paul Westheim, *Helden und Abenteurer* (Berlin, 1931), pp. 188–191.

49
The influence of Schinkel is particularly noticeable in the Wiegand House of 1911–1912. See Wolfram Hoepfner and Fritz Neumeyer, *Das Haus Wiegand von Peter Behrens in Berlin-Dahlem* (Mainz, 1979).

50
Karl Scheffler (1912) as quoted in my article "Klassizismus als Problem," in *Berlin und die Antike* (Berlin, 1979), p. 396, from which I include a short passage here.

51
Franz Mannheimer, "Die deutschen Industriehallen von Professor Peter Behrens auf der Brüsseler Weltausstellung von 1910," *Der Industriebau,* 1, no. 9 (1910), pp. 203ff., supplied the key phrase "elective affinities" that evoked a sensitizing to contemporary formal problems by way of an analogy between modern industrial architecture and early Hellenism, as has been proved by Edmund Schüler in exemplary fashion (compare next footnote).

52
"We made pilgrimages to the giant structures of the Allgemeine Elektrizitäts-Gesellschaft in the Brunnenstrasse and to the Turbine Factory. When someone raved about the 'elective affinity' between new industrial architecture and early Hellenism, a gate to heaven seemed to open up for us, to a new, longed for heaven of our own." Edmund Schüler, "Peter Behrens" (obituary), *Die Kunst im deutschen Reich,* Issue B, 4 (1940), series 4, p. 65.

53
Robert Breuer, "Kleine Kunstnachrichten," *Deutsche Kunst und Dekoration,* 27 (1910–1911), p. 492. On the significance of Behrens's industrial classicism for the development of modernism, compare Tilmann Buddensieg and Henning Rogge, *Industriekultur: Peter Behrens and the AEG 1907–1914,* trans. Iain Boyd Whyte (Cambridge, Mass., 1984). I owe Tilmann Buddensieg decisive stimulation for the question under discussion here.

54
Julius Meier-Graefe, "Peter Behrens—Düsseldorf," *Dekorative Kunst,* 8 (1905), p. 389.

55

Sergius Ruegenberg, "Ein Fünfzigjähriger," *Die Bauwelt,* 27 (1936), p. 346. Mies thanked his former co-worker in a letter:

Dear Mr. Ruegenberg,

I found your greetings to me in Die Bauwelt. I want to thank you sincerely. I was glad to hear that my work was meaningful to some. That is perhaps the significance of such days. It makes me particularly happy that my most-valued co-workers stand so loyally by me.

Your Mies

Beyond that, you also count among the donors of the beautiful painting. [Mies had been given a painting by Max Beckmann, Rückenakt.] I found it much too valuable. But it certainly has delighted me. Not only the possession of it in itself, but the opportunity to test out a painting such as this in the rooms of our imagination.

Again, your Mies.

56

Theodor Heuss, "Brüssel III," *Die Hilfe,* 15, no. 25 (1910), supplement, p. 399, quoted from Fritz Hoeber, *Peter Behrens* (Munich, 1913), p. 239. The remark of Heuss referring to Behrens's Brussels industrial buildings seems to me generally applicable to all of Behrens's industrial architecture and particularly to the Turbine Factory.

57

According to Philip Johnson, "Schinkel im zwanzigsten Jahrhundert," p. 324.

58

Mies van der Rohe, "Was wäre Beton, was Stahl ohne Spiegelglas?" (What Would Concrete, What Would Steel Be without Mirror Glass?), contribution to a prospectus of the Verein Deutscher Spiegelglas-Fabriken of March 13, 1933, following Wolf Tegethoff, *Mies van der Rohe. Die Villen und Landhausprojekte* (Krefeld and Essen, 1981), p. 66f.

59

J. J. P. Oud, "Über die zukünftige Baukunst und ihre architektonischen Möglichkeiten," *Frühlicht,* 1, no. 4 (1922), p. 199.

60

Meier-Graefe, "Peter Behrens—Düsseldorf," p. 385.

61

"In those times it was risky to go to Peter Behrens. Almost the entire architectural world made war on the dilettante Behrens, that bold heretic, who, with only a few like-minded ones, attempted to topple the entire style system corroded for centuries. Whoever turned, at that time, to Behrens knew that he stood in opposition to everyone, to public opinion, and that he would make himself a laughingstock if his enterprise failed." K. E. Osthaus on the occasion of the dedication of the Catholic Gesellenheim in Neuss on November 19, 1910, quoted from Hans-Joachim Kadatz, *Peter Behrens* (Berlin, 1977), p. 129.

62

Meier-Graefe, "Peter Behrens—Düsseldorf," p. 386.

63

Mies van der Rohe, foreword to *Bau und Wohnung* (Stuttgart, 1927), p. 7.

64

In *Der Stil in den technischen und tektonischen Künsten,* vol. 1 (Frankfurt, 1860), p. 508, the Gothic was characterized by Gottfried Semper: "The Gothic building style solved half the problem, namely the mechanical one, albeit in a reckless and all too homemade way by means of support pillars braced against the exterior walls and by flying buttresses. However, it neglects the aesthetic part of the solution. Not only does it leave the eye dissatisfied at the place where the lateral thrust of the vault ribs becomes noticeable, namely in the interior of the vaulted rooms where the external counterthrust is not visible and the eye feels anxiety on account of this unilateral thrust of vault ribs against an external support the adequacy of which cannot be judged from the inside. It also insults the aesthetic sensibility on the outside on account of a seemingly excessive and purely technical pillar and buttress system that exerts thrust against something that cannot even be seen and that therefore, formally speaking, does not exist. For the aesthetic eye easily transfers spatial impressions from something seen earlier to something seen later, but static complements of an overall impression by a not yet seen or no longer seen countereffect of masses are not permissible."

65

Peter Behrens, "Kunst und Technik" (1910), translated in Buddensieg and Rogge, *Industriekultur,* pp. 212–219. See also "Peter Behrens, Schriften zum Problemkreis 'Kunst und Technik,' 1901–1929," ibid., pp. 274ff.

66

Berlage, *Grundlagen,* p. 100; compare also p. 113.

67

In 1904 Behrens wrote several appreciative letters to Berlage, asking him for demonstration material and photographs of his buildings. See Singelenberg, *H. P. Berlage,* p. 158.

68

See Berlage, *Grundlagen,* illustration on pp. 56, 57, "Design of a student of the Kunstgewerbeschule Düsseldorf." One of the works included was by Adolf Meyer, who later worked for Behrens in Berlin and who left the Behrens atelier together with Gropius on occasion of the commission for the Faguswerk in 1910. Behrens had appointed the Dutchman Lauwericks to the school's architectural department, intending to publish with him a study dealing with the laws of proportion in art, as Meier-Graefe ("Peter Behrens—Düsseldorf," pp. 389f.) reports.

69

Arthur Moeller van den Bruck, *Der Preussische Stil* (Breslau, 1916), p. 193.

70

Berlage, *Grundlagen,* p. 4.

71

Peter Behrens, "Was ist monumentale Kunst?," from a lecture published in *Kunstgewerbeblatt,* 20, no. 3 (1908), p. 48. On the significance of circle and square in Behrens's system of design, see Hoepfner and Neumeyer, *Das Haus Wiegand,* pp. 13–24.

72

Meier-Graefe, "Peter Behrens—Düsseldorf," p. 381.

73

Immanuel Kant, *Kritik der reinen Vernunft* (1781; rpt., Berlin and Vienna, 1924) p. 70, here quoted from Karl Popper, *Auf der Suche nach einer besseren Welt* (Munich, 1984), p. 144.

74

Marc-Antoine Laugier, *Essai sur l'architecture* (Paris, 1753), cited in Georg Germann, *Einführung in die Geschichte der Architekturtheorie* (Darmstadt, 1980), p. 200.

75
Friedrich Nietzsche, "On the Uses and Disadvantages of History," in *Untimely Meditations,* translated by R. J. Hollingdale (Cambridge, 1983), p. 62.

76
Piet Mondrian, "Die Neue Gestaltung in der Malerei" (1917–1918), reprinted in Hagen Bächler and Herbert Letsch (eds.), *De Stijl. Schriften und Manifeste zu einem theoretischen Konzept ästhetischer Umweltgestaltung* (Leipzig and Weimar, 1984), p. 77.

77
Berlage, *Grundlagen,* p. 115.

78
Ibid., p. 79.

79
Mies van der Rohe, "Bauen" (Building), in *G,* no. 2 (September 1923), p. 1.

80
Friedrich Nietzsche, "'Reason' in Philosophy,' in *Twilight of the Idols,* in *The Works of Friedrich Nietzsche,* translated by Thomas Common (New York, 1896), vol. 11, p. 121.

81
Friedrich Nietzsche, *The Antichrist,* in *The Works of Friedrich Nietzsche,* vol. 11, p. 344.

82
Friedrich Nietzsche, in *Werke in drei Bänden,* ed. Karl Schlechta (Munich, 1966), vol. 3, p. 526 (unpublished works from the 1880s).

83
Berlage, *Grundlagen,* p. 113.

84
Friedrich Nietzsche, *Richard Wagner in Bayreuth,* quoted from Alois Riehl, *Friedrich Nietzsche der Künstler und Denker* (Stuttgart, 1896), p. 55.

85
Alois Riehl, *Einführung in die Philosophie der Gegenwart* (3d ed., Leipzig, 1908), p. 240.

86
Heinrich Wölfflin, "Eine Revision von 1933 als Nachwort," *Kunstgeschichtliche Grundbegriffe* (Munich, 1915; Dresden, 1983), p. 295.

87
Mies van der Rohe, notebook of 1928, p. 3 (Museum of Modern Art, Manuscripts Folder 1; see Appendix II). The architect Paul Schultze-Naumburg was, as representative of the so-called *Heimatstil* (Homeland Style), one of the sharpest critics of New Building in the conservative camp. In 1928 he was among the founders of the national socialist Kampfbund für deutsche Kultur (KfdK) and became a leading propagandist for "Art and Race." Mies's signature under the "Aufruf der Kulturschaffenden" (Call of the Cultural Workers) that was published in the *Völkische Beobachter,* the official party organ of the NSDAP, on August 18, 1934, is to be found directly beneath Schultze-Naumburg's. On this, see Peter Hahn (ed.), *Bauhaus Berlin: Auflösung Dessau 1932. Schliessung Berlin 1933. Bauhäusler und Drittes Reich* (Weingarten and Berlin, 1985), pp. 147f.

88
Le Corbusier, *Towards a New Architecture,* translated by Frederick Etchells (New York, 1976), p. 31.

89
See note 26.

90
Le Corbusier, "'Température' à l'occasion de la troisième édition" (1928), in *Vers une architecture* (Paris, 1958), p. xi.

91
Le Corbusier, *Towards a New Architecture,* p. 11.

92
Le Corbusier, "'Température,'" p. xi.

93
Friedrich Nietzsche, "Expeditions of an Inopportune Philosopher," in *Twilight of the Idols, The Works of Friedrich Nietzsche,* vol. 11, p. 171. Nietzsche's concept of architecture is derived from Arthur Schopenhauer, *Die Welt als Wille und Vorstellung* (1819); see "Zur Ästhetik der Architektur." Schopenhauer perceives the actual aesthetic material of the building art in the battle between gravity and rigidity. Compare Herman Sörgel, *Theorie der Baukunst. Architektur-Ästhetik* (Munich, 1921), p. 68.

94
Mies van der Rohe, draft of a letter (presumably around 1927), in Museum of Modern Art, Manuscripts Folder 2 (see Appendix I, 17 for text).

95
Friedrich Nietzsche, "Apothegms and Darts," in *Twilight of the Idols, The Works of Friedrich Nietzsche,* vol. 11, p. 104.

IV Elementary Form-Giving: Departure for the Limits of Architecture

1 "Beyond Architecture": On Eternal Building

1
With the exception of the first skyscraper design, which was made for the Friedrichstrasse competition project announced in December 1921, the designs arose more or less out of self-imposed challenges. For the Concrete Country House one can assume, as Wolf Tegethoff shows (*Mies van der Rohe. Die Villen und Landhausprojekte* [Krefeld and Essen, 1981], pp. 17ff.), that Mies had actual building intentions in mind and designed his own residence. The same may hold true for the Brick Country House, which was designed for a lot in Neubabelsberg. The assumption that all projects except for the skyscraper for Friedrichstrasse were ideal designs is incorrect or at least only partially correct. Only for the Office Building is no definite locality provable.

2
Mies van der Rohe, "Arbeitsthesen," *G,* no. 1 (July 1923), p. 3.

3
Mies van der Rohe, "Bauen" (Building), *G,* no. 2 (September 1923), p. 1.

4
Mies van der Rohe, "Bürohaus" (Office Building), text for the *Deutsche Allgemeine Zeitung* of August 2, 1923, not published, in Museum of Modern Art, Manuscripts Folder 3 (see Appendix I, 3).

5
Mies van der Rohe, "Bauen."

6
Compare Mies van der Rohe, "Was wäre Beton, was Stahl ohne Spiegelglas?" (What Would Concrete, What Would Steel Be without Mirror Glass?), contribution to a prospectus of the Verein Deutscher Spiegelglas-Fabriken of March 13, 1933, unpublished (manuscript in the Library of Congress): "The simplicity of construction, clarity of tectonic means, and purity of material reflect the luminosity of original beauty" (text version). "Simplicity of construction, clarity of tectonic means, and purity of material shall be the bearers of a new beauty" (draft version).

7
Mies van der Rohe, "Bürohaus."

8
Ibid.

9
Compare Walter Gropius, "Was ist Baukunst?," pamphlet for the exhibition "Für unbekannte Architekten" (For Unknown Architects) organized by the Arbeitsrat für Kunst, April 1919, republished in Arbeitsrat für Kunst. Berlin 1918–1921, exhibition catalog (Berlin, 1980), p. 90.

10
Mies van der Rohe, "Bürohaus."

11
Mies van der Rohe, "Gelöste Aufgaben. Eine Forderung an unser Bauwesen" (Solved Tasks: A Challenge for Our Building Industry), Die Bauwelt, 14 (1923), p. 719.

12
Gropius, "Was ist Baukunst?," p. 90.

13
Mies's copy of Formprobleme der Gotik (Munich, 1920) carries on the cover the entry "Ludwig Mies." Only in 1922 did Mies enlarge his name to "Mies van der Rohe" by adding his mother's name.

14
Also worth mentioning in this connection are Hans Detlev Rösiger, "Gotik oder Antike," Der Neubau, 6 (1924), pp. 273f., as well as Wilhelm Worringer, Griechentum und Gotik (Munich, 1928).

15
Peter Carter, "Mies van der Rohe," Bauen und Wohnen, 16 (1961), pp. 229f.

16
Mies's two copies of Die Welt des Mittelalters und wir belonged to the third edition of 1925 (the first edition dated from 1922). Apparently Mies did not own Landsberg's second, albeit not quite as well known book Wesen und Bedeutung der platonischen Akademie (Bonn, 1923). It cannot be ruled out that Mies also made the personal acquaintance of Landsberg, who followed Romano Guardini in 1923 as student to Berlin, as Hanna-Barbara Gerl reports in Romano Guardini. 1885–1968 (Mainz, 1985), pp. 130f.

17
Mies van der Rohe, "Baukunst und Zeitwille!" (Building Art and the Will of the Epoch!), Der Querschnitt, 4, no. 1 (1924), pp. 31–32.

18
Landsberg, Die Welt des Mittelalters und wir (1925), pp. 12, 7.

19
Ibid., p. 105.

20
Ibid., p. 28.

21
Ibid., p. 99.

22
Ibid., p. 15.

23
Compare Dagobert Frey, Kunstwissenschaftliche Grundfragen. Prolegomena zu einer Kunstphilosophie (Darmstadt, 1984), pp. 53ff.

24
H. P. Berlage, Gedanken über den Stil in der Baukunst (Leipzig, 1905), p. 48.

25
Mies van der Rohe, "Baukunst und Zeitwille!"

26
Franz Schulze, Mies van der Rohe: A Critical Biography (Chicago and London, 1985), p. 17.

27
A selection of the titles of Raoul H. Francé that can be found in Mies's collection: Das Sinnenleben der Pflanzen (Stuttgart, 1905); Der Wert der Wissenschaft (Zurich, 1908); Bilder aus dem Leben des Waldes (Stuttgart, 1909); Denkmäler der Natur (Leipzig, 1910); Die technischen Leistungen der Pflanzen (Leipzig, 1919); Das Gesetz des Lebens (Leipzig, 1920); München. Die Lebensgesetze einer Stadt (Munich, 1920); Die Pflanze als Erfinder (Stuttgart, 1920); Bios. Die Gesetze der Welt (Munich, 1921); Das Leben im Ackerboden (Stuttgart, 1923); Die Waage des Lebens (Prien, 1923); Die Welt als Erleben (Dresden, 1923); Plasmatik (Stuttgart, 1923); Wege zur Natur (Stuttgart, 1924); Richtiges Leben (Leipzig, 1924); Die Seele der Pflanze (Berlin, 1924); Grundriss der vergleichenden Biologie (Leipzig, 1924); Das Liebesleben der Pflanzen (Stuttgart, 1926); Harmonie in der Natur (Stuttgart, 1926); Welt, Erde und Menschheit (Berlin, 1928); Der Organismus (Munich, 1928); Naturgesetze der Heimat (Vienna and Leipzig, 1928); So musst du leben (Dresden, 1930); Lebender Braunkohlenwald. Eine Reise durch die heutige Urwelt (Stuttgart, 1932); Von der Arbeit zum Erfolg (Dresden, 1934).

In this connection the works of other authors that followed a nature-philosophical-biological conviction and that were represented in Mies's library need to be mentioned: Hans Andre, Der Wesensunterschied von Pflanze, Tier und Mensch (Habelschwerdt, 1924); Leopold Bauke, Werkzeuge der Tiere (Leipzig, 1924) and Streifzüge durch die Tierwelt (Stuttgart, 1926); Frederick Jacobus Johannes Buytendijk, Die Weisheit der Ameisen (Habelschwerdt, 1925) and Über das Verstehen der Lebenserscheinungen (Habelschwerdt, 1925); Heinrich Frieling, Harmonie und Rhythmus in Natur und Kunst (Munich, 1937); Friedrich Herig, Menschenhand und Kulturwerden (Weimar, 1929); Hermann Kranichfeld, Das teleologische Prinzip in der biologischen Forschung (Habelschwerdt, 1925); Paul Krannhals, Das organische Weltbild (Munich, 1936); Maurice Maeterlinck, Die Intelligenz der Blumen (Jena, 1921); Eugène Nielien Marais, Die Seele der weissen Ameise (Berlin, 1939); Martin Philipson, Die Sinne der Pflanzen (Stuttgart,

1912); Helmuth Plessner, *Die Einheit der Sinne* (Bonn, 1923); Remigius Stölzle, *Der Ursprung des Lebens* (Habelschwerdt, 1925) and *Die Finalität in der Natur* (Habelschwerdt, n.d.); Johann Jakob von Uexküll, *Theoretische Biologie* (Berlin, 1920), *Umweit und Innenwelt der Tiere* (Berlin, 1921), and *Der unsterbliche Geist in der Natur* (Hamburg, 1938); Albert Wigand, *Der Individualismus in der Natur* (Habelschwerdt, 1925).

28
Order form, in the Mies van der Rohe Collection, Special Collections, University of Illinois at Chicago.

29
"Die letzten zwei Jahre eines Bauhäuslers. Auszüge aus Briefen des Bauhäuslers Hans Kessler," in Peter Hahn and Christian Wolsdorf (eds.), *Bauhaus Berlin: Auflösung Dessau 1932. Schliessung Berlin 1933. Bauhäusler and Drittes Reich* (Weingarten and Berlin, 1985), p. 179. The author Francé apparently was on the reading list in the early phase of the Bauhaus, in which anthroposophy and cosmology exercised a strong influence. In a letter of May 12, 1933, Kessler reports of a boat excursion to Paretz that had been organized by Mies for his students in order to show them the manor and farmhouse complex erected by David Gilly in 1796. Apparently Mies did not think it superfluous to introduce Bauhaus students to the tradition of classicism. Kessler characterized the Gilly building as "from the outside a very attractive building due to its serene, severe form." Similar qualities also speak from Mies's architecture.

30
R. H. Francé, *Der Wert der Wissenschaft. Aphorismen zu einer Natur- und Lebensphilosophie* (Zurich and Leipzig, 1908), pp. 98, 101, 100, 119. Mies owned *Goethes morphologische Schriften*, edited with an introduction by Wilhelm Troll (Jena, 1926).

31
The following works of Nietzsche are among Mies's books: *Jenseits von Gut und Böse. Zur Genealogie der Moral*, in Nietzsche's *Werke*, First Part, vol. 7 (Leipzig, 1905). (The name Otto Werner on the title page implies that the book was acquired second-hand. Like no other book in Mies's library, it shows many underlinings done by a ruler, a practice that did not correspond to Mies's reading habits, indicating that these markings were from the previous owner. The handwritten remarks in the margin, too, do not appear to be by Mies's hand.) *Friedrich Nietzsches Briefwechsel mit Erwin Rhode*, ed. Elisabeth Förster-Nietzsche and Fritz Schöll (Leipzig, 1902). (According to the name entry on the cover, the owner of this book was Wolfgang Bruhn, presumably a close relative of Ada Bruhn whom Mies married in 1913.) *Gedichte und Sprüche von Friedrich Nietzsche* (Leipzig, 1919). Mies also owned a copy of Friedrich Muckle's *Friedrich Nietzsche und der Zusammenbruch der Kultur* (Munich and Leipzig, 1921), as well as Richard Edmund Benz's *Die Renaissance. Das Verhängnis der deutschen Kultur* (Jena, 1915).

32
Francé, *Der Wert der Wissenschaft*, pp. 119f.

33
Frederick Jacobus Johannes Buytendijk, *Erziehung zur Demut* (Leipzig, 1928). This profusely underlined book that concerns itself with pedagogical questions gave Mies important guidelines for his concept of Bauhaus methods. In his later "Leitgedanken zur Erziehung in der Baukunst" (Principles for Education in the Building Art), too, one can find Buytendijk's principles.

34
Francé, *Richtiges Leben*, p. 8.

35
Ibid., p. 10.

36
Ibid., p. 20.

37
Ibid., p. 73; compare pp. 69ff.

38
Compare v. W., "Hinweis. Henri Bergson," *Frankfurter Allgemeine Zeitung*, no. 177 (August 3, 1985), p. 6.

39
The following books owned by Mies can be listed in this connection: Max Scheler, *Vom Ewigen im Menschen* (Leipzig, 1921), *Vom Umsturz der Werte* (Leipzig, 1923), *Der Formalismus in der Ethik und die materiale Wertethik* (Halle, 1927), *Mensch und Geschichte* (Zurich, 1929); Henri Bergson, *Schöpferische Entwicklung* (Jena, 1921); Dietrich Heinrich Kerler, *Henri Bergson und das Problem des Verhältnisses zwischen Leib und Seele* (Ulm, 1917); Helmuth Plessner, *Die Einheit der Sinne* (Bonn, 1923), *Die Stufen des Organischen und der Mensch* (Berlin and Leipzig, 1928); Fritz Dreuermann, *Naturerkenntnis, Das Weltbild*, vol. 6, ed. Hans Prinzhorn (Potsdam, 1928); Nicolai Hartmann, *Grundzüge einer Metaphysik der Erkenntnis* (Berlin and Leipzig, 1925), *Ethik* (Berlin, 1926), *Das Problem des geistigen Seins* (Berlin, 1933); A. S. Eddington, *Die Naturwissenschaft auf neuen Bahnen* (Brunswick, 1935); Ernst Mossel, *Vom Geheimnis der Form und der Urform des Seins* (Stuttgart, 1938); and later Jacques Maritain, *The Rights of Man and Natural Law* (1943), *Philosophy of Nature* (New York, 1951), *The Range of Reason* (New York, 1953).

40
See the following books in Mies's library: Nils Bohr, *Atomic Physics and Human Knowledge* (New York, 1958); Erwin Schrödinger, *Meine Weltansicht* (Frankfurt, 1963), *Die Natur und die Griechen* (Hamburg, 1956), *Science and Humanism: Physics in Our Time* (Cambridge, Mass., 1952), *What Is Life? and Other Scientific Essays* (1956), *Mind and Matter* (Cambridge, Mass., 1958); Werner Heisenberg, *Das Naturbild der heutigen Physik* (Hamburg, 1955), *Physics and Philosophy* (New York, 1958), *Physik und Philosophie* (Frankfurt, 1959); Karl Jaspers, *Die geistige Situation der Zeit* (Berlin, 1932), *Die Atombombe und die Zukunft des Menschen* (Munich, 1958); Carl Friedrich von Weizsäcker, *The History of Nature* (Chicago, 1949), *The World View of Physics* (Chicago, 1952), *Zum Weltbild der Physik* (Stuttgart, 1963), *Die Tragweite der Wissenschaft* (Stuttgart, 1966); Reginald O. Kapp, *Towards a Unified Cosmology* (New York, 1960); A. I. Oparin, *The Origin of Life* (New York, 1938).

41
Eduard Spranger, "Lebensformen," in *Festschrift für Alois Riehl, von Freunden und Schülern zu seinem 70. Geburtstag dargebracht* (Halle, 1914), pp. 492f. Mies owned Spranger's books *Lebensformen* (Halle, 1922) and *Gedanken zur Daseinsgestaltung* (Munich, 1954).

42
Rudolf Leinen, *Der Wille zum Ganzen* (Leipzig, 1922); Hans Adolf Eduard Driesch, *Philosophie des Organischen* (Leipzig, 1921); Max Scheler, *Vom Ewigen im Menschen* (Leipzig, 1921).

43
Oswald Spengler, *Der Untergang des Abendlandes* (Munich, 1920–1922), vol. 2, *Welthistorische Perspektiven,* p. 26.

44
Hugo Häring, "kunst und strukturprobleme des bauens," *Zentralblatt der Bauverwaltung,* no. 29 (July 15, 1931), quoted from Jürgen Joedicke (ed.), *das andere bauen* (Stuttgart, 1982), p. 22.

45
Compare Mies's "Gelöste Aufgaben," and his lecture of 1926 (see Appendix I, 5 and 11).

46
Häring, "kunst und strukturprobleme des bauens," p. 22.

47
Hugo Häring to Mies, January 22, 1925, in Library of Congress, General Correspondence.

48
Heinrich Lauterbach and Jürgen Joedicke, *Hugo Häring, Schriften, Entwürfe, Bauten* (Stuttgart and Bern, 1965), p. 10.

49
Hugo Häring, "geometrie und organik. eine studie zur genesis des neuen bauens" (1951), in Joedicke, *das andere bauen,* p. 90.

50
Mies van der Rohe, inaugural address as Director of Architecture at Armour Institute of Technology, 1938, manuscript in the Library of Congress (see Appendix III, 14).

51
Mies to Walter Jakstein, Hamburg, November 14, 1923, in Library of Congress, General Correspondence.

52
Mies van der Rohe, lecture, 1924 (place, date, and occasion unknown), manuscript dated Berlin, June 19, 1924, in the collection of Dirk Lohan, Chicago (see Appendix I, 8).

53
Mies to Walter Jakstein, September 13, 1923, in Library of Congress, General Correspondence.

54
Walter Jakstein to Mies, September 21, 1923, in Library of Congress, General Correspondence.

2   Construction as Promise of Art:
Building Art in the Raw

1
Mies van der Rohe, [Skyscrapers], untitled article in *Frühlicht,* 1, no. 4 (1922), p. 122.

2
Norbert Huse, *Neues Bauen. 1918 bis 1933* (Munich, 1975), p. 42.

3
Hermann Obrist, *Neue Möglichkeiten in der bildenden Kunst* (Munich, 1903); Henry van de Velde, *Die Renaissance im modernen Kunstgewerbe* (Leipzig, 1901) and *Vom Neuen Stil* (Leipzig, 1907); Hermann Muthesius, *Stilcharakter und Baukunst* (Mühlheim and Ruhr, 1902).

4
Karl Scheffler, *Moderne Baukunst* (Leipzig, 1908), p. 16. Scheffler's work is not among the books left by Mies. Mies might have found out about this book, a significant one for the prewar period that exercised a sharp critique of nineteenth-century architecture, while still with Peter Behrens.

5
Compare Josef August Lux, *Ingenieur-Ästhetik* (Munich, 1910), p. 5.

6
Scheffler, *Moderne Baukunst,* p. 16.

7
Mies van der Rohe, [Skyscrapers], p. 122.

8
Van de Velde, *Die Renaissance im modernen Kunstgewerbe,* p. 113.

9
Lux, *Ingenieur-Ästhetik,* pp. 12, 30.

10
Friedrich Nietzsche, "On the Uses and Disadvantages of History," in *Untimely Meditations,* translated by R. J. Hollingdale (Cambridge, 1983), p. 84.

11
Mies van der Rohe, "Baukunst und Zeitwille!" (Building Art and the Will of the Epoch!), manuscript of February 7, 1924, in the collection of Dirk Lohan, Chicago.

12
Naum Gabo and Antoine Pevsner, "Das Realistische Manifest, Moskau, 5. August 1920," in *Tendenzen der Zwanziger Jahre,* exhibition catalog (Berlin, 1977), pp. 1/97–100.

13
De Stijl, 6, nos. 6–7 (1924), in front of p. 72 (compare note 31 of chapter I, above).

14
Mies to Walter Jakstein, September 13, 1923 (in Library of Congress): "On my last visit to Hamburg I did not find you at home. I would have liked to discuss important questions with you; also in respect to impressions I received in Weimar. The entire situation, in spite of everything, is so confused that I find it imperative that a clear-cut separation of viewpoints be established. On Sunday, September 16, important discussions on matters of principle are being held by the *G* people here in Berlin. I will take advantage of this occasion to find out where each one stands and I will announce my own point of view quite clearly and unambiguously and we will soon find out who can stick with us and who not. Those we can count on will then take part in further discussions that will serve to establish a precise program of actions. Particularly the atrocious constructivist formalism, that [illegible] in Weimar and the artistic confusion reigning there, have prompted me to reformulate my point of view in *G,* particularly as part of what I had written had been erroneously left out of the first issue. In the new issue it will say: 'We know no forms, only building problems. The form is not the aim. . . .'" Compare Peter Blake, "A Conversation with Mies," in *Four Great Makers of Modern Architecture* (New York, 1963), p. 102. Blake: "What about the constructivists—the Russian Constructivists? Were you interested in their work?" Mies: "No, I was never interested in formalistic ideas. I was very strongly opposed even to Malevich, you know. Very constructivistic. I was interested in constructions, but not in play with forms."

15
Mies to Theo van Doesburg, August 27, 1923, in Library of Congress.

16
Theo van Doesburg to Mies, September 3, 1923, in Library of Congress.

17
"The skeleton nature of iron construction permits a reduction of wall components and leaves mainly empty spaces. This predominance of variously decorated or draped windows does not go well with artful architecture." Max Dessoir, Ästhetik und allgemeine Kunstwissenschaft (1906), quoted in Herman Sörgel, Theorie der Baukunst (Munich, 1921), p. 521.

18
Curt Gravenkamp, "Mies van der Rohe: Glashaus in Berlin (Projekt Adam 1928)," Das Kunstblatt, 14 (1930), p. 111.

19
Compare the analysis of Norbert Huse, Neues Bauen, p. 42.

20
Scheffler, Moderne Baukunst, p. 15.

21
Ibid., p. 19. Paul Fechter, Die Tragödie der Architektur (Weimar, 1922), p. 208, emphasizes in a comparable argumentation the "strong impression of modern apartment buildings under construction" in which "the base plan of the new life with its ordered multiplicity" announces itself "before it disappears under the rigid enclosure of an inherited but now meaningless decor architecture." Compare in this context also Gropius's 1911 lecture "Monumentale Kunst und Industriebau," reprinted in Karin Wilhelm, Walter Gropius. Industriearchitekt (Brunswick, 1983), pp. 116ff.; and Walter Curt Behrendt, "Das Pathos der Monumentalen," Deutsche Kunst und Dekoration, 34 (1914), pp. 219ff., as well as "Über die Deutsche Baukunst der Gegenwart," Kunst und Künstler, 12 (1914), pp. 373ff.

22
Caption to the Friedrichstrasse skyscraper in G, no. 4 (March 1926), p. 7.

23
Adolf Behne, "Kritik des Werkbundes," Die Tat, 9, no. 1 (1917), quoted in Werkbund-Archiv, Jahrbuch, vol. 1 (Berlin, 1972), p. 120.

24
Walter Gropius, "Welche Forderungen muss man von Seiten des Privatarchitekten und Schaffenden Künstlers an eine Reform der Technischen Hochschule stellen?," quoted in Wilhelm, Walter Gropius, p. 89.

25
Mies van der Rohe, "Gelöste Aufgaben. Eine Forderung an das Bauwesen" (Solved Tasks: A Challenge for Our Building Industry), Die Bauwelt, 14 (1923), p. 719.

26
See Reyner Banham, Theory and Design in the First Machine Age (London, 1960), p. 97.

27
Ludwig Hilberseimer, Berliner Architektur der 20er Jahre (Mainz, 1967), p. 20: "One of my friends had the good luck to be able to travel and he brought back from Paris Le Corbusier's book Vers une architecture. It was something special to own this book instead of merely hear about it." Possibly it was Mies who brought this book back from Paris. Opportunity would have offered itself on occasion of the Stijl exhibition in Paris in the fall of 1923, in which Mies also exhibited. This publication might also have alerted Mies to the publication G. Vers une architecture is represented in Mies's library by a copy of the second edition (Paris, 1924), as well as the German version Kommende Baukunst, translated and edited by Hans Hildebrandt (Berlin and Leipzig, 1926), also a second edition. Mies also owned copies of Le Corbusier's Städtebau (Berlin and Leipzig, 1929); Une Maison—Un Palais. A la recherche d'une unité architecturale (Paris, 1928), with a dedication by the author: "à Mies van der Rohe très sympathique-ment, 1928"; and Aircraft (1935).

28
Le Corbusier, Towards a New Architecture, translated by Frederick Etchells (New York, 1976), pp. 83, 41.

29
Compare ibid., the chapter "Regulating Lines" with two illustrations on pp. 66, 67 of a "primitive temple." In The City of Tomorrow (Cambridge, Mass., 1971) Le Corbusier also refers to "the native hut," under the heading "Order" (p. 24). Refer also to Joseph Rykwert, On Adam's House in Paradise: The Idea of the Primitive Hut in Architectural History (New York, 1972).

30
An impression of the one-sided interpretation of Le Corbusier in Germany in the twenties, which turned mainly on the phrase "machine for living," can be gained from the discussion between Roger Ginsburg and Walter Riezler on the theme of purpose and spiritual attitude, occasioned by the debates about Mies's Tugendhat House and published in Die Form, 6, no. 11 (1931).

31
Carl Einstein, "An die Geistigen!," Die Pleite, no. 1 (Berlin, 1919) quoted from Carl Einstein, Werke Band 2, 1919–1928 edited by Marion Schmid (Berlin, 1981), p. 16: "An aim that is too essential to permit intellectuals to dismember it. Decorative glibness covers up for true decisions. We stand by the masses, we are on the march with the simple, uncompromising ones, to a nearby, necessary task. Your complex nuances do not sit well with us. Simple man is fanatical, we reject those second thoughts of the multilateral, hovering intellect. We reject allegory and exaggerated metaphors. Aim and action have long since exceeded the historically burdened, all-too-differentiated ideology of the conditioned bourgeois and his fools. Individualism is finished. . . . The relative is gone. . . ." Walter Gropius formulated his abdication from the old order in quite similar terms: "The intellectual bourgeois of the old kingdom—lukewarm, listless, of sluggish thinking, pompous, and miseducated—has proven his inability to become the bearer of a new German culture. . . . New layers of the populace, not yet spiritually unleashed, are pushing up from the depth. They are the target of our hopes." (Gropius, "Baukunst im freien Volksstaat," in E. Drahn and E. Friedberg, Deutscher Revolutionsalmanach für das Jahr 1919, p. 134.)

32
Mies van der Rohe, "Baukunst und Zeitwille!"

33
Ludwig Hilberseimer, "Konstruktion und Form," G, no. 3 (June 1924), p. 14.

34
Le Corbusier, Towards a New Architecture, p. 195, caption to an illustration: "The Parthenon—Here is something to arouse emotion. We are in the inexorable realm of the mechanical. There are no symbols attached to these forms: they provoke

definite sensations; there is no need of a key in order to understand them. Brutality, intensity, the utmost sweetness, delicacy and great strength. And who discovered the combination of these elements? An inventor of genius. These stones lay inert in the quarries of Pentelicus, unshaped. To group them thus needed not an engineer, but a great sculptor."

35
Mies van der Rohe, lecture manuscript (Chicago, occasion and date unknown), pp. 3, 4 (see Appendix IV, 5).

36
Behrendt, "Über die deutsche Baukunst der Gegenwart," p. 373.

37
Lux, *Ingenieur-Ästhetik,* p. 4.

38
Mies van der Rohe, miscellaneous notes to lectures, manuscript in Library of Congress (see Appendix IV, 6).

39
Werner Gräff, "Ingenieurbauten," *G,* no. 2 (September 1923), p. 4.

40
Werner Gräff, "Es kommt der neue Ingenieur," *G,* no. 1 (July 1923), p. 4.

41
Werner Lindner (in cooperation with Georg Steinmetz), *Die Ingenieurbauten in ihrer guten Gestaltung* (Berlin, 1923), published by the Deutscher Bund Heimatschutz and Deutscher Werkbund in cooperation with the Verein Deutscher Ingenieure and the Deutsche Gesellschaft für Bauingenieurwesen. Lindner later resumed this resonant theme with his *Bauten der Technik. Ihre Form und Wirkung* (Berlin, 1927), published by the Bund Deutscher Heimatschutz and Verein Deutscher Ingenieure.

42
Lindner, *Die Ingenieurbauten,* p. 8.

43
Compare Mies's 1938 inaugural address at the Armour Institute of Technology as well as "Leitgedanken zur Erziehung in der Baukunst" (Principles for Education in the Building Art) of 1965 (see Appendix III, 14, and IV, 17).

44
Lindner, *Die Ingenieurbauten,* p. 87.

45
Ibid., p. 54.

46
Mies van der Rohe to Hermann von Wedderkop (publisher of *Der Querschnitt*), January 18, 1924:

Dear Mr. von Wedderkop. I have in the meantime surveyed all obtainable illustrations of new structures and must admit that the engineer buildings are, almost exclusively, the only structures that reveal the spirit of our time. I therefore suggest including 3 salient illustrations from Ingenieurbauten, *published by Wasmuth. After consulting with the publisher, I have been able to obtain 3 plates at the normal borrowing fee. In case you also want to include one or another of my works, I would be glad to supply you with plates. It would certainly be interesting and sensational to show in this context the architectonic possibilities of our time and demonstrate that the identity of construction and form is an absolute precondition for architectural work. I have the impression that you*

yourself were not convinced by my works. I nevertheless suggest them once more to you for publication as I know of no other works that are so elementarily grasped as buildings and that are so far removed from all that dusty magic without falling into the mistake of artistry.

47
Lindner, *Die Ingenieurbauten,* pp. 11, 87.

48
Ibid., pp. 10, 12.

49
Mies gave a lecture in Bremen on November 27, 1925, under the title "The Spirit of the New Building Art" (manuscript lost). The citation quoted here is derived from a paraphrase of the theme of the lecture in a thank-you letter from the pupils of the Bremen Kunstgewerbeschule, December 11, 1925, in the Library of Congress. (On Mies's lecture in Bremen, see part I, note 43, above.)

50
Piet Mondrian, "Die neue Gestaltung in der Malerei" (1917–1918), quoted in Hagen Bächler and Herbert Letsch (eds.), *De Stijl. Schriften und Manifeste* (Leipzig and Weimar, 1984), pp. 67f.

51
Lindner, *Die Ingenieurbauten,* pp. 11, 12.

52
Erich Mendelsohn, *Amerika. Bilderbuch eines Architekten* (Berlin, 1926), p. 22.

53
Walter Riezler, "Die Baukunst am Scheidewege," in Paul Tillich (ed.), *Kairos. Zur Geisteslage und Geisteswendung* (Darmstadt, 1926), p. 266.

54
Victor Wallerstein, "Negerplastik," *Das Kunstblatt,* February 1917, quoted in Rolf-Peter Baake (ed.), *Carl Einstein, Werke,* vol. 1 (Berlin, 1980), p. 508.

55
Carl Einstein had studied art history under Heinrich Wölfflin and philosophy under Alois Riehl between 1904 and 1908 and wrote in the early twenties for the internationally renowned art journals *Der Querschnitt* and *Das Kunstblatt,* in which Mies, too, published two of his pronouncements. Einstein's *Negerplastik* was published in 1915 (2d ed., Munich, 1920). The duality of orientations that anchored itself in both the primitive and the modern was also in evidence in Einstein's work. One can view *Europa Almanach* (Potsdam, 1925), published by Paul Westheim and Carl Einstein, as a pendant to this work. It practically delivered an anthology of the European avant-garde. Le Corbusier, J. J. P. Oud, Kasimir Malevich, and others were here represented. For the influence of primitivism on the art of the twentieth century, see the exhibition catalog *Primitivism in 20th Century Art* (Museum of Modern Art, New York, 1984), and compare the review of the German-language version by Werner Spies, "Das verlorene Paradies—Anstoss der Erkenntnis," *Frankfurter Allgemeine Zeitung,* no. 255 (November 10, 1984), p. 25.

56
Sergius Ruegenberg, "Ludwig Mies van der Rohe 1886–1969," *Deutsche Bauzeitung,* 103 (1969), p. 660, suggests that Mies took samples from the book of Frobenius for the "only slide lecture in Berlin." Ruegenberg, former co-worker of Mies between 1925 and 1931, further mentions a "book on the prehistory of mankind," *Alteuropa,* to which Mies owed con-

siderable stimulation. This perhaps referred to R. H. Francé's *Die Kultur von Alt-Europa* (Berlin, 1923), which can be found among Mies's books in Chicago. Ruegenberg furthermore has recounted that Hugo Häring called Mies's attention to Carl Schluchardt's *Alteuropa in seiner Kultur- und Stilentwicklung* (Berlin, 1919). In this context the following titles from Mies's library are worth mentioning: Edgar Dacque, *Urwelt, Sage und Menschheit* (Munich, 1924); Moritz Hoernes, *Urgeschichte der bildenden Kunst in Europa* (Vienna, 1925); Richard Uhden, *Erdteile und Kulturen* (Leipzig, 1925); Friedrich Herig, *Menschenhand und Kulturwerden* (Weimar, 1929). Ruegenberg carries Mies's assimilation of primitive building (the African mud hut) to the point that he sees it as the model for the Barcelona Pavilion: "He [Mies] showed the heavy African mud roof on narrow wood supports; it was a model for Barcelona—the construction of the pavilion. The onyx wall in the pavilion corresponded to the freestanding cult wall that, detached from the ceiling, was the focal point of the African room." Ruegenberg also pointed to the designs by Schinkel displayed in Mies's office (the volume *Sommerresidenz des russischen Zaren in Orianda auf der Krim*, drafted in 1838, published in 1878 in four editions: it "lay there forever and was never removed," recounts Ruegenberg). See also Wolf Tegethoff, *Mies van der Rohe. Die Villen und Landhausprojekte* (Krefeld and Essen, 1981), p. 107, as well as his "Orianda-Berlin. Das Vorbild Schinkels im Werk Mies van der Rohes," *Zeitschrift des Deutschen Vereins für Kulturwissenschaft,* 35 (1981), pp. 174–184.

57
Compare Hans Sedlmayr, *Gefahr und Hoffnung des Technischen Zeitalters* (Salzburg, 1970), p. 42.

58
See Vittorio Magnago Lampugnani, "Die abwesende Sprache der Technik. Eine Kritik des Mythos der positivistischen Architektur," in *Freibeuter, Vierteljahrsschrift für Kultur und Politik,* no. 11 (Berlin, 1982), p. 36. Lampugnani refers to the Barcelona Pavilion of Mies as "in this context emblematic." "Instead of setting up a futuristic lightweight building of glued-together short-lived materials or from disassemblable elements, something that would have corresponded to the task, the former co-worker of Behrens built a composition of chrome supports, onyx and glass panels, as well as a wall dressed in travertine, on a heavy travertine base that calls to mind Schinkel, and all beneath a flat ferroconcrete roof—a composition that was as luxurious as it was technically uninteresting. If one were to measure its quality against its degree of constructive innovation, the Barcelona Pavilion would never be included in any architectural history books—something that applies to all great works of the architectural avant-garde of the twenties."

59
William H. Jordy, *American Buildings and Their Architects* (New York, 1972), pp. 221f.

60
Friedrich Nietzsche, "On the Uses and Disadvantages of History," in *Untimely Meditations,* translated by R. J. Hollingdale (Cambridge, 1983), p. 93.

61
Herman Sörgel, *Theorie der Baukunst* (1918), vol. 1, *Architektur-Ästhetik* (Munich, 1921), pp. 256f.

62
Ibid., pp. 174, 175, 176.

63
Lux, *Ingenieur-Ästhetik,* p. 8.

64
Ibid., p. 45.

65
Sörgel, *Theorie der Baukunst,* p. 257.

66
Hilberseimer, *Berliner Architektur der 20er Jahre,* p. 61. For the discussion of Nietzsche in Mies's circle of friends, Hilberseimer appears especially revealing. In his *Grosstadt-Architektur* (Stuttgart, 1927), Hilberseimer gives the last word to Nietzsche. The last sentence of the concluding chapter "Das allgemeine Gesetz" reads: "To form large masses by suppressing multiplicity is what Nietzsche understood as style: the general, the law, is respected and emphasized, the exception is pushed aside, the nuance wiped out, law becomes master, chaos is forced to take on form; logical, unambiguous, mathematics, law" (ibid., p. 103).

67
In the Bauhaus, too, there were many admirers of Nietzsche. Jürgen Krause, *"Märtyrer" und "Prophet." Studien zum Nietzsche-Kult in der bildenden Kunst der Jahrhundertwende* (Berlin and New York, 1984), p. 216, points particularly to Oskar Schlemmer, who called Nietzsche the philosopher of his youth. It is quite conceivable that Schlemmer's Bauhaus emblem of 1923 was intended to symbolize the phrase "right-angled in body and soul."

3   The Building Master of Today

1
Mies van der Rohe, Lecture (1924), manuscript of June 19, 1924, in the collection of Dirk Lohan (see Appendix I, 8).

2
Compare Mies van der Rohe, "Über Sinn und Aufgabe der Kritik" (On the Meaning and Task of Criticism), 1930 (see Appendix III, 6). Mies stood all his life by his conviction that the building art and the civilization of his century were a "chaos" to which one first had to bring order. Compare Peter Blake, "A Conversation with Mies," in *Four Great Makers of Modern Architecture* (New York, 1963), and excerpts from an "Interview des Bayrischen Rundfunks anlässlich des 80. Geburtstages von Mies," *Der Architekt,* 15, no. 10 (1966), p. 324.

3
Walter Gropius, *Internationale Architektur,* the First Bauhausbuch (Munich, 1925), pp. 6ff.

4
Th. van Doesburg, H. Richter, El Lissitzky, K. Maes, and M. Burchartz, "Konstruktivistische Internationale schöpferische Arbeitsgemeinschaft" (manifesto), Weimar, September 1922, in Hagen Bächler and Herbert Letsch (eds.), *De Stijl. Schriften und Manifeste zu einem theoretischen Konzept ästhetischer Umweltgestaltung* (Leipzig and Weimar, 1984), p. 52. Compare also "Manifesto I" of *De Stijl,* 1918 (ibid., p. 49): "The artists of today, driven by the same awareness, have participated in the spiritual realm in the world war against the individual, the arbitrary. They sympathize with all who fight, spiritually or materially, for the formation of an international unity in life, art, and culture."

5
"Neues Bauen" (review of Mies's lecture "Die Voraussetzungen baukünstlerischen Schaffens"), *Berliner Börsenkurier,* March 1, 1928 (see Appendix III, 1, addendum).

6
Compare the review by Christian Wolsdorff of Wolf Tegethoff's *Mies van der Rohe. Die Villen und Landhausprojekte,* in *Die Kunstchronik,* 31 (1984), pp. 407f.

7
See *Der Neubau,* 6, no. 11 (1924), p. 128.

8
Mies van der Rohe, "Über die Form in der Architektur" (On Form in Architecture), *Die Form,* 2, no. 2 (1927), p. 59.

9
Mies van der Rohe, manuscript of June 19, 1924 (see Appendix I, 8).

10
Adolf Behne, *Neues Wohnen—Neues Bauen* (Leipzig, 1927), pp. 15, 17. Compare the entry in Mies's notebook, page 6, that apparently refers to the publication of Walter Curt Behrendt's *Der Sieg des neuen Baustils* (Stuttgart, 1927): "One speaks of the victory of the new building art. I must say that this is entirely out of the question. We have barely begun. In only a few places is the new land visible. What is victorious is perhaps a new formalism. We can only talk of a new building art when [the battle—*crossed out*] new life forms have been formed." (See Appendix II.)

11
This passage reveals the typical fashion in which Mies van der Rohe gradually attempted to objectify his ideas. In a lecture of 1926 (see Appendix I, 11) is a passage speaking of the "chaos of conflicting forces" that is nearly identical to a passage in a lecture of 1924 (see Appendix I, 8); but the later text is made more specific by the addition of a phrase: "One will have to understand that building art as spatial expression is spiritually connected to its times" (1924); "One will have to understand that building art is always the spatial execution of spiritual decisions" (1926).

12
Naum Gabo and Antoine Pevsner, "Das Realistische Manifest, Moskau, 5 August 1920," quoted from *Tendenzen der Zwanziger Jahre,* exhibition catalog (Berlin, 1977), p. 1/100.

13
Louis Henry Sullivan, *Kindergarten Chats and Other Writings* (New York, 1918), p. 46. Compare also August Endell, *Die Schönheit der grossen Stadt* (Stuttgart, 1908), pp. 13ff., chapter "Die Liebe zum Heute und Hier."

14
Mies van der Rohe, "Wohin gehen wir nun?" (Where Do We Go from Here?), *Bauen und Wohnen,* 15 (1960), p. 391.

15
Mies van der Rohe, "Baukunst und Zeitwille!" (Building Art and the Will of the Epoch!), manuscript of February 7, 1924, in the collection of Dirk Lohan (see Appendix I, 6). The following three paragraphs also draw on this text.

16
Mies van der Rohe, notebook of 1928 (Museum of Modern Art, Manuscripts Folder I), p. 7 (see Appendix II).

17
Mies van der Rohe, lecture manuscript of March 17, 1926, in the collection of Dirk Lohan, Chicago (see Appendix I, 11).

18
Ibid.

19
For this paragraph, see Mies van der Rohe, "Baukunst und Zeitwille!," manuscript of February 7, 1924.

20
J. J. P. Oud, "Über die zukünftige Baukunst und ihre architektonischen Möglichkeiten," *Frühlicht,* 1, no. 4 (1922), p. 199.

21
G, no. 5/6 (1926), unpaginated: "The reality of history is not spelled out by 'the facts' but is—constructed. What matters here is consequentiality.—Art History!? What is its point of view, what does it say? Justice toward the individual! Good—but the establishment of a unified view of the world, of a larger context—in order that 'history' can render a world, a world essence the will and expression of which is art—that would be art history—and one, furthermore, that would do justice to living art. . . . You who make art history, listen to this advice: Destroy your manuscripts! Write manifestos for us! Live for the cause of today!—insofar as you can see it. Learn to see reality—insofar as you even want it, and learn to want reality."

22
Compare in this context Josef August Lux, *Ingenieur-Ästhetik* (Munich, 1910), p. 32.

23
Eduard Spanger, *Lebensformen* (3d ed., Halle, 1922), p. 289.

24
Friedrich Nietzsche, "On the Uses and Disadvantages of History," in *Untimely Meditations,* translated by R. J. Hollingdale (Cambridge, 1983), p. 75.

25
Mies van der Rohe, draft of a letter (presumably around 1927), in Museum of Modern Art, Manuscripts Folder 2 (see Appendix I, 17).

26
Mies van der Rohe, lecture at the Immermannbund, Düsseldorf, manuscript of March 14, 1927, in the collection of Dirk Lohan, Chicago (see Appendix I, 16).

27
Friedrich Nietzsche, *Twilight of the Idols,* in *The Works of Friedrich Nietzsche,* translated by Thomas Common (New York, 1896), vol 11, p. 171. See also *The Antichrist,* in ibid., pp. 343–44.

28
See Nietzsche's commentary on the *Twilight of the Idols* in *Ecce Homo* (translated by Clifton P. Fadiman in the Modern Library *Philosophy of Nietzsche* [New York, 1954], p. 868).

29
Hans Richter, "Der neue Baumeister," *Qualität,* 4, no. 1/2 (1925), pp. 7ff. Compare in this context Otto Wagner, *Die Baukunst unsere Zeit* (1896; 4th ed., Vienna, 1914), pp. 33, 137: "The task of art, however, including modern art, has remained the same as it has always been. The art of our time must bring us modern forms created by ourselves, corresponding to our abilities, our doings and nondoings. . . . The art apostles that struggle toward the aims set out here will become what architects of all epochs have always been, children of their time; their works will carry their own characteristics. . . . In their works, the world will glimpse its own reflection and they will be characterized by self-confidence, individuality, and conviction, the trademarks of the artists of all epochs."

30
Mies van der Rohe, "Industrielles Bauen" (Industrial Building), *G,* no. 3 (June 1924), pp. 8ff.

31
Mies van der Rohe, "Baukunst und Zeitwille!," manuscript of February 7, 1924.

32
Mies van der Rohe, "Industrielles Bauen."

33
Compare Fritz Neumeyer, "The Workers' Housing of Peter Behrens," in Tilmann Buddensieg and Henning Rogge, *Industriekultur: Peter Behrens and the AEG*, trans. Iain Boyd Whyte (Cambridge, Mass., 1984), pp. 124–135.

34
Compare Reginald R. Isaacs, *Walter Gropius. Der Mensch und sein Werk*, vol. 1 (Frankfurt, 1985), p. 94.

35
Peter Behrens, "Die Gruppenbauweisen," *Wasmuths Monatshefte für Baukunst*, (1919/1920), pp. 122ff.

36
Mies van der Rohe, "Industrielles Bauen."

37
On this, see Sigfried Giedion, *Die Herrschaft der Mechanisierung* (1948; rpt., Frankfurt, 1982), pp. 141ff.: "Das Fliessband im 20. Jahrhundert."

38
Henry Ford, *My Life and Work* (New York, 1922), p. 3. Frederick Taylor pointed to the expansion of mechanization in the foreword of his book *The Principles of Scientific Management* (New York, 1911), arguing that the principles of scientific management are applicable "with equal justification and with equal success to all human activities."

39
Ford, *My Life and Work*, pp. 13–14.

40
Le Corbusier, *Towards a New Architecture*, translated by Frederick Etchells (New York, 1976), p. 219. Ibid., pp. 215.: "The war has shaken us all up. Contractors have brought new plant, ingenious, patient and rapid. Will the yard soon be a factory? There is talk of houses made in a mould by pouring in liquid concrete from above, completed in one day as you would fill a bottle. One thing leads to another, and as so many cannons, airplanes, lorries and wagons had been made in factories, someone asked the question: 'Why not make houses?'" On the relationship of Le Corbusier to the automobile and the "crossing between avant-garde and industry," see Stanislaus von Moos, "Le Corbusier und Gabriel Voisin," in Stanislaus von Moos and Chris Smeenk (eds.), *Avant-Garde und Industrie* (Delft, 1983), pp. 77ff., as well as Stanislaus von Moos, "Standard und Elite. Le Corbusier, die Industrie und der 'Esprit Nouveau,'" in Tilmann Buddensieg (ed.), *Die nützlichen Künste* (Berlin, 1981), pp. 306ff.

41
Ford, *My Life and Work*, p. 186.

42
Ibid., p. 19.

43
Mies van der Rohe, "Industrielles Bauen."

44
Gottfried Semper, *Vorläufige Bemerkungen über bemalte Architektur und Plastik bei den Alten* (Altona, 1834), quoted from Gottfried Semper, *Wissenschaft, Industrie und Kunst und andere Schriften* (Mainz and Berlin, 1966; Neue Bauhausbücher), p. 16.

45
Mies van der Rohe, "Baukunst und Zeitwille!," manuscript of February 7, 1924.

46
Mies van der Rohe, "Bauen" (Building), *G*, no. 2 (September 1923), p. 1.

47
Le Corbusier, *Towards a New Architecture*, p. 171.

48
H. P. Berlage, *Grundlagen und Entwicklung der Architektur* (Berlin, 1908), p. 116.

49
Mies van der Rohe, "Bauen."

50
Letter from Mies to Dr. Ing. E. Förster, Hamburg, January 12, 1924, in Library of Congress.

51
Henry van de Velde, "Amo," extract from "Vernunftgemässe Schönheit," in *Essays* (Leipzig, 1910), p. 119: "I love the machines, they are like creatures of a higher phase of development."

52
Theo van Doesburg, El Lissitzky, and H. Richter, *Erklärung der internationalen Fraktion der Konstruktivisten* (Düsseldorf, 1922), in Bächler and Letsch, *De Stijl. Schriften und Manifeste*, p. 58.

53
Compare Theo van Doesburg and Cornelis van Eesteren, "Auf dem Weg zu einer kollektiven Konstruktion," in Bächler and Letsch, *De Stijl. Schriften und Manifeste*, pp. 222ff.: "We have to realize that art and life are no longer separate domains. For that reason, the idea of 'art' as an illusion separated from life must disappear. The word 'art' has lost its meaning for us. In its place we demand an environment constructed according to creative laws.... Today one can only talk of the constructors of the new life."

54
Mies van der Rohe, lecture manuscript of June 19, 1924 (see Appendix I, 8).

V From Material through Purpose to Idea: The Long Path to the Building Art

1 Departure from the Will of the Epoch: Building Art as Spiritual Decision

1
Kenneth Frampton, *Modern Architecture, A Critical History* (New York, 1980), pp. 161ff. Under the heading "Mies van der Rohe and the Significance of Facts," Frampton summarizes Mies's work in the period from 1921 to 1933, without, however, explicitly dealing with the change of ideology that became noticeable around 1926.

2
Mies van der Rohe, "Bürohaus" (Office Building), manuscript of August 2, 1923, intended for the *Deutsche Allgemeine Zeitung*, in the Museum of Modern Art (see Appendix I, 3).

3
Theo van Doesburg, "Malerei und Plastik," *De Stijl*, no. 78 (1926–1928), p. 82, quoted from Hagen Bächler and Herbert

Letsch (eds.), *De Stijl. Schriften und Manifeste zu einem theoretischen Konzept ästhetischer Umweltgestaltung* (Leipzig and Weimar, 1984), p. 206. "The elementarist is a spiritual rebel, a rabble-rouser. . . . He does not break with form on a specific half-a-yard-square painting surface, he breaks with form irrevocably on the gigantic scale of human tragedy. He knows: Man is a tragic being that can live life only if supported by tradition and by means of constant repetition. He knows that this precondition, this grace, is based on a lunacy once called religious belief, once duty and honor. If one annuls this lunatic misunderstanding, one simultaneously annuls the vital basis of the bourgeoisie and of their entire superstructure."

4
J. J. P. Oud, *Holländische Architektur* (Munich, 1926, Bauhausbücher, vol. 10; new ed., Mainz and Berlin, 1976), p. 39.

5
Gottfried Semper, *Wissenschaft, Industrie und Kunst. Vorschläge zur Anregung nationalen Kunstgefühls* (Brunswick, 1852), quoted from Gottfried Semper, *Wissenschaft, Industrie und Kunst und andere Schriften* (Mainz and Berlin, 1966; Neue Bauhausbücher), pp. 43ff.

6
Kasimir Malevich, *Die gegenstandslose Welt* (Munich, 1927; Bauhausbücher, vol. 11), p. 59.

7
Le Corbusier, *Towards a New Architecture,* translated by Frederick Etchells (New York, 1976), p. 33.

8
Gottfried Semper, *Vorläufige Bemerkungen über bemalte Architektur und Plastik bei den Alten* (Altona, 1834), quoted from Semper, *Wissenschaft, Industrie und Kunst und andere Schriften,* p. 17 "May the material speak for itself and appear undraped, in that form and under those conditions that experience and science have tested and proven the most suitable. May brick appear as brick, wood as wood, iron as iron, each according to its own law of statics. This is the true simplicity based on which one can then devote oneself lovingly to the innocent needlepoint of decoration." Mies's "building" attempted to turn this principle into fact—albeit without that concession to decor made in the last phrase.

9
Josef August Lux, *Ingenieur-Ästhetik* (Munich, 1910), pp. 10, 44: "According to Semper, the strength of art derives from the weakness and the resistance of the material. Without doubt, a building style is largely determined by the material, with stone and wood each determining their own stylistic laws. . . . From an artistic point of view this means that even beyond immediate function, everything is justified that is permitted by the characteristics of the building material."

10
Theo van Doesburg, "Von der Neuen Ästhetik zur materiellen Verwirklichung" (lecture, Weimar, 1922), published in *De Stijl,* no. 1 (1923), pp. 10–14, quoted from Bächler and Letsch, *De Stijl. Schriften und Manifeste,* pp. 183ff.

11
Ibid.

12
Mies van der Rohe, "Bauen" (Building), *G,* no. 2 (September 1923), p. 1.

13
Le Corbusier, *Towards a New Architecture,* p. 18.

14
Theo van Doesburg, "Von der Neuen Ästhetik," p. 184. Le Corbusier expresses a similar condemnation (*Towards a New Architecture,* pp. 18–19): "Our architects are disillusioned and unemployed, boastful or peevish. This is because there will soon be nothing more for them to do. *We no longer have the money* to erect historical souvenirs. At the same time, we have got to wash! Our engineers provide for these things and they will be our builders." Ibid., p. 101: "There is one profession and one only, namely architecture, in which progress is not considered necessary, where laziness is enthroned, and in which the reference is always to yesterday."

15
Piet Mondrian, contribution to the catalog *Abstrakte Kunst* (Amsterdam, 1938), quoted from H. L. C. Jaffé, *De Stijl 1917–1931* (Berlin, 1965), p. 168.

16
Compare Ludwig Hilberseimer, "Konstruktion und Form," *G,* no. 3 (June 1924), p. 14: "Concrete and ferroconcrete are building materials that set almost no limit to the fantasy of the architect. By that we do not refer to their plasticity, the possibility of overcoming, by means of pouring, all material resistance; quite the contrary: the constructive consequences, the possibility of producing a totally homogeneous building, the fusion of supporting and supported elements, the possibility of sharp delimitation and the possibility of working without wall and roof articulation."

17
Curt Gravenkamp, "Mies van der Rohe. Glashaus in Berlin (Projekt Adam)," *Das Kunstblatt,* 14 (1930), p. 112.

18
Mies van der Rohe, "Baukunst und Zeitwille!" (Building Art and the Will of the Epoch), manuscript version in the collection of Dirk Lohan, Chicago (see Appendix I, 6).

19
Mies van der Rohe, lecture manuscript of June 19, 1924 (see Appendix I, 8).

20
J. J. P. Oud, "Wohin führt das Neue Bauen: Kunst und Standard," *Die Form,* 3 (1928), p. 61.

21
See Mies van der Rohe, inaugural address as Director of Architecture at Armour Institute of Technology, 1938, manuscript in the Library of Congress (see Appendix III, 14).

22
Mies van der Rohe, notebook of 1928 (Museum of Modern Art, Manuscripts Folder 1), p. ?? (see Appendix II).

23
Mies van der Rohe, manuscript for a lecture on art criticism, 1930 (Museum of Modern Art, Manuscripts Folder 4), p. 5 (see Appendix III, 6).

24
Mies van der Rohe, lecture manuscript, Chicago, around 1950 (in Library of Congress), p. 4 (see Appendix IV, 5).

25
J. J. P. Oud, "Über die zukünftige Baukunst und ihre architektonischen Möglichkeiten," *Frühlicht,* 1, no. 4 (1922), rpt. in Bruno Taut, *Frühlicht 1920–1922* (Berlin, 1963), p. 206. In this issue of *Frühlicht* appeared Mies's article "Hochhäuser" (Skyscrapers).

26
Mies van der Rohe, "Bürohaus" (Office Building), G, no. 1 (July 1923), p. 1.

27
For example, the dentil-like line adjacent to the glass skyscraper on the polygonal ground plan (see above, p. 8).

28
In the rendering of the skyscrapers, the formal interest evidently prevailed, for Mies did not show the support system that, with its stenciled regularity, would have schematized the poetic form. He did not publish a plan study in which he attempted to include the supports in the rounded contour of the floor-level plans. This shows the contradictions that presented themselves between free form and regularity of construction.

29
In the lecture manuscript of June 19, 1924 (Appendix I, 8), Mies responds to a criticism that his skyscraper "is not formed, but remains restricted to the schematic treatment." Mies attempts to deal with this reproach, but halfway through his defense he interrupts his argument and, as was his practice at that time, allows the circumstances to speak for themselves: "This reproach is typical. It arises out of another manner of thinking in which one still, even if with modern architectonic concepts . . . [sentence incomplete]. What is overlooked is that the schematic is implied by the task and therefore finds its expression in the form-giving."

30
Leon Battista Alberti, De re aedificatoria, book IX, chap. V.

31
Mies van der Rohe, ["Hochhäuser"] (Skyscrapers), Frühlicht, 1, no. 4 (1922), pp. 122–124.

32
Mies van der Rohe, foreword to Bau und Wohnung, published by the Deutsche Werkbund (Stuttgart, 1927), p. 7. (See Appendix I, 14.)

33
Mies van der Rohe, "Zu meinem Block" (Concerning My Block), in ibid., p. 77.

34
Mies van der Rohe, foreword to Bau und Wohnung, p. 7.

35
Mies van der Rohe, "Industrielles Bauen" (Industrial Building), G, no. 3 (June 1924), pp. 8–13.

36
Mies van der Rohe, introductory remarks to the special issue "Werkbundausstellung: Die Wohnung," Die Form, 2, no. 9 (1927), p. 257. (See Appendix I, 15.)

37
Wohnung der Neuzeit. Denkschrift des Deutschen Werkbundes (Stuttgart, 1926), quoted from Jürgen Joedicke and Christian Plath, Die Weissenhofsiedlung (Stuttgart, 1968; 2d enl. ed., 1977), pp. 10, 11.

38
Mies van der Rohe, foreword to the official catalog of the Werkbund exhibition "Die Wohnung" (Stuttgart, 1927), p. 5 (see Appendix I, 13).

39
Mies van der Rohe, foreword to Bau und Wohnung, p. 7.

40
Ibid.

41
Paul Bonatz already used the comparison "suburb of Jerusalem" in 1929. See Joedicke and Plath, Die Weissenhofsiedlung, p. 63. On the Weissenhof project see Edgar Wedepohl, "Die Weissenhof-Siedlung der Werkbundausstellung 'Die Wohnung,' Stuttgart 1927," Wasmuths Monatsheft für Baukunst, 11 (1927), pp. 391–402. See also Norbert Huse, Neues Bauen 1918 bis 1933, Moderne Architektur in der Weimarer Republik (Munich, 1975), pp. 73–77.

42
There was a full-page illustration, with plans, of Behrens's Project for a Terrace House in Bau und Wohnung, p. 18. Besides Oud, Behrens, and Taut, Mies in his work at Weissenhof made use of Le Corbusier, Ludwig Hilberseimer, Walter Gropius, Mart Stam, Josef Frank, Richard Döcker, Victor Bourgeois, Adolf G. Schneck, Adolf Rading, Hans Poelzig, Hans Scharoun, and Max Taut.

43
Mies van der Rohe, lecture, 1926, occasion and location unknown, manuscript of March 17, 1926, in the collection of Dirk Lohan, Chicago (see Appendix I, 11).

44
Mies van der Rohe, "Über die Form in der Architektur" (On Form in Architecture), Die Form, 2, no. 2 (1927), p. 59 (see Appendix I, 12).

45
Dietrich Heinrich Kerler, Weltwille und Wertwille. Linien des Systems der Philosophie (Leipzig, 1925), pp. 44, 46f., 42.

46
Ibid., pp. 47–49.

47
Mies presumably meant the French philosopher Henri Bergson, whose book Schöpferische Entwicklung (Jena, 1921) he owned. Bergson, philosopher of life associated with the term "élan vital," was popular in Germany around 1920. Compare Max Scheler, Versuche einer Philosophie des Lebens—Nietzsche—Dilthey—Bergson, in his Gesammelte Werke, vol. 3 (Bern, 1955), pp. 323ff. In order to arrive at a "philosophy of the organic," Bergson expounded a philosophy of life emphasizing the perceptive function of feeling and intuition in opposition to the prevailing overemphasis on the intellect. The extraordinary position Mies assigned to the term "life" as original, comprehensive quantity and value may also be due to Bergson's influence. Possibly this also accounts for the relationship to Max Scheler, who occupied himself intensively with the philosophy of life. On the reception of Bergson, see Konstantinos P. Romanos, "Bergson zu seiner Zeit," in Henri Bergson, Denken und schöpferisches Werden (1948; Frankfurt, 1985), pp. 280–286.

48
Le Corbusier, Towards a New Architecture, p. 28.

49
Mies van der Rohe, "Die neue Zeit" (The New Time), Die Form, 5 (1930), p. 406.

50
J. J. P. Oud, Holländische Architektur, p. 9.

51
Peter Behrens, Über die Beziehungen der künstlerischen und technischen Probleme (Berlin, 1917), p. 10.

52
Ibid.

2 1926: Stimuli, Critique, and Orientation

1
The Eichstädt House (1920), Kempner House (1921), Feldmann House (1921–1922), and Mosler House (1924–1925). Alteration of the Urban House, Berlin-Westend, Ulmenallee 32, that had been erected 1911–1912 by the architect Paul Renner; not listed in the index of Mies's work at the Museum of Modern Art, New York, but mentioned in Irmgard Wirth, *Die Bauwerke und Kunstdenkmäler von Berlin, Stadt und Bezirk Charlottenburg* (Berlin, 1961), p. 413.

2
The respective correspondence is in the Library of Congress.

3
First attempts at industrialization were made by Walter Gropius in the Dessau-Törten settlement (1926–1928) and by Ernst May in the Praunheim settlement (1926–1930). A survey of the housing settlements of the twenties is given by Liselotte Unger, *Die Suche nach einer neuen Wohnform. Siedlungen der zwanziger Jahre damals und heute* (Stuttgart, 1983). On the question of industrialization, see Annemarie Jaeggi, "Das Gross-laboratorium für die Volkswohnung. Wagner. Taut. May. Gropius. 1924/25," in Norbert Huse (ed.), *Siedlungen der zwanziger Jahre—heute. Vier Berliner Grossiedlungen 1924–1984* (Berlin, 1984), pp. 27ff. That Mies's skepticism and guardedness were not unjustified is proven by the example of Praunheim. May's experiment with a concrete slab method that was supposed to result in savings turned out more expensive than the traditional methods of raising walls. Compare the Reichsforschungsgesellschaft für Wirtschaftlichkeit im Bau- und Wohnungswesen, *Bericht über die Versuchssiedlung im Frankfurt a.M.—Praunheim,* special issue 4 (April 1929), p. 101. I owe this information to Richard Pommer, whose "Mies van der Rohe and the Political Ideology of the Modern Movement in Architecture," in Franz Schulze (ed.), *Mies van der Rohe: Critical Essays* (New York, 1990), deals intensively with the relationship of the twenties to technology and with attempts in this context to investigate Mies's political position.

4
See Reyner Banham, *Theory and Design in the First Machine Age* (London, 1960), p. 273. Banham calls Mies's blocks on the Afrikanische Strasse "by far the most distinguished of all such buildings architecturally." In this tenor also Julius Posener, "Walter Gropius, Ludwig Mies van der Rohe, Le Corbusier. Drei Meisterarchitekten des 20. Jahrhunderts," in *Die Grossen der Weltgeschichte,* vol. 10 (Zurich, 1978), p. 812: "These houses, built by means of the construction methods and materials . . . employed for all apartment buildings at that time, demonstrate the effect of Mies's discipline. Their proportions are immaculate, they radiate a tranquility and harmony that set them apart from all other apartment buildings of that time." On the Afrikanische Strasse, see my essay "Neues Bauen im Wedding," in *Der Wedding im Wandel der Zeit* (Berlin, 1985), pp. 26–34.

5
Bruno Taut, "Russlands architektonische Situation," manuscript of November 2, 1929, in El Lissitzky, *Russland: Architektur für eine Weltrevolution* (Vienna, 1930; rpt., Berlin, 1965), p. 147.

6
Mies van der Rohe, foreword to the catalog of the Rudolf Schwarz memorial exhibition at Cologne, 1963 (see Appendix IV, 13). Rudolf Schwarz (1897–1961) studied at the Technische Hochschule Berlin, was a graduate student of Hans Poelzig from 1919 to 1923 in the Staatliche Kunstakademie Berlin, and in 1927 became director of the Kunstgewerbe-

schule Aachen. Schwarz joined the directorate of the Deutsche Werkbund, to which Mies also belonged. The relationship between Mies and Schwarz has not yet received scholarly evaluation. The Schwarz papers, in private hands, have not been made accessible to me. Mies also wrote a foreword for Schwarz's *The Church Incarnate* (Chicago, 1958); see Appendix IV, 9.

7
See Schwarz's congratulatory address on Mies's seventy-fifth birthday in 1961, "An Mies van der Rohe," in the catalog of the Rudolf Schwarz memorial exhibition (Cologne, 1963), pp. 7–10; rpt. in Maria Schwarz and Ulrich Conrads (eds.), *Rudolf Schwarz. Wegweisung der Technik und andere Schriften zum Neuen Bauen 1926–1961* (Brunswick and Wiesbaden, 1979), pp. 190–192. Mies is further mentioned on pp. 117, 179, 183f.

8
Mies van der Rohe, notes for acceptance speech on receiving the gold medal of the Royal Institute of British Architects (1959), p. 5, manuscript in Library of Congress (see Appendix IV, 10). To what extent the writings of Max Scheler and Alfred North Whitehead were of significance to Mies by 1926 remains unclear. Preserved in Mies's library are: Max Scheler, *Vom Ewigen im Menschen* (Leipzig, 1921), *Vom Umsturz der Werte* (Leipzig, 1923), *Die Wissensformen und die Gesellschaft* (Leipzig, 1926), *Der Formalismus in der Ethik und die materielle Wertethik* (Halle, 1927), *Menschen und Geschichte* (Zurich, 1929); Alfred North Whitehead, *The Aims of Education and Other Essays* (New York, 1949 [first published 1929]). As far as I know, no writings of Whitehead existed in German translation in 1926.

9
Mies van der Rohe, "Haus H., Magdeburg," *Die Schildgenossen,* 14 (1935), p. 514 (see Appendix III, 13). Rudolf Schwarz had attempted to publish Mies earlier, as can be concluded from a letter dated June 1, 1929, to Werner Becker (Archive Burg Rothenfels), published in Hanna-Barbara Gerl, *Romano Guardini 1885–1968. Leben und Werk* (Mainz, 1985), p. 195: "I for my part suggest asking Mies von der Rohe to furnish a contribution to one of our next issues. He can express himself on the metropolis, for which purpose he can show photos in his possession or he can draw up something new. I could visualize doing this in a generous format with many ground plans and pictures. That man is one of our most valuable acquaintances and like all good Catholics practically unknown in Catholic circles, while others think highly of him." On the relationship of Schwarz and Guardini, see Gerl's book, which has a full chapter on Rudolf Schwarz, pp. 216–223.

10
Compare Rudolf Schwarz, "Die Form ohne Ornament," *Die Schildgenossen,* 6, no. 2 (1926), pp. 83ff.; "Grosstadt als Tatsache und Aufgabe," *Die Schildgenossen,* 7, no. 4 (1926–27), pp. 284ff.; and "Vom Sterben der Anmut," *Die Schildgenossen,* 8, no. 3 (1927–28), pp. 284ff. Mies owned these issues of *Die Schildgenossen* as well as 8, no. 6 (1927–28); 9, no. 2 (1928–29); 11, no. 4 (1930–31). Also of significance were the articles "Neues Bauen?," 9 (1928–29), pp. 207–217, and "Baustelle Deutschland," 12 (1932–33), pp. 1–16. The following writings of Schwarz were in Mies's library: *Wegweisung der Technik* (Potsdam, 1929); *Über die Verfassung einer Werkschule* (Aachen, 1930, published by the Kunstgewerbeschule Aachen): *Gottesdienst* (Würzburg, 1937); *Von der Bebauung der Erde* (Heidelberg, 1949); *Baukunst der Gegenwart* (special ed., Düsseldorf, 1959); *Kirchenbau, Welt vor der Schwelle* (Heidelberg, 1960); *Denken und Bauen* (Heidelberg, 1963). See also the list of the writings of Rudolf Schwarz in the catalog of the 1963 memorial exhibition (cited in Appendix IV, 13), pp. 109ff.

11
Rudolf Schwarz, "Vom Widerstand gegen die Gewalt," lecture given at Castle Rothenfels in 1927, in Manfred Sunderman et al. (eds.), *Rudolf Schwarz* (Düsseldorf, 1981) pp. 99–103.

12
See Mies's foreword to the official catalog of the Werkbund exhibition Die Wohnung (Stuttgart, 1927; see Appendix I, 13), as well as his draft of a letter of about 1927 ("calculating natures work off their excess energies by rationalizing"; Appendix I, 17), and his 1928 notebook, pp. 8, 2 (see Appendix II).

13
Rudolf Schwarz, "Vom Widerstand gegen die Gewalt," p. 103.

14
Ibid.

15
Rudolf Schwarz, *Wegweisung der Technik,* quoted from Schwarz and Conrads, *Rudolf Schwarz,* p. 24.

16
Rudolf Schwarz, "Vom Sterben der Anmut," pp. 286f.: "Does not man, if he fills his narrow and unexpandable historical capacity with [materialistic things], throw away the crown of his spiritual profession? Is there any room left over for the dangerous vision of spiritual insights and for the glowing fervor of works penetrated by spirit? Does not a world arise here that, worse than chaos, is the invention of raw elementary forces and full of naked brutality? This is no anxious fantasy, no mere literary excitement: the ugly slums of the eastern fringes of our large cities are visible facts, and the experience of the great war is not yet forgotten. . . . That poses a task for us more difficult than the tasks of our ancestors . . . the conquest of force."

17
Rudolf Schwarz, "Neues Bauen?," p. 208: "Nothing would be more wrong than to assume that we stand today beyond all historicism. Quite the opposite: we stand right in the middle of it, more than ever before, except that our historicism is fed by true love and has deep roots. History lives more profoundly in us, and thus an immanent historicism has replaced a merely copying type. It still holds the past for real and holds that the past lives in the present. For this reason it supposes that the past could revive at each moment, just as the future could be prefigured. Sometimes it believes that history is simply the expression of an eternal possibility."

18
Rudolf Schwarz, "Vom Sterben der Anmut," pp. 297f.: "Today the humanistic method is no longer as naive as it was thirty years ago. . . . Today humanists have learned to do without embellishments and thus hone closer to their own best tradition. Today one applies decoration with more taste and sophistication: one decorates the intrinsic by covering one's own self with a humanist skin. The crypto-humanist Behrens has 'spiritualized' the light switches of the AEG by freeing them of ornament and giving them a pleasing form, and in Dessau it is being done similarly. The light switch, of course, remains what it was, but it has found a humanist sideline as art work."

19
Mies van der Rohe, foreword to *Bau und Wohnung* (Stuttgart, 1927; see Appendix I, 14).

20
"I beg you, get this text ready and publish it, it is high time," Romano Guardini wrote to Rudolf Schwarz on December 1,

from Potsdam. Quoted in Schwarz and Conrads, *Rudolf Schwarz,* p. 7.

21
Ibid., preface by Ulrich Conrads.

22
Ibid.

23
See Mies's 1928 notebook, p. 14 (Appendix II); and his lecture of about 1950, p. 11 (Appendix IV, 5), where the question "Is the world as it presents itself bearable for man?" and the following sentences are partially verbatim from the preface of Schwarz's *Wegweisung der Technik.*

In the same lecture, p. 15 ("Only 30 lifespans separate us from the Acropolis"), Mies quotes Schwarz's "Baustelle Deutschland," *Die Schildgenossen,* 12, no. 1 (1932–33), according to Maria Schwarz in Schwarz and Conrads, *Rudolf Schwarz,* p. 145. Mies follows the latter essay very closely after 1950 with his main thesis that a mature technology develops of itself into building art. See Mies van der Rohe, "Architecture and Technology," *Arts and Architecture,* 67, no. 10 (1950), p. 30: "Wherever technology reaches its real fulfillment, it transcends into architecture." Compare also the concluding sentence of Mies's miscellaneous lecture notes of around 1950 (Appendix IV, 6)— "We have every reason to assume that, when technology develops into building art, great things will come about"—with Schwarz, "Baustelle Deutschland," p. 145: "The technical becomes beautiful . . . it dissolves into a higher order and becomes building art. By that we mean the immanent redemption."

24
Theo van Doesburg, "Die Neue Architektur und ihre Folgen," *Wasmuths Monatshefte für Baukunst,* 9 (1925), p. 514.

25
Theo van Doesburg, "Von der Neuen Ästhetic zur materiellen Verwirklichung" (lecture, Weimar, 1922), quoted from Hagen Bächler and Herbert Letsch, *De Stijl. Schriften und Manifeste zu einem theoretischen Konzept ästhetischer Umweltgestaltung* (Leipzig and Weimar, 1984), p. 180.

26
Mies van der Rohe, "Bauen" (Building), *G,* no. 2 (September 1923), p. 1.

27
Theo van Doesburg, "Der Wille zum Stil" (lecture, given in Jena, Weimar, and Berlin, 1922), quoted from Bächler and Letsch, *De Stijl. Schriften und Manifeste,* p. 167.

28
Van Doesburg, "Die Neue Architektur und ihre Folgen," p. 514.

29
Theo van Doesburg, "Farben in Raum und Zeit," quoted from Bächler and Letsch, *De Stijl. Schriften und Manifeste,* p. 221.

30
Adolf Behne, *Der Moderne Zweckbau* (Munich, 1926; new ed., Berlin, 1964), p. 68. In a similar vein Rudolf Schwarz wrote against that "stupid and purpose-happy materialism" in "Neues Bauen?" (1929), p. 126: "The national characteristic of the Germans to exaggerate everything and to spoil everything with their melancholic pondering has turned a useful kitchen into an unusable ideology."

31
Behne, *Der Moderne Zweckbau,* p. 6.

32
Edgar Wedepohl, "Die Weissenhof-Siedlung der Werkbund-ausstellung 'Die Wohnung,' Stuttgart 1927," *Wasmuths Monatshefte für Baukunst,* 11 (1927), p. 401: "In the February issue of the Werkbund journal, Mies van der Rohe has spoken out expressly against form as aim, as it always ends in formalism.—Is it not possible that the cause of this fear of form— since we don't want to see in it a confession of inability to create form—arises from the misunderstanding that the purposeful, the technical-constructive and the practical-necessary could even be shaped without form?"

33
Presumably Mies and Oud became acquainted and learned to appreciate each other by way of the Novembergruppe, to which Oud belonged as a foreign member. In 1925 and 1926 he participated in its exhibitions with his own work. How much Mies valued Oud can be seen from a letter to Oud written in September 1930 by Philip Johnson, who was in Europe to prepare the New York exhibition "The International Style": "He talks of you very enthusiastically as of one of his best acquaintances. And Mies rarely is enthusiastic over other architects. Indeed, only you and Le Corbusier were praised by him. . . . He told funny stories about Gropius's respect for technology. He adores it because he understands so little of it. Mies hates that function-mindedness that was carried on at the Bauhaus to such extremes before he arrived. He says it is even more subjective than the purely aesthetic." Quoted from Günther Stamm, *J. J. P. Oud. Bauten und Projekte 1906 bis 1963* (Mainz and Berlin, 1984), p. 110.

34
J. J. P. Oud, "Ja und Nein: Bekenntnisse eines Architekten," *Wasmuths Monatshefte für Baukunst,* 9 (1925), pp. 140–146. Simultaneously appeared in Paul Westheim and Carl Einstein (eds.), *Europa-Almanach* (Potsdam, 1925), p. 8.

35
Le Corbusier, *Towards a New Architecture,* translated by Frederick Etchells (New York, 1976), p. 23, translation slightly modified.

36
Ibid., pp. 102–103.

37
J. J. P. Oud, *Holländische Architektur* (Munich, 1926; new ed., Mainz and Berlin, 1976), pp. 22, 57. Compare Peter Behrens, "Kunst und Technik" (1910): "Technology cannot always merely be viewed as purpose, but gains its ultimate value and meaning when it is recognized as the noblest avenue to culture. But a mature culture speaks the language of art." (Reprinted in Tilmann Buddensieg and Henning Rogge, *Industriekultur: Peter Behrens and the AEG,* trans. Iain Boyd Whyte [Cambridge, Mass., 1984], pp. 212–219.) Stamm, *J. J. P. Oud,* p. 29, reports that Oud "admired" Behrens.

38
J. J. P. Oud, *Holländische Architektur,* pp. 22, 25. The relationship of Oud and Berlage was considerably chilled when the long-revered father figure Berlage, as member of the competition jury for the building of the Rotterdam Stock Exchange in 1926, rejected Oud's design "and supported the obviously mediocre design of Staal, who in the final version even 'borrowed' elements from Oud's project" (according to Stamm, *J. J. P. Oud,* p. 84). Oud characterized Berlage, as related by Helene Kröller-Müller, as an "arrogant aloof Protestant" (ibid.). One should note here that Mies's criticism of Behrens later on, although with a reversed thrust, contained quite similar

reproaches to those of Oud against Berlage. It seemed as if Mies and Oud in their rebellion against the father figure switched roles for awhile. Berlage's student admired Behrens, and Behrens's student admired Berlage.

39
Heinrich de Fries, *Frank Lloyd Wright. Aus dem Lebenswerk eines Architekten* (Berlin, 1926). (Not listed among Mies's books.) The circumstance that this book is not so much a monograph on Wright but a critique of contemporary architecture is excused by the author, who claims that the "extreme contrast in the basic understanding of building . . . practically necessitated constant comparisons." According to him, "this book does not want to improve, it wants to change, from the bottom on up" (p. 33). De Fries carried on his attack with the same radical energy: "All that nonsense about will to style, about the reform of function, about the spirit of the absolute idea, must come to a stop. All this stupid chitchat does not serve to improve human achievement, and above all it does not make it any warmer. . . . When will this building art of the five o'clock teas, of horn-rimmed glasses, and that entire airbag silliness of an alleged cultural caste come to an end? This architecture of the cold hand and the sober heart has nothing to do any more with building art. Any old hearty 'kitsch' is better than that!" (Ibid., pp. 31f.) On the reception of Wright in Europe see also J. J. P. Oud, "Der Einfluss von Frank Lloyd Wright auf die Architektur Europas," in *Holländische Architektur,* pp. 77–83.

40
Mies van der Rohe, "No Dogma," interview in *Interbuild,* 6, no. 6 (1959), p. 10.

41
Ibid., p. 11: "In my interview with the BBC I talked of the three people in Europe who, although I didn't know them, were thinking in 1926 what I was thinking. Their business was to get this thing clear in their minds and to write their books about it." Mies's BBC interview could not be found in its original version. The published excerpts do not mention the three names Mies refers to. If one assumes that he meant respective representatives of three countries, he might have had Le Corbusier, Adolf Behne, and J. J. P. Oud in mind.

42
Sergius Ruegenberg, personal communication. Ruegenberg recalls that this was "in the period of the Stuttgart negotiations" and that Mies asked him, before he left for one of his frequent consultation trips, to throw away the piled-up rolls of drawings.

3   Space for the Unfolding of the Spirit

1
In 1924 Ebeling had already published a special Bauhaus "Young People" issue with the title "Kosmologe Raumzelle" (for this information I thank Mrs. Droste of the Bauhausarchiv Berlin). The book *Der Raum als Membran* (Dessau, 1926) can be viewed as a synchronic expansion of these cosmological ideas for the Bauhaus. The new themes of the Bauhaus after 1924, technology and space, are being viewed from the perspective of the old Bauhaus. For this reason the author might not have wished to publish it as a Bauhaus publication. The frontispiece decoration, recalling Kandinsky, may have been intended to suggest a connection to the Bauhaus.

2
Thus the interpretation of the "spiritual in man," in which the alliance of Nietzsche and Francé is also executed semantically

(p. 19): "The divine-alogical-intoxicated in everything alive that in each moment succumbs to the causality of matter as guarantor of the form-world and simultaneously derides it!"

3
Ebeling, *Der Raum als Membran*, pp. 8, 22.

4
See Joseph Rykwert, *On Adam's House in Paradise: The Idea of the Primitive Hut in Architectural History* (New York, 1972).

5
Ebeling, *Der Raum als Membran*, p. 8.

6
Ibid., p. 11.

7
Ibid., p. 12, with further quotations from Nietzsche. Ebeling calls Nietzsche's "overemphasis on the body" a "triumphant new truth because precisely through this exaggeration we as individuals can obtain access to the profoundest secret that exults in us Dionysiacally: For above us nothing is enthroned: where anything is, it is the whole: and the whole is what it is: that is its fullness and its nature."

8
Le Corbusier, *Towards a New Architecture,* translated by Frederick Etchells (New York, 1976), p. 85.

9
Ebeling, *Der Raum als Membran*, pp. 13, 24, 25.

10
Ibid., pp. 25, 26, underlinings by Mies.

11
Ibid., pp. 11, 14.

12
Ibid., p. 11.

13
Ibid., p. 30.

14
For a similar characterization of modern building see Walter Benjamin, "Die Wiederkehr des Flaneurs" (1929), in *Gesammelte Schriften,* vol. 3 (Frankfurt, 1980), p. 196f.: "Giedion, Mendelsohn, Corbusier make human space above all a space of passage of all imaginable forces and waves of light and air. What takes place stands under the sign of transparence. . . ."

15
See Doesburg's remark quoted in the preceding chapter, at note 24.

16
Ebeling, *Das Raum als Membran,* p. 11.

17
Ibid., p. 31.

18
Ibid.

19
Ibid.

20
Mies van der Rohe, lecture (1924), manuscript of June 19, 1924, in the collection of Dirk Lohan (see Appendix I, 8): "This house, to be executed in brick, shows you the direct opposite of the previous illustration [of the Concrete Country House] as to the influence of material in form-giving. In the ground plan

of this house, I have abandoned the usual concept of enclosed rooms and striven for a series of spatial effects rather than a row of individual rooms. The wall loses its enclosing character and serves only to articulate the house organism."

21
Mies van der Rohe, "Baukunst und Zeitwille!" (Building Art and the Will of the Epoch!), manuscript of February 7, 1924, in the collection of Dirk Lohan (see Appendix I, 6): "Skyscrapers, office buildings, and commercial structures practically call forth clear, comprehensive solutions, and these can only be crippled because one repeatedly attempts to adapt these buildings to outdated attitudes and forms. The same applies to residential building. Here, too, certain house and room concepts lead to impossible results. Instead of simply developing a residence to suit its purpose, namely organizing the activity of living, . . ."

22
Mies van der Rohe, "Die Voraussetzungen baukünstlerischen Schaffens" (The Preconditions of Architectural Work), lecture (1928), manuscript in the collection of Dirk Lohan. See Mies's notebook of 1928, p. 12 (Museum of Modern Art, Manuscripts Folder 1; see Appendix II): "Against the dominance of technology, for serving. Technology as means to freedom."

23
Mies van der Rohe, "Was wäre Beton, was Stahl ohne Spiegelglas?" (What Would Concrete, What Would Steel Be without Mirror Glass?), manuscript of March 13, 1933, in the Library of Congress.

24
Heinrich de Fries, *Frank Lloyd Wright. Aus dem Lebenswerk eines Architekten* (Berlin, 1926), p. 14: "Architecture today, if it is an art at all, is that of a plastic fabric, woven into a beautiful garment, for a room full of rooms."

25
See the reviews of "Die Voraussetzungen baukünstlerischen Schaffens" reprinted in Appendix III, 1.

26
Mies van der Rohe, manuscript of a letter to Walter Riezler, in Museum of Modern Art, Manuscripts Folder 6 (see Appendix I, 12).

27
Ibid. In regard to the dispute with Walter Riezler, see the following chapter.

28
Mies van der Rohe, foreword to the official catalog of the Werkbund exhibition "Die Wohnung" (Stuttgart, 1927), p. 5 (see Appendix I, 13).

29
Adolf Behne, *Neues Wohnen—neues Bauen* (Leipzig, 1927), p. 109.

30
Compare Mies, notebook, p. 34 (see Appendix II).

31
Paul Westheim, "Mies van der Rohe. Entwicklung eines Architekten," *Das Kunstblatt,* 11, no. 2 (1927), pp. 57–58; reprinted as "Mies van der Rohe: Charaktervoll bauen," in Paul Westheim, *Helden und Abenteuer* (Berlin, 1931).

32
Compare Mies van der Rohe, "Zu meinem Block" (Concerning My Block), in *Bau und Wohnung* (Stuttgart, 1927), p. 77 (see Appendix I, 14).

33

Werner Gräff, "Zur Stuttgarter Weissenhofsiedlung," in *Bau und Wohnung,* pp. 8–9. Reprinted with slight alterations under the title "Werkbund-Ausstellung 'Die Wohnung,'" in *Die Form,* 2 (1927), pp. 249–250. Gräff points out that the changes of lifestyle that call for new types of living arrangements are not confined to an elite but "already incipiently concern the masses (especially the younger generation)." Compare in this context Mies's remarks on the "masses" in the letter draft of 1927, in Museum of Modern Art, Manuscripts Folder 2, p. 2 (see Appendix I, 17): "The masses are by no means as character-less as the mass-production clothiers maintain, but we feel particularly in them the strongest impulses for living."

34

The following explanations of Werner Gräff, "Zur Stuttgarter Weissenhofsiedlung," p. 8, are obviously a far cry from the radical utopian changes the modern movement is often accused of; quite to the contrary, one strove for carefully aimed but necessary updating:

However, a clear understanding of the new type of living space has so far not yet emerged; of course not, as these changes are still under way. For the new generation the stan-dard dwelling is unbearably unsuitable, but neither is there a clear-cut understanding of its wishes or an even approximate understanding of its desires. What is worse, it also has not yet been understood by most of the architects. Only very few possess an adequate measure of openness, freedom, and visionary energy—the rest of them are at the present, crucial moment only a type of follower. . . . Even the avant-garde in Germany sees that they still need to exercise patience. . . . Self-understood: a dwelling culture cannot be enforced. But even though the general populace does not yet have a clear understanding of its dwelling preferences, one can still raise consciousness, untie prejudices, awaken instincts—and care-fully observe new sensibilities.

Perhaps the new generation fails to understand its prefer-ences because it has no inkling of the possibilities. One needs to show them the new technological advances, one should acquaint them with functional equipment and machines, and one should introduce them to what the leading architects in the world desire—even if they are only fantastic plans. And as to giving practical examples for living, at this time it is probably best not to overdetermine; on the contrary, to dem-onstrate that everything can still be formed. It will be formed in use (for that reason the variable floor plans). In that way one serves to enlighten domestic life. And that is the meaning of the Weissenhofsiedlung in Stuttgart.

See also Mies van der Rohe, "Zum Thema: Ausstellungen" (On the Theme: Exhibitions), *Die Form,* 3, no. 4 (1928), p. 121. Also: "Programm zur Berliner Bauausstellung" (Program for the Berlin Building Exposition), *Die Form,* 6, no. 7 (1931), p. 241.

35

On the interpretation of spatiality and the difficulties of an adequate conceptualization of the characteristics of Mies's space, see Juan Pablo Bonta, *Über Interpretation von Archi-tektur* (Berlin, 1982), who deals with the history of the reception of the Barcelona Pavilion and its various interpretations up to the present time. Furthermore, Wolf Tegethoff, *Mies van der Rohe. Die Villen und Landhausprojekte* (Krefeld and Essen, 1981), whose nuanced analysis brings the dialectics of space best into focus. On a concept of modern space see Bruno Zevi, *Architecture as Space* (1954; reprint, New York, 1974), and Cornelis van de Ven, *Space in Architecture: The Evolution of a New Idea in the Theory and History of the Modern Move-ments* (Assen, Netherlands, 1980).

36

Gaston Bachelard, *The Poetics of Space,* translated by Maria Jolas (Boston, 1964), p. 184. Regarding the tendency to reduce the limit-setting function of the wall, one could say with Bachelard: "The walls are on vacation" (p. 52). See chap. 2, "House and Universe"; chap. 8, "Intimate Immensity"; chap. 9, "The Dialectics of Outside and Inside."

37

H. P. Berlage, *Schoonheid in Samenleving* (Rotterdam, 1919), p. 31, quoted in Manfred Bock, "Vom Monument zur Städte-planung: Das Neue Bauen," in *Tendenzen der Zwanziger Jahre,* exhibition catalog (Berlin, 1977), pp. 1–32.

38

Herman Sörgel, *Theorie der Baukunst,* vol. 1, *Architektur-Ästhetik* (Munich, 1921), p. 196. Compare also Leo Adler, *Vom Wesen der Baukunst. Die Baukunst als Ereignis und Erschei-nung. Versuch einer Grundlegung der Architekturwissen-schaft* (Leipzig, 1926), p. 5: "Building art is the transposition of an *idea* of space in its visible *form.*"

39

See Dagobert Frey, *Kunstwissenschaftliche Grundfragen. Prolegomena zu einer Kunstphilosophie* (Vienna, 1946; Darmstadt, 1984), esp. "Wesensbestimmung der Architektur," pp. 93ff.

40

Sörgel, *Architektur-Ästhetik,* pp. 225, 193.

41

Nicolas M. Rubio Tuduri, "Le Pavillon de l'Allemagne à l'Ex-position de Barcelona par Mies van der Rohe," *Cahiers d'Art,* 4 (1929), p. 410.

42

Of the writings mentioned, only H. P. Berlage, *Grundlagen und Entwicklung der Baukunst* (Berlin, 1908) is to be found among Mies's books.

43

Aside from the formula "spatially apprehended will of the epoch," Mies made only a few short remarks on space in the following places: his remarks on the design for a Brick Country House, in his lecture of 1924 (see Appendix I, 8); in "Zu meinem Block," 1927 ("the skeleton structure . . . makes a rational production possible and yet permits total freedom of disposition in the interior"); in "Was wäre Beton, was Stahl ohne Spiegelglas?" of 1933; in "Museum for a Small City," 1943; and in his lecture of around 1950, p. 2 (see Appendix IV, 5: "Building, where it became great, was almost always indebted to construction, and construction was almost always the conveyor of its spatial form").

44

August Endell (1871–1925) moved to Berlin in 1901 and obtained a number of building commissions there. See *August Endell. Der Architekt des Photoateliers Elvira, 1871–1925,* exhibition catalog (Museum Villa Stuck, Munich, 1977). Fun-damental on this subject: Tilmann Buddensieg, "Zur Frühzeit von August Endell. Seine Münchner Briefe an Kurt Breysig," in *Festschrift für Eduard Trier zum 60. Geburtstag,* ed. Justus Müller-Hofstede and Werner Spies (Berlin, 1981), pp. 223–250, with a list of Endell's writings. In this context: August Endell, "Über Konstruktion und Schönheit. Vortrag vor der Freien Studentengemeinschaft der Charlottenburger Tech-nischen Hochschule," *Der Kunstwart,* 23 (1909–10), pp. 199–200; Endell, "Architektur-Theorien," *Neudeutsche Bauzeitung,* 10 (1914), pp. 37–39, 53–56; Endell, "Raum und Körper," *Kunst und Künstler,* 23 (1925), pp. 301–306; Endell, *Zauber-*

land des Sichtbaren, vol. 4 of *Der Weltgarten,* edited after his death by Anna Endell (Berlin, 1928).

45

August Endell, *Die Schönheit der grossen Stadt* (Stuttgart, 1908), is not among the books of Mies. See below for the indications that Mies was familiar with this book. The importance of this book is indicated by its reprinting in the exhibition catalog *August Endell,* pp. 87–120, as well as its having been published in pamphlet form in the "architextbook" series (no. 4); there is also a translation into Italian in Massimo Cacciari, *Metropolis, Saggi sulla granda città di Sombart, Endell, Scheffler e Simmel,* Collana di Architettura, 7 (Rome, 1973), pp. 121–164.

46

August Endell, *Die Schönheit der grossen Stadt,* p. 77.

47

Ibid., p. 14: "There is only one healthy foundation for all of culture and that is a passionate love for the here and now, for our time. . . ."

48

Ibid., pp. 11, 12: "One escapes into the past! Not that one understands it or really respects it. From sparse school knowledge and diligent theater visits one dreams up a strangely distorted world. . . . One does not know that the ruins of the past only come to life if one understands the present and that there is no period that we can understand as well as our own."

49

Ibid., pp. 8, 13: "We are ashamed of our own desires and needs. But strangely enough this is exactly the fault of those who rave so loudly against our age and who preach that we should turn our back to it: the romantics of all types who announce that the escape into nature, the escape into art, the escape into the past is the only way out. . . . Romanticism is the archenemy of all that is alive."

50

Ibid., p. 78, "Arbeiter im Rohbau."

51

Ibid., pp. 59f. It is in this sense that one may have to understand Mies's remark that the "building site" has influenced the design, much as a genius loci. See his article on skyscrapers in *Frühlicht,* 1, no. 4 (1922), p. 123.

52

Sörgel, *Architektur-Ästhetik,* pp. 256f.

53

Endell, *Die Schönheit der grossen Stadt,* p. 50.

54

Ibid., p. 63.

55

Theo van Doesburg, *Grundbegriffe der neuen gestaltenden Kunst,* Bauhausbücher, 6 (Munich, 1925), p. 7.

56

Piet Mondrian, "Die neue Gestaltung in der Malerei" (1918), quoted from Hagen Bächler and Herbert Letsch, *De Stijl. Schriften und Manifeste zu einem theoretischen Konzept ästhetischer Umweltgestaltung* (Leipzig and Weimar, 1984), p. 83.

57

Mies van der Rohe, "Museum for a Small City," *Architectural Forum,* 78, no. 5 (1943), pp. 84f.

58

Walter Riezler, "Das Haus Tugendhat in Brünn," *Die Form,* 6 (1931), p. 328. On the Tugendhat House, see Tegethoff, *Mies van der Rohe. Die Villen und Landhausprojekte,* pp. 90–98.

59

In his analysis of spatial delimitation, Tegethoff describes the glass wall as a membrane, without, however, knowing of Ebeling's thesis of "space as membrane": "This transparent membrane cannot simply be interpreted as the end of a room that would continue to exist if there were no wall; it is it that creates the room that is circumscribed but not exactly defined by the overhanging roof" (ibid., p. 109, referring to the design for the Golf Club in Krefeld, 1930).

60

See Grete and Fritz Tugendhat, "Die Bewohner des Hauses Tugendhat äussern sich," *Die Form,* 6 (1931), p. 438: (Grete Tugendhat) "As important as the interconnectedness between inside and outside is, the room is nevertheless closed and reposes in itself—the glass wall functions in that respect truly as delimitation. If it were otherwise, one would experience a feeling of unrest and a lack of privacy. This way, however, the room has, particularly through its rhythm, an especially tranquil air, much more than a totally enclosed room would have."

61

Ebeling, *Das Raum als Membran,* p. 31.

62

Grete and Fritz Tugendhat, "Die Bewohner des Hauses Tugendhat," p. 438: (Grete Tugendhat) "We enjoy very much living in this house, so much, in fact, that we find it difficult to decide on a trip and we feel liberated when we come back from narrow rooms into our wide, tranquil spaces." See Grete Tugendhat, "Zum Bau des Hauses Tugendhat," *Die Bauwelt,* 60 (1969), pp. 1246f.

63

Bachelard, *The Poetics of Space;* see the chapter "House and Universe," pp. 38ff., with numerous images that Bachelard takes over from Baudelaire's "Curiosités esthétiques" and that seem to me illuminating in regard to Miesian space. See for example p. 62: "Housed everywhere but nowhere shut in, this is the motto of the dreamer of dwellings. In the last house as in the actual house, the daydream of inhabiting is thwarted. A daydream of elsewhere should be left open therefore, at all times."

64

Grete and Fritz Tugendhat, "Die Bewohner des Hauses Tugendhat," p. 437: (Grete Tugendhat) "This severity does not forbid a simple 'relaxation' and a letting-oneself-go type of spending the time—and it is especially this urge to something else that man, left exhausted and empty from the exercise of his profession, needs today and experiences as a liberation."

65

See Grete Tugendhat, "Zum Bau des Hauses Tugendhat," p. 1247: "In the dining room we had 24 easy chairs, now called 'Brno chairs,' that were spanned with white parchment; in front of the onyx wall stood two chairs, now so-called 'Tugendhat chairs,' covered by a silver-gray Rodier material, and two Barcelona chairs, spanned with emerald-green leather. In front of the large glass wall stood a reclining chair the upholstery of which was ruby-red velvet. All these color combinations were tried out by Mies together with Mrs. Lilly Reich right on location.

"Belonging to all of this were of course curtains and rugs. In front of the onyx wall was a handwoven rug of light natural wool. . . . The black color of the Shantung curtain in front of the winter garden was also very much in tune with the black velvet curtain next to it and the silver-gray Shantung silk of the front wall. Between entryway and library hung a white velvet curtain. . . ."

66
Ludwig Hilberseimer as reported by Grete Tugendhat, "Zum Bau des Hauses Tugendhat," p. 1247.

67
Riezler, "Das Haus Tugendhat in Brünn," pp. 332, 328.

68
Mies van der Rohe, "Die Voraussetzungen baukünstlerischen Schaffens" (see Appendix III, 1).

69
Mies van der Rohe, "Die neue Zeit" (The New Time), *Die Form*, 5 (1930), p. 406.

70
Mies van der Rohe, "Die Voraussetzungen baukünstlerischen Schaffens."

71
Mies van der Rohe, speech on the occasion of the anniversary meeting of the Deutsche Werkbund (October 1932, in Berlin), manuscript in the collection of Dirk Lohan (see Appendix III, 10).

72
Mies van der Rohe, "Die neue Zeit," p. 406.

VI Architecture for the Search for Knowledge: The Double Way to Order

1
Paul Fechter, *An der Wende der Zeit. Menschen und Begegnungen* (Gütersloh, 1949), pp. 161, 163f. Ibid., p. 164, on Mies: "One of the finest and most talented of the younger generation, a man of such sure instinct for space and proportion that his departure for America has to be viewed as one of the most painful losses the country has experienced through emigration."

2
Walter Riezler, "Das Haus Tugendhat in Brünn," *Die Form*, 6 (1931), p. 332.

3
Mies van der Rohe, notebook of 1928, p. 35 (Museum of Modern Art, Manuscripts Folder 1; see Appendix II).

4
On Mies's lecture in Bremen on November 27, 1925, see chapter I, note 43. In another sense, also, the chances for an encounter with Guardini were, quite literally, nearby. Besides his faculty work, Guardini also held evening lectures at the Berlin Lessing-Hochschule on philosophical-literary subjects that were open to the public and were frequented by the upper-class public. Mies's office (Am Karlsbad, no. 24) was only a few feet away from the Lyceum-Klub on Lützowplatz where the lectures of the Lessing-Hochschule took place.

Fechter, *An der Wende der Zeit,* p. 160f., on Guardini: "The lecture hall on Lützowplatz . . . was packed, the front rows for the most part with older and younger ladies from whose direction a wave of dreamy veneration wafted upward to the speaker. He had at that time some unprofessorial man-

ners. . . . When he talked of a subject that was still not yet resolved in his mind, that was still beset by questions, he used to smile slightly in embarrassment. It was such a charming, winning smile that one could well understand the wave of blissful veneration that arose, almost visibly, from the ranks of the public, just as one could understand that serious Berlin lawyers fell under his spell."

That Mies stood in personal contact with Guardini can be seen from a letter Mies received in 1935 from the art historian Alfred Neumeyer, a pupil of Heinrich Wölfflin and Adolf Goldschmidt. Neumeyer, who had been teaching as a privatdozent in Berlin, had emigrated in 1934 to California and had hoped to have Mies attend one of his summer courses at Mills College. In his letter he reminds Mies of the "evenings at the Glasers' or at Mrs. Kempner's or at Guardini's." See letter, Fred Neumeyer, Mills College, School of Fine Arts, California, of December 15, 1935, in the Library of Congress. Mies could not accept the offer because he could not meet the prerequisite knowledge of the English language. The legacy of Romano Guardini at the Catholic Academy at Munich is not yet researched enough to reveal a possible correspondence with Mies. There is no evidence of such a correspondence among Mies's papers. Aside from Paul Fechter, among those who have written on Guardini only Hanna-Barbara Gerl names Mies (*Romano Guardini 1885–1968. Leben und Werk* [Mainz, 1985], pp. 195, 223f., 279).

5
Mies van der Rohe, draft of a letter to Walter Riezler, in Museum of Modern Art, Manuscript Folder 6; published version as "Über die Form in der Architektur" (On Form in Architecture), *Die Form*, 2, no. 1 (1927), p. 59. (See Appendix I, 12.)

6
Theo van Doesburg, "Der Wille zum Stil" (lecture held in Jena, Weimar, and Berlin, 1922), quoted in Hagen Bächler and Herbert Letsch, *De Stijl. Schriften und Manifeste zu einem theoretischen Konzept ästhetischer Umweltgestaltung* (Leipzig and Weimar, 1984), pp. 164, 165, 168ff.

7
See Peter Blake, "A Conversation with Mies," in *Four Great Makers of Modern Architecture* (New York, 1963), p. 101. Blake: "A lot of art critics claim that your work is very much influenced by De Stijl, by van Doesburg." Mies: "No, that is absolute nonsense, you know." Blake: "Why don't you explain why?" Mies: "Van Doesburg saw these drawings of the office building. I explained it to him, and I said, 'This is skin-and-bones architecture.' After that he called me an anatomical architect. I liked van Doesburg, but not as though he knew very much about architecture."

8
Romano Guardini, *Der Gegensatz. Versuche zu einer Philosophie des Lebendig-Konkreten* (Mainz, 1925), pp. 31, 40, with numerous markings by Mies.

9
Ibid., pp. 44f. The two sentences last quoted were additionally emphasized by Mies by underlining.

10
On this, see Gerl, *Romano Guardini*, pp. 250–266, chapter titled "Die Entdeckung der eigenen Methode: Der Gegensatz und die Weltanschauung."

11
Ibid., p. 255.

12
Mies van der Rohe, "Über die Form in der Architektur," p. 59.

13
Mies van der Rohe, notebook of 1928, p. 26.

14
Guardini, *Der Gegensatz*, p. 48.

15
Mies van der Rohe, speech on the occasion of the anniversary meeting of the Deutsche Werkbund (October 1932 in Berlin), manuscript in the collection of Dirk Lohan (see Appendix III, 10).

16
Guardini, *Die Gegensatz*, p. 74.

17
Gerl, *Romano Guardini*, p. 185. On the relationship of Guardini to Nietzsche see ibid., pp. 61, 312, 338, 370. Also compare Romano Guardini, *Liturgische Bildung* (Rothenfels, 1923), p. 23: "Only now one understands Nietzsche." The bipolarity of Guardini's thinking was also evident in his lectures, attended by "members of all classes" (Gerl, *Romano Guardini*, p. 291). Guardini lectured in the winter semester of 1926–27 on "The Religious in Plato," in the winter semester of 1931–32 on "The Finite and the Eternal. Attempt at an Interpretation of Nietzsche's Zarathustra." The "similarity of inclination" that Hanna-Barbara Gerl sees with Nietzsche may also have been due to the circumstance that Guardini, much like Nietzsche, counted Blaise Pascal and Friedrich Hölderlin as his favorite poets. Guardini may have been in agreement with Nietzsche's opinion that "the most serious Christians were always favorably inclined to me."

18
Guardini, *Der Gegensatz*, p. 14.

19
On this see Gerl, *Romano Guardini*, pp. 126, 262ff. (chapter titled "Offene Haltung und bejahte Grenze"). Also compare the preface by Walter Dirks to the new edition of Romano Guardini's *Briefe vom Comer See* that appeared under the title *Die Technik und der Mensch* (Mainz, 1981). The following recent publications attest the importance of Guardini: Ingeborg Klimmer (ed.), *"Angefochtene Zuversicht". Romano Guardini Lesebuch* (Mainz, 1985); Walter Seidel (ed.), *Christliche Weltanschauung. Wiederbegegnung mit Romano Guardini* (Würzburg, 1985). See also the review of Mathias Schreiber, "Ermutigung zum Blick auf das Ganze, Hanna-Barbara Gerl über Leben und Werk Romano Guardinis," *Frankfurter Allgemeine Zeitung*, no. 131 (June 10, 1985), pp. 11.

20
The following titles by Romano Guardini were among Mies's books: *Aus einem Jugendreich* (Mainz, 1921); *Liturgische Bildung* (Rothenfels, 1923); *Gottes Werkleute* (Rothenfels, 1925); *Der Gegensatz* (Mainz, 1925); *Der Kreuzweg des Herrn und Heilandes* (Mainz, 1926); *Briefe vom Comer See* (Mainz, 1927); *Über Wilhelm Raabes 'Stopfkuchen'* (Mainz, 1932); *Freiheit, Gnade, Schicksal* (Munich, 1948); *Welt und Person* (Würzburg, 1950); *Das Ende der Neuzeit* (Würzburg, 1950); *Die Macht* (Würzburg, 1951); *Der Tod des Sokrates* (Hamburg, 1956).

21
Mies was nominated leading architect for the artistic organization and for the building of presentation space at Barcelona before July 1928; the design work was started September 1928. On May 19, 1929, the opening ceremonies took place. First contact with the clients of the Tugendhat House is doc-umented for the summer of 1928, first design suggestions were ready at the end of that year, and in June 1929 construction was started. See Wolf Tegethoff, *Mies van der Rohe. Die Villen und Landhausprojekte* (Krefeld and Essen, 1981), pp. 73f., 90f.

22
Guardini, *Liturgische Bildung*, pp. 72ff.

23
Mies van der Rohe, notebook in Museum of Modern Art, Manuscripts Folder 7, D.1.15.

24
Guardini, *Liturgische Bildung*, p. 70.

25
Mies van der Rohe, "Die Voraussetzungen baukünstlerischen Schaffens" (The Preconditions of Architectural Work), lecture of February 1928, undated manuscript, in the collection of Dirk Lohan. The following Mies quotations are also from this source unless otherwise identified. A totally unrepresentative, drastically abbreviated excerpt from this widely noted lecture was published under the title "Wir stehen in der Wende der Zeit. Baukunst als Ausdruck geistiger Entscheidung" in *Innendekoration*, 39 (1928), p. 262. This excerpt, published outside of its proper context, creates a totally one-sided view of Mies's lecture.

26
Werner Jaeger, "Platos Stellung im Aufbau der griechischen Bildung, I. Kulturidee und Griechentum," *Die Antike*, 4, no. 1 (1928), pp. 1–13; "II. Der Wandel des Platobildes im neunzehnten Jahrhundert," *Die Antike*, 4, no. 2 (1928), pp. 85–98 (also note pp. 99–102 in this issue: Hugo von Hofmannsthal, "Das Vermächtnis der Antike"); "III. Die platonische Philosophie als Paideia," *Die Antike*, 4, no. 3 (1928), pp. 161–176. Also among the books of Mies: Werner Jaeger, "Die geistige Gegenwart der Antike," offprint from *Die Antike*, 5 (1929). Mies owned copies of Plato, *Die Verteidigung des Sokrates Kriton* (Leipzig, 1922); *Five Dialogues of Plato Bearing on Poetic Inspiration* (London and New York, 1931); and *The Republic of Plato* (New York, 1945).

27
Paul Ludwig Landsberg, *Die Welt des Mittelalters und wir*, 3d ed. (Bonn, 1925), p. 49, underlined by Mies.

28
See ibid., pp. 50, 51, also underlined by Mies: "With the world of his ideas Plato has given orientation to Augustine and thereby to the entire Middle Ages. . . . Leaning on Neoplatonic ideas, especially on Neoplatonic imagery, Augustine has philosophically represented the basic idea of the medieval world view. The spirit, here transposed into entirely novel dimensions, has to be viewed as the most noble legacy of antiquity, whose unsurpassable plasticity derives from it. Much as the church has handed down the most noble practices of antiquity, ecclesiastical philosophy of the Middle Ages has, by way of Augustine, mediated the noblest thoughts of antique philosophy. A sentence such as Augustine's 'Nihil enim est ordinatum, quod non sit pulchrum,' everything well ordered is beautiful, still breathes the noble Greek spirit."

29
Mies could have been pointed to Landsberg by Guardini's *Liturgische Bildung*, p. 84. Vice versa, Landsberg, *Die Welt des Mittelalters und wir*, p. 30, points to Guardini; there are markings by Mies of that passage in which Guardini is mentioned and quoted. The obviously renewed interest in Landsberg is also possibly explained by the circumstance that this book is represented in Mies's library by two copies.

30
Mies van der Rohe: "In the victory of nominalism the victory of a spirit announces itself that is turned toward reality, long before it expresses itself in this reality. This spirit was antimedieval." Landsberg, *Die Welt des Mittelalters und wir*, p. 78 (underlined by Mies): "In the victory of nominalism the victory of a spirit turned toward a so-called 'reality' announces itself, long before it expresses itself in reality itself. But this spirit is antimedieval and antireligious, much as it is antiplatonic and antimetaphysical. . . . The disintegration of the idea of order also already partially expressed itself with Duns Scotus." But Landsberg introduces Scotus and Occam in a totally different sense than Mies. With Landsberg they are examples of "excessive authority and divine will, . . . much as all despotism has the tendency to lead to the gradual death of monarchy. Scotus and Occam, not Luther and Calvin, are the . . . effective destroyers of the medieval religious system. . . . Reason is abased as it never was with Augustine or Thomas." The many reviews of Mies's lecture, some quite exhaustive (see Appendix III, 1, addendum), in which the names quoted by Mies are relayed without Guardini, Landsberg, or Dessauer being mentioned, invites the assumption that Mies attempted to leave his public in the dark as to the author of these thoughts, or even wanted to be himself viewed as such.

31
Mies van der Rohe, notebook of 1928, p. 67 (see Appendix II).

32
See Mies's notebook, p. 70. Also see Mies's excerpts of Leopold Ziegler's *Zwischen Menschen und Wirtschaft* (Darmstadt, 1927) in notebook pp. 71–75, in which Mies pays special attention to the "formation of an organic economy" between capitalism and socialism and traces with great interest the ideas of Emil Rathenau and Karl Marx (pp. 72, 73, "Sentence of Marx, very good . . .").

33
Mies van der Rohe, "Die Voraussetzungen baukünstlerischen Schaffens," manuscript in the collection of Dirk Lohan.

34
Compare Mies's notebook, pp. 52–57, with largely verbatim borrowing of those passages underlined by Mies in Guardini's *Briefe vom Comer See*, pp. 33–41.

35
These headings are set over pp. 25, 35, 46, 56, and 75, respectively, of Mies's copy of *Briefe vom Comer See*.

36
See Mies's notebook, p. 39.

37
Ibid., pp. 39–50.

38
Guardini, *Briefe vom Comer See*, p. 92.

39
Except where otherwise noted, the following paragraphs draw on Mies's "Die Voraussetzungen baukünstlerischen Schaffens" (see Appendix III, 1).

40
See Guardini, *Briefe vom Comer See*, pp. 102–107:

I have a belief in a new image that is in the process of arising. Different from that of antiquity, different from that of the Middle Ages. And thoroughly different above all from that of humanism, classicism, and romanticism. It belongs to that new happening of which we talked. It belongs to that new level on which the battle with the invading forces will be conducted. And there it will be victorious. It is from this depth and from this image that the new epoch will be created [underlined by Mies]. We see its messengers. Most expressly in architecture. . . . I see buildings in which the technical configuration has been subdued into true form. This form has not been brought from the outside but [beginning of underlining by Mies] derives from the same origin as the technical configuration itself, just as true, genuine, and self-evident, so much so that one could think the properly constructed machine and a totally functional house are already on this account also formed artistically—which is of course a fallacy, for the technically correct is by no means yet artistic "form." In that, of course, something greater has occurred insofar as the technical apparatus has been brought in relationship to our living sensibilities [end of Mies's underlining]. . . . And recently I saw in Wasmuths Monatsheft *a design for a future city that has greatly impressed me. The entire form had the transparency of a technical calculation, but it was so austere and so forceful that I felt this belongs to us, as Memphis, Thebes, Nineveh, and Babylon may have belonged to their time.*

Presumably Guardini refers here to Le Corbusier's impressive views of the Cité Contemporaine of 1922.

41
Guardini, *Briefe vom Comer See*, pp. 50ff. with underlining by Mies.

42
To this passage from Mies's lecture, compare Guardini, *Briefe vom Comer See*, pp. 95f.: "By way of authentic work we must penetrate the new to dominate it. We must become master over the unchained forces and build them into a new order that relates to man." (Double markings by Mies in the margin): "What we need is not less technology but more. Better expressed: A stronger, more informed, 'more humane' technology. More science, but more spiritualized, more formed. . . ."

43
See Guardini, *Briefe vom Comer See*, p. 98, with corresponding markings by Mies: "It must be possible to let go of illusions, to see our existence sharply delineated and yet gain a new dimension, a dimension that arises out of the spirit. . . ."

44
Riezler, "Das Haus Tugendhat in Brünn," p. 332; see the discussion of the Tugendhat House in the preceding chapter.

45
Guardini, *Briefe vom Comer See*, p. 98, underlined by Mies.

46
See Mies's notebook, p. 55: "Increased awareness of the body by rhythmical culture. Psychoanalysis has brought a new realm of the living soul into our field of view and revealed deep connections. How the soul has become conscious thereby. . . . There are no more unobserved events. We perceive this as normal." See also Mies van der Rohe, "Wir stehen in der Wende der Zeit. Baukunst als Ausdruck geistiger Entscheidung" (We Stand at the Turning Point of Time: Building Art as the Expression of Spiritual Decisions), *Innendekoration*, 39 (1928), p. 262: "Traffic increases. The world shrinks more and more, it comes more and more into view right into the remotest recesses. World consciousness and consciousness of mankind are the results."

47
See Mies's notebook, pp. 14, 24.

48
Ibid., p. 50: "Culture presupposes a distance from immediate reality. Only from the realm of consciousness can the creative and form-giving hold on the world be set free."

49
Ibid., pp. 46–48.

50
Werner Jaeger, "Die geistige Gegenwart der Antike" (speech given at the first public meeting of the Gesellschaft für antike Kultur), *Die Antike*, 5 (1929), pp. 177, 181ff.

51
See Guardini, *Liturgische Bildung*, p. 80.

52
Guardini, *Briefe vom Comer See*, p. 51: "The direction of the work turns toward the intensive. From the particulars to connectedness, from expanse and survey to profundity" (marked by Mies).

53
Ibid., pp. 60, 79f.

54
See Tegethoff, *Mies van der Rohe. Die Villen und Landhausprojekte*, p. 88: "Mies laid the building across the axis much like a barricade, without, however, interrupting it entirely." See further the valuable analysis differentiating between the axis of movement and the axis of sight in the spatial disposition, ibid., pp. 85–89.

55
Guardini, *Liturgische Bildung*, p. 80.

56
Tegethoff, *Die Villen und Landhausprojekte*, p. 89, concludes the description of the passage through the pavilion: "Only after several changes of direction can one leave the pavilion again on the garden side, and even a previously disinterested visitor will have difficulty ignoring the charm of its architecture."

57
Guardini, *Liturgische Bildung*, p. 23.

58
Compare Mies's notebook, pp. 61–63, with Romano Guardini, *Von heiligen Zeichen* (Würzburg, 1922), pp. 12, 13. Also see my editorial preface to the notebook, in Appendix II.

59
On the irregularities and the significance of this grid, see the analysis of Tegethoff (*Die Villen und Landhausprojekte*, pp. 77f.).

60
Mies van der Rohe, miscellaneous notes to lectures, undated manuscript, around 1950, in Library of Congress (see Appendix IV, 6).

61
See Mies's notebook, p. 63: "The creative. The nature of the thing outside and the answer of man on the inside. . . ."

62
Mies van der Rohe, "Die Voraussetzungen baukünstlerischen Schaffens" (see Appendix III, 1).

63
Mies van der Rohe, "Baukunst unserer Zeit. Meine berufliche Laufbahn" (Building Art of Our Time. My Professional Career),

foreword to Werner Blaser, *Mies van der Rohe. Die Kunst der Struktur* (Zurich and Stuttgart, 1965), p. 6.

64
Wilhelm Lotz, "Die Halle II auf der Bauausstellung," *Die Form*, 6 (1931), p. 247. Under the motto "This is how I live everyday," the publisher Mosse organized on Reichkanzlerplatz a type of counterexposition to the Berlin Building Exposition, for which Mies, in cooperation with Otto Bartning, Otto Haesler, Ludwig Hilberseimer, and Lilly Reich, directed a department of his own under the motto "The apartment of our time."

65
Mies van der Rohe to Herbert Gericke, November 3, 1932, letter in Museum of Modern Art; quoted in Tegethoff, *Die Villen und Landhausprojekte*, p. 119.

66
Adolf Loos, *Von einem armen, reichen Manne* (1900), in Adolf Loos, *Ins Leere gesprochen 1897–1900* (Vienna, 1921, rpt. 1981), pp. 198–203, with the now famous sentence flung triumphantly by the architect at the client who wants to withdraw from the totalist form of the house: "Try to hang a new picture." Justus Bier had posed the question similarly in "Kann man in Haus Tugendhat wohnen?," *Die Form*, 6 (1931), pp. 392ff., and compared Mies to such a dictatorial form-setter "that one did not dare to bring any piece, old or new, into these 'finished' rooms, with walls that do not permit the hanging of pictures because the pattern of the marble, the grain of the woods have replaced art." On this issue, see also the reply of Fritz Tugendhat, ibid., p. 348.

67
W. OE., "Mies van der Rohe entwickelt dem *MM* seine Pläne," *Montag Morgen,* October 1932, quoted in Peter Hahn and Christian Wolsdorf (eds.), *Bauhaus Berlin: Auflösung Dessau 1932. Schliessung Berlin 1933. Bauhäusler und Drittes Reich* (Weingarten and Berlin, 1985), p. 94. This publication also contains the most comprehensive documentation of material for the activities of Mies in the early thirties.

68
Mies van der Rohe, speech on the occasion of the anniversary meeting of the Deutsche Werkbund (see Appendix III, 10). The intellectual morass out of which the attack against the modern was staged can be seen from a caption under Mies's block of the Weissenhof housing project printed in *Deutschen Bauhütte, Zeitschrift der deutschen Architektenschaft,* 36, no. 9 (1932), p. 110: "Apartment Block. Mies van der Rohe (Dessau). Collective type for barracks for supervised Russian Soviet employees."

69
Mies van der Rohe, "Was wäre Beton, was Stahl ohne Spiegelglas?" (What Would Concrete, What Would Steel Be without Mirror Glass?), contribution to a prospectus of the Verein Deutscher Spiegelglas-Fabriken of March 13, 1933; also the following exchange of letters: Mies to the Verein Deutscher Spiegelglas-Fabriken on November 5, 1932: "I would gladly contribute a short article with photos to the pamphlet planned by you. Besides the points stipulated by you, however, I would like to introduce some additional points in order to enrich the theme." The "article" promised by Mies for February 15, barely one typed page, was sent on March 13, 1933, in response to reminders, and was accompanied by a cover letter: "It is shorter than you expected but I only wanted to stimulate building. Everything else will follow."

70
Mies van der Rohe, "Haus H., Magdeburg" (The H. House, Magdeburg), *Die Schildgenossen,* 14 (1935), between pages

514 and 515. For a comparative interpretation of the sky-scraper designs, see Franz Schulze, *Mies van der Rohe: A Critical Biography* (Chicago, 1985), pp. 192f.

71
Written by Friedrich Gilly in the margin of a sketchbook page, according to Alfred Rietdorf, *Gilly. Wiedergeburt der Architektur* (Berlin, 1940), p. 52. For the Friedrich Hölderlin quotation, see ibid., p. 6. Among the books of Mies: *Gedichte von Friedrich Hölderlin* (Leipzig, 1913).

72
On the basis of documentation submitted by Hahn and Wolsdorf (eds.), *Bauhaus Berlin,* justified doubts arise as to the description of the closing of the Bauhaus given by Mies in interviews. (See Mies van der Rohe, "The End of the Bauhaus," in North Carolina State College of Agriculture and Engineering, School of Design Student Publication, vol. 3, no. 3 (1953), pp. 16–18, and also *Mies in Berlin,* phonograph record, Bauwelt Archiv I, 1966.)

73
Replica of the "letter of devotion" in Hahn and Wolsdorf (eds.), *Bauhaus Berlin,* pp. 147f. Ibid. also a letter on this subject, not mailed, from Alfred Rosenberg to Goebbels: "Prof. Mies van der Rohe, the designer of the Liebknecht and Rosa Luxemburg Memorial, has finally consented, but right away apologized to his friends. . . . Now and then, it is depressing to beg for signatures among those against whom we have been fighting, in a cultural-political sense, for years." The restraint Mies imposed on himself must be seen in this light, as he presumably attempted to salvage work possibilities. The negative critique leveled against his work at the Brussels World's Fair of 1935 might have been another reason why he did not want to step in front of the public. See the letter of Mies van der Rohe to George Nelson of July 20, 1935, in the Library of Congress (Nelson wanted to publish an article by Mies in the American architectural journal *Pencil Points* and had asked for some illustrations): "As I already let you know through one of my gentlemen, I do not want to publish in foreign journals at the present time. My stand is firm on that. There is therefore no sense in giving out the requested photos." Of the same order is Mies's refusal to Wilhelm Wagenfeld of October 29, 1935 (Wagenfeld wanted him to deliver a speech on the theme "Glass and Architecture" at the Berlin meeting of the Deutsche Glastechnische Gesellschaft in 1936): "I must beg you to desist, for I can give no time to speeches right now. You will understand this." By contrast, a letter of Lilly Reich of 1935 to J. J. P. Oud offers an insight into the work situation in Mies's office: "At Mies's we have been working on a project for a smaller residence; whether it will be built is unclear . . . such a situation is not nice but we do not know how we can alter it. How sad that it is not much different in your place. What a difficult time we are born in." Quoted in Günther Stamm, *J. J. P. Oud. Bauten und Projekte 1906 bis 1963* (Mainz and Berlin, 1984), pp. 85f.

74
Mies van der Rohe, inaugural address as Director of Architecture at Armour Institute of Technology, held on occasion of the testimonial dinner in Palmer House, Chicago, November 20, 1938; manuscript in the Library of Congress (see Appendix III, 14).

75
Ibid.; the following quotations are from the same source unless otherwise specified. For a differentiation between value and purpose, see the following underlinings by Mies in Alois Riehl, *Zur Einführung in die Philosophie der Gegenwart* (Leipzig, 1908), which seem to stand for Mies's attitude also. Riehl, p.

9: "But there is another perspective than the purely scientific one, and only this second glance that discovers values penetrates to the realm of the spirit. But to discover values means simultaneously to experience values, to create new values." Ibid., p. 183f. (marked by a double line): "Our life grows from values, rests on values. . . . All values are spiritual values. . . . The problems of an ideology are value problems." Ibid., p. 187f.: "All creation is at the same time a destruction and he who erects new tablets must break old ones, we could say with Nietzsche. But the 'good ones' are called the destroyers of old values—criminals. It has never been different in history; he who created new ideals and new norms transgressed established morals, injuring them. It is the tragedy in the life of great leaders and of heroes of the spirit that they must face the sacred convictions, beliefs, and morals of their time in inner conflict. 'The noble one wants to create the new and a new virtue; the good one wants the old and the preservation of the old.' To create values does not mean to invent values or to define them deliberately. Values are not arrived at like scientific insights; one does not invent them, they are revealed. As the stars, those distant suns, shine forth from the dark of the night one after the other, so values enter into the human field of vision, and he who saw them first, experienced them first, lived them first, he is their creator. He points to a higher form of life and pours new spirit into old value concepts. [Double lines:] For in order to be effective he, too, must tie the productive to the historical."

76
See Mies van der Rohe, "Gelöste Aufgaben. Eine Forderung an unser Bauwesen" (Solved Tasks: A Challenge for Our Building Industry), *Die Bauwelt,* 14 (1923), p. 719.

77
See markings by Mies in Eduard Spranger, *Lebensformen. Geisteswissenschaftliche Psychologie und Ethik der Persönlichkeit* (Halle, 1922), pp. 325f.: "The great question that characterizes the cultural fatigue from Rousseau to now, the question of for what purpose this entire effort of forces is set into motion, derives from the technization of life, the leftovers of authentic culture. Indeed most things today are merely technical in nature, that is, efforts to a purpose on the legitimacy and value of which one does not devote any thought. . . . Technology is a brilliant achievement of the human intelligence, persistence, and application. But as long as one fails to establish the purpose of this wonderful instrument, it is nothing but a force of nature that screams for evaluation. Before we can determine *how* we have to live, we must establish *to what purpose* we want to live."

78
See excerpts from the Bavarian Radio interview on the occasion of Mies's eightieth birthday, in *Der Architekt,* 15 (1966), p. 324: "The problem of the building art has really always been the same. The qualitative is achieved through proportions in the building, and proportions do not cost anything. For the most part these are proportions between things. . . . It is of course much work for the architect to articulate the in-between spaces. The artistic is almost always a question of proportions." See Le Corbusier, *Towards a New Architecture,* translated by Frederick Etchells (New York, 1976), p. 223: "As to beauty, this is always present when you have *proportion;* and proportion costs the landlord nothing, it is the charge of the architect!" See also Mies van der Rohe, "Schön und praktisch bauen! Schluss mit der kalten Zweckmässigkeit" (Build Beautifully and Practically! Stop This Cold Functionality), *Duisburger Generalanzeiger,* 49 (January 26, 1930), p. 2: "And what finally is beauty? Certainly nothing that can be calculated or measured. It is always something imponderable, something

that lies in between things." Mies van der Rohe, radio address, 1931, manuscript of August 17, 1931, in the collection of Dirk Lohan: "The artistic expresses itself in the proportions of things, often even in the proportions between things. Essentially it is something immaterial, something spiritual. And thus independent of the material conditions of a period. It is a wealth that even a materially poor period need not renounce, indeed must not renounce."

79
See Mies van der Rohe, "Architecture and Technology," *Arts and Architecture,* 67, no. 10 (1950), p. 30; also published in *Three Addresses at the Blackstone Hotel, April 17, 1950 on the Occasion of the Celebration of the Addition of the Institute of Design to the Illinois Institute of Technology* (Chicago, 1950), pp. 2–3. See also Mies's lecture in Chicago, undated (see Appendix IV, 5), manuscript in the Library of Congress with the remark on the cover sheet: "Manuscript of one important address Mies gave here in German." For Mies's handwritten notes, see the selection in Appendix IV, 6, chosen from the loose-leaf collection of about 130 pages in Library of Congress, Drafts and Speeches.

80
See the works cited in the notes to chapter V.2. Mies presumably obtained his knowledge of Thomas Aquinas and Augustine from the already mentioned writings of Landsberg and Guardini and from *Die Schildgenossen.* Franz Schulze's speculation as to the readings of Mies for the period of around 1930 (*Mies van der Rohe,* p. 172) cannot be documented. Only later can we find in Mies's library books with these titles: Anton C. Pegis (ed.), *The Basic Writings of Thomas Aquinas* (New York, 1945); Saint Augustine, *Divine Providence and the Problem of Evil* (New York, 1942).

81
Friedrich Dessauer, *Philosophie der Technik* (Bonn, 1927), p. 136.

82
See Mies's notebook of 1928 (Appendix II), p. 34.

83
Dessauer, *Philosophie der Technik,* p. 103. See also the passage marked by Mies in ibid., pp. 148f., quoted in Appendix II, note 10.

84
Georg Simmel, "Zur Philosophie der Kultur. Der Begriff und die Tragödie der Kultur," in Georg Simmel, *Philosophische Kultur. Gesammelte Essais* (3d ed., Potsdam, 1923), a book owned by Mies; quoted from the new edition, *Philosophische Kultur. Über das Abenteuer, die Geschlechter und die Krise der Moderne. Gesammelte Essais,* with an afterword by Jürgen Habermas (Berlin, 1983), pp. 203, 187.

85
Mies van der Rohe, "Architecture and Technology."

86
Mies van der Rohe, lecture, Chicago, undated, pp. 17, 18 (see Appendix IV, 5).

87
Mies van der Rohe, quoted from Peter Carter, "Mies van der Rohe," *Bauen und Wohnen,* 16 (1961), p. 239.

88
Mies van der Rohe, undated lecture (Appendix IV, 5), p. 2.

89
Mies in Berlin, phonograph record, Bauwelt Archiv 1, 1966.

90
"If we talk of structure, we think philosophically. Structure is the entire, from top to bottom, down to the last detail—everything subject to the same idea." Mies van der Rohe, quoted from Peter Carter, "Mies van der Rohe," p. 231.

91
Mies van der Rohe, "Ich mache niemals ein Bild," *Die Bauwelt,* 53 (1962), p. 884: "Language in everyday usage is spoken as prose. If one is very adept, one can speak a wonderful prose. And if one masters it, one can become a poet. But it is still the same language, the nature of which is to harbor all possibilities in itself. The physicist Schroedinger says: 'The creative power of a general principle is due to its universality.' That is exactly what I mean when I speak of structure in architecture. Structure is not a specific solution but a general idea."

92
Mies van der Rohe, undated lecture (Appendix IV, 5), p. 7.

93
Georg Simmel, *Philosophische Kultur,* pp. 204f.

94
Mies van der Rohe, miscellaneous notes to lectures, undated manuscript in the Library of Congress (see Appendix IV, 6).

95
Ibid.; likewise in the undated lecture manuscript (Appendix IV, 5), p. 14.

96
Friedrich Nietzsche, "On the Uses and Disadvantages of History," in *Untimely Meditations,* translated by R. J. Hollingdale (Cambridge, 1983), p. 94.

97
Mies van der Rohe, "Geschäftshaus Adam" (The Adam Building), draft of a letter, July 2, 1928, in Museum of Modern Art, Later German Projects (see Appendix III, 4).

98
See Dessauer, *Philosophie der Technik,* p. 169.

99
Rudolf Schwarz, "Vom Sterben der Anmut," *Die Schildgenossen,* 8 (1927–28), pp. 284ff.

100
On this project see Schulze, *Mies van der Rohe,* p. 231.

101
Mies van der Rohe, "Architecture and Technology."

102
Mies van der Rohe, "Museum for a Small City," *Architectural Forum,* 78, no. 5 (1943), p. 84.

103
Romano Guardini, "Die Gefährdung der lebendigen Persönlichkeit," *Die Schildgenossen,* 6, no. 3 (1926), p. 43.

104
Mies van der Rohe, "Museum for a Small City," p. 84.

105
Rudolf Schwarz, "Vom Sterben der Anmut," p. 289.

106
Rudolf Schwarz in a letter to Romano Guardini, January 15, 1928, quoted in Gerl, *Romano Guardini,* p. 222: "Once more, in a very modest way, I remark that the idea of the castle as a series of large, pure, and almost empty rooms was my very own at a time when architects were not aware of it (most of

them do not know it even today) and coziness was trump in the castle. I had to take a thorough thrashing on account of my empty chapel."

107
Ulrich Conrads, who met Mies in Cologne in the sixties on the occasion of a visit to Germany, told me that he spent an entire day with Mies, at the latter's request, visiting the churches of Rudolf Schwarz.

108
Romano Guardini, "Das Leere," *Die Schildgenossen,* 16, no. 2–3 (1936–37), p. 130.

109
Schwarz, "Vom Sterben der Anmut," p. 289.

110
Rudolf Schwarz, *Wegweisung der Technik* (Potsdam, 1929), quoted from Maria Schwarz and Ulrich Conrads (eds.), *Rudolf Schwarz. Wegweisung der Technik und andere Schriften zum Neuen Bauen 1926–1961* (Brunswick and Wiesbaden, 1979), p. 45.

111
Rudolf Schwarz, "Neues Bauen?," *Die Schildgenossen,* 9 (1929), pp. 207ff., quoted from Schwarz and Conrads (eds.), *Rudolf Schwarz,* p. 128.

112
Mies van der Rohe, "Ich mache niemals ein Bild," pp. 884f.

113
Walter Genzmer, "Der Deutsche Reichspavillon auf der Internationalen Ausstellung Barcelona," *Die Baugilde*, 11 (1929), p. 1655: "It was mainly intended to invite passing visitors to the exhibition to a shorter or longer contemplative lingering."

114
Mies van der Rohe, quoted in Christian Norberg-Schulz, "Ein Gespräch mit Mies van der Rohe," *Baukunst und Werkform,* 11 (1958), p. 615.

115
Simmel, *Philosophische Kultur,* p. 207.

116
Friedrich Nietzsche, *The Gay Science,* translated by Walter Kaufmann (New York, 1974), pp. 226f.

117
Guardini, *Briefe vom Comer See,* p. 110.

118
Mies van der Rohe, miscellaneous notes to lectures (see Appendix IV, 6).

Selected Bibliography

Monographs

Philip Johnson, *Mies van der Rohe* (New York, 1947; 3d ed., New York, 1978).

Max Bill, *Ludwig Mies van der Rohe* (Milan, 1955).

Ludwig Hilberseimer, *Mies van der Rohe* (Chicago, 1956).

Arthur Drexler, *Ludwig Mies van der Rohe* (New York, 1960).

Peter Blake, "Mies van der Rohe and the Mastery of Structure," in *The Master Builders* (New York, 1960).

Werner Blaser, *Mies van der Rohe. Die Kunst der Struktur* (Zurich and Stuttgart, 1965; 2d ed. as *Mies van der Rohe,* Zurich, 1973).

James Speyer, *Mies van der Rohe* (ex. cat., Art Institute of Chicago, 1968).

Ludwig Glaeser, *Mies van der Rohe: Drawings in the Collection of the Museum of Modern Art* (New York, 1969).

Martin Pawley, *Mies van der Rohe* (New York, 1970).

Peter Carter, *Mies van der Rohe at Work* (New York, 1974).

Lorenzo Papi, *Ludwig Mies van der Rohe* (Florence, 1974).

Ludwig Glaeser, *Furniture and Furniture Drawings from the Design Collection and the Mies van der Rohe Archive* (New York, 1979).

David A. Spaeth, *Ludwig Mies van der Rohe: An Annotated Bibliography and Chronology* (New York and London, 1979).

Wolf Tegethoff, *Mies van der Rohe. Die Villen und Landhausprojekte* (Krefeld and Essen, 1981).

János Bonta, *Mies van der Rohe* (Budapest, 1983).

David Spaeth, *Mies van der Rohe* (New York, 1985).

Franz Schulze, *Mies van der Rohe: A Critical Biography* (Chicago and London, 1985).

Franz Schulze, ed., *Mies van der Rohe: Critical Essays* (New York, 1989).

Interviews

"'Only the Patient Counts': Some Radical Ideas on Hospital Design by Mies van der Rohe," *The Modern Hospital,* 64, no. 3 (1945), pp. 65–67.

"6 Students Talk with Mies," *Master Builder* (student publication of the School of Design, North Carolina State College), 2 (1952), pp. 21–28.

Christian Norberg-Schulz, "Ein Gespräch mit Mies van der Rohe," *Baukunst und Werkform* 11, no. 11 (1958), pp. 615–618.

H. T. Cadbury-Brown, "Ludwig Mies van der Rohe," *The Architectural Association Journal,* 75, no. 834 (1959), pp. 27–28.

"Mies van der Rohe: No Dogma," *Interbuild,* 6, no. 6 (1959), pp. 9–11.

Graeme Shankland, "Architect of 'the Clear and Reasonable': Mies van der Rohe Considered and Interviewed," *The Listener,* 15 (October 1959), pp. 620–623.

Peter Carter, "Mies van der Rohe," *Bauen und Wohnen,* 16, no. 7 (1961), pp. 229–248 (includes excerpts from an interview).

"Mies van der Rohe: Ich mache niemals ein Bild," *Die Bauwelt,* 53, no. 32 (1962), pp. 884–885.

Mies in Berlin (phonograph record), Bauwelt Archiv I (Berlin, 1966; records an interview on RIAS Berlin, October 1964).

Katherine Kuh, "Mies van der Rohe: Modern Classicist," *Saturday Review,* 48, no. 4 (1965), pp. 22–23, 61.

Excerpts of an interview on Bayrischen Rundfunk on the occasion of Mies's eightieth birthday, published in *Der Architekt,* 15, no. 10 (1966), p. 324.

Franz Schulze, "'I Really Always Wanted to Know about Truth,'" *Chicago Daily News,* "Panorama" supplement, 27 April 1968.

Illustration Credits

Citations are by page number.

Lenders

AEG-Foto: 75 top
Akademie der Künste Berlin: 6, 212, 323 top
Author: 43 center, 48 top left and top right, 49 bottom, 67 top, 80 center right, 173, 229
Gerd von Bassewitz: 90, 153 right
Bauaufsichtsamt Wilmersdorf, Berlin: 84
Bauhaus-Archiv, Berlin: 22
Berliner Bildbericht, Berlin: 186, 190, 192, 227 top
Eichstädt, Berlin: 86
Germanisches Nationalmuseum Nürnberg: 55
Hedrich-Blessing Studio, Chicago: 218 center right, 219, 227 bottom, 230 all, 232, 328
David L. Hirsch, New York: 234 bottom
Knoll Associates Inc., New York: 205
Balthasar Korab, Troy, Michigan: 233
Kunstbibliothek Berlin: 3, 4, 5, 7, 187, 189 bottom, 191, 193, 240
Landesarchiv Berlin: 85
Landesbildstelle Berlin: 78 center right, 184 top
Library of Congress, Washington, D.C.: 25, 37, 165 center, 244, 326, 330
Museum of Modern Art, New York: 8, 11, 40, 75 bottom, 78 top, 113, 131, 152 right, 153 left, 189 top, 216, 231, 241, 242, 256, 262, 266, 269, 274, 276, 281, 288, 291, 292, 294, 314, 315, 320, 322
Sergius Ruegenberg, Berlin: 10, 12, 16, 17, 18, 20 bottom, 164, 238, 248
Staatliche Schlösser und Gärten, Berlin: 78 center left
Staatsbibliothek Berlin: 58
University of Illinois at Chicago: 102, 103, 203, 207, 286
Renate Werner, Berlin: 47, 48 center left
Williams & Meyer Co., Chicago: 74, 323 center

Publications

Architectural Review, 151 (1972): 224–225
Bau und Wohnung (Stuttgart: Deutsche Werkbund, 1927): 156, 159, 188 bottom, 258, 260, 261
Bauhaus Berlin, ed. Peter Hahn (Weingarten and Berlin, 1985): 303 top right
Bauhaus, advertisement for first exhibition (Weimar, 1923): 133
Adolf Behne, Der moderne Zweckbau (Munich, 1926): 158 bottom
Werner Blaser, Mies van der Rohe (Zurich, 1973): 215 top left, 218 all but center right, 335
Tilmann Buddensieg and Henning Rogge, Industriekultur (Berlin, 1979): 65 bottom
Deutsche Kunst und Dekoration, 32 (1913): 48 center right
Theo van Doesburg, Grundbegriffe der neuen gestaltenden Kunst (Munich, 1925): 149 top
Festschrift für Alois Riehl (Halle, 1914): 38
Festschrift der Firma Hermann Schäler (Berlin, 1930): 9, 83
Die Form, 6 (1931): 215 top right, 310 all
Heinrich de Fries, Moderne Villen und Landhäuser (Berlin, 1924): 81 right
Leo Frobenius, Das unbekannte Afrika (Munich, 1923): 117
Frühlicht, 1 (1921–22): 155
Hanna-Barbara Gerl, Romano Guardini 1885–1968 (Mainz, 1985): 199
Fritz Hoeber, Peter Behrens (Munich, 1913): 44, 46 right, 53, 65 top left, 73 all
Innendekoration, 21 (1910): 41 bottom, 42 both
Jahrbuch des Deutsches Werkbundes 1913: 148 top left
Katalog der Grossen Berliner Kunstausstellung (ex. cat., Berlin, 1924): 13 top
Kunstblatt, 10, 11, 14 (1926, 1927, 1930): 78 bottom right, 188 top left, 306
Marc-Antoine Laugier, Essai sur l'architecture, 2d ed. (Paris, 1755): 130
Le Corbusier, Oeuvre Complet, 8 vols. (Zurich, 1930ff.): 132 top, 148 bottom
Le Corbusier, Städtebau (Stuttgart, 1926): 118
Le Corbusier, Vers une architecture (Paris, 1923): 121
Werner Lindner, Die Ingenieurbauten in ihrer guten Gestaltung (Berlin, 1923): 122, 125, 126
Moderne Bauformen, 9 (1910): 41 top, 43 top, 45
George Nelson, Industrial Architecture of Albert Kahn Inc. (New York, 1939): 227 center
J. J. P. Oud, Holländische Architektur (Munich, 1926): 72, 158 center
Wolfgang Pehnt, Neue deutsche Architektur (Stuttgart, 1970): 132 center
Josef Popp, Bruno Paul (Munich, 1916): 46 left
Qualität, 4 (1925): 13 center and bottom
Der Querschnitt, 4 (1924): 185, 245
Alois Riehl, Einführung in die Philosophie der Gegenwart (Leipzig, 1908): 59
Rudolf-Schwarz-Gedächtnisausstellung Köln (ex. cat., Heidelberg, 1963): 165 top
Karl Friedrich Schinkel, Sammlung architektonischer Entwürfe, 3 vols. (Berlin, 1858): 77, 152 left, 234 top

Franz Schulze, *Mies van der Rohe* (Chicago and London, 1985): 39, 78 bottom left, 301, 302, 303 left, 321, 324, 332, 340

Larissa A. Shadowa, *Suche und Experiment* (Dresden, 1978): 149 bottom

Albert Sigrist, *Das Buch vom Bauen* (Berlin, 1930): 19

Pieter Singelenberg, *H. P. Berlage* (Utrecht, 1972): 65 top right, 67 bottom

David Spaeth, *Mies van der Rohe* (London, 1985): 112

Stadt und Utopie (ex. cat., Berlin, 1982): 148 top right

Wolf Tegethoff, *Mies van der Rohe* (Krefeld and Essen, 1981): 188 top right

Stanley Tigerman, *Versus* (New York, 1982): xvi

Wasmuths Monatsheft für Baukunst, 11 (1927): 80 all but center right, 81 right, 259

Zeitschrift des Vereins Deutscher Ingenieure, 58 (1913): 120 both

Zentralblatt der Bauverwaltung, 49 (1929): 91

2. Sonderheft der Stadtbaukunst alter und neuer Zeit (Berlin, 1922): 184 bottom

Index

Page numbers in italics refer to illustrations.